AUSTRALIAN ENVIRONMENTAL POLICY 2

AUSTRALIAN ENVIRONMENTAL POLICY 2

STUDIES IN DECLINE + DEVOLUTION

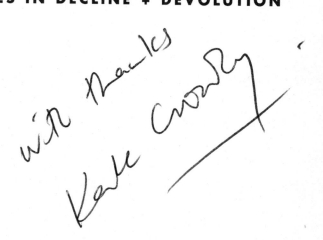

with thanks
Kate Crowley

EDITED BY
K.J WALKER + K. CROWLEY

UNSW PRESS

A UNSW Press book

Published by
University of New South Wales Press Ltd
University of New South Wales
Sydney 2052 Australia
www.unswpress.com.au

National Library of Australia
Cataloguing-in-Publication entry:

Australian environmental policy 2: studies in decline and devolution.

Bibliography.
Includes index.
ISBN 0 86840 673 2.

1. Environmental policy — Australia.
I. Walker, K. J. (Kenneth James), 1940– .
II. Crowley, K. (Kate), 1956– .

333.70994

Printer Griffin Press, Adelaide

CONTENTS

PREFACE

This book's predecessor, *Australian Environmental Policy*, was well received when it was published in 1992. Much of its analysis and data is still relevant. But the need for studies of the environmental policy process in Australia has, if anything, grown. It is still rare for environmental policy issues to be written up comprehensively and analytically; yet dozens of interesting cases still beg for such treatment. The dead hand of statist developmentalism remains dominant in government policy making. Mainstream political parties and the media still attempt to downplay and minimise the importance of environmental issues. And while major policy and institutional changes have occurred, they have served to exclude environmental concerns. World politics is nowadays dominated by a very different, and potentially highly damaging agenda.

These developments require description and analysis. This new collection of essays attempts to situate the developments in environmental policy and politics in Australia, both positive and negative, within the changes that have taken place during the 1990s. Its stance,

VIII • AUSTRALIAN ENVIRONMENTAL POLICY 2

inevitably, is critical. It seeks to dissect, analyse and explain, not to endorse or celebrate. It is not a reprint of its predecessor, nor is it a rehash. The focus has shifted, just as its subject has.

None of the following chapters has been published before, though some have appeared as conference papers.

The editors would like to thank the contributors, the bulk of whom met — or at least did not fall far behind — very tight deadlines. They would also like to thank their nearest and dearest, who as usual put up with considerable dislocation. Mary Heath carefully proofread most chapters and contributed numerous valuable suggestions.

EDITORS and CONTRIBUTORS

EDITORS

Dr Kate Crowley is lecturer in the School of Government, University of Tasmania, where she teaches environmental policy and politics. She is co-editor of *Governing in Minority: Tasmanian Politics & Policy 1996–1999* with Dr Marcus Haward (1999). Her research interests span ecopolitical theory, green politics, environmental employment and Australian environmental policy. She has published articles in journals such as *Environmental Politics, Local Environment* and *Just Policy*, review articles in *Environmental Politics, Local Environment, Alternatives Journal,* the *Canberra Bulletin of Public Administration* and the *Australian & New Zealand Journal of Sociology,* and is a book reviewer for numerous journals. She has also written book chapters on power theory and ecopolitics. She is a member of the Editorial Panel for the *Australian Journal of Environmental Management,* and convenes the Austral-Ecopol email discussion list.

Dr Kenneth Walker is an independent researcher. According to a recent reviewer, he "pioneered the study of environmental politics in Australia". He edited the collection *Australian Environmental Policy*, and is author of the textbook *The Political Ecology of Environmental Policy: An Australian Introduction*, published in 1992 and 1994 respectively by UNSW Press. He has taught at Melbourne, Monash, Flinders, Adelaide, Case Western Reserve, Cleveland State, Griffith and Macquarie Universities. He has developed and taught ground-breaking interdisciplinary courses in environmental policy and politics. He writes mainly in the fields of environmental policy and environmental political theory, but has subsidiary interests in technology, technology transfer and technology history in its social context. He is currently at work on a further book, *The State in Environmental Management*, and a number of papers.

CONTRIBUTORS

Graham Adams (BA, Dip.Ed., M.Env. St., MEIA) was author of a guideline handbook for local government published in 1992 by the South Australian Government's environment agency, on developing and implementing environmental management plans at the local level. Since that time he has played an active part in promoting and facilitating the rôle of local authorities and their communities in shaping and delivering environment policy. On behalf of his department he initiated and fostered the establishment of SA's original, landmark Partnership for Local Agenda 21. As an acknowledged leader in this field he has represented the South Australian Government in national forums and international conferences and has provided consultancy services to interstate local authorities. Currently his work is focussed on Environmental Management Systems and the take-up of the International Standard by public sector agencies.

Dr Mark Carden has a Doctorate in Environmental Politics from Griffith University. He has played an active rôle in environmental politics in Australia since the early 1980s. He has lectured at the University of Melbourne in both the School of Environmental Planning and the Department of Geography and Environmental Studies. He has since been employed by the Victorian Department of Natural Resources and Environment, where he worked on the development of community and regionally oriented Decision Support Systems for improving environmental decision making. He has recently accepted an appointment with the Murray-Darling Basin Commission. His ground-breaking work in linking biophysical conditions to politico-economic processes also appeared in the first edition of *Australian Environmental Policy*.

Dr Stephen Dovers is Research Fellow at the Centre for Resource and Environmental Studies at the Australian National University. His research themes include: theoretical, policy and institutional dimensions of sustainability, decision making in the face of uncertainty, biodiversity conservation and environmental history. He is consultant to the Australian government on a wide range of topics, including currently on establishment of research funding portfolio in policy-related R&D on land and water management. He has written some eighty articles, papers, reports, books, etc. in these and other areas. He is co-author of *Our Biosphere Under Threat* (Oxford, 1990), editor of *Australian Environmental History* (Oxford, 1994) and *Sustainable Energy Systems* (Cambridge, 1994), co-editor of *Ecology and Sustainability of Southern Temperate Ecosystems* (CSIRO, 1994). At present he is editing a further volume on Australian environmental history and policy, and co-editing a volume of South African environmental history essays.

Dr Tim Doyle is Senior Lecturer in the Mawson Graduate Centre for Environmental Studies at the University of Adelaide. He is also the President of the Conservation Council of South Australia, the major peak environment body in that State. His most recent works include the books *Environmental Politics and Policy Making in Australia*, co-authored with A.J. Kellow; and *Environment and Politics*, co-authored with D. McEachern. He is currently working on a book for UNSW Press on the experience of the environmental movement in Australia.

Nicholas Economou is a lecturer in Australian Politics in the Arts Faculty at Monash University, Melbourne. He has published on Australian politics and environmental policy.

Maggie Hine (BA Com. Hons., Post Grad. Cert. Ed.) has ten years' working experience in local government in Britain and Australia in the fields of community development and environmental management. Since 1995 she has worked in the area of Local Agenda 21 programme development and delivery in both local and State government in South Australia. She has also worked for five years as an environmental campaigner for non-government organisations and focussed on the development and implementation of environmental policy at a national, state and local level. She is presently employed as the Team Leader Environment at the City of Marion in South Australia.

Tony McCall is a lecturer in Government and Public Policy in the School of Government at the University of Tasmania. He is completing a Doctorate on environmental policy in Australia. His research interests are in environmental policy and regional development. Before joining the university he was an advisor to the Green Independents during the Labor/Green Accord in Tasmania 1989–92.

Dr David Mercer is Associate Professor in the Department of Geography & Environmental Science at Monash University, Clayton. He teaches courses in environmental policy and management and has published extensively in these areas.

Dr Roslyn Taplin is currently Principal Consultant, Taplin Ecoconsulting, and carries out contract research in areas including urban sustainability and climate change. Before establishing her own business she was Director of the Climatic Impacts Centre, Macquarie University, Sydney, which she first joined in 1991. With seven years spent in the climate change field and ten years before that in environmental research and teaching, she has an extensive background in environmental policy matters.

I

INTRODUCTION

K. Crowley & K.J. Walker

The *Living Planet Report*, released in October 1998, made the startling claim that over the 30 years from 1970, more than 30% of the productivity of the natural world had been destroyed. This was not alarmism. The report emanated from reputable bodies: the World Wide Fund for Nature, the New Economics Foundation and the World Conservation Monitoring Centre at Cambridge.[1] While the report's comprehensive review of the processes of degradation was groundbreaking, neither its approach nor its message was especially new. Human beings now appropriate some 40% of total global *biological* productivity. Other species are being driven into extinction at unprecedented rates. This might seem unimportant, if humans did not depend critically on biological processes — and hence the existence of some at least of those species — to produce their basic needs. When human activity disrupts them, these processes can overload and break down. Without ecology, there is no economy — and no human society.

Overpopulation, serious epidemiological risks, resource depletion and climatic modification have already led many scientists to conclude that resource demand is already unsustainable, and that only by "living on capital" — depleting valuable non-renewable resources — can current populations and standards of living be maintained.[2] With exponential growth in population, it becomes increasingly urgent to reverse current trends before "natural" checks such as famine and disease come into play, and before "the point of no return" arrives, at which resources have to be devoted to survival and can no longer be used to find "escape routes".[3]

Occasional concerned citizens and scientists have been blowing the whistle on environmental damage since well before the Industrial Revolution; even Marx noted the dangers, blaming them on the rapacity of capitalism.[4] Warnings of resource exhaustion, species extinction, declining biodiversity, hazards to human health and numerous other symptoms of "planetary overload" have been accumulating.[5] Since the massive awakening of interest in environmental questions in the late 1960s and early 1970s, there have been dozens of books, numerous comprehensive overviews and some influential reports to government.[6]

Scientists have united in a positively Aristophanian chorus to repeat the message of environmental concern and the lessons of ecology. Many scientists in the 1960s predicted the onset of serious global environmental problems by the early 1990s.[7] It became fashionable to deride these predictions, which were based on simple models and linear extrapolation of existing trends. But crude as those predictions were, they pinpointed disturbing changes. Those same concerns were echoed in 1992 by 1,700 senior scientists from seventy-one nations in "The World Scientists' Warning to Humanity" claiming, in part, that

> Human beings and the natural world are on a collision course. Human activities inflict harsh and often irreversible damage on the environment and on critical resources. If not checked, many of our current practices put at serious risk the future that we wish for human society and the plant and animal kingdoms, and may so alter the living world that it will be unable to sustain life in the manner that we know. Fundamental changes are urgent, if we are to avoid the collision our present course will bring about.[8]

To worries about resources, population and the productivity of agriculture, there have recently been added concerns about climatic change and the "greenhouse effect". Yet the *Living Planet Report* suggests that policy responses have been far from sufficient, and that more ground has been lost than gained. That is certainly true in

Australia. The 1996 *State of the Environment* report, while underlining some positive aspects of Australian environmental management, drew attention to numerous deficiencies, and the threats they posed to sustainability. There has been no serious attempt to take up and implement its recommendations.

When this book's predecessor, the first edition of *Australian Environmental Policy*, was published in 1992, it was possible to speak of "policy learning", slow, even faltering, though it was. Since that time, under the Keating and Howard Governments, policy learning has been subverted, then thrown to the winds. Keating made promises — such as the "phasing out" of woodchipping within five years — which were never kept. One of the Howard Government's first acts was to double the rate of woodchipping. The press, having decided that environment was "old hat", failed to spell out the implications. Howard's Government has since gone to the Kyoto conference with a policy dictated by mining interests and guaranteed to make Australia a laughing stock. It has dragged its feet on every aspect of environmental management. As Economou, McCall and Doyle show, this is policy, not inadvertence. Paradoxically, therefore, although political scientists, lobbyists and commentators have frequently announced that "green" or environmental politics has "arrived" and is "here to stay", not only is the hold of environmental considerations in Australian politics now more precarious, but determined attempts have been and continue to be made to ignore and obliterate them. Interestingly, however, more than 60% of Australian voters have consistently placed environment high on their list of concerns for the last two decades.

Describing environmental policy in Australia is therefore not simply a question of identifying policy processes, institutions and legislation, and then showing how they all work. It must necessarily identify missed opportunities and failed initiatives, and ask why and how. It must consider non-decisions as well as decisions; the issues that have been ignored and repressed, as well as those that have been taken up with enthusiasm. It must account for policy dissonance, as well as policy process.

There is no established methodology for doing this. The radical changes in Australian politics in the 1980s and 1990s have made the study of environmental policy more difficult. Furthermore, the scope of such study overstresses existing methodologies, which assume a stability and regularity to political processes that, in a time of policy upheaval, has been absent. Consequently, the study of environmental policy entails not merely the consideration of ecology, climatic and physical constraints and so on, but also political economy, and the dynamics of the socio-economic system. As might be expected for such a fundamental enterprise, it necessarily casts a wide net.

Appreciation is steadily growing that, far from being "lifestyle" issues of interest primarily to an idealistic, politically powerless fringe, environmental issues are critical. Dramatic disputes, such as those over Lake Pedder (1972), the Gordon/Franklin Dam (1983), the battles over the Great Barrier Reef (1980s) and the wet tropical rainforests in Queensland (1970s–80s) and mining at Coronation Hill in the Kakadu National Park (1991) now compete with "browner" questions. These more fundamental issues include the desultory debate about population policy; soil erosion, salination and degradation; forest management, in particular woodchipping for foreign markets; the very similar issues in mineral "development" and export; problems of pollution and toxic waste disposal; urban planning and amenities; and the not unrelated question of what standard of living and satisfactions future Australian populations will be able to enjoy. Looming over all, and as yet unknown in impact, is the certainty of some future climatic modification.

The major Australian political parties have long found environmental issues an embarrassment. They do not fit into their nineteenth century political philosophies, and are consequently intractable as objects of policy. Labor in particular was not slow to exploit them for electoral gain; but both parties have had difficulty in taking them seriously and in appreciating their importance. Recognition of the "last chance" nature of some issues, and of their importance to a wide range of people, battled with "practical" considerations such as jobs and economic growth. Failure to appreciate that ecological responsibility and sustainability could be job-creating still persists. The consequences of these deficiencies are starkly dramatised by policies which overcommit resources for the benefit of foreign corporations through "resource guarantees" for extractive industries, and suchlike.

Labor remains bogged down, paralysed by the apparent collapse of Left political thought and by its own traditional commitments to industry and "development". Labor leaders have described Green policies as "poison"; in Tasmania, Labor even conspired with conservatives to reduce the power of minor parties. The libertarian Right, as Doyle shows, has responded with dogmas which legitimise continued flat-out exploitation in terms of "freedom", private property and a perverted interpretation of stewardship, all under the "wise use" banner. This dogma underpins the increasing tendency of conservative governments to ignore important environmental constraints and to downplay issues such as ecosystem stability.

This is especially bizarre in view of the urgency of contemporary environmental pressures, and in view of the fact that many scientists have become frantic over political neglect of them.[9] Modern industrial societies are living on biological capital to a dangerous degree. Few politicians appreciate the significance of the "natural" checks on population, through famine, pestilence and war, which are already in operation. Such dangers were dramatised by the Gulf War and its attendant oil spills. Environmental damage in places as far apart as Tibet, Bosnia and Alaska further underlines the risks.

Whether human socio-economic activity must *necessarily* degrade the natural environment irretrievably remains a hotly debated topic.[10] Because human adaptation is radically different from that of other species, through sociality, language and tool making, it inevitably modifies the natural environment far more extensively. Only if all human impacts were benign could we be certain that they were not detrimental. Human systems of social choice, embedded for the last 9000 years in state societies, are not geared to cope with such problems. They have emerged through selective processes — particularly intersocietal competition — which stress growth and environmental modification as essential survival characteristics.[11] Stability and rationality in *ecological* terms are low priorities; consequently state information systems are poorly adapted to recognise important symptoms of ecological destabilisation.

Environmental issues are intrinsically ecological, stemming as they do from human disruption of otherwise self-regulating and resilient natural ecosystems. But ecology sits awkwardly with traditional policy concerns: there is no received wisdom on its relationship to other issues, and widely accepted theories and world views have no room for it. Politicians, most of them untrained in science, find ecology difficult to fit into pre-existing conceptual frameworks. Especially on the conservative side of politics, ecological considerations have often been dismissed as secondary to the "important" business of economic policy; and environmental issues are often seen as "frills", for attention once "fundamentals" such as economic growth have been secured.

These attitudes result in part from ignorance and prejudice. There is no *necessary* incompatibility between wise environmental management and many forms of economic growth, at least at low levels of environmental impact. It is failure to cooperate, poor planning, lack of foresight and myopia that cause environmental problems, not a fundamental conflict between economic and environmental values.

For example, soil conservation — perhaps the most serious of all our environmental challenges — is a classic **public good**, with its accompanying problems of collective action and cooperation; the failure of political coordination is predictable, but entirely remediable. Similarly, serious inroads on scarce native forest could have been avoided had policies of creating extensive plantations of commercially valuable native species been adopted in good time. But government policy and planning was not forthcoming. Recurrent crises over pesticide residues in exports have been entirely avoidable, since the overseas standards were known, and the necessary scientific knowledge had been repeatedly urged on government. Similar myopia inhibits positive policies to maximise the retention of aesthetically attractive, scientifically useful and globally unique resources.

It is true, too, that although it has had major setbacks — for example the loss of Lake Pedder, the failure to stop uranium mining, the massive damage to forests from woodchipping — the environmental movement has also had major successes. But whether the movement is adjudged effective, and Australian environmental policy adequate and appropriate, depends entirely on the evaluative criteria used.

If politics is seen in the usual democratic pluralist framework, in which compromise and horse-trading are the daily norms, the environmental movement has been very effective in introducing environmental themes to politics, in arousing public concern, and in gaining political recognition. From this standpoint, environmental issues are here to stay, at least as long as public interest exists.

But if environmental policy is seen in an ecological framework, with the focus of concern the survival of particular biomes, species or habitats, or even effective policies for halting and reversing threats to production such as soil erosion, the picture is far less satisfactory. Very often compromise politics results in smaller changes than were necessary in the first place. A further problem results from the application of unsuitable techniques; cost-benefit analysis (CBA), for example, has been shown to produce sub-optimal results, and the deficiencies of environmental impact analysis (EIA) remain controversial. Endangered species and ecological processes do not understand economics, politics or compromise; they do not respond to "half-a-loaf" measures.[12] Continuing pressure for exploitation generates successive compromises, steadily "whittling away" what little has been gained. This is the real danger of **incrementalism** in decision making; everywhere the result has been steady decline in forests, growth of soil erosion, desertification and flooding, with accelerating rates of species extinction.[13] This poses a potential threat, not merely to further economic growth, but also to ultimate human survival.

Nevertheless, popular environmental political activity in Australia has often been unusual and unprecedented, both in nature and style. The "Green Bans" of the 1960s, for example, contributed to the preservation of a significant area of bush in Sydney, but also sparked a widespread awareness of environmental issues in the trade unions and the community.[14] The importance of such novelties lies in their capacity to counter the long established dominance of economic ideas and "practical", growth-oriented prejudices among decision makers.[15]

For the environmental movement, the need continually to defend past gains and to attempt to prevent new losses is rather like attempting to plug a dyke which continually springs more leaks. This is especially so where State governments remain bent on exploitation at any cost, promoting "fast-track" development schemes, in which proper social and environmental assessment has been eliminated.[16]

But, in the present-day context, it is abundantly clear that good management can greatly slow degradation processes in the short to medium term, given foresight and effective management. In the longer term, the ideal of the stable, "steady-state" society, in which high standards of living and human dignity are reconciled with a rich natural environment, still beckons.

For political scientists, interest in the processes of environmental policy-making is a natural development; as too, are attempts to determine whether it serves rational ecological goals. The capacity to answer these questions, however, depends on a more fundamental issue: identification of the common, policy-relevant features of environmental problems.

ECOLOGY AND ENVIRONMENTAL POLICY

There are two scholarly views of the place of ecology and of environmental policy. The first has tended to treat environmental issues as of fundamental importance, seeking ways of integrating scientific and technical knowledge with an understanding of political process and exploring the philosophical problems posed by human impacts on the environment.[17] The second has treated environmental issues as similar in nature to others, ranging from Stretton's description of them as "fit for regular politics" to the explicit claim that issues in environmental politics are no different from others.[18]

The first approach is unconventional, highly diverse, combative, opinionated — and fun. The second, though common, is inadequate and inappropriate for analysis of environmental issues, failing to appreciate their fundamental significance and importance. It has focussed mainly on attitudinal research, by contrast with the "concerned" school's predominant emphasis on policy and philosophy. By applying a relativistic, pluralist and unproven methodology to the explanation of environmentalism, this school of thought has come under suspicion of serving the conservative political agenda.

WHY ECOLOGY IS IMPORTANT

Ecology differs from other foci of political interest precisely because it is both complex and fundamental. All living things are bound together by a common dependence. Plants use the sun's energy to convert chemical nutrients to biomass, in the process called **photosynthesis**. Animals eat the plants, and each other. When they die, plants and animals are broken back down by **bacteria** into nutrients, and the cycle continues. The distinctive patterns of interaction which this generates are called **ecosystems**. Most ecosystems are distinguished by specificity — each is evolved to fit a particular place, with distinct physical characteristics — and by a very high degree of complexity. Most ecosystems have many hundreds and even thousands of species, all delicately balanced in a dynamic equilibrium. While scientists disagree about the precise degree of equilibrium required, as well as about ecosystem resilience, all agree that ecosystems lose their self-regulating, self-adjusting properties if disrupted.

Taken together, all the world's ecosystems are known as the **biosphere**. The **connectivity** of the biosphere is so far-reaching as to make Commoner's maxim that "everything is connected to everything else" far more than a metaphor, if not literally true in every case.[19] Apparently harmless impacts — such as low levels of environmental exposure to chemicals or radiation — can have unsuspected, long term consequences. The consequences of specific actions may impact at places or times remote from them.

Synergism is a consequence: substances and processes in the environment may (and frequently do) interact with each other in unpredictable, complex ways. Often scientists are ignorant of synergistic effects until they occur, because they jump disciplinary boundaries and produce unpredicted reactions. Risk and exposure calculations frequently omit them: each risk to the public is calculated in isolation from other similar risks at the same time, thus ignoring likely synergisms with consequent aggravation of impacts.

Many ecological systems are subject to **threshold effects**. Below a certain level, for example of pollution, no adverse effect can be detected. Above that level, the onset of undesirable effects is rapid and dramatic. The eutrophication of lakes is a much-quoted example.

Specific, emergent ecological phenomena can also present problems. One such is **biomagnification** in the food chain. Toxins such as heavy metals may be widely dispersed in the environment, but particular species may tend to concentrate them. Oysters, for example, by filter-feeding, accumulate heavy metals at levels hundreds of times those found in their immediate environment.[20] Humans, eating "high" up the food chain, are especially vulnerable to biomagnification. Looming over all is the problem of exponential growth: increase by a constant percentage of the total in a constant time period, like compound interest.[21] Though common in nature, it cannot continue indefinitely in any finite environment; if not checked, it will result in **overshoot**, where, for example, a population outstrips available resources. **Crash** follows: if a population outgrows its food supply, equilibrium will be restored by starvation. With human global population growth rates themselves increasing, overshoot must be forestalled, or famine and epidemic disease will do the culling.[22] Exponential growth in demand may lead to exponential **rates of depletion**, which continually increase, as is happening to global rainforest reserves.

Despite the achievements of modern technology, scientific knowledge is remarkably sketchy where a wide range of natural phenomena is concerned. While physics disposes of a powerful theoretical base capable of impressive predictive feats, biology and ecology are "softer", more observational and markedly less powerful theoretically. This is of exceptional importance, because, whereas the power of modern physics tends to obscure the many unanswered questions which it still has to tackle, gaps in knowledge are all too evident in ecology. Furthermore, it is important to bear in mind at all times that scientific knowledge is *never final*. At any time, it is no more than a combination of observation, interpretation, theory (in the sense of structured, relational process models) and informed guesses. At any time, it may be drastically revised by better observations, novel interpretations, improved (and occasionally very different) theory, or better guesses. It is very often the best knowledge available. But while it may be authoritative, it remains uncertain. This **scientific uncertainty** necessarily plays an immense part in policy in any science-dependent society.

Social and political thinking about environmental issues must take account of all the foregoing factors. The social effects of environmental problems are extensive and far-reaching; often they too interact in novel ways.

FROM ECOLOGY TO POLICY

Ecological threats to human societies are not new. Several ancient civilisations collapsed from irreversible problems which are all too familiar today. Evidence of failure due to declining soil fertility, salination of irrigation systems and collapsing rural productivity is now available for numerous ancient state systems.[23] While these once posed insoluble problems, in modern times the assumption is that, with superior knowledge and better tools for policy-making, such catastrophes could not occur. That assumption could not be more wrong. Ecological problems pose a critical threat to modern statecraft, placing enormous stresses on the policy system, and reviving, often in sharpened and urgent forms, some of the thorniest unresolved questions of political philosophy.

Furthermore, many problems of environmental policy arise from attempts to treat it in the same way as, say, industrial relations, and from a failure to appreciate how and why it differs. But the characteristics noted above suggest how very differently it must be handled. Uniquely, environmental policy treats "nonhuman beneficiaries of policy as prominent target groups", regulates human activity to benefit plants and animals, and redistributes the benefits to future human generations. It is also atypical in policy terms for granting science "a strong voice in agenda setting, formulation, and evaluation", though science is often used expediently by policy makers "to justify or legitimate their existing preferences".[24]

Because environmental problems, as commonly understood, are the social manifestations of underlying ecological malfunctions, their impacts are noticed only by scientists until they disrupt human activity. Pollution, for example, interferes with natural ecosystems, destroying some species and at times permitting others to increase to excess. By inhibiting the self-regenerating, waste-disposing processes in ecological cycles, it becomes evident as polluted land, water or air, with impacts on human health, productivity and amenity.

"Solving" such problems may involve a genuine attempt at amelioration by investigating the disruption to the ecosystem and establishing a new ecological equilibrium; or it may simply displace the problem to another time or locality. The dumping of chemical, nuclear or manufacturing waste or the disposal of domestic sewage by direct discharge into the sea are examples of **displacement**, likely simply to postpone (and perhaps worsen) the disposal problem they represent. Factories commonly dispose of wastes into the immediate environment, leaving them for someone else to clean up. This is known as an **externality**; it too is a form of displacement.

Many features of the contemporary world environmental crisis — excessive population, shortages of renewable and non-renewable resources, decline in number of many species and extinction of others, regional collapses of ecosystems through pollution, destruction of soil and fertility — are, in whole or part, consequences of displacement. Wishful thinking often plays a significant part: better technology, it is assumed, will make possible extraction of minerals which are now inaccessible, thus economy now is unjustified.

Nuclear waste is not a problem, enthusiasts claim, because by the time it has accumulated to serious levels, effective disposal techniques will have been developed. Such attitudes depend critically on an assumption of *progress*: that the better technologies will be found, that technological "fixes" for growing problems do exist, that the "limitless ingenuity of man" will always forestall the diseconomies and dislocations. It is sometimes implicitly assumed that failures — accidents and oil spills, for example — will simply not occur, or that their cost will be negligible. If, as is so often the case, the assumption proves false, the potential problems are horrendous.

Technology, in fact, is no substitute for political, lifestyle and institutional reform:

> We have only to consider the unforeseen consequences of chlorofluorocarbons — once touted for their environmental virtues — as evidence of the dark shadows behind well-intentioned technological innovations. The quest for ecological freedom is in fact an invitation to reduce unbounded faith in technological solutions and in the ability of nature to heal itself. While new technologies will unquestionably be needed to repair and mitigate the environmental damage inflicted by old ones, it is highly improbable that advances in technology alone will be able to preserve the kind of choices that will matter most in the next century.[25]

Ignorance, compounded by scientific illiteracy, is an unavoidable consequence of scientific uncertainty. Unknown and uncalculated risks are continually being taken — for instance, thousands of novel chemicals are introduced into the biosphere annually, with only minimal research into their impact.[26] The history of nuclear weaponry and energy has been a string of unpleasant surprises.[27] The most important outcome of ignorance is the emergence of unexpected, unintended consequences of particular courses of action, social trends or public policies.

In addition, ecological problems are frequently not susceptible to "technological fixes". Often an apparent fix merely displaces the problem. This is a consequence of the **interpenetration** of ecological systems: disruptions can set up chain reactions of great length. Displacement often appears in the form of an externality, as in the factory waste case.

Very frequently, environmental "bads" are **invisible**, in the sense that the society's information systems are not geared to their detection.

Technical invisibility can result when particular professions or trades are inconsiderate of or blind to the consequences of their actions: bricklayers walking on garden beds, engineers oblivious of their environmental and aesthetic impacts. *Economic* invisibility often manifests itself in the form of externalities; there is now an extensive literature on their correction or elimination.[28] Environmental issues can also be socially or politically invisible: socially, if there is no general concern, or if the culture is inimical, politically if there is no concern among population or ruling élite, and no immediate pressures for solution of the problem. The attention of politicians to environmental issues displays clear cycles, often based on threats to the productive system as they emerge from ecological disruptions.

The **irreversibility** of ecological damage has highly specific policy consequences. Not only must environmental policy address remedial action, it must also leave ample margins for error, as a "safety net", and accept that some "worst cases" will occur. Irreversibility mandates careful attention to the implications of ignorance and uncertainty, and the adoption of the "cautionary principle", which states that "worst case" outcomes should always be considered, policies which court danger treated with the greatest of care, and reversible options preferred.

The central message of ecology is **holism**. Connectivity and complexity mean that the behaviour of whole systems is often not reducible to that of the components, and so must be understood at the system level. Ecosystems often behave counter-intuitively, reacting in unexpected and unpredicted ways.

Environmental policy issues are frequently unfit for compromise, not least because ecological systems do not understand political constraints: if critical thresholds are passed, destabilisation is inevitable. Thus the **incrementalist** test for the "best" policy, that all concerned can agree on it regardless of their particular goals, is invalid, because non-human interests are not represented, and, in principle, never can be. The "rational" test, that the means chosen be the most appropriate to the ends sought, seems more apt. A utilitarian, or more correctly, "consequentialist" approach, in which the probable outcomes are properly evaluated, seems unavoidable. This dovetails with the precautionary principle.

THE STUDY OF ENVIRONMENTAL POLICY

A collection such as this can do no more than present a series of "snapshots" of particular issues or problems. It cannot resolve complex methodological problems, nor can it offer a fully comprehensive overview of environmental policy.[29] But many of the political problems raised by environmental issues display similarities. They are rarely central to policy and planning. They pose novel and thorny difficulties for policy makers, as a direct consequence of ecosystem complexity, connectivity and unpredictability.

Many issues in social and economic policy unfold in a well-understood context, requiring only a minimum of "backgrounding" by the researcher in order to elucidate the processes under study. By contrast, given widespread ignorance of ecology, and the importance of technical and scientific data, there is a clear need for researchers in environmental policy not merely to understand the links from the environmental to the social system, but to interpret them intelligibly to the reader. A central puzzle is to determine whether (and how) they have been taken into account in the policy-making process; for this, the daily tools of policy analysis are frequently inadequate.

In addition, environmental policy explicitly requires an evaluative stance, with clear criteria, consistent over a range of issues and constant over a reasonable length of time. There is less *relativity* to environmental issues than to many social ones, despite the large element of *uncertainty*. One decision is often nowhere near as good as another; as a result incomplete analysis or expedient adoption of policy may harbour danger. The technique of **satisficing** — ceasing the analysis when the first satisfactory policy appears — becomes much more dubious, and frequently will be inadequate. Because present actions may have adverse future consequences, unforeseen through ignorance or uncertainty, there is more need for prudence, foresight, self-critical attitudes and lateral thinking. The centrality of scientific knowledge aggravates problems in handling it and judging its implications. These can be acute: the 1987 Helsham enquiry into the logging of Tasmanian rainforests was marked by a dramatic split between the scientific and other personnel.

But even scientific evidence, though often better than outright bias, is far from "objective", and is rarely conclusive. Experts have their biases, and by its nature, scientific evidence is open to revision and changed judgements. It can rarely give a "yes" or "no" answer; the sheer complexity of ecological systems, and our limited understanding of them, means that uncertainty is especially rife in such circumstances. But scientists are no more competent than ordinary citizens in judging many issues involving ethical outcomes of scientific decisions, where it is highly appropriate for citizens to participate and hold views.

Nor is that all. Ecologically rational decision making throws substantial burdens both on the cognitive systems of governments, and on their will and ability to devise and follow through suitable policies.

All types of social choice mechanisms are stressed in this way. To the degree that political systems are "polyarchal", combining several decision mechanisms, and allowing open debate on policy issues, they often fall down particularly badly on consistency and coordination. Environmental policy problems tend to demand more of the most desirable qualities — prudence, foresight, altruism, statesmanship and so on — than most systems have available. They place in doubt features of "democratic" systems — such as the capacity to compromise, the assumption that individuals are the best judges of their own needs, or rights over property — which have been lauded as their most positive.

COLLECTIVE ACTION AND COMMON GOODS

Connectivity means that most environmental problems are **collective**: they cannot be remedied by uncoordinated individual action. Instead they require collective action, which can be costly. If one person or group gains by behaving selfishly, but the effect on the bulk of the population is small, though irritating, it may be difficult to motivate resistance.[30] This problem is typical of air or water pollution. Often the only genuine solutions require collective action. For example, if two cities border a lake, a situation may arise where the lake will be clean only if both refrain from discharging sewage into it. One defector can jeopardise water quality; cooperation of both is required to maintain it.[31] Coercive powers may be needed to enforce compliance with rules about collective action, though such powers do not necessarily imply political dictatorship.[32] Worse, not only are environmental problems political, but they trigger some intractable paradoxes of social choice. Frequently, simply counting heads will produce distributional conflicts — especially if all concerned consider only their own immediate gain — in which collective goods are neglected. Common systems of social choice, such as voting, are not immune to the problem.[33]

Further, many environmental goods are **exclusive**, meaning that they cannot be available to all: compare, for example, access to wilderness with an increase in wages for all members of a trade, an example of an **inclusive** (or non-rival) good, the enjoyment of which by one member of the group does not exclude the others.[34] Exclusive goods are particularly sensitive to congestion.

The dominance of economics in modern public policy making creates particular difficulties because of its insensitivity. Neoclassical economic theory prices natural resources at zero; when they become scarce, their price rises according to the dictates of the market, not the intrinsic worth of the resource, nor its ecological status. And market mechanisms can only react. Markets are also poor coordinators, especially where public goods are concerned. They cannot conserve, nor can they detect and plan for approaching shortages. Furthermore, the total economic value of "ecosystem services" to the global economy is of the order of $US33,000,000,000; roughly double the annual GNP of all the world's economic systems.[35] Nothing could underline human dependence on the natural environment more starkly.

A further insensitivity is the assumption that all resources are substitutable, and thus that there is no cause for concern about the depletion of any one of them. Lurking behind this is the further assumption that the natural environment is an infinite source of potentially exploitable resources, directly contradicting the findings of biology and ecology. A derived assumption is of reversibility: that mistakes can be rectified or erased. This is not so for many important environmental problems, such as species extinction, soil degradation, persistent pollutants and so on. Furthermore, most economists assume that indiscriminate economic growth (and hence resource consumption) can go on indefinitely.[36] It is not possible, as the economists assume, to run the system close to its limits — "maximum efficiency" in economic terms may be excessively close to disaster ecologically, especially when humans are appropriating very large percentages of natural productivity.

REGULATION

Economists and political scientists, especially in the United States of America, have stressed the difficulties of regulation to the point that conservative policies now overstress markets and seek to minimise regulation. But regulation is more central to environmental management than resource ownership, direct government participation in the economy, or even "economic transformation", long seen as a critical government responsibility. This is not to downplay the difficulties of regulation. Government may have to contend with hostility, indifference and ignorance. Its decrees may be ignored, distorted or deliberately flouted. It may encounter serious "enforcement costs", raising the expense incurred by the policies in question.

Governments have often responded to environmental questions by seeking to regulate or forbid activities with environmental impacts. Britain's Alkali Inspectors were endowed with sweeping powers during the mid-nineteenth century, in response to industrial contamination of streams and rivers. Much pollution legislation has followed this model. An alternative approach has been to attempt the development of comprehensive policy mechanisms, generally built about the notion of ecological sustainability. Grabosky and others have explored regulatory mechanisms which are developed in coop-eration with firms involved, and "arm's length", in the sense that reg-ulation is not punitive so much as anticipatory. They suggest that firms often appreciate clear rules, known well before project planning commences, more than "open slather" with attendant risks of public objection or prosecution.[37]

POLICY, REGULATION AND SUSTAINABILITY IN AUSTRALIA

Evidence that stresses on Australia's environment have reached crisis point has been accumulating rapidly. Particularly at risk are the frag-ile and unique ecosystems which make Australia distinctive and which represent an important resource for future economic activity. The need for regulation of human environmental impact is rehearsed again and again in the pages that follow.

Australia is the only inhabited continent lying exclusively in the southern hemisphere. It lies between 10 and 43 degrees south, it is the driest continent in the world, and has the lowest average eleva-tion. The continent is geologically stable, parts having been so for 400 million years. Its area is about 7.6 million sq km, nearly equiva-lent to the United States of America without Alaska. Two thirds of Australia's land mass is arid and semi-arid. Eighty percent of its 18 million inhabitants have settled within the 1% of its area along the eastern seaboard between the uplands and the coast. Although the effects of coastal settlement have dominated environmental impacts, no part of the continent, even its extensive, sparsely populated arid zone, has been spared.[38]

In the 200 years since European invasion and settlement, Australia has achieved one of the highest rates of ecosystem destruction in the world, radically altering both its natural habitat and the habitation and culture of its indigenous people. "Nowhere else on earth have so few people pauperised such a large proportion of the world's surface in such a brief period of time".[39] By contrast, some 60,000 or more years of occupation by Australia's indigenous peoples had left no impact vis-ible to the European eye. Until overturned by the High Court's 1992 *Mabo* decision, the country had been officially declared *terra nullius*, an empty wilderness belonging to no one.

Whilst relatively low population density, limited air pollution, clean drinking water and healthy coastal regions in more remote areas tend to present an impression that problems are only minor, the Australian environment still faces serious problems of degradation. These include habitat destruction, urban environmental problems, poor inland water management, ozone depletion, land degradation, old growth forest logging and complex environmental and social justice issues for indigenous Australians.[40] One third of Australia's woodlands have been cleared, one half of its forests, 95% of its temperate woodlands, mallee and native grasslands, 75% of its tropical and sub-tropical rainforest, and much of its coastal wetlands. Species extinctions, agricultural pollution, soil salinity and erosion continue unabated. Australia is also the highest per capita greenhouse gas emitter, domestic garbage producer and fuel consumer.[41]

Most of these problems are well known. The Australian Conservation Foundation (ACF) lists major current threats to Australian biodiversity as: the impact of irrigation, river regulation and pollution on rivers and wetlands; the effect of logging, wood-chipping, mining and associated damage to forests and woodlands; the grazing, cultivation and urban development impacts upon grasslands; the extinction costs of overgrazing; the effects of ferals, mining and soil erosion on mammal species; the damage to coastal ecosystems including mangrove, seagrass beds, coral reefs, coastal waters and oceans from urban development, tourism, pollution, dredging, overfishing and introduced organisms.[42]

Contemporary environmental problems originate with the early colonial settlement ethic. In Australia, heavy dependence on exports, especially of wool and wheat in the nineteenth century, led to an early emphasis on extractive considerations, and a pervasive concern with "development". The first settlers, rejecting Australian species as "useless", deliberately introduced European varieties and techniques. Yet even the adoption of wheat and wool were themselves constrained by environmental criteria: they were the only export produce available which were adapted to extensive dryland farming and which were relatively imperishable and hence transportable to Britain. Though later supplemented by meat exports (as refrigeration became available) and minerals, their continuing predominance is in part a reflection of ongoing ecological constraints: viable alternatives remain undiscovered.[43]

Australia's unique and fragile ecosystems have been acutely stressed ever since Europeans settled. Alien techniques of cultivation, with their attendant exotic species, were joined by deliberate introductions designed to make the landscape more European or even to afford sport; their environmental impact was unanticipated, and, even in the nineteenth century, most unwelcome.[44] In consequence, unresolved, often urgent problems exist in every area, from the lack of a coherent population policy through soil degradation, habitat loss and numerous other issues, down to the space requirements, noise impact and ecological implications of recreational activities.

The complexity and fragility of Australian ecosystems has been a standard argument for conservation and preservation for the last century. Their variability is of particular relevance as highly standardised "agri-business" penetrates farming, imposing unsuitable practices in many areas. The impact of such practices is very often uncertain, precisely because of extensive ignorance.

In fact, ecological research in Australia is radically incomplete. The ecology and biology of many native species, both faunal and floral, is unknown; many species have not even been described. Extinction of useful species has already occurred; many others are virtually certain, given the present accelerating extinction rates. In 200 years, some 78 species of plants, 1 of birds and 12 of mammals are known to have become extinct; but a further 812, 18 and 23 respectively, plus 2 reptiles, are now endangered.[45] In many cases a relatively small investment in management would contribute markedly to survival. Given the enormous economic importance of natural sources for many important products — rainforests, for example, are an important source of pharmaceuticals — this is an important concern.

These problems are often connected; soil fertility, for example, is affected by the presence or absence of native species, to the point that some farmers now plant windbreaks and "corridors" of native trees to encourage beneficent animal and bird species.

Nor, despite relative isolation, is Australia immune from important global environmental issues such as oceanic and atmospheric pollution, and most importantly at present, climatic modification and its effects. The concentration of population on the coastline, in fact, renders Australia disproportionately vulnerable to the rising oceans and storms predicted as consequences of the greenhouse effect. There is extensive and legitimate disagreement about the extent, severity and policy implications, but they are cause for serious concern.

SUSTAINABILITY

The emerging threats to the sustainability both of the productive system and of Australia's position in global trade stem from a number of sources. Soil loss to wind and water erosion continues. Soil nutrients are lost when crops are harvested, and are either exported or dumped in the sea by urban sewage systems; few farmers replace them fully, some not at all. Yet available, tried technology can contribute both to water conservation and nutrient replenishment. While depletion rates of minerals are controversial, and do not appear to pose an *immediate* threat, depletion of biological resources such as timber and fish stocks is already severe. Loss of ecological diversity, especially through extinctions, threatens the resilience of the underlying ecosystems. Population growth places pressures on water supply, intensifies the impact of industrial pollution (which is growing more severe in any case) and sharpens land-use conflicts.[46] Australian lifestyles are highly demanding of space for residential and recreational purposes, depleting available fertile land and competing with alternative land uses.

Ecological stresses, even when they do not conflict with economic or social "necessities", frequently do not translate readily into obvious policy measures. Poor knowledge of many aspects of ecology means that necessary data is often unavailable. Uncertainty about the relationships among species, or impacts of human economic activity, is common. Scientific uncertainty is often a barrier to clear-cut policy making. Frequently the only rational option is to adopt a policy that does not foreclose future outcomes — the "cautionary principle" — and to seek further information. Global warming is a case in point: not everyone agrees that it is happening at all, and no one can offer cut and dried policy nostrums.

Even where scientific knowledge is reasonably adequate, countermeasures can require policies which are politically unpalatable. Clearing controls, for example, can prevent loss of rare species as well as of forest cover, but are unpopular among farmers; so far, they have been successfully implemented only in South Australia (SA).[47]

Dovers finds sustainability problems are significantly different from other policy problems due to their temporal and spatial scale, limits, irreversibility, urgency, connectivity and complexity, uncertainty, cumulation; moral and ethical dimensions; and novelty.[48] This complexity leads to difficulty in interpreting the idea in practice.

The concept of Ecologically Sustainable Development (ESD) has been heavily criticised, both for vagueness, and, importantly, for allegedly "fudging" the conflict between expansionist industrialism and a finite globe. The latter charge, however, is not proven, in the sense that, should industrial techniques which are sustainable emerge, and a steady-state society in ecological terms develop, it would prove false. In all probability, the only way to find out is to conduct the experiment; in this venture, the very ambiguity of ESD may prove advantageous, permitting the reconciliation of differing viewpoints and sustaining institutional and policy diversity.[49] However, development of clear policy lines for ecologically sustainable development is a chicken-and-egg problem in many ways. Until the problems are tackled, options will not become clear, nor directions for policy development apparent. Thus recognition of problems, big and small, may be an essential prerequisite for their effective resolution.

HOLISM AND CASE STUDIES

This collection mingles case-study material with essays in interpretation. Both classes of material are still scarce. While it is possible to assemble a more comprehensive array of material than in the early 1990s, there is still much to be done. This is particularly so because of the heavier than normal interpretative demands of environmental policy analysis.

The interpenetration and synergistic qualities of ecosystems require from their student a "pragmatic holism": a commitment to seeing problems as wholes, and in their broader context, for the most practical of reasons. But holism can impose unmanageable burdens on the analyst, and exploration of the "fine grain" of problems may tend to reveal unexpected complications. As complex systems are often "counter-intuitive", such surprises must be expected, and empirical research will be essential to ferret them out. Even though sceptical of reductionism, pragmatic holism is entirely compatible with a sensitive use of reductionist *techniques* for understanding interactions in detail. By eschewing the conventional tendency to break down problems into discrete specialisations with attendant tunnel vision and problem displacement, it can keep all interactions in perspective. Nor does it necessarily imply any particular policy stance. Combining holism with case studies can help reduce the risk of excluding the very phenomena of most interest, especially where they cluster at the boundaries of conventional classifications. Boundary problems are always rather intractable; one solution is to treat phenomena as networks rather than as bounded entities, and to allow the importance of each element in the network to determine its place in the analysis.[50]

In the following chapters, a series of themes will be taken up. Walker's chapter stresses the persistence of a developmentalist policy régime in Australian politics, and suggests that, in environmental terms, this fact has been more important than changing fashions in economic management. Crowley investigates some of the paradoxes of environmental policy-making; in particular the challenge offered to standard single-level, linear process models by the complexities and multidimensionality of environmental issues, and offers a unified analytical theory. Economou explores federal environmental policy in the light of recent moves to return responsibility for it to the States, where, as he points out, it mainly lay before it rose to national prominence under the Hawke Labor Government. Doyle offers a cutting critique of conservative "wise use" policies as they have actually been applied to arid land management in SA, and points to a disturbing trend away from state brokerage and towards corporate controlled environmental "round table" decision making. Carden's critique of Queensland development policy, and of the sugar industry in particular, focusses both on mismatched European-derived agricultural technology under tropical and semi-tropical conditions, and the persisting irrationality of attempts to make such technologies work where they have already failed. McCall examines the McArthur River mine fiasco in the Northern Territory, against the background of mining industry demands, environmental impact and Aboriginal land rights. He pinpoints this development as a key turning point in the Keating transition away from "Hawkean" adhocery and toward "proactive" environmental decision making. Mercer examines the increasingly important area of tourism and coastal management, showing how there has been a comprehensive failure to plan and manage such areas effectively, and describing the ecological and political consequences. Taplin's review of Sydney's sustainability catalogues the many missed opportunities, as well as sketching ways forward. Its analysis is innovative both for its urban critique, and its pursuit of the local implementation of a slippery, contested political notion. Adams and Hine continue the local theme, reviewing the implementation of the Agenda 21 programme at the municipal level in SA. They note the surge in local level programmes, but also the problems of benchmarking local environmental activity. Dovers addresses the issue of sustainability, tracking the remarkable amount of bureaucratic activity it has generated, exploring the weaknesses and deficiencies in the sustainability policy process, and offering much needed suggestions for its working application and administration.

The conclusion takes up many of these themes, reflecting on their common characteristics. It suggests an overall framework, incorporating a political economy perspective, for their evaluation.

STATIST DEVELOPMENTALISM IN AUSTRALIA

K.J. Walker

INTRODUCTION

Public policy in Australia since 1788 has been persistently developmentalist. Imported from Europe and geared to European expectations, developmentalism has tended to ignore or belittle environmental constraints. The resulting pattern of development has been subsidised by the running down of Australia's natural resources, unsustainably in the medium term. And the institutionalised pattern of activity which this has generated tends to inhibit change in the direction of greater environmental sensitivity and consequently sustainability.

Most of these points have been argued separately, and in more depth, elsewhere.[1] But they are related far more closely than conventional scholarship allows. Bringing them together makes possible a more comprehensive as well as a clearer overview of the Australian policy régime of the last 200 years.

Explanations of Australia's developmental pattern have tended to rely on a mixture of geographical and economic data: thus

failures are explained in terms of remoteness and aridity, while successes are celebrated as consequences of a rich endowment of natural resources.[2] But these explanations have tended to be incomplete
and *ad hoc*. They need a broader context, geopolitically and ecologically sensitive, for a full understanding of Australian development
since 1788.

The concept of the *policy régime* is of great utility here. régimes
encompass policies and the processes by which they are made, but
additionally incorporate an understanding of the cultural background,
the guiding assumptions and the political economy — the whole environment of policy, in short. Australia's developmentalist régime has
proved remarkably durable, its basic tenets unquestioned even when
major changes in policy direction are implemented. It has always
applied a European developmentalist attitude, grounded in nineteenth-
century notions of "progress", to an ecological system in which climate, soils, flora and fauna were all incompatible with the implicit
model of development to a greater or lesser degree. Most developmental "successes" can be explained in terms of incompatibilities which
(if only for the time being) are not fatal; the failures in terms of severe
mismatches of natural resources with European visions.

European imperialism has taken two forms. The first, domination
and political control of existing political systems, impacted mainly
Asian and tropical regions such as India or the Dutch East Indies.
The second was the settlement by Europeans of "underpopulated"
regions of temperate climate to which European agricultural technologies could relatively easily be introduced.[3]

Australia was one of the latter, the "Neo-Europes", but the last
to be settled and least tractable in biophysical terms.

The violent displacement of indigenous hunter-gatherer societies
which accompanied European settlement in the New World and in
Australasia aimed specifically at "opening up" land for denser modes
of production, such as agriculture, pastoralism, mining and forestry.[4]
The initial impacts were primarily extractive. In Australia, whaling,
sealing and exploitation of exotic timbers such as cedar and sandal-
wood were followed by wool, minerals and wheat.[5] Imperial trade, by
establishing niches for the new societies as suppliers of food, fibres
and minerals, underwrote continuing population growth. Relatively
low population densities delayed impacts from congestion and pollution, permitting the ignoring or displacing of environmental problems for long periods.

Ecological conditions in Western Europe differ radically from
Australia. Reliable annual rainfall, deep alluvial soils and a temperate
climate mean greater resistance to ecological abuse and symptoms

which were less noticeable and more easily repaired. European patterns of environmental exploitation relied on predictable returns and the consequent expectation of steady annual incomes. Australia presented particularly difficult problems to settlers guided by assumptions derived from these conditions. They encountered a climate in which drought was the norm, populated by flora and fauna they did not understand and hence could not attempt to use sensitively or sustainably.[6] They responded, not by accommodation, but by redoubling their attempts to impose a European development pattern.

AUSTRALIAN DEVELOPMENTALISM

Australia's development pattern strongly resembles those of Canada, New Zealand, Argentina and Brazil, dubbed "settler capitalist" or "dominion capitalist" societies. Like them, its economy

> ... exhibits ... a substantial degree of industrialisation under conditions of dependent development, a concentration on raw materials and first-stage processing for export industries, a predominance of manufactures among imported products, and reliance on foreign capital and technology.[7]

The service sector is proportionately larger than in "metropolitan" countries such as those of Western Europe. Strong pressures on governments for economic growth, mythologised as "development", are characteristic.[8]

Australian farms have tended to specialise in no more than three or four crops, predominantly for export, making them inordinately sensitive to market fluctuations.[9] "Broad acre" farming on the European model required extensive clearing, encouraged by deliberate government policy; loss of soil fertility resulted. Pastoralists consistently overstocked, "flogging" land to recoup costs which were often a result of overcapitalisation in the first place.[10] Holdings were unrealistically sized. The banking system, geared to regular repayments and the assumption of reliable annual crops, made no allowance for fluctuating production. Australia's ecology, radically different from Europe's in respect of soils, rainfall, fauna and flora, responded poorly.[11] Scientific knowledge of soil properties — such as the need for trace elements — has been hard-won, but has been exploited almost exclusively to extend cultivation of European crops.[12]

In Australia as in the other "settler capitalist" societies, development has deeply involved government. Lack of private infrastructure provision meant that government provision of communications, encouragement of land clearance and subsidisation of infant industries was required to "open up" the country.[13]

The effect was to institutionalise the developmentalist policy régime, in an expression of the Australian "talent for bureaucracy".[14] This régime is best characterised as "statist developmentalism", in recognition of the nation-state's rôle in attempting to speed up economic growth. Statist developmentalism has appeared in at least four distinct guises. In the earliest, colonial stage, economic development was rudimentary, and government's stimulation of economic activity was direct but haphazard. The second phase is that dubbed "colonial socialism" by Butlin, in which the state played an important part in stimulating economic development and became a major participant in the economy. The third phase, lasting much of the twentieth century, was a sort of half-hearted developmentalist Keynesianism, as yet unendowed with a catchy name. The current phase of "state-sponsored marketisation" is a fourth. Though quite distinct as economic policy, marked by privatisation and deregulation, it is not a departure from developmentalism, nor is the state's rôle as stimulator of economic activity as much on the wane as it might seem.

Successive fashions in economic policy have tended seriously to exacerbate the environmental impact of the productive system in Australia. As conflicts over competing land uses increase with population and intensity of exploitation, the importance of regulation by government grows. Statist developmentalism in all its forms stresses exploitation rather than regulation. It has resulted in significant and serious erosion of ecosystem resources, posing a medium and long-term threat to sustainability.

THE EARLIEST DAYS

Little needs to be said about the years immediately following 1788, nor about Aboriginal land use. Both subjects are extensively researched and are the focus of numerous fascinating scholarly controversies. Frawley comments that

> ... The development of colonial Australia was closely tied to the needs of the British Empire and took place within a capitalist world economy where the "core" industrialised countries of Western Europe invested in "peripheral" states whose rôle was to provide cheap raw materials and foodstuffs, a market for manufactured products and profitable avenues for investment of surplus capital.[15]

What was important in the small and fragmented Australian economy was the early establishment and persistence of radical environmental modification, a tendency to authoritarianism in government, and the broad culture of developmentalism, in which the interests of the professional classes and government became closely entwined.[16]

Many issues dominant in Australian historical analysis turn out to be largely beside the point from an environmental perspective. Clashes between pastoralism and "closer settlement" have often been constructed in terms of class antagonisms and the clash of opportunity with privilege; yet the environmental impacts of both activities were equally serious. Pastoralism's introduction of hoofed livestock damaged flora, fouled creeks and in all probability was responsible for the early extinction of succulent plant species, selectively grazed by sheep in particular.[17] But the broad acre agriculture associated with "closer settlement" cleared and modified forests and savannah, with serious, adverse, ongoing impacts on both native species and soil fertility. More relevant to both is the failure of government to control or regulate pastoral settlement, and the Lockean insistence on land clearing as a measure of "improvement", contrary to evidence that it adversely affected productivity and ecology.

Australia's capacity to provide a steady stream of repatriated wealth was, however, constrained by distance. At first only durable, high-value commodities, such as gold and wool, were profitable in the face of costly, inefficient inland transport and months in transit to Europe by sea. Lower value commodities such as wheat and base metals joined them as internal transport improved, but meat and dairy products had to await the introduction of refrigeration in the last decades of the nineteenth century.[18] As a supplier of primary produce and an importer of manufactured products, Australia financed its imports by the exploitation of its natural resources.[19] It was the institutional arrangements for carrying out this rôle, and their ecological impact, that were distinctive.

NINETEENTH CENTURY DEVELOPMENTALISM

During the "long boom" from the 1860s to 1890, the Australian economy became more unified, and grew at an extraordinary rate, due in part to the gold rushes and the accompanying increases in population and wealth. During this period the pattern of developmentalism that Butlin has labelled "colonial socialism" was consolidated, though most of its elements had already emerged. It was to remain dominant into the following century.

COLONIAL SOCIALISM

The encouragement of "national capital", common in capitalist countries during the nineteenth century, sought both to enhance national capabilities in a growing international market, and to protect state power by inhibiting the already well-developed internationalism of mercantile capital. In creating sheltered trading networks based in colonial empires, European governments intervened not merely in the provision of infrastructure such as transport and communications, but also in fields such as education, social welfare and even direct investment in and promotion of industry. Australia may have done no more than follow these precedents, but what was unique was the sheer scale of government involvement.[20] It was so great as to distort, during the nineteenth century in particular, the "normal" pattern of State revenue.

> This late nineteenth-century pattern of public and private relations depended first on large-scale public action to attract resources of capital and labour into the economy from outside (essentially Britain), enhancing rates of increase beyond those that the private market was capable of delivering, and second on the direct participation by public institutions in investment and the delivery of marketed output on a scale that was rare in the Western world. Combined with these activities, governments were the landlords of most of the Australian continent. A central motif in this pattern was that governments became highly market-oriented and their revenues were predominantly from government enterprise, land and customs receipts.[21]

INSTITUTIONAL INNOVATIONS

Most Australian governments founded departments with specific infrastructure functions such as posts and telegraphs, railways, urban transport and energy supply. Communications especially have long been a common function of the nation-state, so this in itself is not so remarkable; what is special about Australia is the presence of all such functions, and the depth of government involvement. At various times, all of these functions — and sometimes even their day-to-day commercial activities — have been incorporated directly in departments and have been subject to political control. The problems arising from departmental control of commercial enterprises, leading to the emergence of statutory corporations from the 1880s, are especially well documented. The consequential policy issues became dominant, especially in State politics.[22]

Political interference, corruption and mismanagement were often triggers for centralisation, frequently via the setting up of quasi-governmental authorities at State level. Large numbers of localised irrigation and water supply trusts marked the early years of irrigation in Victoria, in accordance with liberal dogmas of the time. These were later departmentalised as a result of serious conflicts, inadequate planning, poor financial management and ineffective coordination.[23] Other examples have tended to be state-wide or even greater in scope. Marketing boards have been an important tool in the procurement and marketing of primary produce as well as regulation of production, which has been quite draconian in industries such as sugar and fresh fruit.

These proliferating government departments, semi-government authorities, statutory authorities and inquiries of various kinds indulged in considerable political and bureaucratic infighting. This contributed to policy paralysis, stagnation and the making of policy "on the run". In a system with seven governments, the complications can barely be imagined.

ENVIRONMENTAL IMPACTS

"Colonial socialism's" emphasis on physical development was inherently insensitive to Australia's fragile and unique natural environment. Encouragement of "closer settlement", irrigation and land clearance had direct and measurable impacts.[24] State assistance to rural industry, from provision of infrastructure such as railways, grain elevators and marketing schemes to purchase of ailing mines, further subsidised these impacts. Drought "relief" helps perpetuate the myth that bad years are exceptional; continuation of unsustainable farming practices then increases stresses on soils and flora.

SOCIALISM — OR DEVELOPMENTALISM?

Butlin's coinage conformed with a considerable body of writing which equated state involvement in the economy with socialism.[25] But Reeves, for example, frequently uses the term "governmentalism".[26] Others reject the characterisation outright.[27] For this was developmentalism; it had nothing to do with socialist political objectives such as income equality, social welfare and a "fair go" for working people. The "colonial socialist" policy pattern emerged during the "long boom" of 1860–90. While trade union activity did take place in Australia from the 1830s onward, it was neither well organised nor did it involve a very large part of the workforce. Strong politically active unions, and parliamentary representation of Labour, were delayed until the depression of the 1890s. While there can be no denying that a social welfare element enters public policy — though largely under a *liberal* guise — in the last two decades of the century, it was not especially egalitarian and is viewed by some as quite elitist.[28] McQueen, indeed, complains that socialist ideas were neither widely disseminated nor well understood even by the 1890s.[29]

In short, although egalitarianism and welfare-statism were early and important elements in Australian political thinking, their widespread acceptance postdates the "long boom". "Colonial socialism" was firmly established well before the rise of a strong Labour move-ment, long before Labor as a political party had any significant say in policy, and before socialist ideas were widely diffused in Australia.

Furthermore, when Labor did begin to influence public policy in Australia, its one area of agreement with its conservative opponents was developmentalism. Labor did place a stronger emphasis on direct government investment and hence state ownership and delivery of marketable goods and services. But, with statism well established, the difference was one of degree rather than of kind; nor did Labor, always reformist, seriously challenge the encouragement of private investment.

Thus "colonial socialism" was inherently neither socialist nor welfare-statist. It expressed a strong convergence of interest between government and capital, in a consensus on "development". Government and industry agreed on subsidies, government invest-ment, protectionism and "closer settlement", just as they now agree on deregulation.[30] To describe this as a form of socialism significant-ly misrepresents and misunderstands the rôle of government in Australia. It overemphasises the fact of government participation in the market economy, in the process underplaying the significance of "development" and the importance of the associated commitment to infrastructure provision. Alternative descriptions such as "state capi-talism" or "the state mode of production" also fail adequately to recognise the developmentalist dimension.[31] By substituting "devel-opmentalism" for "socialism", the new term "colonial developmen-talism" sufficiently emphasises the rôle of government while underlining its persistent developmentalist purpose.

THE IMPACT OF FEDERATION

Thus the creation of an Australian federation in 1901 heralded no break with the existing policy régime; rather it sought merely to resolve intercolonial stresses. Creation of a national market aimed to stimulate economic growth, and provision for an Interstate Commission and a High Court was expected to address cooperation as well as adjudication. The new Commonwealth's inherited tasks included construction of the Transcontinental Railway, a condition of Western Australia's entry to the federation. The extensive pro-gramme of dam construction, weirs and locking which followed the Murray Waters Agreement of 1914 and the establishment of the Murray River Commission in 1917 was also unfinished federation business.

Federation reapportioned but did not change governmenta func-tions. With posts, telegraphs and later broadcasting, the Commonwealth gained most communication infrastructure. Transport, especially rail-ways, remained predominantly with the States, as did urban transport, irrigation, water supply and marketing of primary produce. The Commonwealth rôle grew as it became involved with various major works and investment projects including various dam, railway standardi-sation and electricity supply projects. The grandest of all was the Snowy Mountains scheme of the 1940s, in which the Commonwealth, from being a participant, became the leader. Since the 1970s, Commonwealth "leadership", through fiscal power and bureaucratic control of imple-mentation, spread to transport, power supply and education.

Federation thus extended statist developmentalism. Major inter-state and Commonwealth-State instrumentalities such as the Murray River Commission and the Joint Coal Board set political pacts in con-crete: the Murray Waters Agreement of 1914, for example, though amended a score of times over minor issues, proved so durable in respect of the water-sharing arrangements that it "effectively estab-lished a legal gridlock which could not be broken for 70 years".[32]

PHASE THREE: HALF-HEARTED KEYNESIANISM

Classic "colonial socialism" began to weaken after 1918, as the "nat-ural monopolies" which had previously underpinned it were under-mined. In transport, motor vehicles began to challenge the railways for freight after 1918, and universal car ownership devastated for-merly profitable urban public transport monopolies from the late 1940s. But Keynesianism in Australia was half-hearted at best. It licensed politicians to run deficits — but they never realised its pos-sibilities for effective economic management.

SHIFTING PATTERNS

Within the envelope of persisting developmentalist trends, there were shifts in economic policy and in the "culture" of public policy. Immediately following Federation, some significant policy innova-tions — such as the introduction of White Australia, the first income supports such as pensions, and the arbitration system — emerged. It was also during this period that the general trend to welfare statism began to gain momentum, expressed in a growing acceptance of the state's rôle in cushioning the vagaries of economic change and in providing "positive" freedoms for citizens. This came to its full flow-ering *after* (but not during) the Great Depression of the 1930s, in the form of Keynesian interventionism. This in turn lost its momen-tum in the "stagflation" that followed the post-war economic boom.

Accordingly, priorities for public investment changed, both to reflect contemporary intellectual trends and to meet changing needs.

Although, from the 1920s onwards, government's most profitable market activities progressively decayed, private investment did not exceed State until the 1930s.[33] Not only was change slow, but substantial investment in various "infrastructure" and developmentalist activities continued. There was a general shift after 1945 from transport and communications to electric power generation as the primary focus for state government investment. With a doubling of Australia's population between 1950 and 1990, most States found themselves hard pressed to keep up with the demand for services, especially in the cities, where electricity supply, sewage and roads made substantial demands. Major rural development schemes, such as the Brigalow, the "light lands" in the south-west of Western Australia (WA) and the Ord and Burdekin irrigation schemes, were undertaken. The Federal Government weighed in with the Snowy, conceived originally as a post-war rehabilitation activity as well as a major development project.

Thus in seeking to stimulate economic growth, Australian governments have continued to rely primarily on infrastructure provision, in the inclusive sense underlined by Butlin, Barnard and Pincus. This has constituted a subsidy to "development".[34]

States depend on Canberra for the bulk of their revenue, and among the few sources of discretionary income capable of rapid expansion is natural resources. Thus, States tend to favour their exploitation, even at the expense of good husbandry. Wayne Goss, the Premier of Queensland, said during 1991 that the new Century zinc mine proposal in the Gulf country was "too exciting and too worthwhile" to let anything stand in its way; the Beattie Government, elected in 1998, soon found itself threatening to compulsorily acquire land under title claim so as to "guarantee" the project. One of its first acts had been to pass a Native Title Act that completed the Coalition's programme of dispossession.[35] The difficulties of challenging government over "development" projects are so great that, except in New South Wales (NSW), the courts are virtually closed both to individuals and to voluntary organisations.[36] Attempts to insulate mining and other "major developments" from any form of environmental impact assessment are in the same mould. Liberal governments in NSW, Victoria and Tasmania have persistently attempted to expand logging. And "technocratic dreaming" whether of multifunction polises, Very Fast Trains, or "information superhighways", remains an important thread in developmentalism.[37] Nor is recent state government interest in the "intellectual property" represented by genetic material found within their boundaries a departure from the pattern of resource exploitation; rather, it is a novel extension, well within the tradition of "statist developmentalism", and fully compatible with exploitative "wise use".

Politically, identification of development with votes leads to an emphasis on "projects" intended to gain electoral approval. But the assumption of electoral popularity may reflect significant cognitive dissonance between the politicians and public. Recent public opinion polls have suggested that most citizens now put environmental preservation ahead of growth and "development".

POLICY FAILURES

Extensive government infrastructure provision did not always stimulate economic growth or even increase net welfare. Not only did taxpayers frequently see no significant return on their investment; sometimes they were actually "taken for a ride" by private investors.

The problem lies both in the nature of anticipatory state investment, and in dogged persistence in policies of dubious utility. The "booster" mentality of developmentalist doctrine fails to recognise that state investment in infrastructure *in advance* of private interest or proved demand is essentially speculative, and must be considered risky. Its precariousness, historically, was increased both by poor evaluation of projects before their acceptance and poor assessment once completed.

Many Australian railways, for example, were built with little or no critical scrutiny. Some never covered their operating costs, generating no detectable stimulus to economic activity. Repayment of capital as well as interest on moneys borrowed for these investments had to come either from taxes or from receipts from other, more profitable activities. Cross subsidy of this kind, of course, is unobjectionable when it leads to genuine improvement in welfare over the long run; but the risk inherent in poorly evaluated investment was precisely that too many miscalculations would overextend State capabilities and resources. If the expected spurt in economic growth did not take place, the investment would prove a dud, and eventually a white elephant. The net effect is a reduction in overall welfare.

The "Giblin model" of development for Tasmania exemplifies both poor policy evaluation and persistence. First enunciated in the second decade of the century, it involved the use of the Commonwealth Government's subventions — tax reimbursements, equalisation grants and the like — to build infrastructure in order to progressively emancipate Tasmania from dependence on the mainland, and to underwrite development within the State. The model was most importantly applied to hydroindustrialisation, intended as the lynchpin of a comprehensive approach to "development"; subsidies were also offered to industry either directly or via provision of cheap power. But Giblin's strategy backfired. Tighe showed that the Tasmanian Hydro Electric Commission's policies were economically unviable as well as ecologically damaging, and that power projects had been co-opted by "brokerage" politics, in which regional political support is secured by judicious use of political patronage, generally of a tangible nature.[38] Crowley's study of the attempted revival of the Electrona smelter underlined the risks — and costs — of unsuccessful subsidy.[39] In both cases, politicians and bureaucrats displayed acute hostility to demands for more thorough project evaluation, and to any questioning of their developmentalist justification. In sum, rather than using the windfall of Commonwealth tax reimbursement and equalisation grants to develop a sustainable economic infrastructure, successive Tasmanian governments instead employed it to underwrite costly and ineffective policies which had become articles of faith, but which at best served only short-term political ends.

Similar fiscal irresponsibility afflicts other States. The West Australian Government's reckless pursuit of the Ord River scheme has been blamed on the fact that federal funds were available for northern development, but not for more worthwhile schemes further south.[40] Additionally, the mere existence of federal funding made State commitments to grandiose plans easier.[41] Lowe has ruthlessly documented the rôle of political myth in electricity supply over-investment.[42] Overspending has also contributed, especially when interest rates were high, to the States' chronic debt problems.

DIFFUSED RESPONSIBILITY AND SECTORAL DISSONANCE

The failure of Keynesian measures is in part a consequence of the diffusion of responsibility inherent in Australia's particular form of federalism, which has led to policy confusion and frequently to a paralysis of planning and innovation.[43] Government's capacity for overall economic management is still hotly disputed; fragmentation has tended to exacerbate the dissonance between the various sectors of the system.

Bell's discussion of industrial policy emphasises the paradox of a highly statist political system in which government has frequently played a powerful rôle, but at the same time an ideology of liberalism and *laissez-faire* has remained dominant. The Australian state consequently displays

> ... simultaneous elements of state strength and weakness in the economy; a pattern marked by what at times has been substantial intervention, but of a kind featuring classic weak state characteristics, particularly the proclivity of state élites not to challenge the autonomy

of firms and not to become too involved in the detailed workings of the economy...[44]

He also stresses the compartmentalisation, both of politics and the economy. Statism can coexist with liberalism because they dominate different sectors, and hence the inconsistencies between them never become intractable: institutionalised "sectoral dissonance". But what results is a sort of policy schizophrenia. Not only is government planning a constant hostage to private investment decisions, but its success depends on the relative power of the affected sectors of the economy. In some areas the state will be positively incompetent, while in others "... bouts of state activism will tend to be built around areas of administrative capacity".[45] These uneven capacities are at the heart of government weakness and fragmentation. Because policy is facilitative in intent, not only is there a risk of "garbage can" policy-making, but in addition policies may be inconsistent, lacking coordination and impeding overall environmental management and regulation.

The involvement of multiple governments, as well as multiple interests in the community, serves to deepen the complexities. The more parties are involved, the more likely it is that policies will be compromised, and the process of policy-making will be riddled with short cuts, *ad hoc* approaches and exclusion of parties with legitimate interests. This paralysis was not significantly affected by the next major policy change.

"STATE-ASSISTED MARKETISATION"

Australian public policy underwent what appeared to be a major change in direction from the 1980s on. Rather than attempt to insulate the economy from global trends, a policy of "openness" to global markets emerged, underpinned by New Right rhetoric which was repeated unanimously, uncritically and ad nauseam by the mass media. Part of the trend to globalisation of the world economy, this saw the mass movement of wage labouring employment to low-wage countries, and a vast expansion of contract, sweatshop and casual labour, seriously undermining the political power of the traditional Labour movements. Giving priority to economic criteria and especially to corporate profit seriously undermined previously promising environmental policy trends.

These trends were widely seen as marking a revolution in public policy, and in particular as an absolute contraction in the rôle of the Australian state. Yet, paradoxically, the rôle of government remains large.

CHANGES IN THE 1980s AND 1990s

In the 1980s and 1990s, under the banner of "deregulation", some state enterprises, ranging from banks to communications, were sold off, and a philosophy of state withdrawal from directly marketed services was widely accepted. The motivation was allegedly to stimulate competition, widely and uncritically accepted as bringing reduced costs to consumers. However, the underlying "New Right" economic philosophy, which had become especially dominant in the Commonwealth Public Service, paid little attention to verifying this claim, and none to environmental costs or sustainability. Nor did the extent of government commitment to capital investment greatly change, despite much rhetoric about "smaller government". Communications and road building expenditure, for example, grew, though social services were generally cut. Government remained willing to contemplate huge infrastructure expenditures, especially in "sunrise" technologies such as digital communications.

Bell and Head have characterised this trend as "state-assisted marketisation" of the economy, stressing the partial withdrawal of government from regulation, especially in areas such as banking and finance.[46] Though the segmental nature of the economy selectively constrains the capacity of government to direct and control, they point at the same time to the continuing importance of government, both in setting overall goals and objectives (though within clearly defined constraints arising from global forces) and in creating the framework for the "new" economic order.

But dramatic changes in economic policy may have very little impact on development policy, at best altering its emphasis. There remains an element of pump-priming — now called neo-Keynesian — and there continues to be a fairly wide acceptance of the "need" for government to provide infrastructure. focussing attention on the decline of old infrastructure and subsidy obscures the rise of new. Road transport, for example, continues to be massively subsidised; the social costs are ignored; and the application of "level playing field" criteria to transport is virtually never discussed. Attempts to improve the balance of payments by exporting larger volumes of the traditional unprocessed exports have led to massively increased environmental impacts, as increased volume attempts to make up for falling prices. Alternative strategies involving greater intrinsic value and higher employment — such as export of cabinet timbers rather than woodchips — have not been adopted; "value added" tends to mean large, foreign-owned plants such as pulp mills. The highly economistic emphasis of the new policy direction pays little attention to the environmental issues, continuing to treat natural resources as free goods, and ecological damage as trivial and reversible. This points, not to the supplanting of "statist developmentalism" by market-oriented philosophies, but to its persistence in a changed form.

DISTRIBUTION AND REGULATION

This persistence may be a last gasp. Nearly all discussions of Australian government note a swing to increased regulatory activity during the twentieth century. The Right have tended to interpret this as a bad thing, to be reversed if possible. They ground this in a crude, ideological "size of government" model, implicitly postulating that governmental size continually increases unless restrained, while neglecting variables such as population growth and resource depletion. Lowi offers a more sophisticated explanation in terms of a changing frontier régime in which gradual maturation accompanies a decline in freely available, abundant resources.[47] This latter model attributes the growth in government regulation to increased conflict between potential uses. Implicitly, it recognises the importance of *scale*: that is, the relative size of the polity, and consequently the opportunities for conflict. The significance of this is that the number of possible conflicts ("connections" in network theory) is a geometrical function of the number of elements in the system. A telephone system with two subscribers has only two possible calls; three subscribers generate six, four generate twelve, five generate twenty, and so on. In other words, as *any* system grows larger, the number of possible interactions will increase geometrically — *not* linearly. We should expect a polity with twice the population to need four times as much government; governments that are not four times larger have been successful in choking off input and restricting output, not at maintaining their liberal credentials! The Australia of the 1990s, with over 15,000,000 citizens, would generate far more conflicts over resources than that of 1950, with a mere 8,000,000, *even if* cunning foreigners were not attempting to get their hands on them as well. An expanded rôle for government, in which distribution itself requires greater regulation, is a clear cost of growth.

Developmentalism thus becomes a liability when resources are no longer abundant and cheap, and competition develops not only for the resources themselves, but from alternative uses, ranging from other, "cleaner" industries to recreation and wilderness. The environment can no longer be freely exploited: the end of formerly "inexhaustible" resources is in sight. Investment no longer expands employment in direct proportion; instead, the biggest, most capital-intensive projects create the most disruption and the fewest jobs. As the effects of development increasingly impose diseconomies on the population, the benefits are no longer "self-evident", and the associated policies fall dramatically in popularity. In other words, when "ecological scarcity" begins to bite, and the resource régime has to change from distributive to regulatory, developmentalist policies become increasingly irrelevant and even harmful.

The significance of this for Australian public policy is that the "capture" or subversion by vested interests of attempts to define policy more broadly or to establish advisory institutions aggravates the already haphazard, *ad hoc* and piecemeal nature of regulation. Arguably, an example of capture was the Ecologically Sustainable Development (ESD) process at federal level; the Resources Assessment Commission (RAC) survived a mere four years; apparently enlightened initiatives in Victoria have been stifled at or shortly after birth; and so on. In this light, the "change of mind" represented by the "free market" policies of the 1980s and 1990s delays the onset of effective regulation, doing untold damage in the process. Indeed, "state-assisted marketisation" can be interpreted as the last gasp of the frontier, and with it the political Right: the denial of the importance of regulation in favour of an attempt to restore distributionism — by accelerated environmental exploitation.

THE ROLE OF THE AUSTRALIAN STATE

Governments in Australia have acted historically as licensers of plunder, sometimes quite blatantly: unable to control squatting, for example, governments settled for formalising the squatters' status in leases. The pastoralists later became dominant in colonial legislatures, effectively setting the leases in concrete. The government rôle in infrastructure provision, marketing and provision of services can be seen as an important element in that process. Policies have not been consistent over time: rather, they have been indecisive, piecemeal and frequently *ad hoc* in nature. The most enduring element has been a commitment to developmentalism in various forms. In the prevailing economic and geographic circumstances, this has translated into a commitment to accelerated economic growth through depletion of natural resources.

The persistent failure to develop a capacity for planning or direction of the economy stems from the facilitative rationale for Australian statism. As noted above, this mindset grants hostages to private "enterprise", since the hands-off approach makes government dependent on private investment to round out and complete its plans.[48] This in turn exacerbates the consequences of diffused responsibility, governmental fragmentation and policy schizophrenia, all of which contribute to failure at the highest levels of policy.

POLICY PATTERNS

These factors also underlie the pursuit of entrenched policies regardless of their real worth. Policy "hangovers", in which particular strategies are pursued long after they have lost their efficacy, are frequent even when the objections are well known and crippling. The Tasmanian pursuit of hydro-industrialisation is the most quoted, but the promotion of irrigation in the Murray-Darling Basin is another; the all-time favourite, perhaps, is the Bradfield scheme to divert North Queensland rivers inland, still regularly revived despite its economic unviability, marginal practicability in engineering terms, and the lack of profitable crops for tropical agriculture. Policy persistence is reinforced by some specific features of the Australian political and fiscal systems.

Firstly, there is poor and inadequate project evaluation, to which the dynamics of federalism contribute. Diffusion of responsibility is inherent in a system in which one level of government raises funds, but another spends them. The availability of Commonwealth funding makes it worth a State's while to put forward projects even when their worth is in doubt. As the granting body, the Commonwealth has to act as "gatekeeper". If it refuses funding, it can be blamed while the State claims to be "doing its best". The merits of the project are less important in this case than its political utility to the State. The Commonwealth, if it sets up criteria for approval, may be tempted — as it was in the Ord case — to abandon them for political advantage.[49] In short, the political relationship of granter and grantee has the effect of distorting project evaluation away from economic or ecological rationality towards political. There are clear political disadvantages to rigorous project analysis as long as "development" is seen as electorally popular.

Secondly, in a context in which planning is *ad hoc* or nonexistent, and in which conflict between competing bureaucratic empires is common, misallocation of resources, waste and ecological damage easily occur. Since natural resources are undervalued, often to the point of being treated as a free good, governments, for the fiscal reasons noted above, often subsidise their exploitation. For example, forestry departments offer free advice and services. Charges do not recover the full costs; coupled with government-provided infrastructure such as roads, the effect is to subsidise timber extraction.[50] Similarly, the "resources boom" relies, among other inputs, on the extensive surveys undertaken at taxpayers' expense since the 1950s.

Thirdly, there is the cargo-cultism of States, particularly when small and remote. The textbook example is Tasmania, where the Giblin strategy's degeneration to a caricature of itself has recently been characterised as a form of parasitism.[51] Commonwealth funds underwrite unsuccessful State policies, permitting their continuation, regardless of the consequences, which are often economically disastrous, quite apart from their environmental impacts.[52]

Finally, "statist developmentalism" tends to construct political discourse in its own terms. Deep government involvement in the economy focusses political discourse not only on economic management, but on galaxies of specific demands for services, infrastructure and major projects. Politics concerns itself predominantly with "bricks and mortar", neglecting other issues, especially social welfare. Issues are reduced to "projects", the bigger the better. Though not untypical of other nation-states, gigantism and "projectism" are especially harmfully embedded in Australian political culture. Discrete, visible "projects" offer political advantages: they are thought to be electorally attractive, and they are amenable to handling through budgets and bureaucracies. Where political panacea-hunting seeks a "grand plan" to eliminate economic and budgetary headaches for the foreseeable future, politicians can become addicted to "quick fixes", making them easy targets for grandiose, "high-tech", gimmicky plans which exploit the latest buzz-words and fashions. Spaceports, Very Fast Trains, nuclear power, car races and of course dams and irrigation schemes have all occupied this privileged position.[53] Kellow attributes this phenomenon to lack of policy options for States:

> ... since the Commonwealth government has such a stranglehold on macro economic policy and the states are forbidden from using tariffs or bounties to foster development, the application of cheap loans to public works to provide private goods such as electricity or irrigation water, which are then priced below their true economic value, is one of the few means at the disposal of state governments to be seen to be doing something to improve the welfare of their citizens. The resulting "edifice complex" is good news for the engineering profession, but bad news for the nation as social returns are bidded [sic] down by the competition between states to attract development.[54]

While nearly all democracies develop a "politics of distribution", statist developmentalism in Australia, given the central importance of government infrastructure provision, is distributive in the stronger sense implied by Lowi's distinction between distributive and regulatory policies. The progression of Australian "development" policy agrees well with Lowi's identification of distributive policies with a "frontier" stage of economic development, in which abundant natural resources are wastefully exploited.

SMALL TYRANNIES: DEVELOPMENTALISM AS A STATE OF MIND

Statist developmentalism is as much a state of mind as a development strategy. It embodies the assumptions that "development" is (1) imperative, (2) popular, and (3) has self-evident advantages. This ignores evidence that development damages ecologies and diminishes amenity for the population at large. Instead, it assumes that ecologically rational policies will be costly and will eliminate jobs. The resulting conflict is unnecessary and damaging, frequently causing policy makers to reject perfectly viable options out of hand.

A further problem is that, if "development" is always assumed to be good, then the onus of disproof is thrown onto objectors. Projects, big or small, are assumed to be beneficial unless it can be clearly shown that serious ill-effects will follow. This can be difficult for technical reasons, since objectors are often attempting to prove damage of a social or ecological nature, where proof may be difficult or delayed, while proponents claim more tangible and immediately visible economic benefits. Thus not only can objectors expect frequently to fail, but their claims are more likely to be dismissed as trivial or ill-founded regardless of their objective merits or the weakness of the proponents' claims. Furthermore, this attitude leads regularly to a situation in which the "tyranny of small decisions" subjects common goods to the "death of a thousand cuts" by perpetual erosion. A well-known example is urban parkland, where excision of a plot here for a bowling club and a spot there for a footy pavilion progressively subdivides the amenity and reserves it for specialised subgroups, while steadily diminishing its attractiveness in other ways.[55] This problem is particularly strong where issues of habitat size — for flora as well as fauna — are concerned. Most species cannot survive in a habitat below a specific minimum size which is unknown in many cases, if not the majority. Ehrlich demonstrated in some pivotal research that many assumptions about habitat size underestimate the needed area, and suggested that a "safety first" policy, making very generous assumptions about habitat needs, was the only safe course.[56]

Where projects of a significant size are concerned, policy fragmentation is further aggravated by piecemeal evaluation. In Australia, as in the United States of America, the present law requires that all but very small projects be evaluated by a process of Environmental Impact Assessment (EIA), which has a number of well-documented defects. Obviously, unless case-by-case assessment is fitted into a broader policy picture in which some serious attempt is made to impose overall control, "tyranny of small decisions" is very likely to occur. Amenities will be whittled away until it is no longer practicable to attempt to restore the status quo ante, and they disappear.

A dramatic example of just this problem is the debate over the impact of domestic pets in the Dandenong ranges east of Melbourne, where they have had a devastating effect on native fauna, even within sanctuaries such as Sherbrooke Forest. The inherent tendency of EIA to favour project proponents is a good ground for concluding that the legal requirement for EIA itself has a built-in developmentalist bias.[57]

The minimal long-term protection for most environmental features under law underlines the pervasiveness of developmentalism. A simple Cabinet decision to rescind a National Park for mining, for example, is often all that is required. Given that private individuals and groups articulating issues of public concern generally lack the standing in the courts enjoyed by bodies with direct financial interests, the law is a very weak defence against "whittling away".[58]

CONSEQUENCES

Intervention by States to attract industry and investment in competition with each other and with foreign nations leads to direct subsidy as well as lavish infrastructure provision. A telling example was an attempt by a nominally "dry" Liberal government in Victoria to subsidise an airline flying to China in an attempt to bring more trade to the state, a departure so far from its normal "slash and burn" policies as to attract criticism from a right-wing "thinktank".[59]

At the national level, indiscriminate industry subsidies can lead to a net loss in economic terms, creating increasing dependency as balance of payments problems worsen progressively.[60] Financial dependence brings with it technological dependence and a "branch-plant" economy, controlled by remote overseas owners. Suppression of domestic initiative — especially research and development — and strategic restriction of access to foreign markets often follow.[61] Eagerness for foreign investment can lead to unwillingness to consider such impacts, as well as neglect of environmental damage and undesirable social effects. Urgent pressures, for example to reduce overseas debt, can then lead to short-sighted, exploitative policies.

CRITICISMS OF "DEVELOPMENT"

The "development" ideology, though it never lacked critics, always assumed that its benefits were self-evident. The demand for greater emphasis on equality or social welfare was disarmed with the argument, in one form or another, that "wealth creation" came first. Though a small but vocal minority persistently pointed out the devastating effects of European settlement on the Australian environment, they lacked, in the main, access to the ruling circles and the machinery of opinion.[62] As a result, their critiques were detached from accepted constructions of reality and perceived as irrelevant to social and economic wellbeing. A direct consequence is that governments frequently ignored well-founded policy advice, as the saga of Goyder's Line in SA so graphically illustrates.[63] In this, governments were often out of touch with reality: Pope, for example, shows that a major obstacle to "closer settlement" in the early twentieth century was lack of suitable land.[64]

Warnings that Australian developmentalism is both ecologically and economically unviable have grown in frequency in the last fifty years; a recognition which is at last slowly spreading from scientists to politicians.[65] Most importantly, perhaps, is the "proof of the pudding": Australians had the highest standard of living in the world in 1900. It has been declining steadily ever since.

CONCLUSION: STATISM UNBOWED

By emphasising the pivotal rôle of the state in Australian development, the critique of statist developmentalism helps considerably in the analysis of the extensive governmental intervention in the economy that has characterised Australian development. It also throws into sharp relief the environmental costs of development, and suggests both why they have been incurred and why they have been ignored. In particular, the systematic failure to appreciate the implications of an unusual and "difficult" environment has caused a stream of agricultural and pastoral disasters, "mining" soil and resources and withdrawing minerals and nutrients without replacement. Present profits have repeatedly been bought at the cost of future decline. In response to economic crisis, governments tend to increase the rate of exploitation of natural resources, offsetting chronic mismanagement with increased cash flow.

The federal system underwrote statist developmentalism, both in the States and federally. The larger States gained both from Commonwealth infrastructure provision and from participation in such programmes as the Murray-Darling irrigation works. Smaller States exploited the opportunities provided by tax reimbursement and later equalisation grants underwriting grand development programmes.

Statist developmentalism's distributive approach to public policy is geared to big "projects", often with substantial government investment. All have involved committing large lump sums, the beneficiaries being contractors engaged in construction work, and their employees, or recipients of subsidy, such as farmers benefiting from cheap water or fertiliser. Frequently, for political reasons, State governments in particular would espouse grandiose schemes for which they had few resources. Often, like the Burdekin scheme in

Queensland, these would be undertaken in dribs and drabs, a little capital being allotted in each year's budget. States found themselves paying interest on loans for schemes which would not yield revenue until far in the future, if at all. That in turn increased the tax burden and tied up funds that might have been used for other, more useful purposes.

Statist developmentalism faces growing obsolescence as distributionism fails to solve problems that increasingly require regulation. Limited policy change toward regulation is necessarily occurring, reflecting, *inter alia*, ecological scarcity. But the policy dilemma for government is that in order to break out from the old pattern, new and radical ways of looking at economic management are needed. No Australian government, state or federal, has yet seriously attempted the transition. The sole comprehensive exploration of the problem, the "Greenprint" for Tasmania, was ignored and shelved by the very government that had commissioned it.[66] Worse, the wave of imitative economic irrationalist policy since the 1980s has temporarily reversed the trend, in the right-wing backlash against changing conditions.

This analysis consequently implies a rôle for the state different from both the New Right and the Old Left positions. It suggests that government has little business in bricks and mortar "development", and its participation in the economy, especially in the context of the global capitalist régime, really has little impact either way. Its most important and most neglected rôle is regulatory, especially in environmental policy. Implied are comprehensive policies for land use, pollution, population and social welfare.[67] These would require complementation by more effective, finer-grained tools for regulation, especially of manufacturing and commerce. These tools would attempt to encourage investment and economic activity in truly productive and worthwhile activity, while restraining the environmentally destructive or economically futile. It is now almost a cliché to point out that ecologically sound policies can generate far more jobs than mere quarrying; but that would be the precise point of targeted regulation.

The institutional consequences may include a future move away from dedicated single-purpose authorities towards broader policy-related oversight; considerably greater emphasis on techniques for regulation and evaluation of economic activity, especially where it has significant environmental impact; and a move away from emphasis on physical infrastructure and production of goods. The effective achievement of these goals would require substantial institutional change, as well as significant innovation, especially in mechanisms for accountability.

But the importance of government participation in the economy has lain not simply in the characteristic economic and political institutions to which it has given rise, but also in the pattern of policy, its impact on the Australian political culture and the interactions with the biophysical environment. The latter, largely detrimental, affect the long-term sustainability of Australia's economic activity. Given a steady decline in the standard of living of all Australians relative to the rest of the world since its peak as the highest at the turn of the century, this is an issue of immediate importance.

EXPLAINING ENVIRONMENTAL POLICY: CHALLENGES, CONSTRAINTS AND CAPACITY[1]

K. Crowley

INTRODUCTION

"Neither our market economy nor our methods of public decision making were designed with environmental concerns in mind. The political economy responds to those concerns on the basis of well-established private interests, distribution of power, lines of authority, and ideologies. Its *instinctive* response to the expression of environmental concerns is to limit the definition of problems according to the capacity of existing institutions to deal with them".[2] Leiss' remarks, while concerned with Canada, apply almost without modification to Australia.

The last decade has seen a remarkable development in environmental policy theory, with increasing focus upon implementation analysis in the search for improved policy learning and outcomes, and increasing reflection upon the need to "green up" democratic structures of governance. Given the persistence of ecological concerns, now made plain by state of environment reporting and renewed environmental activism around the country, notions of improved policy and more ecologically accountable governance enjoy renewed relevance in Australia. These notions also run directly counter to the contemporary, conservative, political trend of downplaying ecological problems and dismantling federal environmental powers, if not moral responsibility. In such circumstances there is little sense in environmental policy explanations that neglect the broader analytical context. It is necessary to consider, given all that has been learned in scientific, institutional and political terms over the last several decades, why ecology remains such a challenge to policy even in the late 1990s, and why the state would assume a self-diminished rôle in ecological governance at this critical time. This is not to suggest that detailed empirical analysis is any the less valuable, nor that its relative neglect in Australian terms should not be remedied, but to assert that its value is limited without broader contextualising. How else could institutional capacity be properly assessed at a time when Australian neo-conservatism is hotly denying ecological problems, marginalising ecopolitical actors and reducing state influence in the policy process?

It is important to stress that there has never been a consensual approach to environmental policy analysis in Australia, neither in earlier times post-World War Two when "wise use" policies were taking hold, nor since the emergence of contemporary environmentalism in the late 1960s. Even so, a number of common approaches have been employed. These include the broad categories of historical, institutional, legal, electoral, political, sociological and geographical case study analyses; with the most critical, contested accounts coming from political economists and, more recently, from ecopolitical analysts. There has been a tendency in the political and policy literature to focus upon "deep green" natural area and wilderness issues and disputes at the expense of other "lighter" green and "brown" concerns, though the latter remain significant policy undercurrents. The deeper green focus is understandable given the need to explain (if disparagingly, as some of the literature does), the intriguing influence of conservation, wilderness and green politics, more recently in terms of its failing electoral impact in the late 1990s. Nevertheless, just as it is imprecise to say that conservation is an issue born of the radical 1960s in Australia, given the concern about resource depletion dating back at least a century, so is it misleading to portray environmental politics and policy demands in Australia narrowly as deep green. Indeed the platform of the United Tasmania Group, the world's first green party, founded in 1972, addressed not only natural resources, but alternate technology and work, social justice and equality, participatory institutional design, freedom in thought, speech and action, human dignity and cultural heritage.[3]

However, the waning electoral influence of Australian environmentalists may tend to lend colour to the traditional political science view that environmental policy concerns are easily incorporated into, and resolved by, existing institutions and processes. And in fact there may well be good grounds for arguing this, if for instance one's focus is simply and narrowly upon the politics of issue agendas and management rather than upon the improvement of ecological outcomes and the evaluation of environmental policy processes. The approach taken in this chapter, however, is not so narrow. On the contrary, it is argued that, for all the beliefs of traditional political science, environmental policy still represents a distinctive institutional and political challenge, unlike health, education or even women's policy. In these terms, environmental policy needs complex, critical explanation, able to reflect upon the nature, priorities, policy capacity and political economy of modern industrial society — even more so where it remains dependent, as Australia does, upon natural resource exploitation. There are many reasons why ecology remains an atypical policy challenge.[4] Ecological problems have been around for centuries, but are occurring and recurring at an intensifying rate. Everything about ecological concern is challenging to our economic priorities and offers very little room for compromise. For all the various phases of institution building in Australia, political solutions to ecological problems remain elusive. And for all the efforts of the green movement, there has been no political shift towards ecological rationality, nor is one likely.

For some, this may sufficiently explain how it is that Australia's recent environmental policy roll-back has been so swiftly executed, and how the honest environmental policy broker of international fora in the 1980s could be such an ecological disgrace at the December 1997 Kyoto negotiations on climate change. Indeed, even the historic translation of Australia's global environmental goodwill into domestic policy arrangements, Agenda 21 included, has continually been fraught with ideological, political, economic, bureaucratic and petty, unforeseen yet often practical obstacles. Such difficulties beset policy translation globally, and were specifically considered at the 1992 Rio Earth Summit when attention focussed upon implementation mechanisms and environmental policy capacity in the hope of better embodying ecology within policy processes. Yet even as nation-states were making rhetorical commitments at the Summit via Agenda 21 to an improved global environment,[5] albeit within the context of enhanced economic growth, their ability to do so was coming under question from key policy theorists. Weale[6] observed at the time that the scale of environmental problems appeared to have outgrown the institutional capacity to deal with them; Dryzek[7] argued that Western capitalism, liberal democracy and the administrative state have simply proven unable to cope with the ecological challenge; and Janicke[8] found that the higher the international level of commitment, the more environmental policy is reduced to mere verbal declarations. Again the need to review basic institutional arrangements and the constraints upon them is highlighted by global environmental policy implementation deficits and the state ecological failures of the previous decade.[9]

Interest in reviewing Australia's environmental institutional arrangements has risen since the late 1980s for political reasons. There has been a need to explain how the institutions established to mediate resource conflict (the Resource Assessment Commission — RAC) and achieve ecologically sustainable development (the Ecologically~Sustainable Development process — ESD) in the late 1980s, could be dismissed on a political whim (see below). Australian implementation analysis has also, in the last couple of years, explained the steady dismantling of state environmental procedures and protection; the difficulties of realising policy substance from policy rhetoric; and the fledgling administrative steps, where these are being taken, towards ecological sustainability.[10] Elsewhere policy evaluation has already drawn attention to the clear gap between environmental policy rhetoric, activity and intent on the one hand, and reality, outcome and practice, on the other; a gap that has become known as an implementation deficit.[11] This notion, which arose in the European context and examines the pursuit of policy commitment, has led to theoretical explorations of related concepts such as policy capacity, policy learning and policy innovation[12] (which for reasons of scope cannot be pursued here). These explanatory concepts do not need to focus exclusively upon minuscule details: they can be placed, as they are by the likes of Weale, within broader social and political contexts, where policy is recognised as subject to "meso" and "macro" influences.[13] Implementation treated in this way makes great sense in the Australian context, but it also suits environmental policy analysis generally for reasons of ecological challenge and complexity, discussed below.[14]

In 1992, while the Rio Earth Summit was still inspiring policy communities around the globe, Toyne was describing Australia as a "reluctant nation", one that shies away from intervening in matters of great environmental significance despite its constitutional power to do so.[15] This does not bode well for domestic environmental protection, the adoption of precautionary development policy, nor the ecological provision for future generations, all Agenda 21 responsibilities that Australia has subsequently seemed intent upon shirking. Despite recognising the environment as a central political issue (at the same time as becoming rhetorically committed to global environmental improvement), Australian politicians were described, also in 1992, as having had difficulty both in taking it seriously and in assimilating it.[16] These views are significant for coinciding, not only with the Summit, but with the peak of environmental policy ascendancy that had been achieved under the Hawke Labor Government and that has been in a sharp tailspin ever since.[17] It had been felt that the expansionary, if *ad hoc* and politically expedient, environmental policy style of Hawke as Prime Minister had led to measurable gains for environmental protection that could then be built upon. However the Keating Labor Government, after abandoning the RAC and sidelining the ESD process, then devised the 1992 Intergovernmental Agreement on the Environment. This effectively relegated the environment, and its political challenges and headaches in particular, to the State domain where most politicians of both major parties had long felt they had always belonged.

Today notions of federal environmental policy responsibility have sunk to previously unknown depths under the conservative Howard Coalition Government, even as it claims to be staking out new policy terrain with its funding cuts, outsourcing and devolution of responsibility, if not power, to local levels. The purpose of this chapter is to consider Australian environmental policy challenges, constraint and performance, given the historical reluctance to accept environmental responsibility which is being exacerbated by Howard's accelerated devolution of responsibility along the trail blazed by Keating. Keating's neo-liberal agenda, including the fiscal and functional hollowing out of the state and its policy responsibilities, has proceeded apace since the 1996 election, and the narrow 1998 re-election, of the Howard Government. The difference with Howard's environmental agenda is the rightist radicalism driving it, its proposed legislative legitimisation of environmental policy devolution (via the *Environment Protection and Biodiversity* Bill) and its brutal assault on natural resources with scant regard for protective status. At the time of writing, the *Environment Protection and Biodiversity* Bill was being condemned for weakening the capacity for national leadership on the environment.[18] Yet environmental policy administration is being so reorganised, with such redefined funding and regional emphasis under the Coalition, that, ironically, it may well stand as a period of extraordinary policy redesign and innovation. At the same time, the Coalition has shown a curious discursive dedication to solving environmental problems via synergistic fiscal, political and community arrangements, including the newly created Natural Heritage Trust, that remain as yet unproven.[19]

No wonder that so many Australian theorists fail to focus upon micro detail in circumstances such as these when politics is so clearly driving environmental policy performance, and indeed where policy resolutions of previous decades have been so clearly tied to the shifting politics of federalism. This chapter goes back to basics by considering why it is in the first place that environmental politics is so problematic and why the Australian state may find itself constrained in responding to environmental demands, before reflecting upon Australian environmental policy performance. It adopts a theoretical, multi-dimensional approach, discussed immediately below, to explaining environmental policy in general, and to analysing Australian environmental policy in particular. It places its consideration of policy performance within the context of broader political and institutional contexts, and adopts an approach that admits complexity in environmental problems, politics and policy, and encourages flexibility in analysis. The chapter is broadly analytic rather than empirically descriptive, and asks the difficult why, rather than detailing the obvious what, of environmental policy formation. There are clearly many more problems with this approach than can be identified here. The attempt to bridge the broad distance between theory and policy detail is difficult, and may mislead. Identification of major constraints at the political economy level may appear deterministic, though this is not the intention. And high-level analysis may fail to benefit from the enlightened, practical feedback offered by an empirical approach. But a deliberately broad focus maximises the potential to explain endemic problems with Australian environmental policy formation.

ENVIRONMENTAL POLICY COMPLEXITIES

Environmental policy analysis has long been characterised by anarchic eclecticism in a manner easily recognisable firstly as reflecting the complexity of ecological concerns themselves, and secondly as confirming the need for a degree of complexity in policy analysis. In more recent times, various authors have consciously acknowledged this, and the concomitant need for what can be termed multi-dimensionality and complexity in analytic focus and style.[20] Hempel is all for debunking the simple, rational, linear process model, with its unreliable compartmentalised "conveyor belt" model, in favour of environmental policy process models that acknowledge overlap and repetition in dizzying combinations.[21] Others place the fine detail of policy process, after Simeon, within a broader set of categories that acknowledge the political, economic and social frameworks within which environmental policy makers operate and which will ultimately limit the policy alternatives considered.[22] Whether theorists employ Simeon's different analytic categories, or Weale's rather less well defined "idioms" of analysis,[23] it is clear that there are many kinds of analysis used to abstract, simplify, discuss and analyse environmental policy. In terms of explaining constrained policy circumstances and the difficulties of achieving policy change, there has been recent refocus, discussed below, upon paradigmatic analysis. But Weale prefers not to employ approaches to policy analysis that claim the coherence of a model, or the conceptual presuppositions of a paradigm. His idioms are rather less formal, concerned with the shifting ways in which environmental policy is discussed and therefore executed.[24]

The range of environmental policy approaches that can be discerned today reflects a trend, though by no means a universal one, in the general field of policy theory toward greater analytic freedom and complexity.[25] "What is needed," Howlett and Ramesh argue, "is an analytical framework that permits consideration of the entire range of factors affecting public policy".[26] Contemporary analysis of this sort means shifting away, as Hempel does, from abstract linear interpretation that fails to explain complexity, and moving "towards a more nuanced position on the investigation and conceptualisation of the public policy process".[27] Following this trend, some do devise elaborate multi-dimensional, multi-levelled models,[28] others borrow, adapt and sometimes transform otherwise limited insights,[29] whilst many simply acknowledge the value of analytic eclecticism.[30] This is a counter-empirical trend, that necessarily admits normative dimensions in policy analysis, and considers no one policy solution better than any other.[31] It has parallels with post-positivism, which, in Fischer's sense, does not descend into postmodernist relativism, but does allow normative practices to be assessed in terms of the processes and practices by which they are selected.[32] Analytic complexity and multi-dimensionality offer great potential in the environmental policy context, and no doubt will sometimes see explanatory approaches inextricably intertwined. The complexity metaphor seems appropriate to ecology itself, which was once considered "ordered and predictable" in scientific thought, and is now recognised more for its "baffling complexity", impermanence and an instability that commands both policy precaution and an enhanced respect from human nature.[33]

Multi-dimensionality suits the Australian context too, since environmental policy processes are in any case rarely considered in isolation

from environmental values and politics (for instance) or from the economic and resource development pressures that constrain policy innovation, formulation and implementation.[34] Australian policy analysis in
general does commonly range across the macro-political, the meso-
institutional and the micro-empirical levels of policy detail; though not
necessarily in any systematic fashion, nor with any agreement on the
significance of policy influence at the various levels.[35] Most Australian
policy analysts would agree with Ham and Hill that they "should give
due consideration to the social, political and economic contexts within
which problems are tackled" or otherwise accept that they are undertaking, at best, a partial exercise. Again these authors suggest three
appropriate levels of analysis: the macro-level analysis of political systems, including the examination of the rôle of the state; the middle
range analysis of policy formulation; and the micro-level of decision
making within organisations.[36] For Australia, this approach ranges
from the larger political context, through the institutional level and
down to the local policy arena. The assumption is that different explanations are required at different levels as the analyst's perspective
moves closer and closer to the specific.[37]

The question for environmental policy analysis seems not to be
whether or not multi-dimensionality is a feasible approach, since
multi-faceted, multi-levelled analysis is relatively common, but how
to admit ecology and environmental values into the equation.
Simeon's multi-dimensional approach simply introduces the categories of context and ideology that automatically admit both, and
that Downey adopts to explain environmental policy. Weale admits
belief systems into his analysis with his "policy discourse idiom", a
notion that is flourishing in environmental scholarship.[38] He argues
that there are coalitions of actors, opposed to one another in a policy system, whose disagreements, and ability to reach agreement, are
based upon belief systems and understandings.[39] Paehlke recalls
Easton's definition of politics as "the authoritative allocation of values". He also treats environmental politics as an expression of a set
of values, identifying some of "the difficult issues that the wide
acceptance of these values urges onto the political agenda".[40] Both
approaches are not dissimilar to Sabatier's notion of policy "advocacy coalitions", which he and others use to explain environmental policy in particular, and to identify the resilience of core beliefs as a key
frustration to policy formation and change.[41] This notion of ideological resilience is reinforced by Bell's proposition, in the Australian
context, that prevailing ideology and dominant policy discourse will
shape economic policy choice and thus the rôle of the state in the
economy.[42] From this one can conclude that environmental policy

choices, which invariably suggest some revising of both economic and political priorities, often towards more ecologically responsible concerns, will be therefore be constrained.

Returning to the Australian policy context, we find that in an earlier edition of their work, Davis et al also adopt Simeon's multi-dimensional approach to identify macro-economics and federal-state political complexities as key constraining influences upon policy formulation and implementation.[43] Whilst their approach succeeds in integrating political science concerns with public policy analysis, which for decades has been the aim of the multi-dimensional approach, it fails to overtly stress prevailing ideology and dominant policy discourse as limiting variables. However it should still be relatively straightforward, in terms of approaches adopted elsewhere, to admit ecology and environmental values into public policy analysis, even if the practice is not welcomed by those Australian theorists who remain sceptical of ecopolitical critique. The Australian ecopolitical critique is typically multi-disciplinary, conveying a concern for ecology itself, a healthy scepticism about the ability of the state to protect it, and a sense that contemporary environmentalism is politically unique. It has in common with political economy a desire to pin down and analyse the powerful influence of social, political and corporate actors, but also explores clashes of belief, values and political practice between environmental advocates and their political opponents. It is fair to say that ecopolitical notions of environmental policy and politics as ideologically distinctive do remain theoretically contested in Australia. Nevertheless, the unique Australian environment, the environmental activism and politics that it inspires, and ideologically generated economic obstacles to innovative environmental policy, would be significant in a Simeonesque multi-dimensional policy approach.

ISSUE PERSISTENCE: ECOLOGY AS A POLICY PROBLEM?

Despite the breadth and lack of consensus in Australian environmental policy analysis, three broad approaches can still be discerned: the ecopolitical, the traditional and the radical right. Each has a quite different view of ecology as a policy problem, and, in Weale's terms, each discusses it (and expects it to be executed) differently. As mentioned, the ecopolitical school of environmental policy theory treats ecology critically as a significant, persistent policy problem for modern industrial societies, and its advocates as posing a challenge to established politics that is not easily accommodated. The traditional school of environmental policy theory treats ecology fairly neutrally as a routine, easily resolvable policy problem, and its advocates as

players jostling pluralistically for issue attention on a level policy playing field. The radical right school of environmental policy theory
portrays ecology as an abstract, market-based concept. It advocates
the market as best able to solve environmental problems, and sees
environmental activists as outsiders in modern industrial society.
However, this categorisation is abstract, and does not preclude the
possibility, say, of a radical right ecopolitical approach, or of traditional analysis with ecopolitical overtones, or of any other number of
analytic variations. The point of devising categories at all is merely to
highlight the key differences between approaches that will affect how
seriously ecology is perceived as a policy problem.

The point of categorisation is also to stress that the ecological
problems and the challenges of environmental politics which preoccupy ecopolitical scholarship will not necessarily preoccupy mainstream political scientists, and will often be denied altogether by
radical right theorists. Nor will mainstream and radical right theorists
necessarily be as concerned about the need for policy changes to
improve the state of the environment, nor about the need for
enhanced democratisation of environmental policy processes, as
ecopolitical theorists and environmental activists increasingly are.
Mainstream political science may also record the environmental policy adhocery that has plagued countries like Australia as the inevitable
end result of politicians and policy makers muddling incrementally
though; whereas ecopolitical theorists will try to discern patterns to it.
Whilst realising only too well that policy making is never as rational as
theorists would like, Downey still cannot accept incrementalism as an
adequate explanation of environmental policy adhocery, nor of erratic environmental funding levels, nor the injudicious policy selection
that exacerbates environmental problems. He cannot accept that
politicians and their advisers are less rational, less intelligent and less
concerned than the rest of us. So he adopts Simeon's approach to look
behind what the traditionalists call "public policy pragmatism" and
"policy makers doing the best they can", to argue that environmental
policy is not formed in an idea-less vacuum as pragmatism implies. He
concludes that "the term pragmatism is nothing more than a handy
excuse for avoiding more difficult questions and for failing to attempt
more comprehensive and incisive explanations".[44]

It seems entirely predictable that Simeon, Downey and, in more
recent times, environmental policy analysts like Fiorino and Vig,
would turn partly to paradigmatic explanations to show the difficulty
of achieving ecologically rational policy outcomes within constrained
circumstances that they identify. As Bell explains, the policy paradigm
"suggests that, at the most fundamental level, policy makers at any

given time tend to work within an overarching set of ideas, standards and goals that structure the way they see and interpret" their policy choices.[45] Whilst this analysis offers a very clear means of "admitting the ideological" into environmental policy analysis, Downey is at pains to point out that policy paradigms can be issue specific — less grand, that is, than ideology or even dominant ideas — and can apply narrowly to circumstances where broad orientation operates to limit the range of policy options. The notion of policy paradigm not only emphasises how the limits to rational environmental decision making can be reached, but also it suggests how radically the overarching terms of policy discourse would need to change for there to be a shift in these limits.[46] The notion of policy paradigm is well suited to the Australian environmental policy context if one is convinced, for instance, that resource exploitation has served not only as a tool of national development, but as a cultural ethos that persists in thwarting innovative environmental policy. Dominant paradigms also serve to spawn counter-paradigms as their anomalies are gradually realised, hence the emergence of an active green political culture of complaint in Australia which has greatly influenced policy over the years, essentially by contesting statist developmentalism.[47]

Environmental theorists have long been drawn to paradigmatic analysis as a means of describing the ideological nature of environmentalism so that the challenge of environmentalism to conventional societal values can be appreciated.[48] To understand environmental policy in these terms, we need to know where environmental demands come from and what challenge they offer to established politics and policy processes, before we can appreciate the likelihood of their ever becoming policy.

Environmental paradigmatic analysis is somewhat dated, and has been criticised — even by those who favour it — for juxtaposing "materialism" too bluntly against environmentalism, which is now perceived to comprise not one but many various shades of green. But even whilst agreeing with this criticism, one can still appreciate the value of paradigmatic analysis for revealing how world views, ideological reference points and schemes for understanding reality can narrowly confine policy. However one describes it, the dominant industrial paradigm does manifest anti-ecological characteristics, partly by viewing nature as a resource, but also by legitimating those institutions and processes consistent with, and not undermining, this view.[49] The significance of ecology as a counter-paradigm, critical of industrial society yet expecting sympathy from its instrument of governance, the state, becomes apparent. In the late 1990s, environmentalists are struggling more than ever for legitimacy within political and economic systems that are geared towards the ongoing destruction of non-human nature.[50] Paradigmatic analysis is still valuable for seeing prevailing economic values as the dominant influence and prevailing policy discourse in this power struggle between economy and ecology.[51]

At the extreme opposite of this paradigmatic approach is Downs' oft-quoted "issue-attention" analysis, which suggests, as an economist would, that environmental concern rises from self-interest, and falls, essentially from cost realisation and issue displacement.[52] Accordingly environmental concern rose to prominence in Australia in the late 1960s and 1970s, inspired an era of institution-building into the late 1980s, hit the barrier of economic rationalism into the 1990s, and has now been displaced by other policy "imperatives". Whilst appealing to traditional policy theorists for its simplicity, and to radical right theorists for dispensing with environmentalism, this is only a superficially accurate description. "Issue-attention" analysis reduces environmental concern to self-interest and a single issue; it assumes that fall from political prominence equates to lack of public concern and issue decline; and it reads this as a shift of attention onto more pressing problems. Whilst environmental concerns may have first gained prominence as single issues, they have always been complex and multifaceted, ecologically and politically. As Australian public polling continues to show, the environment has not declined as a key public concern, but has arguably been eclipsed and marginalised by an emphasis on mainstream economic imperatives during the 1990s. Indeed the shift of political issue attention away from the environment begs closer examination given the public support for environmental issues and environmental political reinvention at the local level. Issue-attention also fails spectacularly to explain how what was a single issue politics in the 1960s has unfolded into the historic, scientific, social, political, philosophical and global concerns of today.[53]

In fact ecological concern has not declined if the scientists, public pollsters, environmental activists and ecopolitical theorists are to be believed, but will persist as a policy problem well into the new millennium. It does not merely jostle in a pluralistic way for issue attention at the policy level by such accounts, but is still raising fundamental questions and ethical issues that continue to challenge social, political, cultural and institutional norms.[54] Over two decades ago, the environment was first recognised by policy theorists, not as a conventional, easily accommodated political issue, but as a threat to cherished assumptions, not easily reducible to self-interest, bounded only by ignorance and thus ever-expanding, and a challenge to the narrow specialisation of industrial society.[55] In the 1990s, however, ecology is as perplexing and novel a policy concern as ever, in the same terms of threat, ignorance, boundlessness and complexity that still defy traditional issue accommodation measures. By following the ecopolitical notion of ecology as challenging and contentious, rather than the traditional notion of single issue politics, the policy context as a whole, most notably its political economy, becomes critical to evaluating environmental institutional capacity and state response to environmental concern. No other policy context is such a blend of science and politics, of ideology and grass roots activism, of concern, not only for the present and future, but for human and non-human beneficiaries.[56] Despite a greening at the institutional level (complete with expedient, illusory, placatory, rhetorical and symbolic policy solutions), ecology persists as a policy concern precisely because of the difficulties in accommodating it within industrial society.

POLICY CONSTRAINT: STATE CAPACITY AND RESPONSE

If environment could be convincingly portrayed as single issue politics, sporadically generated by idea-less, self-interested individuals, in a society where all can equally influence policy, then it would be easily resolved by the state despite federal political obstacles. This has certainly not been the Australian experience. In fact as environmentalists have increasingly turned to the state with their concerns (albeit, as Victor[57] suggests they would, with varying degrees of scepticism), they have bluntly encountered the limits and contradictions of liberal democratic governance: the tension, that is, between expectations that the state should "create and maintain economic growth" on the one hand, and conserve the natural environment and "husband resources" on the other.[58] This has made it increasingly difficult, say, to achieve the protection of remnant old-growth forest, or to expand world heritage areas to include significant adjacent sites, or to see Australia reduce its fossil fuel dependence. Moreover, in the late 1990s, the protective measures of earlier decades are being slackened so that mining, development, damming, eco-tourism, privatisation and luxury resort building now threaten remnant natural, world heritage and wilderness areas.[59] Nevertheless it is still true to say that at any given time in recent Australian history, environmental policy trends, both positive and negative, have been closely intertwined with the shifting politics of federalism and to federal policy agendas. The complex task of negotiating environmental policy across multi-levelled government should never be underestimated; all the more so for the lack of an environmental head of power formally spelling out federal environmental responsibilities in the country's Constitution.[60]

Much Australian environmental policy literature, therefore, necessarily focusses upon federalism as a key component in environmental policy performance and political outcomes (as discussed below). But there are also more critical explanations concerning the rôle of the state, employed by policy theorists to describe prior constraints operating upon state action, that are also useful in the Australian context. From both the political economy and ecopolitical perspectives, the constrained rôle of the state is crucial to explaining environmental policy. For example, the expectation that the state will respond impartially to policy concerns is replaced by Bell's political economy conception of the state as a constrained actor because of its links to capital; and thus in the position of approving only limited, uncontroversial environmental reforms.[61] From the ecopolitical standpoint, Eckersley also describes the environmental policy capacity of the state as constrained, with her conception of the modern state as fiscally dependent on accumulation, thus leaving environmental protection vulnerable to political bargaining and trade-offs against human interests.[62] Bearing in mind that both of these accounts are the most contested in Australian environmental policy literature, they still do reflect a broader concern in policy theory to critically question the policy capacity of the modern state. The theoretical questions that bear upon the state's environmental policy capacity include these:

- What are the various rôles of the state?
- Are there any contradictions in these rôles? If so, how can these contradictions be resolved?
- Is the state predisposed to favour any of its rôles?
- How can liberal states be brought to account for their environmental decision making?[63]

These are the sorts of questions that are preoccupying critical Australian policy theorists as it becomes increasingly clear that environmental policy problems are, for the short term at least, here to stay. They are consistent both with the notion of an overarching policy context or paradigm that constrains contentious demands, and Vig's notion that environmental policy change is not impossible, but that change at the broadest level of paradigmatic influence is the most difficult.[64] In theory, the modern liberal democratic state will respond impartially to the policy demands upon it; whilst in practice the state's response to ecological demands is very often dictated by economic and strategic necessity.[65] The state would need to further revise its already contradictory rôles of accumulating capital (promoting economic efficiency) and satisfying human needs (protecting social equity),[66] to consider how best to plan for the protection of the environment. There is already considerable tension between these rôles; tension that was held in increasingly tenuous check for thirteen years under Australian Labor Governments with their corporatist policy régimes. The environment is a recent concern that has presented the state with further dilemmas, in particular the need to disentangle itself from the interests of capital, and to consider the notion of non-human state beneficiaries. If the state has come to recognise that its accumulation function will be undermined if its exhausts its social capital, it is still far from appreciating a similar need not to exhaust its ecological capital. The best that liberal democratic states have managed is a rhetorical commitment to sustainable development, all the while remaining "committed above all else to the pursuit of economic growth".[67]

Despite these notions of constrained state capacity, the Australian experience (during the early Hawke years in particular) has shown that, if faced with a threatening decline in popularity, liberal democratic governments may revise their close links with capital. In order to secure environmental protection beyond limited reforms, Australian conservationists have learned to play sophisticated electoral politics, to their benefit at the federal level in the 1980s, but to their increasing cost in terms of state, industry and general political backlash into the 1990s.[68] This electoral behaviour can be seen in historical terms to have emerged out of a frustration with continued ecological loss, combined with a dissatisfaction with the state's institutional responses. It might be supposed, by those theorists who fail to appreciate the remoteness of environmental politics from the traditional political left and right, that Australian conservationists forged electoral deals with the Australian Labor Party in the 1980s because of a natural affinity with its social justice agenda. Nothing could be further from the truth, as three decades' experience demonstrates.

When the reformist Whitlam Labor Government was swept to power in 1972, Labor had been out of office federally for over two decades. Whitlam was dramatically dismissed from office three years later,[69] leaving a chequered environmental record, notably for failing to save Lake Pedder,[70] but also for using his expansionist environmental policy agenda for what was seen as "an attempt to tilt the federal-state balance in the direction of the Commonwealth".[71]

Whitlam's environmental institutions were perceived by the States, not as ecologically rational, but as a radical political encroachment upon their territory, even though his conservative successor largely persisted with them.[72] Whitlam's expansionist environmental approach was subsequently toned down by his Coalition successor,

Fraser, who adopted a painstakingly slow "cooperative federalism" that still achieved some significant ecological outcomes over the next eight years.[73] In the turbulent days of the Franklin River controversy, during which Fraser was equivocating about how far to intervene in a State environmental issue, Bob Hawke snatched the Opposition leadership from Bill Hayden and rode to power on a promise to save the Franklin from hydro-inundation. This was the first of his electorally based environmental policy interventions that secured significant, yet *ad hoc*, ecological outcomes, and thus failed to clarify Commonwealth environmental powers. Theorists commonly consider the early years of the Hawke Government as his most environmentally interventionist, and his latter years as returning to traditional Labor policy arrangements, with corporatism dominating after the failure on environmental grounds of the Wesley Vale pulp mill proposal.[74] This shift in the Federal Government's policy approach toward reintegrating the environment within Labor's economic priorities paved the way for an even more enthusiastic return to cooperative, "new" federalism under Hawke's political successors. Labor had never fully embraced environmentalism, for all the reasons typically described by ecopolitical theorists; but also because Labor had led the 1980s charge towards economic liberalism that further distanced the Party from ecological rationality. Environmentalists who had come to believe that Labor had accepted its environmental responsibilities following the institutional and electoral gains of the 1980s, ended up bitterly disillusioned a short decade later.

For all the differences in Labor and Coalition environmental policy approaches over the last thirty years, all federal governments have displayed considerable reluctance to exercise their environmental policy powers.[75] The influence of environmental bureaucracy, and the reach of federal environmental powers, have waxed and waned with the shifting political tides since the late 1960s. Where Labor federal governments have aggressively asserted Commonwealth environmental powers and blatantly courted green electoral support, they have achieved more spectacular results than otherwise, but always with a lack of natural affinity with environmentalism. These governments have varied from sharply expansionist (1972–75); to stridently *ad hoc* (1983-89); back to "cooperative federalist" (1989–96). Conservative Coalition federal governments (pre-1972; 1975–83; post-1996) have, on the other hand, been more cooperative with the States, rigidly non-interventionist and, until 1996, uninterested in chasing green supporters. There have been distinctive environmental policy rôles played by federal governments (1970s institution-building; 1980s electoral expediency; and 1990s policy reintegration) with the 1990s seeing the Coalition legitimising Labor's devolution of environmental control back to the States. Devolution is a perfect "out" for the federal government in terms of resolving the contradictory economic-environmental demands upon it, and minimises its own environmental political difficulties.[76] But it does suggest that ecological management is not considered a legitimate demand to place upon national government, save for the narrow scope of matters now nominated as nationally significant.[77] It casts environmentalism out from federal policy processes.

CONCLUSIONS

If we see environmental concerns as complex ecologically and politically, difficult to accommodate within mainstream policy processes, and challenging to dominant macro-economic objectives, then the obstacles to improved environmental policy performance can be appreciated. This is the more so as the measure of improved performance swings toward ecological rather than institutional outcomes. It is not only traditional policy theorists who under-appreciate, ignore and sometimes deny the complex problems of ecology, but also policy makers who operate within politically constrained circumstances and are looking for bureaucratically expedient solutions. There is much scepticism amongst critical theorists about the sort of policy performance that can be expected in such circumstances. There is no doubt that policy rhetoric has become more eco-friendly recently, with the adoption of notions such as ecological integrity, sustainability, diversity, precaution, synergism, whole-of-life-cycle planning and best practice environmental management. But in Australia these terms are invariably sandwiched between prior commitments to enhanced economic growth, property rights, certainty for industry and cooperative decision making between levels of governments, all of which tend to undercut ecological objectives. The economically fundamentalist policy push since the 1980s,[78] embraced by Labor and accelerated by the Coalition, now presents the "reformist" environmental policy material of the Howard Government blatantly in this fashion. For all the improved policy rhetoric, the Australian political response to environmental concerns still arguably remains electoral, superficial, reactive, narrowly conceived, short-sighted, ineffective and without lasting institutional benefits.[79]

Australia's capacity to improve its environmental policy performance would be greatly enhanced by attention to what implementation analysis has been concluded to date. The *State of the Environment* report has found no consensus on ecological degradation, nor on how to approach environmental policy analysis, and no coherent institutional mechanism for addressing and resolving issues.[80] Where national policy principles have been determined, such as the commitment to ecologically sustainable development, little evidence has been found of their integration into decision making. Dovers and Lindenmayer conclude that Australia's environmental policies "are usually vague, lacking measurable goals, overwhelmingly non-binding, and not underpinned by substantial institutional or statutory provision".[81] There has long been criticism of Australia's environmental institutions; environmental impact procedures have offered developers greater protection than the environment.[82] The Australian Heritage Commission has been criticised for its limited application (to Commonwealth agencies and actions), and for the Commonwealth's failure to use its processes to minimise damage to heritage values.[83] The intergovernmental mechanisms that manage the Great Barrier Reef[84] and the Murray Darling River Basin[85] are both admired internationally, but are proving no safeguard against steady ecological decline. Criticism of these relatively early institutions has been steadily joined by criticism of the failure of more recent institutions and policy arrangements, such as World Heritage obligations, the Intergovernmental Agreement on the Environment and the much contested Regional Forestry process, to actually protect the environment.

The positive, if *ad hoc*, environmental policy record of the 1980s is fading into history now as an aberration with short-lived institutional outcomes, rather than a period in which ecological rationality was integrated into public decision making. But the contemporary process of environmental policy abandonment clearly began with Keating's shift of "metapolicy" toward economic imperatives and away from the environment after he deposed Hawke in 1991.[86] He then shook himself free from the green hand upon governance that had derailed traditional economic initiatives under Hawke. He set about alienating Labor's environmental constituency to the point of ignoring increased woodchipping as a critical issue in a Canberra by-election, which Labor lost.[87] On gaining power, he abandoned initiatives only recently established to resolve resource conflict. He used his Intergovernmental Agreement on the Environment, not to better coordinate environmental protection, but to fast-track the MacArthur River Mine against environmental advice.[88] Conservationists could not interest him in exercising federal environmental powers against the development excesses of the States, even where these threatened World Heritage. His decision-making style was aloof rather than consensual. He retained environmentalists on policy forums, but berated them in public, claiming that "[t]he environmental lobbies have no moral lien over the environment".[89] The deteriorating relationship between Keating and environmentalists was critical to Howard's ability to drive an electoral wedge between them with his promise to spend $1.25 billion "saving our natural heritage".[90] Once in office, Howard accelerated Keating's shift to economic "rationalism", and again environmentalists felt betrayed.

Many are marvelling at how far and how fast environmental policy and politics have sunk as national priorities. The simple, conventional view is that issue attention has been exhausted and just moved on. Thus the policy platforms of both Labor and the Coalition in the lead-up to the 1998 Election were noticeably thin on environmental content. The Coalition was seeking re-election after two years of environmental policy roll-backs that were barely remarked upon by Labor in Opposition. Even the controversy stirred up by the Natural Heritage Trust's funding process could not shift Labor into gear. Meanwhile, the environment suffered. Woodchip export quotas were lifted, greenhouse gas reduction targets were abandoned, developments were supported in World Heritage areas and longstanding bans on uranium mining were overturned.[91] Institutional arrangements and prior commitments offered no protection against these purely political decisions. Indeed, the shift in environmental policy tactics from Hawke to Keating to Howard shows how political will can stunt institutional capacity. Hawke expanded, then expediently applied, federal environmental powers; Keating devolved such powers, reserving only the option to exercise them; whilst Howard wants to divest the federal government of them almost totally. Once the era of green electoralism in the early 1980s dimmed, so too did the environmental differences between Labor and the Coalition. Green demands now tend to drive these antagonists together, just as ecopolitical theorists would expect them to. And the defence of capital interests as a shared imperative has blurred their policy differences just as the political economists would expect. In a political system driven by the wealth imperative, environmentalists have long recognised themselves as ideological outsiders whose best hope is to keep vigilant watch over the state's environmental policy performance.

Perhaps other political systems have different environmental policy experiences that would benefit from different theoretical explanations from those used here for Australia. Some political systems lack the complication of federalism, for instance. In others, there may be greater acceptance of environmentalism because they are less dependent upon resource exploitation. Some systems have more sophisticated environmental institutional design which has been relatively more effective than Australia's. In many countries, the bipartisan political commitment may be for, rather than against, environmental improvement. Some of these countries may have participative electoral structures that more accurately reflect public concern. Some countries may have made such enduring environmental commitments that micro-policy critique actually proves worthwhile. But Australia's environmental policy is greatly constrained by its disproportionate reliance on natural resource exploitation.[92] Even our supposedly less advanced regional neighbours are increasingly pursuing better environmental policy régimes. Environmental policy analysis in these terms must convey a sense of the persistence of ecological problems, the limits to policy and the bipartisan obstacles to better environmental protection. Policy failure should be recognised as responsible for the resurgence, if in a more marginal fashion now than in the 1980s, of Australian environmental activism. There are many more ecopolitical contests to come — most notably over arid land use, the land rights of indigenous peoples and the economic rationalisation of environmental policy administration. It will make no sense at all to argue that these contests, and the media attention they will generate, are simply environmental policy reclaiming its lost place on the issue agenda.

BACKWARDS INTO THE FUTURE: NATIONAL POLICY MAKING, DEVOLUTION AND THE RISE AND FALL OF THE ENVIRONMENT

N. Economou

The 1980s were important years in the recent history of Australian environmental politics. In 1983, the Australian Labor Party was elected to national government with a policy manifesto that promised, amongst other things, to prevent the construction of the Franklin-below-Gordon hydro-electric scheme proposed by Tasmania's Hydro Electric Commission (HEC). A year later, the High Court of Australia validated the Commonwealth's *World Heritage Properties Protection Act 1983*, thereby legitimising the Hawke Government's anti-dams policy.[1] At the same time this decision established a new beachhead in the expansion of the Commonwealth's power to make land-use decisions in the name of environmental protection, despite the opposition of the States. This, in turn, was to be the basis of a period of quite important Commonwealth policy-making that resulted in the conservation of some significant forest and land areas, and which even resulted in the prevention of some major industrial and mining projects on the grounds that their environmental and/or cultural costs were too great for the community to pay. In short, this was a golden period, at least for those in the environmental movement motivated by a desire to achieve the conservation of some of Australia's more significant wilderness and land areas, and opposed to uranium mining. So, too, was it a period in which the environment arrived as a permanent presence on the national political agenda — a major achievement for those seeking to have such matters break out of the regionally parochial confines of State-based land-use decision making.

By the 1990s, however, the nature of the national environmental debate changed again, notwithstanding the fact that the issue still enjoyed significant public recognition and was still being addressed in the election manifestos of the mainstream political parties.[2] One particularly noticeable feature of the national debate at this time was the way in which policy actors — government, developer interests, the unions and the environmental movement — were preoccupied less with the sort of specific land-use disputes that had dominated the debate in previous times, but rather with more involved discussions about decision-making procedure and the technical question of how long-term decision making might seek to achieve a "balance" between environmentalist and developer positions on the ecological sustainability of growth and development. In a sense, this shift involved a transition in the national environmental policy debate away from short-term addressing of land-use disputes as they arose, to instead become a debate about what Dror once described as "metapolicy"[3] — the debate institutional actors conduct amongst themselves as to how the mechanisms and processes of policy decision may be constructed, or improved on the basis of past experience.

There was an important political consequence associated with this shift in the environmental debate from specific issues to metapolicy, which was to persist through the change in national government from Labor to Coalition in 1996. The shift provided scope for governmental actors to exert leadership over the issue, primarily at the expense of the environmental movement generally, and its organisational core of environmental interest groups in particular. Up until this point, the environmental movement had been very successful in defining the debate's parameters, particularly through their ability to exploit heightened community awareness about the aesthetic qualities of some of the specific land areas that environmentalists were seeking to protect from development and exploitation. Admittedly, these campaigns were assisted by the ascendancy of a Federal Environment Minister willing to associate his ministerial career with the nature conservation battles being brought to national attention.[4] In many ways, this alteration in the nature of the national debate was as much a response from within the Hawke Cabinet to Senator Richardson's method of dealing with the environment issue as it was a deliberate attempt by institutional actors to reassert their control over the external politics of environmental policy-making.

Here, then, lies the basis upon which the "roll back" of environmentalism's impact on the national political debate has occurred. Interestingly, this decline in the environmental movement's ability to impact on the political process owes much to its initial success in having environmental matters addressed at the national level in the first place. It will be argued below that the environmental movement's achievement in this area was based on the willingness of the Hawke Government in particular to use the interventionist powers of the Australian state to address environmental matters at a time in which neo-liberal notions of state minimalism were beginning to take root in the overall policy approach of what was supposed to be a social democratic government. The process of redefining the national environmental debate — and, through it, the Commonwealth's rôle in that debate — commenced after the 1990 Federal Election, and was carried on by the Keating Labor Government. The election of the Liberal-National Coalition simply completed the devolutionary process. Despite paying lip-service to the importance of the environmental agenda (especially with regard to the uncontentious issue of regenerating agricultural lands), the Coalition Government simply refused to entertain central aspects of the environmentalist agenda, including the opposition to development at Port Hinchinbrook and mining in the Kakadu National Park Conservation Zone, and the repudiation of the "green" position on "Greenhouse" gas emissions at the World Climate Summit held in Kyoto, Japan.

THE ENVIRONMENTALIST ASCENDANCY: NATIONAL POLICY UNDER THE HAWKE GOVERNMENT

Notwithstanding the periodic eruptions of discord and occasional threats to dissolve the mutually supportive relationship that had formed between Labor and the core environmental interest groups, particularly after the Tasmanian dams controversy, the period between the 1983 and 1990 Federal elections was one of almost unprecedented environmentalist influence on the national political debate. Whilst it is very true that both the Whitlam (Labor) and Fraser (Liberal-National) Governments had, at some point during their incumbency, enacted significant environmental policy, it was the Hawke Labor Government that was the most consistent in its willingness to respond to the environmental movement's political agenda. Commencing with the use of federal powers to prevent the hydro-development of Tasmania's south-west wilderness region, the Hawke Government also made decisions that extended Commonwealth protection of forest areas in Tasmania, Queensland and Victoria,[5] prevented mining at Coronation Hill in the Kakadu National Park Conservation Zone, and even prevented the development of a major new pulp mill at Wesley Vale in northern Tasmania.[6]

Each of these specific land-use issues has been the subject of extensive research and discussion, and does not require retelling here. Controversy continues to surround the reasons why the Hawke Government was so proactive in the field of environmental protection, however, particularly in the light of the high value the Labor Government and its trade union-based constituency has historically placed on economic growth and development as a precursor to employment growth.[7] In a very real sense, the Hawke Government's willingness to embrace the environmentalist agenda as it pertained to some of the more spectacular disputes reflected a triumph of a more sophisticated politics over a more traditionally developmentalist blue-collar approach. However, the point has been made that Labor's activism in this field coincided with a decline in the national unemployment rate, suggesting that the Hawke Government could afford to respond to the conservation agenda.[8] In other words, the Hawke Government's interest in environmentalism was of an extent necessary to assuage a "middle class" interest, particularly in the conservation of spectacular natural areas under threat from development. From this approach developed the view that Labor's interest in the environment was based on electoral considerations, particularly where environmental interest groups involved themselves in the process of endorsing candidates involved in federal contests.[9]

It is also important to note that the Hawke Government's approach to environmental matters was a classic example of traditional state interventionism at a time when neoclassical liberal notions about the economic and social desirability of state minimalism were beginning to have a major impact on the policy debate.[10] Not even Labor, as a social democratic party in government, was able to resist the hegemony of neoclassical liberal arguments about the need for economic liberalisation based on deregulation and a reduction in the size of government.[11] Whilst debate exists as to the extent to which it embraced these arguments, the Hawke Government certainly sought to apply neoclassical liberal ideas to economic policy and reduced the provision of government services in a bid to return budget surpluses. By de-emphasising tariffs in preference for a "level playing field" in industry policy, the Hawke Government also embraced the deregulatory agenda of economic rationalism. Yet at

the same time that it was applying economic rationalism to economic policy, its increasing activism on environmental matters required
more regulatory intervention and, as the Commonwealth sought to
enhance its ability to make land-use decisions on a sounder technical
and scientific basis subjected to the processes of public and interest
group mediation, plus some significant institution-building as well.
In this policy area, at least, Labor's record of state interventionism
was akin to traditional social democratic practice.

The coincidence of Labor's proactive period in environmental
policy-making with the tenure of Senator Graham Richardson as
Environment Minister was also an important factor, reflecting the
extent to which the support of a powerful institutional actor can
assist interest groups in having their agendas addressed by the institutionalised policy-making process. By being motivated primarily by
short-term political considerations (including judgements about the
electoral implications of decisions), Senator Richardson was particularly amenable to those agenda items that enjoyed strong public
recognition and sympathy. This dovetailed very nicely with the way
the environmental movement conducted its anti-development campaigns, particularly in the midst of aesthetically spectacular disputed
land areas. Indeed, the extent to which land-use debates could be
influenced by aesthetics led developer interests and pro-development
ministers in the Hawke Government to decry what they saw as a
debate excessively dominated by "emotion" rather than "rational
economic" considerations.

Interestingly, Senator Richardson's actions in the environment
field could infuriate environmental leaders almost as much as they did
developer interests and even his Cabinet colleagues. Motivated by
short-term considerations, the Environment Minister remained
impervious to demands from both developers and environmental
leaders for a more systematic approach to incorporating as wide a
range of value inputs as possible in land use and resource decision
making. The reasons why both environmentalists and developers
should place a high value on decision-making process are worth
reflecting upon, for this issue would later result in a reorientation of
the national environment debate. The tendency for developers to
consider economistic perspectives as inherently rational has already
been alluded to. In a similar vein, environmentalist perspectives tend
to be dominated by the high value they place on an "ecological rationality".[12] This is based on notions that, first, humanity needs to find
ways in which it can live in balance with the environment and, secondly, that ecological considerations are a matter of decision-making
urgency that can and should be applied to a wide range of policy

debates.[13] Motivated by a view that their rationality should prevail in long-term decision making, both environmentalists and developers were quite willing to address the environmental issue as a debate on entrenching long-term principles in decision making, rather than just as short-term debates about specific land uses when and if disputes arose.

These approaches were particularly noticeable in the "Ecologically Sustainable Development" (ESD) debate that was commenced by the Commonwealth in 1990.[14] Originating as a concept developed by the Brundlandt Commission under the auspices of the United Nations Educational, Scientific and Cultural Organisation (UNESCO) as part of its multilateral development of an international approach to "balancing" development and environmental demands, the Australian ESD debate was discharged through a series of Working Groups — organised around seven broad economic functions — in which capital, unions, government and government-invited environmental interest group leaders were participants. Their brief was to find ways in which ecological values could be included in policy-making, and environmental leaders certainly invested enormous amounts of energy and time in these debates. A similar view that environmental matters should be the subject of a more complex and broad based approach as distinct from the tendency to undertake short-term decision making underpinned the Hawke Government's development of the Resource Assessment Commission (RAC).[15] Together with the ESD process, the creation of the RAC was at the forefront of the Government's attempt to transform the national environmental debate. Herein lay the basis of the way the national debate would change, and the environmental movement's ability to impact on the national debate via specific land-use disputes was to be modified accordingly.

Whilst political considerations influenced the change in the direction of the environmental debate (and especially the political tensions that existed between Senator Richardson and his pro-development colleagues in the Hawke Cabinet), the shift in emphasis towards thematic discussions about ways ecological values could be incorporated into long-term policy-making still assuaged some important environmental demands. First and foremost, the Hawke Government was prepared to take a leading rôle in the debate, thereby offering environmentalists the hope of national intervention as a panacea to the tendency for close relations between developers and State agencies. Second, the Hawke Government's approach was still one based on the notion that government intervention was an appropriate response as a way of countering the dominance of materialist values in a more market-rationalist approach to land use. Finally, the ESD and RAC developments indicated the extent to which the Hawke Government was prepared to create new national institutions that could provide the intellectual and technical work required to supplement the Commonwealth's enhanced rôle in the national environmental debate. It was these three aspects that were to be notable casualties as the Hawke leadership fell before the Paul Keating challenge in 1991.

COMMENCING DEVOLUTION: THE KEATING GOVERNMENT AND THE ENVIRONMENT

After its election to government in 1993, the Keating Government commenced the process of devolving Commonwealth influence over environmental matters. This began with the Government's decision to dismantle the RAC — a decision announced as part of the money-saving measures in the 1993 budget. While the politics surrounding this decision were complex (an account may be found elsewhere[16]), the dismantling of the RAC represented a major repudiation by the Keating Government of the Hawke Government's approach to reforming national environmental policy-making by state interventionism and institution building. The decision could also be interpreted as an indication of the influence of state minimalism and economic rationalism on the Keating Government, although a more likely explanation is that the dismantling of the Commission was an indication of the lower priority the environment was given by this Government.

With the ESD process wound down and the RAC dismantled, the finalisation of the Intergovernmental Agreement on the Environment (IGAE)[17] and the subsequent policy positions on forestry became the primary arenas for the national environmental debate. Paralleling the notion of seeking ways in which the States could be incorporated into the land-use decision-making process as cooperative partners (rather than, as in the past, as adversaries) was a reform to the operation of the Australian Heritage Commission (AHC). Central to this reform was the formulation of the so-called "regionalisation" method by which the AHC would undertake analyses of disputed areas of land in order to determine what, if any, national estate properties were at risk from development. During the Hawke years, AHC findings had developed a significant political dimension, and were often used by environmentalists as the basis for appeals to the Commonwealth for federal government intervention on land-use matters particularly to counter the support State governments would give to development proposals. Herein lay the basis on which relations between the AHC and counterpart State agencies had become strained, State governments in some cases directing their agencies not to cooperate with Commonwealth investigations.[18]

Regionalisation and the IGAE were initiatives commenced under the Hawke Government, but carried on to fruition by the Keating administration. The major difference between the two Labor approaches to this issue was that, under the Hawke Government, these initiatives designed to bring cooperation to federal-state environmental relations would have occurred in parallel with the operation of the RAC. Under the Keating approach, the absence of the RAC meant that the impetus in cooperative federal-state relations on environmental matters would be with the States, primarily because of the great reservoir of technical, scientific and administrative experience held by State land-use agencies who had been operating in this policy area over the long term. In his campaign to win the Labor leadership, Keating had been critical of the notion of returning responsibilities to the States contained in Hawke's "New Federalism" policy.[19] Somewhat ironically, once in power, his approach to environmental metapolicy (dominated by the RAC closure) put in place the administrative environment in which the Commonwealth would surrender its ability to compete with the States in the process of garnering information and coordinating competing interest group demands in this field.

A second important political development unfolded during this transition period that exacerbated the trend to devolution. At the time that Hawke was formulating his New Federalism policy, Labor was in government in the States of Victoria, Queensland, SA and WA, and the Green-Labor Accord Government was also operating in Tasmania. By 1993, however, the political landscape of the States had changed dramatically and the Liberal Party was in government in all States, either in its own right, or in coalition with the National Party. This major shift in the party alignment of the various State governments also influenced the environmental debate by virtue of the tendency for the Coalition parties to be more firmly committed to the developer agenda than the Labor governments they displaced. With the ascendancy of a federal government with an agenda dominated by a host of social issues other than the environment, and the rise of pro-development Coalition governments in the States, the political environment in which land-use and resource policies were to be debated had undergone a major shift in favour of developer interests.

Although it was not in itself the direct result of the Keating Government's metapolicy approach, the extent to which the environment was permitted to languish as a matter of importance under the new Labor administration was revealed in the woodchip export licence dispute that was to have a major influence on relations between Labor and environmental interest groups during the 1996 Federal Election campaign. This dispute arose from the procedure by which federal and state agencies facilitated the annual issuing of export licences to timber harvesting interests seeking to meet demands for the woodchip industry — a particularly sensitive area of the timber resource debate given the importance that the environmental movement has historically placed on opposing woodchipping.[20]

Particularly because the dispute erupted as a result of the Resources Minister's attempt to assert his credentials with his department's timber industry constituency, it was not just damaging to Labor-environmental relations. It also revealed the gulf that had emerged between the Hawke and Keating administrations on the matter of managing the policy-making process. The Hawke Government's interest in reforming the land-use and resource decision-making process had been based on the objective of preventing disputes such as these from erupting onto the public agenda. Without a commensurate interest in decision-making processes, the Keating Government was caught out by a dispute caused by a problem in the way licence applications were evaluated and expedited. Yet this simple procedural problem was quickly overwhelmed by an escalation of the dispute into a debate about the future of the timber industry. An ALP-affiliated union — the Construction, Forestry, Mining and Energy Union (CFMEU) — became a participant when it convened a blockade of the national parliament that became a serious embarrassment for the Keating Government. As if this wasn't enough, the dispute was to reverberate some time later during the by-election for the federal seat of Canberra caused by the retirement of former Environment Minister, Ros Kelly. A "green" candidate won some 20% of the primary vote, after which the distribution of preferences led to the election of a Liberal representative. Here, "green" politics — in the form of a non-major-party-aligned green candidate, along with a disgruntled environmental interest group constituency — contributed to the dealing of a major electoral blow to the Keating Government.[21]

The poor electoral relations between green politics and the Keating-led ALP in the Canberra election was a portent for a deterioration in Labor-environmental relations during the 1996 Federal Election campaign. The Coalition meanwhile undertook a concerted effort to drive a wedge between Labor and the core environmental interest groups such as the Wilderness Society, the Australian Conservation Foundation (ACF) and the World-Wide Fund for

Nature (WWF). The promise to use funds accrued from the partial privatisation of Telstra to finance a land conservation fund as part of the Coalition's *Saving Our Natural Heritage* environment policy manifesto was the main instrument used by the Coalition in this task. The success of this strategy was revealed when a couple of environmental groups, including the Wilderness Society, gave tacit approval to the Coalition's proposal.[22] Not only did this outcome indicate the extent to which the rift between the Keating Government and sections of the environmental lobby had grown (especially in the light of the woodchip dispute), it also revealed that the Coalition had made the strategic decision to abandon its previous hostility towards the environmental movement. Instead, the Coalition indicated that it now viewed the environment as a major national political issue to which it now sought to respond with offers of policy concessions — a far cry from a previous period in which the environmental movement was vilified by successive Liberal shadow environment ministers as either a front for the Labor Party, political extremism, or a combination of the two.

The 1996 Federal Election was to be a major turning point as the Coalition swept into government in an electoral landslide; the entire policy debate would change considerably. Although the 1996 defeat was interpreted as the end of a Labor-dominated era of national politics,[23] the qualitative change in the nature of the environmental policy debate had actually begun with the transition of the Labor leadership from Hawke to Keating, and all areas of policy — including environment policy — were affected. This transition involved more than just changing priorities on the policy agenda. At the heart of the transition from Hawke to Keating was a qualitative change in Labor's approach to the politics of policy making in which neo-corporatist notions of the need to incorporate key interest groups into the policy-creation process were eschewed for a much more fragmented and adversarial approach.[24] Under the Keating leadership, policy matters were thrashed out in a much more competitive and conflict-oriented environment — a reflection of Keating's greater willingness to undertake an adversarial rôle as Prime Minister than his consensus-oriented predecessor.

The problem for some policy areas to which the Hawke Government's neo-corporatist approach to decision making was applied (such as the environment) was that the fall of Hawke and his normative approach to politics also meant a decline in Labor's interest in institutional reform, particularly where the Commonwealth was seeking to improve its ability to make "good" policy in a given area. Here the environmental policy area suffered particularly. Just as

Keating was willing to risk the Labor-environmental relationship that Hawke had put together in the 1983 Election in response to the anti-Franklin Dam campaign, so, too, the new Prime Minister's relative indifference to developing new national policy-making institutions that could enhance Canberra's ability to make environmental policy was a contributing factor to the environment's decline in the national debate after 1991. With the closure of the RAC, and the election of a host of Coalition State governments, the tendency towards devolution was well under way prior to the 1996 Federal Election. The election of the Howard Coalition Government in that poll simply completed the devolutionary process.

DEVOLUTION COMPLETE: THE ENVIRONMENT AND THE FEDERAL COALITION GOVERNMENT

Notwithstanding the effort it had gone to break up the ALP-environmental alliance by wooing environmental interest groups via its *Saving Our Natural Heritage* policy, the Coalition's victory in the 1996 Federal Election represented a major shift in the balance of power in the environmental debate in favour of developer interests — a fact acknowledged by the National Association of Forest Industries (NAFI) in its official exultation of the appointment of the National Party's John Sharp as Minister for Primary Industries.[25] The basis of this shift lay in three important political givens about the nature of the Coalition's response to the environment issue. First, the evolution during the 1980s of a closer relationship between the environmental movement and the social democratic parties on the Australian spectrum (the ALP and the Democrats) meant that much antipathy existed between the Coalition and environmental interest groups. The National Party in particular were, and continue to be, fundamental opponents of "green" politics. With the Coalition now in power and able to rely on parliamentary alliances that could exclude the Democrats and the Greens to get its legislation through the Senate, the likelihood of there being cooperative relations between the Howard Government and the leading environmental interest groups was extremely remote.

Indeed, the notion that the Coalition would treat environmental interest groups in ways very different from the previous Labor administrations was a second important factor. It reflected the degree to which the Liberal Party in particular had been influenced by the critique of traditional pluralist approaches to interest group politics popular in Thatcherite Britain. Here the influence of public choice theory (as interpreted by the Right) is important, for the Coalition used the argument that governance should seek to keep sectional interest groups at arm's length from the policy-making process — as a means of ensuring that it is government, and not interest groups, that defines the "national interest" — as a basis for its critique of the Hawke approach in particular.[26] Indeed, Labor's willingness to seek to include environmental interest groups in its neo-corporatist approach to managing policy debates was singled out by the Coalition as an example of the degree to which Labor had been captured by sectional interests. Similar criticisms were made with regard to Labor's relationship with "ethnic groups" and the formation of multiculturalism, and with the ACTU in formulation of economic and industrial relations policy.[27] Implicit in the Coalition's "For All of Us" slogan for the 1996 campaign was the claim that Labor had become the captive of vested interests to the exclusion of a presumably greater silent majority. So, despite the wooing of environmental interest groups that went on during the campaign, the election of the Coalition to government signalled a period in which groups viewed as too closely aligned with the ALP in the previous administrative era could expect to have their access to institutional actors substantially diminished.

Finally, the notion of devolving policy-making particularly in those areas historically viewed as a regional responsibility away from the Commonwealth and back to the States is a major feature of the Coalition's normative commitment to federalism. Philosophically, the federalist ideal fits neatly with traditional liberal notions about the need to devolve the power of the state as a means of assuring individual liberty.[28] There are many examples of practical inconsistencies in the Coalition's normative position, and instances where it has exercised central power over the States when in government. But its stand on the need to preserve the distinction between national and regional policy bailiwicks in order to preserve Australian federalism has assisted it in opposing centralist intervention on environmental matters. Whilst the Keating administration allowed devolution to occur as a result of neglect, the Coalition's devolutionary approach has had a much firmer ideological and philosophical basis. Ever since the Franklin Dam dispute, the Coalition has been highly critical of the increased rôle Canberra has played in a policy matter that the Liberal and National parties believe should be primarily the responsibility of the States.

In the two and half years of the first term of the Howard Coalition Government, the main themes present in the Coalition's approach to environmental matters were clearly evident in three broad policy debates — the question of how and to which projects the funds acquired from the Telstra privatisation would be distributed through the *Saving Our Natural Heritage* policy (which has been directed primarily at land regeneration programmes that enjoy conservationist-developer consensus), the formulation and finalisation of joint Commonwealth-State forestry use agreements through the Regional Forest Agreement (RFA) mechanism, and the position Australia would take on global greenhouse gas emission levels at the World Climate Summit held at Kyoto in Japan. Before any of these broad, metapolicy-oriented matters could be fully addressed, however, an insight to the Coalition's approach to nature conservation was provided in a dispute over a tourist development at Port Hinchinbrook in northern Queensland. This development in an area adjacent to a World Heritage conservation area had been the subject of environmentalist-developer dispute for some time, and the previous Labor Environment Minister, Senator John Faulkner, had succeeded in having the development stopped pending further environmental impact assessment. This approach was overturned by the Coalition, with Tim Fischer, the National Party leader and Deputy Prime Minister (rather than the Liberal Environment Minister, Senator Robert Hill) making a public declaration of the federal government's support for the developer. This was an early indication of the extent to which the balance in land-use politics had now tipped back in favour of developers, and little transpired in the following two years of the Howard administration to mitigate this sense of a developer ascendancy.

The Howard Government's approach to the world climate debate was a further manifestation of this ascendancy. In the face of a growing international acceptance of the need to impose global limits to the amount of "greenhouse" gases produced by economic activity particularly in the developed world, the Australian government successfully applied for an increase in greenhouse emission levels. As Fenna and Economou point out,[29] this position was interpreted by the government (and especially Prime Minister Howard and his National Party colleague, Tim Fischer) as a victory for the government's commitment to securing employment particularly in the resources sector, and reflected a very important attitude prevalent in the approach of institutional actors in the debate: that environmental protection is achieved at the expense of economic and employment growth. Significantly, the government's position was formulated in the face of great criticism by the core environmental interest groups such as the ACF, who were strong advocates of Australia conforming to the gas reduction approach being accepted by other industrial nations. The environmentalist position had been more influential on the approach taken by the previous Labor government during the 1992 Earth Summit at Rio de Janeiro.

It has been in the area of forestry policy, however, that the clearest signs of devolution have been discernible, and where the environmentalist gains that had been achieved during the time of the Hawke Government have been subjected to a substantial roll-back. Once again, the antecedents of national forestry policy under the Coalition are to be found in the previous Keating Labor Government. It was the Labor government that articulated its National Forestry Policy Strategy (NFPS), encompassing the Comprehensive Regional Assessment (CRA) and Regional Forest Agreement (RFA) mechanisms, which would figure prominently in the subsequent trend toward devolution. Briefly, the CRA process was designed to undertake a thorough investigation of a wide-ranging set of evaluative criteria by which decisions about forest usage could be made. The CRA would then feed in to the RFA which, in turn, would involve the Commonwealth and the respective States working together to formulate a set of long-term forest use agreements. Protagonist interest groups would gain access, but would also have to accept the outcome of the process.[30] Formulated by the Keating Government, the CRA-RFA process was actually utilised by the Howard Government, and agreements with the Coalition government in Victoria over East Gippsland, and the Liberal government in Tasmania, were finalised by the end of 1997.

To its proponents, the CRA-RFA process represented an extension of the rational comprehensive approach to national environmental policy-making that had been initiated by the Hawke Government back in the post-Wesley Vale pulp mill dispute period. As such, the process was designed to allow institutional policy makers the opportunity to evaluate a range of inputs (including environmental perspectives) in making their decisions on forestry matters, and provide the basis upon which environmentalist and developer demands could be "balanced".[31] To its critics, however, the CRA-RFA process looked very suspiciously like the resource security process that had also emerged as a controversial issue during the last months of the Hawke Government and which had been vigorously opposed by the environmental lobby.[32] Environmental leaders were also angered at what they perceived to be a set of outcomes from the policy that allowed for the realisation of some longstanding items on the timber industry's agenda. These included the abolition of Commonwealth-set quotas on woodchip harvesting in Tasmania and the introduction of a woodchip component to the Victorian industry where previously none had been allowed to exist. The extent of the environmental movement's anger at these decisions was evidenced in the resumption of direct protest activity, particularly in the East

Gippsland region.[33] Whatever goodwill might have existed between the Coalition and the environmental interest groups in the lead-up to the 1996 Election was comprehensively lost in the CRA-RFA debate, and the environmental movement's perception that the impetus in forestry policy had been regained by the timber industry was a reflection of the extent to which the environmental "lobby" had been frozen out of the institutional policy-making process under a pro-developer conservative government.

National environmental politics underwent a significant change as a result of the election of the Howard Government. The return of greater latitude to the States to make land-use and resource decisions, at the expense of the growth in Commonwealth influence that had been developed especially by the Hawke Government, was an important part of this transformation. This dovetailed with other instances of the way in which the Coalition was more hostile to the environmentalist agenda than both the previous Hawke and Keating administrations. This was particularly noticeable over the Port Hinchinbrook controversy, the stand the Australian government took on greenhouse gas emissions, and, later, a resurfacing of a robust anti-uranium campaign in response to the government's decision to allow mining to proceed at the Jabiluka site in the Northern Territory. This in itself was not really surprising, given the historical antipathy between the Coalition and the environmental movement. The attempt by the Howard-led Liberals to try to regain some of the ground lost in Coalition-environmental relations during the 1996 campaign was noteworthy, however, not so much for what it said about the Liberal Party's attempt to define environmentalism to be something more acceptable to the conservative side of politics — rather, its significance lay in what it indicated about the souring of the Labor-environmental relationship under Keating's prime ministership.

CONCLUSION

In a dynamic closely resembling the cyclical tendency in policy debates once forecast by Downs in his "issue-attention cycle",[34] the environmental policy debate in Australia has turned something of a circle. From its previous incarnation as a regional issue debated primarily at the State level, the environment rose to a position of great national prominence, particularly under the Hawke Labor Government. Whilst it still figures on the national agenda, the high point of achievement for the environmental movement occurred when the Hawke Government was making decisions designed to appease the core environmental interest groups. After the Wesley Vale pulp mill dispute, however, the nature of the debate shifted from addressing specific issues to explore the mechanisms by which long-term policies that would seek to balance developer and ecological outlooks could be made. This approach was, in turn, undermined by the Keating Government's lack of interest in institutional design, which resulted in the collapse of the RAC. The formation of mechanisms such as the CRA-RFA process based on returning a major evaluative rôle to the States, was in fact, a carry-over from the Hawke Government's interest in cooperative federal-state relations as part of the then Prime Minister's "New Federalism" policy. Keating's contribution to devolution was to strip the RAC from the IGAE process, and the election of a pro-developer, States'-rights oriented Coalition government simply completed this process.

It is interesting to note that the rise of the environment as a major national issue to which substantial federal governmental attention was directed occurred against a broader backdrop in which neoclassical notions about the centrality of the market to decision making, and the desirability of state minimalism, were predominant. There was a sense in which the environment became an important arena in which the Hawke Government could continue to be a government in the social democratic tradition — an arena in which notions of equity could be brought in as a counter to the crude materialism of the marketplace, and where the state could involve itself in the process of institution-building in order to improve its ability to intervene in issues via the policy-making process. The attempt to build up the Commonwealth's ability to make policy in this area by undertaking the task of investigating how a concept such as ESD could be applied to policy making, by putting more resources into the AHC, and building an institution such as the RAC, all required the central government to seeks ways in which it could mitigate the monopoly over metapolicy held by the States.

This was meant to be an important legacy of the Hawke Government, yet the dismantling of these bodies began with the very next Labor administration and was carried over into the subsequent Coalition government. The environment continues to figure prominently in the minds of the national electorate as an important issue, and the major parties continue to pay it lip-service in election campaigns via the formulation of environmental policy manifestos. Yet the reality is that the golden age of Commonwealth activity in this area has passed and, thanks to devolution of responsibilities back to the States, the metapolicy debate has returned to the position it was in before the intrusion of the Tasmanian dams dispute into the national agenda back in 1982–83.

UNSUSTAINABLE DEVELOPMENT IN QUEENSLAND

M.F. Carden

INTRODUCTION

Queensland's political and economic problems have been highly persistent. At Federation Queensland was considered to have very good prospects, yet for most of the twentieth century it has lagged politically, economically and socio-culturally behind its southern cousins in NSW, Victoria and SA. A particularly striking feature of its political culture has been a persistence with uneconomic or failing industries, and a dogged refusal to re-examine the developmental premises of its policies. These have underlain periodic scandals and political repression.

The fundamental reason for these failures has been a persistent mismatch between European-derived development policies, predicated on broad acre farming dependent on reliable rainfall and fertile soils, and the realities of a fragile, predominantly tropical environment, in which drought is the norm and ecological disturbance easier to achieve than European "development". Political cargo-cultism, encouraging large-scale, capital-intensive development to "solve" the State's budgetary problems, has intensified environmental impacts.[1]

In short, underlying the economic and political failures is a more fundamental ecological disruption, manifested as a series of intractable environmental problems. Land degradation is serious, especially on the Darling Downs, which account for 25% of Australia's agricultural exports. Governments have been reluctant to tackle this politically explosive problem. Conflicts over fishing have become progressively more acute, with recreational and commercial fishermen at loggerheads, and conservationists concerned over fish stocks. The Great Barrier Reef is affected, and it is also thought that run-off from agriculture has been polluting it. But the major source of run-off is the cossetted sugar industry. Environmental impacts from mining have largely been ignored, or accepted as the "price" of "progress". Along the coast, and especially in the south-east, ribbon development and urban sprawl are generating energy, water supply and sewage disposal problems of truly Augean proportions.[2]

Tasmania and WA, with similar failings, have also performed relatively poorly this century. As a result there are two Australias: one made up of NSW, Victoria and SA; and the other consisting of Queensland, Tasmania and WA. The latter are all renowned for their conservatism and anti-environmental policies. Indeed, the radicalisation of the environmental movement in Australia was largely due to the ecological intransigence and undemocratic behaviour of these three States. The genesis of the radical green movement of the 1980s lay in the conflicts over the damming of Lake Pedder (Tasmania), oil and mineral prospecting on the Great Barrier Reef (Queensland) and logging in native jarrah forests (WA). By contrast with Queensland and its recalcitrant cousins, governments in the progressive States responded to environmental conflict in a more conciliatory and democratic manner, often leading to favourable decisions and institutional reforms.

As argued elsewhere,[3] public policy outcomes normally result from complex interactions between:

1 existing legal, political, institutional, economic and socio-cultural legacies;
2 negotiations within government institutions; and
3 constrained negotiations between state agents (including politicians) and representatives of key interest groups.

Such interactions commonly yield decisions that are not ecologically or economically rational, emphasising instead political or social acceptability. Where policy legacies have significant political or social support, policy innovations, however important or necessary, are easily stifled.

Tighe has shown that the problems in Tasmania were (and still are) due to numerous institutional, economic and political legacies.[4] The interaction between these legacies, and support from particular interest groups, made the Tasmanian State resistant to environmental, economic and political reforms. Similarly, the causes of the poor economic performance of Queensland, and its conflict-ridden, ecologically irrational policy process, derive from a suite of legacies supported by key interests and actors. To understand and explain the "Queensland problem", therefore, it is necessary to (1) identify the relevant policy legacies; and (2) determine why support for them has been maintained.

Consequently, a historical analysis of the development of Queensland's contemporary political economy is required. But more is needed.

Tighe also demonstrated that hydro-industrialisation was failing Tasmania economically.[5] Indeed, its persistence was largely due to significant financial subsidies from the Commonwealth government.[6] From a public policy perspective, it is important to evaluate the ecological and economic rationality of development policies. It enables the analysis of political conflicts and economic problems to be understood in terms of failure within the public policy process. This provides insights useful for reforming and improving the policy process, rather than merely reporting on contentious issues or presenting historical facts of varying significance.[7]

Reflecting the points raised above, this chapter argues that Queensland has developed in an unsustainable fashion due to three interacting, ecologically irrational policy legacies: decentralism, agrarianism and northern development. These legacies have persisted due to the support of an alliance of electorally powerful interests, particularly in the north of the State. The ensuing policy networks have locked out change and innovation.

The case is developed in three steps. First, the problems and constraints the biophysical environment of Queensland poses for European-style development are described: are there significant constraints acting on decentralism, agrarianism and northern development? If so what are they? Second, the political and economic history of Queensland is reviewed and analysed, to: determine critical events in the evolution of the development policy process; understand how policy legacies initially emerged; and comprehend the processes and structures that permit their persistence. Finally, the implications for reform of the development and environment policy process in Queensland are briefly discussed.

BIOPHYSICAL AND ECONOMIC CONSTRAINTS ON DECENTRALISM, AGRARIANISM AND NORTHERN DEVELOPMENT

Australia is the most arid, infertile and topographically flat inhabited continent on Earth. Nine major constraints inhibit intensive European-style development in Australia:

1 low rainfall;
2 highly variable and unreliable rainfall;
3 high temperature and evaporation rates;
4 infertile soils;
5 the continent's massive area;
6 the large distance from significant potential markets;
7 the flat topography of the continent;
8 the absence of large navigable rivers connecting the inland with the coast; and
9 the lack of easily domesticated native plants and animals.

These biophysical constraints restrict intensive European settlement to 14% of mainland Australia, mainly in a crescent-shaped region on the eastern and southern parts of the continent.[8] Along the eastern coast this region stretches from south of Bowen (in Queensland) around to Adelaide (in SA). Inland it forms a long thin band close to the coastal ranges, beginning at the cracking clay plains of Queensland and running down through the agricultural heartland of NSW, Victoria and SA. It is in this crescent-shaped region that most of the country's population currently lives, and where the most intensive agricultural and other development has occurred since European settlement. Even here, adverse environmental effects have been significant.[9]

This fertile crescent is a little over 1 million sq km in size; roughly equivalent to the combined area of NSW and Victoria. Of the three eastern States Queensland has the smallest proportion of its area in the fertile crescent. In contrast, Victoria is the only State that lies almost entirely within it. In WA only the south-west corner is favourable for European development and in Tasmania it is largely the eastern and northern regions that are favourable.

In Queensland, the biophysical constraints tend to be more extreme, since a significant part of the State lies in the tropics. The tropical climate, topography and insect pests are all significant obstacles to agriculture and intensive development in north Queensland. High temperatures and evaporation rates, plus seasonal and erratic rainfall, make water scarce for long periods. Conditions are so severe that tropical plants have had to develop special strategies to survive. Different photosynthetic processes — the C4 pathway — evolved to cope with increased temperatures and solar radiation. European plants, which use the C3 pathway, do poorly north of the Tropic of Capricorn. The very existence of these special adaptations to heat and intense light demonstrates just how different the tropics are from the temperate south.

Rainfall occurs in the summer months, between January and March, and is normally intense, with large runoff volumes. Along the east coast, rivers are short and fast flowing, discharging their waters rapidly into the sea; westward they rapidly dry out after the summer rains are finished. Natural water storages are rare and little water is retained over the winter months. This limits the amount of moisture available for plants and animals, restricting the range of crops and livestock suitable for the north.[10] Queensland has large areas where soil fertility is either moderate or high, but they are very arid most of the time. Agricultural development west of the ranges is heavily reliant upon artesian water supplies.

But the feasibility of irrigation is limited. During winter, rainfall is low while temperatures and evaporation rates remain high, so water stress is a major problem. Consequently, water is limited when it is most needed for irrigation purposes, demanding larger than normal water storage facilities. However, the flat topography of the State means that most of the good sites for dams lie in the south.

These biophysical attributes are major economic obstacles for decentralised or intensive agrarian development in Queensland. Tropical pests and the harsh climate increase the cost and quantity of agricultural inputs required by primary producers. Consequently, only high-value crops which cannot be produced more cheaply by southern States are likely to succeed. Indeed, as Davidson has noted:

> Past experience simply shows that any pastoral or agricultural industry founded north of the tropic must be one in which a high output per man [sic] can be obtained and that output per acre may be far less important.[11]

Thus widespread European-style development in large parts of Queensland requires labour intensive industries. However, the biophysical attributes of the north act against the development of agricultural industries that employ large numbers of people. Davidson[12] and Holmes[13] have both noted that intensive northern development is also inhibited by three other factors:

1 significant competition from southern States;
2 high transport costs to suitable markets, as well as minimal transit infrastructure including an absence of navigable rivers into the
interior; and
3 high labour costs, as skilled people must be recruited from elsewhere.

Thus, as a late developer, Queensland has always suffered relatively high startup costs and diseconomies of scale. Their impact is
exacerbated by the biophysical constraints, which grow progressively
more severe to the north. Consequently, both biophysical and economic constraints north of the Tropic essentially divide Queensland
into two different bio-economic regions. In the south-east conditions are favourable for intensive western style development, whereas in the north (and west) they are not. This distinction has never
been appreciated by the State, which has consistently attempted to
develop the north as aggressively, and in the same way, as the south.
In order to understand this policy régime, it is important to analyse
the evolution of the development policy process in Queensland.

DECENTRALISM AND NORTHERN DEVELOPMENT

The extensive settlement of the north and north-west of Queensland
owes much to successive governments desperate for tax revenues and
votes. When Queensland gained self-government in 1859 it was close
to bankruptcy, as NSW had sent the new Government a bill for all
public works built until then. Consequently, rapid economic growth
was urgently needed to raise tax revenue: resource mobilisation was
an overarching priority. This had three long term outcomes:

1 it stimulated a decentralised agrarian settlement pattern;
2 it promoted rapid and widespread development in the north of
the State despite the biophysical constraints acting there; and
3 it dispersed economic and political strength, inhibiting the concentration of wealth or power.

PASTORALISM AND RAILWAY DEVELOPMENT

Pastoralism was initially promoted, although it was seen by many as
an interim measure pending closer settlement[14] in the future.[15]
Squatters moved rapidly northward, but by 1866 pastoral expansion
was slowed by number of factors. First, establishing a run was expensive, requiring substantial credit. Second, disease, unreliable water
and drought caused considerable stock losses. Third, labour was
expensive and in short supply because of isolation, distance from

other urban centres and Aboriginal attacks. Fourth, cattle production quickly exceeded the demand of local markets, while distance from southern markets hampered export of cattle or meat.[16] Finally, in 1866 the major English and European financial houses collapsed, leaving the government without the financial resources necessary to meet its commitments. Credit for pastoralists also dried up and the land boom ended.

The general economic crisis increased the pressure from pastoralists for improved transport facilities. The first three railways in the south-east were built to 3ft 6in (1067mm or "Cape") gauge, isolating Queensland's rail system from NSW. While this minimised construction costs, it did not yield the expected returns. Narrow gauge and light track restricted economic development because:

1 speeds were slow compared to other States;
2 trainloads were comparatively small; and
3 maintenance costs were high, inflating freight charges and soaking up limited government resources.

Although the economic case for rushing ahead with cheap solutions was sound, the locations of the initial rail lines were chosen to pacify pastoral interests, not satisfy economic or engineering concerns.[17]

The extensive nature of pastoralism, and the perishability of most agricultural products, demanded an efficient, yet decentralised transport system. However, lack of funds and an inexperienced legislature led to an *ad hoc* and partisan approach to railway and road construction.[18] After the initial construction of the first rail lines in the south, priority was given to the construction of railways from regional centres such as Rockhampton and Townsville. The resulting unplanned and uncoordinated rail system entrenched an economic and political system unique to Queensland: "... unlike other Australian colonies, economic life did not revolve around the capital. Railway construction both reflected and preserved this phenomenon."[19]

GOLD

Decentralism and northern settlement was also stimulated by gold.[20] The financial crisis of 1866 was resolved by the discovery of gold at Mount Morgan in the same year, and at Gympie in 1867. Gold was found across the State, especially in the north and west of the ranges. Large, prosperous and politically active mining towns emerged, and their demands for food and fibre stimulated the growth of pastoralism and agriculture in the north. By the turn of the century nearly 24% of Queensland's population lived in the north, while less than

40% lived in the fertile south-eastern corner. Railway development was now sought to service the goldfields.

Gold, and the population it brought, stimulated the desire for a separate northern State. A major feature of political and social life in Queensland was (and still is) regionalism. In its mildest form it expressed itself as a split between urban and rural interests (town versus country), and at its most extreme, separatism (north versus south). Separatism posed a major challenge to the new State. *Ad hoc*, shoestring development had a profound long-term impact. In contrast to the other colonial capitals, Brisbane did not become the economic centre of Queensland. Although it was the major source of imports, it was second to Rockhampton in the export of wool, minerals, meat and sugar.[21] In 1896 Brisbane handled only 37% of Queensland's seagoing trade, whereas Sydney accounted for 77% of NSW's and Melbourne 87% of Victoria's.[22] This inhibited the concentration of capital in any given Queensland centre, leaving the new colony more dependent on outside capital. Consequently, successive governments were dependent on a diverse range of interests to survive. This situation was difficult to manage, but dissent and most political demands were easily satisfied while the gold boom lasted.

By the 1890s the alluvial gold ore deposits were near exhaustion. This slowly drove out the small independent miner, concentrating mine ownership and reducing employment opportunities.[23] Between 1876 and 1891 the number of people employed in mining fell from 12,000 to 7,000.[24] By 1901 slightly over 9,200 people were employed in mining, a value not exceeded until 1976.[25] Working conditions in the new and deeper mines were poor; disease and accidents were common. Poor management meant that new technology, which might have kept mines open, was not adopted.[26] Exploration was sparse and few new mines or shafts were built. Many mines, purchased at inflated prices in the 1880s by overseas investors, were unable to cover their costs.[27] The employment problems within the industry were largely ignored as gold production continued to rise throughout the 1890s, peaking in 1899.[28] However, in the period 1904 to 1907 production fell rapidly.[29]

SUGAR

Sugar was the final stimulus to northern settlement. It prospered with the assistance of successive governments who aimed to consolidate the economic gains of mining, and find some combination of agricultural activities that would facilitate closer settlement by being capital and labour intensive, as well as earn export earnings for the colony. As explained earlier, the latter was an impossible objective, for in the north only agricultural industries that use large amounts of land with little labour can succeed.

The single most important fact about sugar as an export industry is that international sugar prices have fallen slowly but steadily over the past century, interrupted only by "unusual and unrelated events" such as bad seasons and political crises, which temporarily boosted demand and hence prices.[30] Ironically, a major disruption could occur to sugar production worldwide in the medium-term future as a result of global warming and consequent extreme climatic conditions, but in that case the Queensland industry is itself likely to suffer.

In 1864 the government stimulated the sugar industry by making land available for sugar at one shilling per acre per annum.[31] It was quickly discovered that the highest yields were obtained on the alluvial plains of north Queensland. However, labour costs were especially high there:

> ... the problem of high wages was even more acute in Northern Queensland. The rich soils of the north were covered with jungle ... the stumps of which could not be burnt out. All cultivation had to be carried out with a hoe, a task that Europeans refused to do ... but even [in Southern] regions a labour force was needed to control weeds and harvest the cane.[32]

Sugar was a labour intensive crop. Overseas, success had depended on cheap indigenous labour. Labour costs in north Queensland were comparatively high for three reasons.[33] First, the distance between urban centres and rural areas made it difficult for migrants to reach areas of prospective employment, although many managed the long and arduous journeys during gold rushes. Second, most migrants were artisans and tradespeople from the cities and towns of Britain, unsuited to frontier rural life. Although wages were higher in the bush, wages and conditions in the settled urban areas were still superior to those in Europe, so there was no incentive to work in the bush. Finally, sugar growing required skills few European farm labourers possessed: they were inefficient and unskilled workers.

In response the government permitted the import of labour from the New Hebrides — the so-called kanakas. These people had been used by the failed cotton industry. While kanaka labour was often no more experienced or skilled, it was initially significantly cheaper.[34] Cheap kanaka labour enabled sugar to rapidly develop and expand; it was part of the overall system of financial assistance to the industry, effectively an unofficial subsidy of £42 per annum per labourer in the boom years.[35]

While the industry grew rapidly, especially in the north, it was threatened by a range of political and economic forces after the mid-1880s. Cheap imported labour was favoured by conservative northern rural interests, but opposed by labour interests and many southern urban groups. As the prospects for mining soured, many miners moved into sugar, either as growers or labourers. They were well received because the hot arduous conditions of the mines suited them to work in the sugar fields.[36] The perception rapidly grew that sugar was the safety net for northern miners: but Europeans were not prepared to work for the same wages and conditions as kanakas. In 1885 the Liberal government decided to phase out importation and use of kanakas, despite opposition from sugar growers and worsening sugar prices.[37]

By 1900, the north contained a significant proportion of the State's population, many of whom favoured separation from southern Queensland. The northern economy was dependent on pastoralism, gold mining and sugar, all of which were either in decline or reliant on government aid. The long-term success of European settlement north of the Tropic was dependent on finding a major new industry or securing the continuation of economic assistance. However, the ensuing economic decline did little to stem the political power of northern interests; if anything it increased it.

DEVELOPMENT POLICY AND POLITICS: 1900 TO 1958

Before federation Queensland had a large and diversified manufacturing sector, protected by tariffs. After 1900 the State had to compete openly with the industrial centres in NSW and Victoria. As the government later acknowledged:

> The state ... received a bad knock. It entered the union unconditionally, and immediately its local tariff walls were removed, it became the dumping ground for southern products. The mass production and lower wage levels of New South Wales and Victoria have proved a great handicap to the State's secondary industries ever since the inception of Federation.[38]

The decline in manufacturing was rapid.[39] By 1907 the number of factories per capita had fallen by over 50% compared to NSW. While the other States benefited from World War One, Queensland's manufacturing sector failed to keep pace with the others, and by 1927 the number of factories per capita stood at 63% of that in NSW.[40] Despite the stimulus to manufacturing provided by World War Two, Queensland once again failed to keep pace, and by 1948 the number of factories per capita was only 65% of the figure for NSW.[41] Apart from a minor revival in the early 1950s, manufacturing in Queensland never recovered from the impact of federation.

Employment in manufacturing also suffered.[42] At federation Queensland had the lowest percentage of the population employed in manufacturing. Its manufacturing work force initially kept pace with the main industrial States (NSW, Victoria and SA); however, after 1913 growth stagnated. By 1939 Queensland had the second smallest manufacturing work force, at 6% of the population. After the war this remained unchanged, with Queensland and WA competing for last place.

The immediate impact of federation was to remove the smaller, less efficient factories in the State, especially those that had survived only through protection.[43] This did not initially reduce employment in manufacturing, but the main areas of growth were associated with primary production, not heavy industry.[44] In contrast, the other States were expanding their textile and heavy industry sectors, especially after 1913 and 1939.[45]

At the same time as manufacturing was declining the northern economy also suffered problems. In 1911 the gold industry was in serious trouble, and by 1921 employment in mining had crashed to its lowest level since its inception.[46] Without gold to underwrite the northern economy other rural industries began to suffer as towns shrank and closed.

The sugar industry absorbed some of this burden, but it was facing new problems. In its inaugural year the new Commonwealth Parliament ordered the end of the kanaka trade and their repatriation. This decision, and competition from cheap overseas imports, meant that now the whole northern economy was threatened. Sugar was rescued by a Commonwealth embargo on imports and a home price scheme; but it would never employ the same numbers nor yield the wealth that gold had. The ability of sugar to support the north was limited because it was confined to a few areas on the east coast, unlike gold, which had been dispersed throughout the north. By 1915 it was clear to many that the northern economy was in decline and the dream of closer settlement threatened.

LABOR'S NORTHERN OBSESSION: 1915 TO 1958

Queensland's economic problems at the turn of the century combined with past political scandals to undermine confidence in the traditional parliamentary alternatives. Since the 1870s the Labour movement had been growing in strength and political credibility. By federation the Labor Party had widespread support among mining, rural and urban labour interests.[47] Sugar growers had previously voted with other agriculturalists against the Liberals and Labor. However, the monopoly of Colonial Sugar Refineries (CSR) meant that cane growers received low prices for their produce from mills.[48] Consequently, small farmers were unable to afford demands from unions for higher wages and shorter hours.[49] Labor promised to break CSR's monopoly and increase the prices paid to small growers so they could afford the labour costs in the post-kanaka era. Labor's support for small growers also made sense because many were retired miners who had once been unionists and Labor supporters. The electoral appeal of Labor's sugar policies was fairly uniform throughout the industry.[50] Similarly, its proposals for shoring up the mining industry gained wide acceptance. Unsurprisingly, an overwhelming majority of northern electorates fell to Labor in the 1915 State Election: Labor won with a 5% swing and obtained 52% of the votes cast.[51] They secured all but three of the twenty-six seats in the north and west of the State, the Party's heartland.[52] In all the Party won forty-five seats.[53] Significantly, Labor failed to gain any seats in the relatively wealthy Darling Downs, a conservative stronghold even today.[54]

Queensland was in desperate need of reform in 1915. On gaining office Labor implemented three separate types of programmes:

1   those necessary to improve the conditions of electoral supporters;
2   those intended to promote industrialism and re-energise the economy; and
3   those designed to promote socialist objectives.

Labor was quickly forced to reinterpret its policy agendas to favour its northern voters at the expense of the ailing industrial south-eastern sector. However, many programmes, such as the State-owned hotels and butchers' shops, and unemployment insurance, were innovative attempts to realise their wider aims and socialist ideals.[55]

Economic restructuring and socialist idealism rapidly gave way to political pragmatism and pork-barrelling. Little wonder too, given the fact that they had aligned themselves with the interests of the stagnating north. Although these interests now voted for Labor, many traditionally had not, or had once been political antagonists. Such an electoral coalition was unstable, requiring active management and appeasement by parliamentary Labor leaders. This ensured that rural and northern interests remained central to the State's policy processes. This effect is best illustrated by four examples.

The first was the "Mungana Affair". This followed from Labor's attempt to revitalise mining and closer settlement in the north. As part of its election platform Labor had promised to create a state mining enterprise centred at Chillagoe, an economically important town supporting 20,000 people.[56] The closure of its smelters in 1914 had caused widespread hardship.[57]

In 1918 the Government acquired railways, mines and equipment from the Chillagoe Company.[58] The financial success of the project depended on high ore prices available during the war, and the optimistic belief that new deposits would be discovered. In addition to the Chillagoe Company, the Government acquired leases and equipment from the Mungana Mining Company. This venture into mining proved a disastrous failure: after the war mineral prices fell and no new deposits were found.

The scandal surfaced in 1926 when the Opposition revealed that the government-owned mines and smelters were in severe financial difficulty.[59] In 1927 they demonstrated that records were being faked, the enterprise mismanaged and preferential treatment given to the previous owner of the Mungana operation.[60] In 1929 the Premier of the day was shown to have been a shareholder of the Mungana Company, and to have shared the profits of the sale with other Members of Parliament.[61] In 1929 the Labor Government fell.

The second example involved the economic blockade of Queensland by English financiers in the early 1920s.[62] This occurred when the Labor Government raised rents on pastoral leases. Traditionally pastoralists had paid a smaller rental per unit area than other agriculturalists using leasehold land. In 1920 three influential and reactionary members of the conservative political élite of Queensland convinced English financiers that the Labor Government was a bad risk, as well as a threat to established values and the existing political order. The State Government's consequent inability to raise loans on the London market led to dramatic cutbacks in spending, and the entire economy suffered; unemployment rose sharply and the basic wage was cut. By 1922 the Parliamentary Labor Party began backing away from its more radical agendas and economic restructuring policies.

The blockade and continued problems in the north encouraged Labor to rapidly pursue "an extraordinarily comprehensive programme of agrarian reform, encompassing not only improved distribution and marketing schemes, but the establishment of an institutional basis for policy-advising and industry control by delegation to the farmers themselves".[63] Even before the blockade Labor had quickly negotiated the embargo on imported sugar and fixed the price paid to growers by mills. The Department of Agriculture was established in 1922 to provide scientific advice to farmers, and to find methods for improving production and quality. By 1923 there were fourteen Acts of Parliament relating to primary production, designed to stimulate and protect agriculture.[64] In 1926, in response to farmers' demands, Labor reorganised the Queensland Producers Association along commodity lines.

The economic crisis caused by the investment strike slowed economic growth, stopped industrial diversification and forced Labor to abandon many of its radical programmes of economic and social reform. Consequently, the State maintained its commitment to decentralised and agrarian development. Thirteen years after the economic blockade the problems with these development policies were publicly recognised by Forgan-Smith's government:

> The sparse population and large area of the state have been factors militating against development of manufacturing to an extent comparable to Victoria for instance.[65]

The third example concerns the ill-fated state iron and steel works. The steel works were first proposed in 1917, but conservative, agricultural interests in the upper house initially defeated the Bill needed to empower the Labor government to proceed, although there was strong bipartisan support in the lower chamber.[66] Such a project would have been of immense benefit to the State's stagnating industrial sector, potentially placing it on an equal footing with the south. At the time Australia was importing almost twice as much steel and pig iron as it was domestically producing, so there existed a guaranteed market close by. Due to the political opposition in the upper house and the economic effects of the blockade, the mill was delayed, and finally abandoned.

There are good reasons for believing that the project was designed to placate the northern electorate. It was to be located in Bowen.[67] Placing the mill there would have helped the local coal industry and unemployed miners. However, it would have been isolated from Brisbane, the main manufacturing region of the State, increasing freight costs to factories there. Secondly, without the economies of scale present in southern ports, shipping costs would also have been high. Consequently, the mill would have had little economic advantage over foreign or southern competitors. Indeed, the interim manager of the project opposed the proposed site for these reasons and recommended a site in Bulimba, near the mouth of the Brisbane river.[68] Undoubtedly, the real objective was not to stimulate Queensland's manufacturing sector, but provide assistance to the northern mining industry and Labor's electoral heartland.

The final example involved attempts to combine hydro-electricity development with irrigation. In 1938, J.J.C. Bradfield, the supervising engineer for the Sydney Harbour Bridge, suggested that the Tully, Herbert and Burdekin Rivers should be dammed, and their waters used for hydro-electricity and irrigation purposes.[69] He also proposed that water from these rivers be diverted over the ranges to supplement the flows of the river systems in the arid interior, providing a year-long supply and making the desert bloom. Diversion schemes were in vogue at the time, and Bradfield's idea was just one of many, including his Snowy River proposal.[70] Bradfield's proposal was an instant success with people in the north, and many quickly leapt to the cause. Further investigation by state and federal bodies found that the proposal was based on inadequate data and inappropriate assumptions about rainfall, evaporation and runoff.[71] Consequently, the estimates for the cost of the project dramatically escalated: the scheme was scientifically flawed and grossly uneconomic. This has not prevented it from reappearing on party political platforms as late as the 1990s.

Undeterred, and spurred on by public support and interest, Labor went ahead with smaller projects which might one day become part of this grand scheme. In 1950 the government passed a Bill to build the Barron Falls Dam on the Tully River, near Cairns. This was completed in 1958 and has been used to generate hydro-electricity since then. The Burdekin River irrigation project was begun in 1951 and was intended to be a major irrigation, hydro-electric and flood mitigation scheme. This was to be a four-stage project, with actual construction dependent on available finance and Commonwealth support. Indeed, in 1983 the Commonwealth finally provided the funds needed to build the main irrigation dam on the Burdekin. However, economically the scheme will never pay its way because of cost overruns, the presence of saline aquifers, and indigenous nematode and insect pests.[72]

THE ECONOMIC IMPACT OF UNSUSTAINABLE DEVELOPMENT

Queensland governments have faced considerable added expense providing and maintaining infrastructure and social services to a dispersed population. By 1923–24 Queensland had the highest taxation of any of the States.[73] In addition, the relative income-tax paying capacity fell rapidly from being the highest in 1914–15 to an Australian low in 1927–28.[74] By 1933, the population and local companies had a lower average income than NSW and Victoria, although nominal and effective wage rates were high.[75] The State's high taxation rates and freight costs (due to decentralisation and an inefficient railway system) acted as disincentive to prospective investors from the south, further impoverishing the Queensland economy.[76]

Between 1925 and 1949 living costs across the State slowly rose, while wages failed to keep up with the rest of the country.[77] Effective wages improved in comparative terms during the 1930s and early 1940s,[78] but this was due to adverse economic conditions in the rest of the Commonwealth, which effectively joined Queensland in depression. The State benefited during World War Two, but by 1949 its relative position was worsening once again.

Development policy in Queensland was, therefore, not as successful at increasing or maintaining per capita incomes as in the other States. By the end of World War Two the northern economy was not significantly better off, despite years of government assistance after the collapse of mining. The neglect of manufacturing in the southeast and the pursuit of irrational development projects in the north also stifled economic growth in the greater Brisbane region, and retarded the performance of Queensland as a whole.

CHANGING THE RULES

Labor's leaders quickly realised that their electoral base was fragile. After gaining office in 1915 Labor encountered fierce opposition from conservative forces, especially southern rural capital. Nowhere was this more frustrating than in the upper House of the Parliament, the Legislative Council. The Governor appointed its members for life; after federation this was on advice from the government of the day. The composition of the Legislative Council in 1915 closely reflected the earlier domination of politics by conservative rural interests, presenting a formidable obstacle to reform, of which Labor was acutely aware.[79] As approximately 50% of Queenslanders were in the workforce, Labor expected continuing domination of the lower House; the upper House, in whatever form, would remain an obstacle. On winning power Labor immediately initiated the process of abolition, which culminated in 1922.

Although Labor's following was strong in urban areas, especially Brisbane, it was support in north Queensland that kept it in power. Labor had come to victory in the north by promising revitalisation; mining was a strong source of Labor support precisely because it was failing. Employment opportunities in mining and agriculture were declining. Although the percentage employed in the north was greater than the State average until the 1960s, the values were rapidly converging after 1911. Consequently, Labor's stronger support in the north could not last.

In 1949 the Hanlon Labor Government abandoned its commitment to an electoral system based on one value for each vote, and created the zonal system, over-representing the rural areas. This was justified by the claim that the problems in the rural sector required special representation and compensation in Parliament, and that urban interests should be balanced against rural needs. But this claim was false:

> The true reason was political expediency. The population in the country areas, where the ALP at the time enjoyed strong political support (especially in mining areas), was diminishing. In the face of this eroding electoral base the government reasoned that to preserve itself in office it needed to increase the value of country votes and, thus, the number of Labor seats in state parliament. The experiment worked impressively, enabling the government to retain office in 1950 by a margin of nine seats ... despite being outpolled in primary votes by their political opponents (46.9% to 49.2%).[80]

This tactic ultimately backfired on the Labor Party. The changing conditions in the rural sector and the north strained the alliance between northern rural capital and labour. The rural sector now accepted the structural reforms of the Labor Party and they were no longer a political issue. In the stable environment that these reforms produced, farming and mining became increasingly capital intensive, and employment steadily declined. Rural groups (especially farmers) no longer saw a link between their interests and labour. The Labor Party's difficulties with the Industrial Groups caused a rift between the right and left, losing it the support of the Roman Catholic church and triggering the split of 1957 in which it lost government.

THE CONSERVATIVE REVIVAL: 1958 TO THE 1980s

The conservative coalition of the Country and Liberal parties which won government in 1957 represented a new alliance between rural and urban capital. The Country Party's support base lay with farmers, pastoralists and miners, and the Liberal Party represented local urban capital, especially small business. The split in the Labor Party disillusioned a great number of workers, further adding to the new government's support. A new dominant coalition of interests, similar to that which had supported Labor, now backed the conservatives' promises to revive the ailing Queensland economy.

By the early 1960s the State's economy was in severe trouble, with the highest unemployment rate in the country. The new conservative coalition State Government failed to make any radical policy changes: agrarianism remained while decentralism was modified to emphasise industrial growth in regional centres.[81] In 1964 the appearance of the book *Queensland: Industrial Enigma* offered the first independent review of development policies in the State. In particular, it explained the negative impact of decentralisation on the State's economy.[82]

However, it failed to have any effect on government policy: decentralism, agrarianism and northern development persisted.

Like Labor before them they strongly supported the sugar industry, despite growing evidence that it was failing to stimulate widespread closer settlement across the north. From the 1950s the industry rapidly mechanised. This process of mechanisation began at the waterfront, concentrating the export of sugar on the five major northern ports.[83] Between 1960 and 1981 the average farm size rose from 18 to 63 hectares, or 250%.[84] This trend in the growth of farm size is continuing. Over the same period the proportion of the sugar crop mechanically harvested rose from 2.7% to approximately 100%.[85] Consequently, unemployment in sugar districts grew dramatically, and by the late 1970s in sugar districts it was running as high as 50%.[86] So although the total workforce in the north was rising slowly there was a contraction in the sugar labour force. Between 1949 and 1981 there was also a 16% decline in the primary industry labour force.[87] Overall, mechanisation was recreating the old plantations but "in modern guise, with mechanical slaves instead of the muscle-power of Pacific Islanders".[88] Thus, the billions of dollars diverted to the sugar growing since 1922 had failed to generate a labour intensive and spatially extensive economic base for the north. Sugar growers remained the major beneficiaries.

The historical data reveals how misguided this policy framework was. From 1949 to 1985 Queensland usually had the second-lowest household income of all the States.[89] After 1949 there was a rapid and sustained decline in per capita incomes. This followed on from a fall in income levels after World War One. Matters improved in the early 1970s during the resource boom; but compared with WA, the gains were not as substantial or as prolonged.[90] Total performance of the rural sector was also unexceptional, despite the priority given it by successive governments. Queensland agriculturalists did not obtain higher incomes than those in the other mainland States.[91] Indeed, Victorian agriculturalists usually fared better. In addition, the State with the highest average value for Gross Farm Product (GFP) over the period 1949 to 1981 was WA.[92] Queensland, however, tied second with Victoria, with SA following closely.[93]

The performance of Queensland's rural sector is surprising for two reasons. Firstly, WA is a predominantly rural State like Queensland, but does not have the same:

1 range of agricultural products;
2 quantity of land in production; or
3 access to potential and existing markets.

Secondly, both Victoria and SA have been pursuing industrial development policies since the depression and especially after World War Two, unlike Queensland. After a century of government policies designed to boost agriculture, at the expense of manufacturing, surely Queensland should have managed to outperform the more industrialised States.

The political response to the continuing economic problems was to make minor changes to the zonal electoral system, not to re-evaluate the development policy mix. Continual alteration to the electoral laws strengthened the position of the Country Party, as well as rural and northern interests in the policy process.[94] In 1963 the Government introduced preferential voting which, with the zonal malapportionment, further enhanced the electoral prospects of the Country Party, entrenching it as the dominant member of the coalition Government while undermining the Liberal and Labor parties. In 1966 it won 27 seats with only 18.9% of the primary vote. In contrast, the Liberals secured 20 seats with 25.6%, and Labor 26 seats from 43.8% of the primary vote.[95] This success inspired the Country Party to strive to govern without the Liberals, but first it was necessary to change their electoral image and widen their support base. Further stimulating this ambition was the continuing decline in the rural population, slowly making their support unreliable. In 1974 the Country Party changed its name to the National Party and began wooing urban voters with new policies. In 1983 the Nationals broke the coalition with the Liberals and won government.[96] The collapse of the coalition was due to a number of deep and significant divisions:

> ... the Liberals maintained an uneasy alliance with the Nationals. This was because the formers' "liberal conservatism" clashed with the Nationals' right radicalism. Moreover, liberal conservatism was southern based, for it emerged from manufacturing capitalists, the dominant fraction of the Australian bourgeoisie — concentrated in the south — and the fraction that has held a competitive relationship with mining capital since the 1960s. In coalition, then, Queensland Liberals split their loyalties between southern-based manufacturing capital, which had done little or nothing to develop the state, and mining capital which, though foreign, was seen as aiding Queensland development. Such political schizophrenia expresses well — and helps explain — the perennial conflicts between the Liberals and Nationals in coalition and why the coalition eventually split in 1983.[97]

After changing its name, the Country/National Party still relied on rural support to stay in office. This perpetuated the prominent rôle of farmers and pastoralists in policy formulation, ensuring the continuation of the economic and developmental priorities of previous years.

During the 1960s one group within rural capital, foreign mining, was on the ascendant. The growing importance of the mineral sector meant that the Coalition government, and especially the Country/National Party, was willing to assist it. The National Party also courted foreign capital for financial support.

The diverse support base of the Nationals, foreign mining capital, farmers and pastoralists, small business and sections of labour, produced tensions within and between the interests involved. The Nationals were better able to manage these tensions than the Liberals. They were always quick to support development projects, especially in rural or northern areas, maintaining widespread support there. They consistently placed developmental concerns above environmental considerations, even when such action was clearly detrimental to the long-term interests of their electoral supporters or when no real economic gains existed.[98] The National Party was also a keen promoter of tourism. This industry, while dominated by foreign interests, heavily involved local capital and labour, offering gains for all concerned.

In addition to development fetishism, the Nationals tried to retain and consolidate power by crudely suppressing dissent.[99] Dissent in any form was a threat to the maintenance of the coalition of interests backing the Government. Despite the illusion of strength portrayed by the conservative (National Party) government, its position was increasingly fragile. It failed repeatedly in negotiations with its supporters concerning politically sensitive issues: for example, land degradation persisted in rural Queensland, the heartland of the National Party.[100] Overall, the tactics employed by the National Party to resolve the inherent conflicts within its support base permitted the continuation of agrarianism and decentralisation within the State's policy process.[101]

In this environment corruption thrived.[102] While in the short term assisting the conservative government, it eventually brought it into disrepute, destabilising the alliance of interests that supported it. It was not the only cause for their failure, as corruption is no stranger to Queensland and was accepted by many as the normal way to conduct business. The demographic changes that displaced the Labor Party were continuing. The population of the urbanised south-east was continuing to grow, and the interests of the eastern urban centres were rapidly diverging from those of the agriculturalists. The controversy over daylight saving typified this divergence. When major urban centres and business interests threatened to "go it alone" and implement daylight saving, the legitimacy of the Government was undermined severely. The impact of these factors, in combination with irrefutable evidence of widespread corruption and a comparatively sluggish economy, resulted in a massive defection of conservative voters to Labor in the 1989 State Election.

CONCLUSION

Queensland's tripartite policy structure emerged in response to the State's pre-federation political economy. This framework, and the network of interests that supported it, arose in response to:

1   the fate of the gold mining and sugar industries in the late nineteenth and early twentieth centuries;
2   the impact of federation on the State's manufacturing economy; and
3   the persistent failure within the development policy process to understand the relationship between the State's physical environment and economic development.

The early economic development of Queensland created a dispersed settlement pattern that was environmentally and economically unsustainable. By federation the State had split into two regions: the south-east which contained the manufacturing heartland, and the north with its gold and sugar interests.

This split created irreconcilable tensions that undermined economic performance, created political corruption and caused biophysical constraints to be ignored by policy makers and the community.

The development policy process that emerged allowed the manufacturing sector to wither, while remaining focussed on propping up the north, and satisfying economically and electorally powerful rural interests. The political and policy response was to stimulate the sugar industry and pursue grand water resource projects, although neither provided returns on the investments made. Consequently, they did nothing to reverse Queensland's uninspiring economic performance, and despite the agrarian policy focus, failed to create an outstanding rural sector.

This analysis reveals that the anti-environmental development fetishism and political intolerance of successive Queensland governments derives from the combined legacy of unsustainable development and dispersion of economic and political power.

Together these policy legacies prevented the State of Queensland from developing:

1   effective infrastructural power and
2   a strategically and ecologically rational coordinating capacity.

Consequently, it was unable to resist the short-term demands of economically and electorally important interests: the State has constantly negotiated from a position of weakness.

The outcome for environmentalists has been ridicule and repression, because they have questioned the fundamentals of the settled tripartite development framework, and in large part exposed it as flawed. But while they tacitly recognise that environment policy is the "flip side" of development policy, and requires an understanding of it, the fundamental implications of this fact are not yet fully understood by the Queensland environment movement. They continue to focus on wilderness, at the same time self-indulgently forming alliances with groups seeking fundamental political change.[103]

Correcting the problems in Queensland will not be easy while the State remains politically weak, and a servant of traditional vested interests. Reform must focus on:

1 freeing the State from their dominant influence; and
2 developing wealth-generating industries compatible with biophysical realities.

In practice this will require finally abolishing the zonal electoral system: its retention by the Goss Government was clearly a mistake. Active promotion of diversified, environmentally responsible economic development in the coastal strip from Rockhampton to the NSW border is also needed.[104] This would involve such measures as harnessing of the State's abundant sunlight for heat and power; recycling water and sewage; adopting high-value crops adapted to tropical conditions, often in small-scale, environmentally sensitive applications; and exploiting the remaining natural resources with greater sensitivity than has been shown heretofore. These are necessary conditions for the revitalisation of Queensland.

Such reforms would effectively concentrate political and economic power in the region most suitable for Western style development. These changes will not be easy, given that existing policy, political and institutional legacies undermine the infrastructural power of the Queensland State, as well as weakening the bargaining position of its political leaders. It is in the interest of the environmental movement, therefore, to work with and support such reforms and their parliamentary advocates. The alternative is the continuation in Queensland of the existing anti-environmental, economically suboptimal development policies and associated repressive politics.

DEVOLUTION IN EMBRYO: THE McARTHUR RIVER MINE

T. McCall

INTRODUCTION

Australian environmental policy underwent a number of funda-mental changes during the period 1990–93. There were three significant policy shifts. Firstly, the Commonwealth Government was moving away from the reactive, *ad hoc* approach that had dominated the previous fifteen years, and instead was responding more proactively to resource management conflict. Secondly, this response took two forms: a more cooperative approach within a federal political framework through the establishment of agreements between the State, Territory and Commonwealth governments, and the formulation of institutional policy approaches with the specific intention of ameliorating the political conflict that arose over resource management issues. Thirdly, this institutional approach allowed the Commonwealth government to align resource management policy to its broader macro and micro economic reform agenda.

The most important policy initiatives that emerged during this period were Ecologically Sustainable Development (ESD) and the cooperative federal environmental agreement, the Intergovernmental Agreement on the Environment (IGAE). ESD was essentially an attempt to integrate environmental issues within resource management policy approaches. It followed worldwide commitments to notions of sustainable development developed in response to the Brundtland Commission report of 1987. The IGAE endorses continuing devolution of control over resource management issues from the Commonwealth to the States and Territories, a central theme of the new "cooperative federalism".

This chapter's purpose is analytical rather than descriptive. It attempts to place the McArthur River project in the broader policy perspective of the time, to which it is pivotal.[1] Its significance lies in its emergence during the ESD process, while the IGAE was being concluded, and coincident with the High Court's *Mabo* decision and the period of the *Native Title Act*. It provides a unique opportunity to examine the rhetoric of ESD, enshrined within the IGAE, and the political realities of Australian environmental policy in the post-Wesley Vale period. In particular, McArthur River provides an insight into how the IGAE framework might operate in a highly proactive policy environment as distinct from the *ad hoc* and reactive approaches that had prevailed in Australia prior to Wesley Vale and Coronation Hill. This changing policy context was accentuated by the change of leadership in the Labor Government which saw a marked shift in governmental priorities in relation to environmental outcomes and approaches to resource management.

McArthur River provides an insight into how the IGAE framework may work in the near future. It clearly demonstrates the impact the devolution of power from a central agency (Commonwealth government) to a peripheral agency (Northern Territory government) can have on the management of a large resource based project. The relevance of the McArthur River project today is that it affords an early "bird's eye view" of the framing of environmental issues and social justice issues under continuing devolution of Commonwealth involvement in environmental regulation to the States and Territories. The processes attached to the McArthur River project raise some critical concerns regarding the proposed future direction of environment policy in Australia. This is particularly pertinent in the light of the current Commonwealth review of federal environment legislation and the proposed enactment of a new *Environment Protection Act*.

McArthur River demonstrates that little was learnt from the Wesley Vale pulp mill project in terms of project management. Crucial issues that emerged during Wesley Vale, such as the critical importance of establishing adequate baseline studies in the formation of Environmental Impact Statements (EIS), were lost within the devolutionary process established for the McArthur River project. An analysis of the McArthur River project should ring alarm bells in relation to commitments embodying continued devolution of management responsibility. Importantly, it should not be seen as a model for the broadening of such processes envisaged under the Commonwealth review of 1998: quite the contrary. Finally, as the first major mining project after the High Court *Mabo* decision the McArthur River project presents an insightful look at the politics of native title deliberations over resource projects such as mining.

THE MCARTHUR RIVER MINE — BACKGROUND

The McArthur River flows 120 km to the Gulf of Carpentaria, crossing the Barkly Tablelands, in the Northern Territory. Zinc-lead-silver deposits, estimated at 220 million tonnes of high quality ore, were discovered in 1955, situated within the McArthur River basin. Mount Isa Mines (MIM) secured the leases to the deposits in 1959.

The $250 million underground mine project commenced in early 1993. Over 20 years, it is expected to generate between $200 to 300 million per year of export revenue. The project is a joint venture between MIM (70%) and a Japanese consortium, ANT minerals (30%), employing 250. The first zinc-lead concentrate commissioning began in May 1995. August 1995 saw the first export shipment. In September 1998, MIM announced that despite some difficulties with regrind capacity and ongoing problems with the blocking of discharge grates, the mine was now approaching its target of 350,000 tonnes of mixed concentrate a year, containing 160,000 tonnes of zinc, 45,000 tonnes of lead and 1.6 million ounces of silver. This mine at full production is potentially the largest zinc-lead-silver mine in the world.[2]

The McArthur River mine was the first significant development proposal since the "failed" Wesley Vale pulp mill project in Tasmania. Though smaller in scale, it was attractive to the Commonwealth Government because it was export-oriented. The foreign investment component meant that Commonwealth approval was required. Commonwealth involvement was secured through a 1990 bilateral agreement between the Commonwealth and the Northern Territory governments. There was general support for the project within government circles as it was considered to be of national importance. However, a range of issues emerged, including environmental concerns and social justice issues relating to indigenous rights, that complicated matters and raised serious questions about the legitimacy of the processes leading to the project's approval. The project faced intense scrutiny in relation to the *Mabo* High Court decision of 1992 and deliberations leading up to the *Native Title Act*.

Resource management strategies in Australia were changing at the time of the McArthur River project's emergence. The ESD process led to the National Strategy for Ecologically Sustainable Development (NSESD), which was endorsed in December 1992 by the Council of Australian Governments (COAG) and formed the foundation for the IGAE. Announced in the *One Nation* Statement on 26 February 1992, the latter was hailed as an important outcome for a new cooperative federalism.

In addition, this project coincided with the Commonwealth Government's reassessment of its attitude towards resource management. The new Keating Government was intent on restoring "development" and the economy (in the narrower sense) to first priority in the light of its broader micro and macro reform agenda.[3] The McArthur River project was to benefit. It was treated as a model project, the first assisted under the newly created Major Projects Facilitation Unit (MPFU) located in the Department of Prime Minister and Cabinet and headed by the Parliamentary Secretary, Laurie Brereton. Brereton's response to the "success" of projects such as McArthur River and Mount Todd, also in the Northern Territory, underlines the project's perceived importance. Brereton suggested that:

> These results, I know are ones that Australia has been waiting for, for many years, and I would think that they will be a model for years ahead and will guarantee the prosperity of Australia and, at the same time, make sure that all environmental safeguards are met.[4]

THE POLICY CONTEXT

Continued devolution of Commonwealth involvement in resource management issues is proposed in the Howard Government's recent consultation paper on the reform of Commonwealth environment legislation. The unfolding of the McArthur River policy process is indicative of likely future methods.

ESD AS A POLICY PROCESS

The failure of the Wesley Vale pulp mill project in northern Tasmania triggered significant changes in environmental policy in Australia. This was the largest industrial project in the Australia since the Snowy Mountains Scheme: a proposed investment of $1000 million. However, choice of technology, available supplies of pulpwood, the effects of pollution on other industries in the area and hazards to public health all became contentious. Neither the State nor the federal government was able to resolve these issues authoritatively, let alone to the satisfaction of the objectors. Economou comments:

> The processes by which the Wesley Vale project was planned, approved, presented to the community, reviewed, and finally put to rest by State and Federal institutional actors was riddled with inconsistencies, ad-hoc decision making, disputes between the State and the Commonwealth over divisions of decision-making power, and scientific investigations that were, at best, open to serious questioning. It was indeed significant that environmentalist and corporate protagonists who agreed on very little throughout the debate should find common ground in their expression of dismay with the decision-making process.[5]

Intergovernmental indecision and conflict over pollution guidelines for the mill's effluent was effectively exploited by grass-roots community opposition. Wedging itself between competing claims, it gained important strategic leverage, especially over contentious issues such as the siting of the mill, a range of environmental issues, particularly the effluent discharge into Bass Strait that contained organochlorines, and wood supply issues. In March 1989, the proponents abandoned the proposal, unprepared to accept the stringent new guidelines attached to the project's approval.

There are strong reasons to think that the assessment process never addressed the most substantial objection: that such a large mill was inappropriate for Tasmania. It was a typical "footloose" industry, consuming Tasmanian resources at a low price, and adding value to foreign investors' dividends. It competed with smaller operators for access to forest resources, in a political climate where significant reduction of rates of exploitation was a live issue. The proposed technology was itself contentious. The mill's "loss" or "failure" in that context was by no means a disaster. Unfortunately, in a policy environment dominated by cargo-cultist encouragement of "value-added" industries, it was thought to send "all the wrong messages" to overseas investors.

The Hawke Labor Government had been committed to substantial economic restructuring, with (as Economou notes in Chapter 4) a policy strategy which emphasised metapolicy: principles and institutions for handling particular classes of problems. Hawke's emphasis on consensus found the reactive approach that had dominated the environmental policy in the 1980s repugnant. Conflicts such as the Franklin Dam in Tasmania, Coronation Hill in the Northern Territory and continuing forestry management antagonism, principally over continued logging of old growth forests in Tasmania, Victoria and NSW, needed to be fitted into a consistent framework.[6]

Occurring at a time of economic restructuring, when the federal government was attempting to lay the foundations for the emergence of an "internationally competitive" economy by creating a "sound investment climate", continuing political conflict was perceived as undermining the broader economic agenda of government. This was especially so in the case of Wesley Vale, where the "loss" of an export oriented, value-adding industry — a world competitive pulp and paper mill — undermined the macro economic reform agenda.

"Sustainable development" was adopted as the framework, responding to international initiatives aimed at integrating economic development imperatives with environmental concerns. In Australia, it was labelled Ecologically Sustainable Development.[7]

ESD was envisaged as a policy process which would channel diverse viewpoints into a negotiating forum where broad objectives could be agreed and a sense of shared responsibility for outcomes encouraged, through the acceptance of agreed frameworks and processes. In the first round, a series of Working Parties were established, to report back with suggested policy frameworks. In the consensus mould of the Hawke Labor Government, it attempted to integrate concern over environmental degradation with the requirements of economic development, on the assumption that integration would promote economic and productive efficiency. The key here was not a continued commitment to growth per se but a determination of what sort of growth would be acceptable. In principle, this could imply government "vetting" of specific technologies. Once established, the objectives and principles of ESD could be linked to the larger economic reform agenda through their adoption in legislative frameworks addressing resource management conflict.

ESD incorporated two critically important aspects that were strategically vital for government. First, it was ambiguous and, secondly, as a policy process it effectively "institutionalised" political conflict, in the special sense that conflict was resolved by bureaucratic institutions to which decision responsibility was transferred.

Ambiguity is an important political tool, promoting compromise and cooperation through lack of clarity. By masking dissonance, it allows policy makers to placate antagonists in a political conflict by promoting "win-win" outcomes, which *appear* to offer gains to all sides. Most significantly, in a strategic sense, ambiguity enables political leaders to satisfy demands that "they do something" about a political problem by endorsing "an agreement" with ambiguous meaning and then allowing administrative agencies to capture the process by sorting out the more conflictual details behind the scenes.[8]

Ambiguity has the additional benefit of concealing the liberal democratic state's continuing pursuit of its structural imperatives in the face of political challenges such as those of environmentalism. These imperatives, as noted in Chapter 2, require liberal democratic states, as a minimum, to secure economic stability and growth (the accumulative imperative); keep order, largely by legitimising the prevailing political/social/economic system; and "stay afloat" in a hostile international political economy.[9]

Within ambiguous policy frameworks, political conflict is effectively neutralised by inviting stakeholders into a policy environment where they do not control the agenda, have no control of procedure, and cannot determine authoritatively what constitutes evidence or acceptable argument. This can dilute and even negate the influence of citizen and other "public interest" community groups; it is often a very alien terrain for activists best suited to the highly emotional environment of a contested political site, such as a forest coupe or a threatened wilderness area.

Ambiguous hegemonic discourses, such as that concerning ESD, consequently became an effective policy approach for the resolution — or, more accurately, displacement — of the environment/development conflict. This was especially important for a government intent on structural economic adjustments aimed at dragging Australia — against significant, deeply concerned resistance — into the new globalised international economy, where investment confidence is strongly linked to established governance processes that demonstrably placate potentially destabilising political conflict.

Following the ESD exercise, as noted, a National Strategy for Ecologically Sustainable Development was endorsed by the Council of Australian Governments. The ensuing Intergovernmental Agreement on the Environment was to become the framework for establishing acceptable principles and objectives that would be incorporated into state government legislative responses to resource management planning. Cooperation and institutionalisation were seen as keys to reduction of the intense intergovernmental conflict of the past. As Keating succeeded Hawke, and the Howard coalition Keating, this approach would provide both the basis and the argument for reduced Commonwealth intervention in resource management conflict within State jurisdictions.

The IGAE set out the rôles of the parties and established the "ground rules" under which the Commonwealth, State, Territory and local governments were to interact on the environment. It included a broad set of principles to guide the development of environment policies and, in a series of schedules, set out cooperative arrangements which mirrored those forming the basis of the bilateral agreement established between the Commonwealth and Northern Territory to oversee the McArthur River project. These include a commitment to:

- a national approach to the collection and handling of environmental data;
- joint collaborative efforts to facilitate national and environmentally sound land-use decisions and approvals processes;
- a common set of principles for environmental impact assessment;
- a cooperative Commonwealth/State/Territory process for developing national environmental standards, guidelines and goals;
- closer cooperation between governments in preserving the national estate; and
- cooperative arrangements on a wide range of nature conservation issues.

Some of these issues became foci of criticism during the approval process for McArthur River.

ESD AND MCARTHUR RIVER

The significance of the ESD process in relation to the McArthur River project is that it is contemporary with its assessment and approval. However there is little evidence that the two-year ESD process impacted on the approval procedures for this project, nor is there much evidence that those ESD principles and objectives specifically addressing the mining sector were incorporated into the evaluation and approval.

The NSESD, endorsed by COAG on 7 December 1992, included 88 recommendations in relation to the mining sector, qualified by the escape clause: "implementation would be subject to budgetary priorities and constraints on individual jurisdictions".[10] This caveat reflected the general antagonism of State governments to the ESD process, which they felt was largely driven by the Commonwealth Government's agenda.

But the language of the ESD recommendations is indicative rather than prescriptive. The second ESD mining recommendation clearly demonstrates the extent of the gap between what actually happened at McArthur River and the integrated approach espoused by ESD. This recommendation outlines a series of principles that should apply to various decision-making processes in relation to new major mineral resource development projects:

1   decision-making processes should seek to integrate economic and non-economic considerations;

2   decision-making processes should *be more transparent and open to scrutiny and participation by industry and the public to the greatest extent possible*;

3   *information should be made available from an early stage* to ensure major issues can be identified and addressed in a timely fashion in project planning;

4   *the exercise of discretionary powers should be minimised.* Where discretionary powers are judged necessary, the criteria against which the discretion may be exercised should be made explicit from the outset and the processes should provide for a statement of reasons for the decision;

5   decision-making processes should be embodied in legislation or regulatory arrangements *which include ESD objectives*; and

6   there should be a sensible standardisation of process. *This should not be on the basis of the lowest common denominator.* (emphasis added)[11]

The lack of mandatory procedures opened up a discretionary space which permitted the subversion of effective assessment.

FAST-TRACKING: THE IGAE AND THE MPFU

Another highly significant policy development which occurred during the establishment period of the McArthur River Mine Project was contained in the *One Nation* Statement of 26 February 1992, issued by the then Prime Minister, Paul Keating. The change of leadership from Hawke to Keating marked a shift of governmental priorities from the integrative principles of ESD to a renewed emphasis on the economy and growth. The *One Nation* Statement announced the introduction of the IGAE and most significantly for the McArthur River project, it launched the MPFU.[12]

The establishment of the MPFU flowed directly from the "failure" of the Wesley Vale project and the Keating Government's view that the economy must be re-established as a priority in policy terms. Essentially the rôle of the MPFU was to fast-track projects of $50 million and more. The official position was that the MPFU was established to assist developers in ensuring that various elements in approval processes were handled simultaneously, rather than sequentially. The Prime Minister's Parliamentary Secretary, Laurie Brereton , was charged with ensuring that there was no duplication in the assessment of major projects. It was widely reported that MIM executives met with Brereton in Canberra the day after the announcement of the establishment of the unit and as a consequence, McArthur River was the first project sanctioned under the "fast-track" provisions facilitated by the MPFU.[13]

MCARTHUR RIVER — ANALYSING THE ISSUES

The McArthur River project proposal raised numerous interlocking issues affecting both the biophysical environment and the indigenous inhabitants.

ENVIRONMENTAL ISSUES: THE INTERGOVERNMENTAL PROCESS AND THE EIS

Environmental concerns focus principally on the potential for long-term heavy metal pollution from the mine site and also from the port and loading facility in the Gulf of Carpentaria. These could affect the shallow marine areas of the coast adjacent to the mouth of the McArthur River and the islands in its estuary. In addition, the construction of the port facility threatened the extensive seagrass beds that are important for dugong and turtle populations. These species are also important to the maintenance of the day-to-day lifestyle of the traditional owners. There is also a potential pollution threat to the barramundi and tiger-prawn fishery in that part of the Gulf.[14] Because the ore is transferred by barge to offshore shipping facilities one of the principal environmental concerns is that a spill caused by accident or a cyclone would cause serious environmental impacts. The fear is that any significant loss of ore could create a toxic cocktail in the marine environment and enter the food chain.

The environmental impact assessment required under the Foreign Investment Review Board (FIRB) was facilitated by the two governments — Commonwealth and Territory — under a 1990 bilateral agreement. This agreement provided for a hybrid assessment, combining some elements of each government's EIS legislation and practice.[15] The question here was how this assessment was to be conducted and to what extent the Commonwealth would prevail if disagreement emerged. This conflict of jurisdiction had been at the heart of the Wesley Vale controversy.

Significantly, the bilateral agreement included several elements that set a precedent for the IGAE. Firstly, in an attempt to overcome areas of duplication, it emphasised cooperative, as distinct from coordinate approaches to federalism. Secondly, it established a process of further devolution of responsibilities away from the Commonwealth to the States and Territories.

The initial advice that the Federal Minister, Ros Kelly, received from her department was to follow the Northern Territory assessment process as "there is no reason to suggest that the NT process will not meet the Commonwealth requirements".[16] This decision was taken on 16 April 1992, a month before the IGAE came into effect, and the Northern Territory was so advised.[17] Its significance was that, despite concerns with the Northern Territory legislative process, it embodied the fast-tracking intentions which had prompted the establishment of the MPFU only two months earlier. In fact, the Northern Terrritory Conservation Commission (CCNT) had directed MIM to prepare an EIS for the project under the Northern Territory Act, a week earlier on 7 April 1992.[18]

This EIS was prepared in just over a month and released on 23 May with only a 30-day public response period.[19] The draft EIS met with vigorous criticism. A government agency, the Australian National Parks and Wildlife Service, mirrored most of the major concerns, pointing to a number of deficiencies in the draft relating to:

- transport methods for the ore;
- monitoring programmes;
- potential contamination from the fine-grained nature of the ore;
- potential for lead poisoning in Aboriginal people consuming marine mammals;
- lack of baseline studies;
- safe mooring in the event of cyclone activity;
- dredging the channel through the seagrass beds;
- compliance with international obligations to provide habitat protection under the Bonn Convention for five of the six species of turtles in the region, as well as the dugong;
- inadequate description of the environment of the area of the loading facility;
- the impact of the proposed de-watering system.[20]

The most central criticism of the EIS was over its support for the establishment of the marine loading facility in the fragile seagrass ecosystem. The inadequacy of baseline studies had made it impossible to determine the impact of the facility properly. There was simply a lack of quality data: no core samples had been taken nor had any adequate survey been made of the area that was to be affected by dredging. Dr Sam Lake, a marine ecologist at Monash University, was highly critical of the EIS:

> The data is of low taxonomic quality … I would suggest that the data is not of sufficient quality to allow you to form a good baseline survey, let alone use that data to design some form of reliable, ecologically sensitive monitoring program.

> If this EIS is going to be, and this project is going to be held up as a good
> example of rapid fast track assessment … in terms of detecting poten-
> tial impacts on the environment, the procedure seems to be very crude
> indeed. I mean, no details are given so that you have any sense of eco-
> logical security as to whether the mine is going to damage the system
> or not.[21]

The critical linkage between the fast-track provisions and the
inadequacy of the EIS extended to concerns about the implications
this arrangement had for the implementation of the IGAE in the
oversight of future resource projects. The intended use of the bilateral arrangement agreement covering the McArthur River project as
a model for future devolution under the provisions of the IGAE
raised several issues. Three were critical. Firstly, the extent and quality of the scientific data that formed the basis of the EIS was clearly
inadequate. Secondly, the Northern Territory approvals process
lacked transparency, potentially both ignoring and restricting community input. Thirdly, the Commonwealth appeared to wash its
hands of responsibility when concerns were raised about the adequa-
cy of the approvals process. At no stage did it overrule the Northern
Territory, despite the NT's own conservation department raising
concerns over the restricted time limits imposed on the approval
process. The timetable appeared largely to be determined by the
requirements of MIM's board rather than the time needed for preparation of an adequate EIS.

Mike Krockenberger, biodiversity coordinator for the Australian
Conservation Foundation (ACF), commented explicitly:

> What the fast tracking has done in relation to the intergovernmental
> agreement on the environment is to simply delegate the Commonwealth
> responsibilities to, in this case, the Northern Territory. What they did was
> they said to the States and the Territories, through the IGAE, we are pre-
> pared to give full faith and credit — and that was the terms used — to
> your process. In other words, we will recognise your processes. We will
> not intervene in your processes, and we will enable major projects to go
> ahead through your processes, and we'll stand back and simply give them
> a tick. … some States and Territories do not have the processes that are
> required to ensure good decision making. And in the case of the
> Northern Territory, it's issues such as lack of freedom of information leg-
> islation, the lack of a Land and Environment Court, or an environmental
> protection authority or agency, basically the lack of checks and balances
> that is the main problem. And more specifically, in the case of the
> McArthur River, a lot of the things that should have been done in terms
> of an environmental impact statement up front were simply pushed to a
> post environmental impact statement situation.[22]

This assessment was backed up by policy analysts working in environmental law. Rob Fowler, Associate Professor of Law at the University of Adelaide, commented that:

> ... if this is the way the Commonwealth process is going to apply whenever a project is deemed to be urgent in the future, in effect it's worthless, because the Commonwealth simply sits back and says to the State or the Territory concerned: Look, you go about your business of assessing this, and we'll essentially just watch you and probably we will accept the outcomes of your process.[23]

On 17 July MIM released a "Supplement to the Draft Environmental Impact Statement" which addressed comments received on the draft EIS. This supplement and the draft constituted the final EIS.[24]

On the 16 November 1992, MIM and its Japanese partner gave the development the go-ahead. This agreement had its legislative outcome in the *McArthur River Project Agreement Ratification Act 1992*, receiving Royal Assent on 1 December 1992. On 5 January 1993, the Northern Territory Minister for Mines and Energy issued a 25-year mining lease to MIM. The entire process had taken less than 12 months.[25]

Brereton defended the process:

> If you look at the McArthur River zinc mine, you found that in the process of assessment, the loading facilities were moved from the McArthur River itself to a new port constructed in the gulf. There was a whole new process for guaranteeing the water at the mine did not spill into the McArthur River. A whole road was constructed around the township of Borroloola for environmental reasons. In addition to all that, of course we had a great study on the native dugong population.[26]

Toyne concludes that the rushed approval process for the McArthur River project indicates that economic imperatives overrode any substantive environmental concerns. This was exacerbated by the Federal Government's endorsement of a fast-track process. His concerns that the fast-tracking of a number of additional projects under the MPFU, might become the norm rather than the exception were prophetic:

> It is not clear how many of these are resource projects, tourism projects or others that might require Federal Government approval or EIS evaluation. It is reasonable to assume there will be many and that is deeply worrying when the McArthur River has proved to be such a flawed illustration of the procedures invoked to date. It should not stand as an adequate precedent for the future.[27]

INDIGENOUS ISSUES

Another key issue in the approval process of the mine was the process of negotiation with the indigenous owners of the mine site. As Toyne makes clear, the Yanyuwa, Mara and Kurdanji people have strong cultural and religious interests in both the mine area and the coastal site of the port. Their attachment to the land was indicated through an unsuccessful claim under the Commonwealth's *Northern Territory Land Rights Act 1976*.[28] The marine species most likely to be affected by the project form a significant part of their food supply.

The High Court decided the *Mabo* case in June 1992, just as the mining company and the local people had reached agreement that the mine would go ahead. The Court's rejection of the *terra nullius* doctrine had the effect of recognising native title as of right. Negotiations failed to reach agreement over compensation and the subsequent threat of a claim under *Mabo* led the company to deliver an ultimatum: secure title by 1 July 1993 or the project would be scrapped.

Mabo produced nervousness about the security of their titles amongst developers generally. In response to the McArthur River joint venturers' concerns, on 23 May 1993, the Northern Territory Government introduced a Bill to amend the *McArthur River Project Ratification Act 1992* to validate leases and simply provide compensation for native title holders who might subsequently be found to be disadvantaged.[29] The intent was to extinguish native title in the interest of confirming the mining leases and securing the future of the project. This Bill created tension between the Northern Territory Government and the Commonwealth Government, which latter had to balance support for the project with finding a workable response to the *Mabo* decision. The then Prime Minister, Keating, was fully aware of the dilemmas facing his Government:

> Were the project not to proceed, you can imagine the noise which would be around. People would be saying "Well, here's Mabo at its first blush a $300 million project hits the fence". You'd have the worst elements of conservative interests in this country up there blackguarding the Mabo decision and all it stands for. So what we're doing is doing no more than the Aboriginal community offered us, that is, a validation of these titles, protecting its revival, allowing a discussion about just terms, getting it off the stocks so it doesn't complicate the broader Mabo principles.[30]

Lawyer, commentator and spokesperson for the Catholic Centre for Social Research Action, Frank Brennan observed:

> What you have there is a major mining project where all parties are agreed that it would be a good thing for the mine to proceed. Mining

leases had been issued by the Northern Territory Government under Northern Territory legislation prior to Mabo but because of some of the legal advice around, and with excess of scrutiny of Japanese investors, it's been said that there's a need to legislate again and to re-issue the leases. Now the Aboriginal groups have fairly been saying: "Well, if you want that degree of certainty, and in doing so, if you're extinguishing our rights you should at least contemplate the Commonwealth solution which is that you have minimal interference with our rights, namely that you suspend our rights for the duration of the mine but once the mine has completed that our rights be restored and that we be allowed to restore a traditional relationship with the land ..."[31]

In the event, the Commonwealth supported the validation of leases but not, as requested by the Northern Territory Government, the extinguishing of native title. The Prime Minister indicated that the Commonwealth would reserve its right of remedial action in relation to *Mabo*. The subsequent Commonwealth *Native Title Act*, passed in December 1993, gave effect to the validations, providing for the suspension of the native title interest, compensation for its impairment, and its revival at the completion of the mining.[32]

The Northern Land Council (NLC) felt that the indigenous people had been excluded from the negotiations at a critical period. It urged Commonwealth intervention to facilitate a broader settlement between traditional owners, the mining company and both governments. Wes Miller, of the NLC, speaking on behalf of the traditional landowners in the area, made it clear what the range of claims included:

Well, we've been talking and holding consultations with them. There's a range of things they want: land, environmental issues, site protection. They want employment, economic development, opportunities.[33]

In November 1993 the Commonwealth purchased a pastoral lease for the Kurdanji, paying more than $1.7 million. In addition, $1.5 million was committed to the establishment of an Employment and Enterprise Development Plan for Borroloola, the closest settlement to the project site — some 50km away. In return, the Aboriginal groups involved agreed to forego any compensation claims against the Commonwealth they may have been entitled to arising from any native title interest.[34]

MIM's contribution included a January 1994 contract to transport the ore by barge to a joint venture comprising the Aboriginal and Torres Strait Islander Commercial Development Corporation (CDC) and Burns Philp Shipping. This means that the local Yanyuwa people could eventually secure 50% of the barging business as they buy back the CDC's stake.[35]

DISCUSSION

It is worth reiterating that the McArthur River project was initiated at a time when environmental conflicts were generating consequent policy shifts. The project emerges from a background dominated by the Resource Assessment Commission's (RAC) assessment of Coronation Hill, the rejection of that project and the abandonment of Wesley Vale. The two-year ESD process was beginning. A change of political leadership in the government in Canberra saw the subsequent elevation of the economy to centre stage in policy. Priority was given to development within the development/environment discourse, illustrated by the signing of the IGAE and the announcement of the *One Nation* measures together with the establishment of the MPFU within the Department of Prime Minister and Cabinet. Brereton's endorsement of the process shows that the Keating Government saw the McArthur River mine as the prototype of a devolved resource management process, lending the States and Territories more autonomy.

All these conflicts and processes should have provided sufficient impetus for the development of proactive, integrated approach to resource based management issues, processes and planning legislation. McArthur River was a complete negation of the consensual ESD goal. Some commentators have suggested that the fast-tracking of the McArthur River project can be seen as an important political strategy for the Keating Government, providing an opportunity for the government to restore its pro-development credentials by "paying back" the mining sector for the "loss" of Coronation Hill.[36]

The McArthur River project was the first practical application of the devolutionary philosophy of the IGAE, and of the MPFU's facilitation of "fast-tracking". The Commonwealth could have demanded that the EIS process be more transparent than in normal Northern Territory practice. This was not done, and the effectiveness of the actual EIS, judged against the outcomes, was dubious. As Toyne stresses, the integrity of the process was undermined by the fact that after the go-ahead was given, the proponent decided to locate the port 3km up the coast from the site designated in the EIS. Its impact, particularly on the sensitive seagrass beds, could now only be monitored after the event.[37]

Fast-tracking, and the neglect of proper EIS procedures, had the effect of obscuring procedural deficiencies which had been thrown into sharp relief in the Wesley Vale case. A central failure of the latter's EIS was the lack of recognition that unless baseline studies are done prior to the project it is simply impossible to determine or even estimate the environmental impact. For Wesley Vale, effluent disposal in Bass Strait was critical. Ignorance of baseline environmental conditions fatally inhibited assessment of the impact of effluent, particularly that carrying organochlorines. Subsequently, the Commonwealth Government engaged the CSIRO to undertake the appropriate research into tidal patterns and biodiversity within Bass Strait so that future projects could treat the results as baseline studies. This research helped set the framework for Commonwealth guidelines for future kraft chlorine pulp and paper mill projects. It also defined essential prerequisites for thorough, proper and legitimate environmental impact statements for large industrial projects. Thus, although EIA is itself a flawed and highly unreliable technique, proper guidelines for its application existed.

But even this disappeared with the McArthur River project, which was approved, and proceeded, without any complete picture of the environmental impact risks. A basic requirement of EIA philosophy — that impacts must be assessed prior to approval in order to evaluate their costs and benefits — was ignored. Establishment of a satisfactory régime for monitoring project implementation was made immeasurably more difficult. As Krockenberger explained, none of this was necessary or justifiable:

> We've seen McArthur River being approved on what really was an extremely poor environmental impact statement, and one that should not have been produced in the 1990s. And let me make it clear here: it isn't an issue of whether that project went ahead or not. We're not talking about a Coronation Hill situation where it was a question of yes or no. It was a question under what conditions that project went ahead, what safeguards were in place for the environment.[38]

It seems that the concern of both levels of government was with expediency rather than legitimacy. The fast-tracking of the process under the MPFU saw the final approval rushed through in indecent haste.

CONCLUSION: RHETORIC VERSUS REALITY

The McArthur River Mine Project highlighted a number of significant issues for environmental policy in Australia. Firstly, despite the ESD rhetoric about integration of environmental and development concerns, this project clearly emphasises its irrelevance. The actual outcomes were driven by political considerations, derived from the traditional structural imperatives of liberal democratic political systems. When faced with the complexities of resource management issues, liberal democratic governments will rely on growth, ignoring its costs. The resulting policy strategy has been highly successful, but at the cost of potentially aggravating environmental problems. It exploits issue ambiguity by taking issues "out of politics", institutionalising them in bureaucracies and agreements. This is a short-term displacement strategy. Rather than solving the problem, it pushes it into the future. This temporarily defuses public conflict; but risks deeper, more damaging clashes once public perceptions of environmental damage or economic loss are triggered.

Secondly, the McArthur River project raises some serious concerns about ongoing adoption of the IGAE as a framework for dispute resolution within the federal system, particularly if the "price" of cooperative federalism is a lowest common denominator response at the EIS stage in particular. This is particularly pertinent at a time when the Howard Government, narrowly re-elected in October 1998, is committed to pursuing a new legislative framework for an environmental régime that would involve the "efficient" discharge of Commonwealth responsibilities. This framework will address "problems" in the existing laws which are criticised for failing to deliver "certainty" for the proponents of development projects and involving too much potential for unnecessary delay or duplication.[39] The November 1997 COAG agreement that forms the basis of the government's consultation paper endorsed the view that the Commonwealth rôle in environment matters should be confined to regulating those proposals having a *significant impact* on "matters of national environmental significance".[40] McArthur River may have been the model. The paper states that the proposed new Commonwealth law will seek to "maximise reliance upon State process which will meet appropriate standards" by means of bilateral agreements which will accredit State environmental impact assessment régimes.[41] It also suggests a resort to "case-by-case" assessment of specific development projects. Finally, just to complete the sense of *déja vu*, decisions within the legislation are to be based on the principles of ESD.

Thirdly, although mentioned only briefly here, the McArthur River project also highlights the importance of political "leadership" in resource management. The elevation of Keating to the position of Prime Minister brought with it a renewed emphasis on growth and economic issues as pre-eminent over, and distinct from, environment. Hawke's consensual ESD strategy had been to institutionalise conflict, bending it to the integration of development and environment. But any environmental gains were subverted under Keating. Reinstatement of the economy and economic growth as a priority pushed ESD off the political agenda, to be captured once again by the bureaucracy, particularly within the intergovernmental ESD Steering Committee (ESDSC) and reclaimed by the State governments who, under Hawke's endorsement of ESD, had felt marginalised.

Fourthly, the McArthur River project highlights the political nature of the continued conflict over native title aspirations between traditional people on the one hand, and miners and pastoralists on the other. In the case of McArthur River and Mount Todd, difficult and stressful conflicts were resolved through negotiation rather than direct action — blocking mining projects, for example — or resorting to the High Court. This approach was forgotten in the highly politicised environment of the Century zinc mine in Queensland where "States' rights" rhetoric found a bedfellow in that of "property rights". The tactics of divide and rule create stress and division, but have the perceived political benefit of creating divisions between environmental groups and traditional owners over strategies and outcomes. They also capitalise upon bigotry and prejudice.

Finally, if McArthur River represents the likely outcome of resource management processes such as ESD within the IGAE, then it may be time for participants — particularly environmental groups — to reconsider their involvement in such time-consuming and resource depleting processes. The institutionalisation of political conflict permits government to exploit ambiguity through control of the deliberative process. Under these conditions, even the clearer principles and objectives of ESD are lost to sight. Failure to apply the available, if imperfect, instruments of assessment inhibits discussion and analysis. Development of policy instruments that would allow projects to be evaluated against indicators of sustainability has been neglected.

ROUNDTABLE DECISION MAKING IN ARID LANDS UNDER CONSERVATIVE GOVERNMENTS: THE EMERGENCE OF "WISE USE"

T. Doyle

Resource decisions made in the arid lands of SA are increasingly dominated by "wise use" movement strategies. These strategies are currently particularly powerful in SA due to the existence of conservative governments at both state and federal levels. This industry-led, right wing movement, which has emerged from the United States of America, shares much ideological baggage with Australian conservative governments. Perhaps this explains, at least in part, the ease and earnestness of adoption of "wise use" decision making by these conservative governments.

Apart from assailing the notion of "the commons", the "wise use" movement advocates a range of instrumental attacks on environmental movements. These have been ably documented by their critics.[1] They include the creation of right-wing think tanks which produce propaganda which challenges dominant myths of green movements; it uses "dirty-tricks" campaigns (designed to "smear" the reputations of its opponents); and it has created anti-green front groups, masquerading as environmental groups, to confuse the "general public".

The critique offered in this chapter further contends that the "wise use" movement has also championed a particular style of decision making which it believes gives it more power over decisions relating to the utilisation of nature, whilst masquerading behind a sales pitch singing the praises of its supposedly democratic nature.

Two particular cases are studied here: Coongie Lakes in SA's far north-east and Roxby Downs uranium mine with its associated bore-fields in the State's centre. Both include land-use interests and conflicts synonymous with the management of Australia's arid lands: pastoral, mining, irrigation (water), conservation and indigenous peoples. Both provide very different practical examples of "wise use" decision making, whilst sharing the core tenets of "wise use" ideology.

This chapter draws on a number of methods of data collation, which demand mention here. First, the author has directly participated in various ways in the decision-making processes featured in the two case studies. He is a member of the Olympic Dam Community Consultative Forum (CCF), and in his capacity as President of the Conservation Council of South Australia (CCSA) he has been involved in different levels of negotiation relating to Coongie Lakes. As well as ethnographic material, this chapter is based on both official and informal correspondence which provides extra, and more verifiable primary information. By cross-referencing this material, this study provides a clear and rich picture of the actual mechanics and organics of the policy-making processes.

THE "WISE USE" MOVEMENT

The "wise use" movement emerged in the late 1980s in the United States of America. One of the key founders of the movement was Ron Arnold, who argued that business could not survive the attacks made on it by environmentalists unless it, too, took on the attributes of a social movement. This movement is largely rural-based, "anti-environmentalist", "localist" and populist. It shares some salient features with other right-wing movements — or lobbies — which have evolved out of America's West in recent times. For example, it shares with "The Freemen" and the powerful gun lobby the notion that the "gumment" (government) is a tool which almost always serves the interests of liberals "back east", and that government, per se, is something which impinges upon individual rights, such as the right to bear arms, or the right to do anything to privately owned property. Indeed, public ownership of forest lands, for example, is also "anti-constitutional" according to these lobbies and, in this sense, the "wise use" movement is profoundly radical libertarian in its economic focus, and pathologically conservative in its morality.

Proof of the "wise use" movement's advocacy of radical libertarian economic systems is abundant. Arnold, for example, has also served as Executive Director of the Centre for the Defense of Free Enterprise (CDFE). This think tank, according Mark Dowie, an American critic of "wise use", formulates "an ideology for a grass roots insurrection he [Arnold] believes will save free enterprise capitalism from the scourge of environmentalism".[2] An enticing aside here is that these sentiments are expressed so similarly by Hugh Morgan, Managing Director of WMC, the company responsible for uranium mining at Roxby Downs. He writes:

> The road to power for ambitious revolutionaries is no longer the socialist road. But the environmentalist road, today, offers great opportunities for the ambitious, power-seeking revolutionary. Environmentalism offers perhaps even better opportunities for undermining private property than socialism.[3]

The "wise use" movement is backed by large corporations active in extractive industries. Some of these include Exxon, Louisiana Pacific and Boise Cascade.[4] The key movers on the ground, however, are right wing lobby groups, including the Moon-affiliated American Freedom Coalition[5] and thousands of "populist, small-town, and rural citizens' groups".[6]

"WISE USE" AND MULTIPLE USE MODELS OF RESOURCE MANAGEMENT

Arnold and others co-opted the term "wise use" from Gifford Pinchot, an early twentieth century icon of the forest service. It was deliberately chosen by Arnold for its ambiguous meaning, and the positive connotations of "wisdom" inherently attached to it. Pinchot championed "multiple use" as a way of resolving land-use conflicts. This model was firmly rooted in notions of nature as constituting a series of resources for human use. Nature itself was not of value outside of these utilitarian notions: the classic Lockean position demanding "improvement". Multiple use, despite its serious intellectual incoherence, has been dominant as a resource allocation model in many parts of the world, including Australia. It emerged most vociferously in the language which framed the establishment of the Great Barrier Reef Marine Park in the 1970s.

Multiple-use planning imagines nature divided into a pie. All possible uses of nature — as pie to be consumed — are known and explored, as all of nature is a commodity.

In addition to nature being construed as a series of pie segments, so too is society itself. Multiple use is very much reliant on pluralist and neo-pluralist concepts of power and the state. The round table is a symbolic representation of the pie, the table itself being provided by the state. People (or, in present day fashion, "stakeholders") are physical manifestations of possible resource use and conflict. Environmental managers using this multiple-use model argue that most environmental processes are reversible, and that all sectors can pursue diverse goals for resource use without unnecessary conflict. All that it takes to succeed is that conflicting sectors produce end positions based on compromise and negotiation. This point will be developed later in this chapter.

Multiple-use decision making has enormous weaknesses. In true pluralist terms, all interest groups are perceived as equal stakeholders, whilst the state perceives and portrays itself as an objective middle-person, attempting to provide a working compromise between conflicting sets of "values". Values, of course, are important; but by concentrating solely on reconciling values, power differentials between conflicting positions are almost totally denied and neglected.

Free marketeers see multiple-use models of decision making as essential to promote market-based and market-advantaged outcomes. Indeed, one of the "birthdays" of the "wise use" movement occurred at a three-day "Multiple-Use Strategy Conference" in August 1988 organised by the aforementioned "Centre for Defense of Free Enterprise" at the Nugget Hotel in Reno, Nevada.[7]

To be fair to multiple-use resource allocation and decision making, when genuinely interpreted as a conservation régime it can achieve results. What is essential to good multiple-use decision making is the open recognition that some interests, some values, are more paramount than others. Also, that depending on context, sometimes not all resource issues are "win-win" situations. In fact, on many occasions, certain interests are more successful than others. The example of Australia's Great Barrier Reef, though a long way from the arid zone, is an excellent example. Central to the Reef's management is the existence of marine national parks, or no-take areas.[8] The benefits of no-take areas are widely recognised by scientists attempting to maintain some "control" areas which allow the development of successful management strategies. The majority of the Barrier Reef is not so exclusively protected. Most of its Marine Protected Areas (MPAs) allow commercial interests to enter into the Reserve. Multiple use can only work from a conservation perspective, when these multiple access areas are coupled with a strong sample of representative habitats which are "no-go" zones for commercial interests such as mining. Frameworks which do not explicitly provide any exclusiveness to any interests are at best ecologically useless; and, at worst, promoters of commercial, anti-ecological interests. These systems cease to be multiple use and take on the tag: "wise use".

"WISE USE", SEQUENTIAL USE AND THE GANG BANG THEORY OF NATURE

"Wise use" shares many similarities to multiple use. In some ways it is simply a recent re-invention of multiple use, but this time it is larger than life; a more brutal, less subtle manifestation which deliberately distorts its multiple use cousin. First, in "wise use" roundtables there is no Labour stakeholder. In post-Hawke Accord processes union interests were seen as integral to resource decision making. Under "wise use" they are usually absent, seen now as a non-constituency, a non-stakeholder.

Second, the rôle of the state is almost non-existent under "wise use". In many multiple-use models, the state is portrayed as neutral arbiter at the centre of the wheel or table. But the central rôle of the state within pluralist models (or even the pretence of centralised neutrality) is currently bypassed in "wise use" decision making. The state is usually just another participant in roundtable discussions, or, worse still, the interests of large business and the state are so closely intertwined that the two are indistinguishable. The state as axis-point, as convenor, is now dead.

Penultimately, and carrying on directly from the last point, corporations are now the carpenters of the roundtables, initiating and controlling agendas and terms of reference. Worse still, they are largely self-monitoring and self-regulating.

Finally, as mentioned, "no-take areas", exclusion zones, scientific control zones and ecological buffer zones are now increasingly obsolete. Under "wise use" decision making, these areas are now referred to as resource "lock-ups". The Minister for Environment under the Howard Ministry, Robert Hill, has made this quite plain. In an ABC radio broadcast from Port Lincoln in September 1998, Mr Hill addressed the management of the Great Australian Bight. He stated that "MPAs (Marine Protected Areas) which exclude use are an old-fashioned view …".[9] Any ecological "use" is only considered after business interests have deemed it appropriate insofar as they have no further utilisation for the areas in question. Other "wise use" jargon refers to this as "sequential use", which promotes a strict hierarchy in the order of access to the "resources". The biosphere, in this view, can be used over and over again, fulfilling all the demands placed on it by the multitude of stakeholders, with no long-term negative consequences. This can be better understood as the Gang Bang Theory of Nature. It is not necessary to labour the point that environmental interests and those of indigenous peoples are most often given access last.

"ROUNDTABLE" DECISION MAKING

The "wise use" movement has been assiduous in its sale of round-table, consensus decision making. As mentioned, the round table itself represents the imagined non-conflictual notion of pluralist political models which, in turn, promotes the win-win models of unfettered markets. A fine example of this championing of non-conflictual roundtables occurs with the Quincy Library Group. The town of Quincy, in the Sierra Nevada range, formed this group in 1993, ostensibly to resolve resource conflicts between timber and environmental interests, as well as government agencies.[10] It was held in the town library so people would not yell at each other. As touched upon previously, wise and multiple use models are based on the premise that everyone — including the environment, conceived of as a stakeholder — will win in the market, if quiet negotiation between conflicting interests and values takes place. The Quincy Library Group has been extremely successful in promoting its "wise use" round table, the end result being victories to resource extractive industries. In fact, it has been hailed as a model of resource decision making right across the United States of America. Emerging from this process was *The Quincy Library Group Forest Recovery and Economic Stability Act 1997*. It orders the US Secretary of Agriculture to hold a five year pilot project based on Quincy style decision making on three national forests in the Sierra.

The round table, although appearing to uphold pluralist notions of democracy, is deeply exclusive. All decisions are handed over to "local" people. The definition of local is telling, as it includes multi-national companies and their management teams (as they are employers in the local community); but it excludes representation from national environmental organisations. Consequently, industry representatives are markedly over-represented; create agendas and bottom lines; set terms of reference; and, simultaneously, receive acclaim as achievers of community consensus with all the legitimising imprimaturs which are associated with this process. The notion of "localism", of course, fits in nicely with the discourses revolving around "bioregions", "grass-roots" and "participative decision making" — concepts widely endorsed by many environmentalists. This further defuses opposition. Sierra Club Chair Michael McCloskey's November 1995 memo to the club's Board comments on this cleverly contrived exclusionist process:

> Industry thinks its odds are better in these forums … It has ways to generate pressures on communities where it is strong, which it doesn't have at the national level … This re-distribution of power is designed

to disempower our (national environmental) constituency, which is
heavily urban ... Big business has a game-plan of pursuing this approach
to get out of the clutches of the tough federal agencies ... A lot of people on the left have been taken in because it is a touchy, feely approach
that plays to those with romantic notions about localism and self-con-
trol. They forget they're disempowering most of the people who have a
stake in the issue.[11]

Consensus, of course, is more easily achieved by limiting the
domain of stakeholders. Additionally, these roundtables are built by
business; not the state (although sometimes it is a shared task, with
the division between private and public sectors almost impercepti-
ble). The pluralist and even corporatist notions of state-initiated
coordination, mediation and monitoring of such processes are no
longer useful in understanding these recent innovations to conservative environmental decision making.

The work of wise-user Patrick Moore is of interest here. Moore is
North American and an ex-Greenpeace professional now working for
industry. In 1998 Moore visited Australia as a guest of the Forest
Protection Society, which is an Australian "wise use" style front
group for the National Association of Forest Industries.[12] Moore was
vociferous in advocating the prevention of the "locking up" of forests
in "no-go" zones in national parks and reserves which, as aforesaid,
is the key "wise use" mantra.

In his website entitled "Green Spirit" Moore co-opts green and
democratic language to further industry's gains. In the website much
attention and acclaim is given to successful roundtable decision making. Advice is given on achieving agreement on membership and
terms of reference. Moore describes the purpose of these roundtables:

The job of the facilitator, in the final analysis, is to help the roundtable
produce a consensus document, which expresses the areas of unani-
mous agreement among the participants, and where there is not unan-
imous agreement, an explanation of that disagreement, in words that
are unanimously agreed to by all the participants.[13]

Win-win, non-conflictual decision making imagines government
in limited economic terms. This neo-liberalism and radical libertari-
anism sits neatly in the discourse of sustainable development which
argues that all environmental problems can be resolved by increasing
efficiencies at the political, social, economic, scientific and organisational levels.[14] In this vein, all environmental problems can be
resolved with better management. Whereas the Club of Rome imagined Malthusian limits, advocates of sustainable development pursue
increased growth by bypassing concepts of a finite biosphere through

arguments of increased efficiency and "best practice management". Growth is good for the environment. All environmental problems just need to be addressed using professional conflict resolution techniques. Britell supports this contention when he argues:

> A defining characteristic of this approach is a reluctance to ascribe the cause of any problem to pervasive and systemic corruption, or to the ability of the rich and the strong to take advantage of the poor and the weak.[15]

These Quincy style roundtables are replicated in the two case studies which follow. Three issues are discussed in both cases: exclusiveness of roundtable proceedings; definition and limitations of terms of reference; and restriction and bias of information.

ROXBY DOWNS

The uranium and copper mine at Roxby Downs is undergoing an enormous expansion. In the first instance, it is enlarging its production from 85,000 tonnes of ore per year to 150,000 tonnes. Its ultimate projected output is 200,000 to 350,000 tonnes. During this expansion phase, Western Mining Corporation (WMC) has been issued legal rights to increase its extraction of fossil waters from the Great Artesian Basin from 14 to 42 megalitres per day. Roxby Downs is fast becoming one of the biggest uranium mines in the world.

The uranium mine at Roxby Downs has been chastised from a wide variety of angles by environmentalists. In the "Report of the Public Inquiry into Uranium" (which largely focussed on Roxby's operation) widespread criticisms were levelled at the industry's operation in five main areas: health and safety; uranium tailings management; information access; water management; and its contribution to the nuclear fuel cycle.[16]

WMC's mismanagement of uranium mining and milling has been well documented and consequently is not the focus of attention here. This study will chiefly interest itself in the creation and operation of the Olympic Dam Community Consultative Forum (CCF). In the literature jointly provided by WMC and the SA Government, the CCF was set up to "be an important mechanism for liaison and information exchange between the Commonwealth government, State government, representatives of Aboriginal interests, conservation groups, pastoralists, the Roxby Downs community and WMC".[17]

EXCLUSIVENESS

There are several interesting parallels with the American experience with "wise use" roundtables in the selection of membership for the CCF. The process was exclusive on four counts. The first count, as discussed, is obviously the inbuilt bias of such roundtables in favour of the market, as the process reflects the neo-liberal politics of the market place. The final three counts, however, are far more easily identified: the supposedly outdated and less sophisticated models of elitist and instrumentalist models of power seem more useful as tools of analysis in this context.

For example, there were attempts to exclude one particularly dedicated but "unfriendly" environmental activist, Dr Dennis Matthews, from being a representative of the CCSA on the Forum. As President of the CCSA, the author received a telephone call from the Department of Primary Industries during which he was asked, most uncomfortably, if he would not nominate Matthews for the Forum. Next, there were simply no representatives included in the Forum from the working population of Roxby Downs (over 1000 workers) at any level lower than management. Both the Construction Forestry Mining and Energy Union (CFMEU) and the Australian Workers Union (AWU) operate on the site, but neither union or non-union workers were asked to sit on the Community Consultative Forum.

It is the issue of the exclusion of indigenous people, however, which is most bone-chilling. This exclusion has occurred both within the CCF and in the broader context of all "negotiations" between WMC and local indigenous peoples. At the general level, prior assessment of the cultural significance of the mine sites, the mound springs, associated waterways and surrounding lands to the local indigenous peoples has been insufficient. It is not appropriate to list the details of many of these issues here, as they are the business of the indigenous peoples themselves. What is included is information already in the public domain.[18]

The Kokotha people's traditional lands include the Roxby Downs mining site. As evidence of Aboriginal exclusion one only has to refer to the process which led to the initial Environmental Impact Statement (EIS). The anthropological report prepared in association with the Kokotha people was not included in the EIS. Rod Hagan, the anthropologist working with the Kokotha, recalls:

> Apart from the problems of disclosure of confidential information, the company were also demanding some form of assessment of the Aboriginality of the people involved in the survey, the Kokotha themselves. The Kokotha (who are very much traditional people; most of the people involved in the survey are initiated men), found this sort of approach really quite insulting.[19]

The Kokotha people have had to directly confront WMC on certain occasions in the past, particularly in association with road and pipeline construction. In addition, there have been numerous land claim disputes around the mine.

The treatment of the Arabunna people by WMC shares a similar disrespectful resonance with the Kokotha case. A large part of Wellfield A and B areas are part of Arabunna lands. The facts seem to lead to the conclusion that the WMC financed the Diera Mitha Council to bring people from the Northern Territory 1600 km away to hold a ceremony on Arabunna land, in January 1995. This was an attempt to prove that the Dieri Mitha are the traditional custodians and are still linked to the land, proof of which is needed to support any native title claim. It would also support WMC's contention that they consulted with the appropriate Aboriginal group with regard to the pipeline corridor and borefield. During the "ceremonies" the Diera Mitha Council were assisted in this action by employees of WMC. The Arabunna consider this to be a sacrilege, and were out-raged that a mining company has used Aboriginal culture for its own gain. Hine writes:

> The suggestion of back door deals appears to be substantiated as members of the Dieri Association and WMC have signed a co-operation agreement. The Dieri Association is not to be confused with the Dieri Land Council based at Birdsville … So why is Finniss Springs so important to WMC and Roxby's future? There's liquid gold in that piece of desert, namely the artesian waters … WMC now wants to expand Roxby's operations and security of water supply is vitally important. This is borne out by the South Australian Government's announcement that it would do everything in its power to protect Roxby from any Mabo-style land claim.[20]

It appears WMC has supported the establishment of small Aboriginal groups that have challenged the rights of the Kokotha and Arabunna peoples. Regardless of the manoeuvrings of WMC, on June 1994, eighty elders from various regions of central Australia met at Port Augusta and decided definitively that it was the Arabunna people who were the traditional custodians of the area in question. In association with the SA Government a committee of spokespeople and elders was nominated and confirmed. WMC has not satisfactorily consulted with this committee.

This process of exclusion is also in evidence in the actual mechanics of Aboriginal representative selection on the CCF. Only one Aboriginal representative was chosen from the indigenous community, and this was done without consultation. Responding to a letter from the CCSA to the Department of Primary Industries, Natural Resources and Regional Development (PIRSA) in February 1998, the Minister justified the selection of one Aboriginal member on the CCF as follows:

> It was not easy to resolve the matter of an appropriate level of Aboriginal representation on the CCF. I am advised that there are at least seven different Aboriginal organisations with substantial interest in the matters to be discussed by the CCF. I believe it would be impractical to include representatives from all the organisations and choosing only two or three groups could offend those omitted.[21]

The Minister resolved his dilemma by appointing Garnet Wilson, who was not a member of any of the claimant peoples involved with the mine sites and their borefields. Mr Wilson is a highly regarded Aboriginal leader and he was placed in an extremely difficult position. It must be said, however, that his sole selection on the CCF was entirely inappropriate. How can it be a Community Consultative Forum when there are no Aboriginal members from the community? The Minister, of course, was placed in a very difficult position due to the prior activities of WMC. In its rôle of clouding traditional ownership issues, WMC had produced such a state of confusion that this, at last, was used this as justification for non-consultation with "local blacks". This long litany of indigenous complaints against WMC now continues in the Philippines.

LIMITATIONS TO TERMS OF REFERENCE

It cannot be said that Australian responsibility ends at the wharf, since payment for exports is accepted and used by Australian companies and by the Australian government. "… concepts of liability and duty of care are well developed and accepted in our commercial, social and legal systems. It seems inconceivable that we should ignore them in the case of uranium exports".[22]

Terms of reference (ToR) under "wise use" management are either notoriously narrow, or so loose and ambiguous as to defy useful definition. In case of the CCF it is the former scenario. The CCF is limited to considering impacts "on the environment of the Olympic Dam region".[23] It was an issue in itself in getting the CCF to include within its rubric of concern items relating to the proper management of borefields, and movement of mined uranium to South Australian ports. Questions which relate to the connections between uranium mining and the full nuclear fuel cycle are deemed "moral" questions and, therefore, irrelevant. The statements of Richard Yeeles, the Manager of Corporate Affairs for WMC (and ex-State Liberal Party ministerial minder) are living proof that paying public relations executives exorbitant wages does not guarantee quality of argument. In correspondence with the author, Yeeles refers to what he imagines is a flaw in the logic of anti-uranium campaigners. He produces an embarrassingly deficient metaphor, by comparing the long-term effects of the nuclear fuel cycle with car accidents. He writes:

> However, [environmentalists] using this type of reasoning, practically everything that mankind does should be stopped. To extend the logic, cars kill people therefore iron ore mining should be stopped.[24]

Yeeles misses the point that car accidents do not remain danger-ously radioactive for up to half a million years; or that nuclear war is substantially more explosive than a large number of car collisions. Regardless of logical inadequacies, in a political milieu where there is no alternative information, such arguments enjoy unprecedented currency.

In "wise use" decision making, early agreement from all parties is sought relating to the ToR in a bid to focus and limit future debate. The terms of reference for the CCF were set in advance and simulta-neously by WMC, and the State and Federal Governments. These terms of reference for the CCF are overseen by another commit-tee: the Olympic Dam Environmental Consultative Committee (ODECC). This latter committee is the one with the real power, at least at the formal level. This shadow committee's membership is exactly the same as the CCF, except for the "community stakehold-ers" — that is, pastoralists, townspeople, traditional owners, environ-mentalists and so on. This means that this smaller and more restricted group of company, state and federal government employees meet, usually a week or so before the larger committee, to discuss strategy. As one consequence, when the second, larger meeting is convened, government and corporate employees usually speak as one; their united position finely honed.

At a meeting of this shadow committee the power of the Community Consultative Forum was severely restricted before it had even congregated for the first time. It was decided at this meeting that the CCF should not be awarded sitting fees, as the "CCF is intended to be a consultative forum only and would not be required to make significant decisions".[25]

No significant decisions would be made by the CCF in relation to their narrow terms of reference.

INFORMATION RESTRICTION

Community groups which do attend these "consultation meetings" often justify "poor process" under "wise use" on the basis that they have been given singular access to important information. Unfortunately, this justification is not appropriate in relation to

Roxby. Information provided to the CCF is usually taken from the WMC public relations "showbag"; ranging from readily accessible annual reports to documents with colourful covers presenting the results of corporate self-monitoring. Sharon Beder writes:

> Community Advisory Panels ... tend to be dependent on the company for technical information and expertise ... The resulting panel begins with little knowledge of the environmental problems and the politics of the issues surrounding those problems. They learn only what the company tells them in closed meetings or gives them to read ... This information is explained and interpreted by company officers or those sympathetic to the company. It is not surprising that the panels often become great supporters and advocates for the company.[26]

As with the issue of indigenous representation, this procedural malaise reflects a much larger secretive context. The *Roxby Downs (Indenture Ratification) Act 1982* prohibits the disclosure of any material passed between the State government and WMC to be made public without their mutual consent. The implications of confidentiality arrangements are significant, to say the least.

Shared secrets lead to further shared arrangements. One excellent example, again at a broader societal level, is the process which led to the writing of the "Olympic Dam and Roxby Downs Curriculum Guide". This information package was prepared for South Australian secondary schools by WMC. Apart from being extremely disparaging to environmental groups, it does not provide a balanced summary of differing points of view relating to mining and borefield operations. Furthermore, there are serious holes in the document. For example, five million cubic metres of water had leaked from the tailings retention system at Roxby up until February 1994. The "curriculum document" does not reference the Roxby Downs water leakage, nor the South Australian parliamentary committee which "investigated" it.

Instead of embarking on a critical review of the document before allowing it to become part of SA's curriculum, the then Department of Environment and Natural Resources (DENR) did its best to usher the company's public relations document through the administrative hoops. Michelle Grady (Executive Officer of the CCSA) writes of her astonishment at the government's rôle (or lack of) in this curriculum process:

> Overall, we find it astounding that DENR are accepting of this material from WMC, on what seems to be face value. DENR should exercise its own critical review in editing this material ... the document simply amounts to a PR exercise for the company involved. We would strongly advise DENR to seriously review and rewrite this material.[27]

The end result of this flawed curriculum process is unknown at the time of writing. Within this cargo-culture of secrecy, however, it is evident that the state no longer plays the rôle of policeman. Community groups fill this void, and are then labelled pariahs.

COONGIE LAKES

The Coongie Lakes are situated in the north-east corner of SA, on the Cooper Creek. The Lakes, or Wetlands, have been recognised under a number of State, Commonwealth and international protection schemes. The area has also been rated by the CSIRO as constituting World Heritage status on three of the possible four criteria. One of the international mechanisms which has been designed, in the first instance, to protect some of these wetlands is the Convention on Wetlands of International Importance (the Ramsar Convention). This is the roundtable process which will be the focus of the following discussion. Ramsar promotes wetlands conservation and cooperation between countries with a particular emphasis on the welfare of birds. The Convention designated the Coongie Wetlands a Ramsar site in 1987.

Coongie Lakes are experiencing three major threats to their ongoing ecological survival: grazing from pastoral leases; Queensland government supported upstream irrigation of the Cooper catchment; and mining exploration and petroleum drilling from Santos Ltd.[28]

Conservative governments at both state and federal levels have refused to list Coongie as World Heritage. The Labor Opposition has been silent on the issue, fearing a backlash against it if the party is perceived as "anti-developmental". Instead, the federal government awarded the SA Government $100,000 to develop a Ramsar Management Plan for the Wetlands in 1997. In part, this was to deflect attention away from its failure to recognise the Lake Eyre Basin as World Heritage. Even more attractive, however, was the "wise use" language already incorporated into the Ramsar management process. The Convention's own promotional materials describes it as a "flagship for demonstrating best practice management and 'wise use' of wetlands".[29]

Its wise and sequential use goals have proven to be extremely business-friendly. All parts of the wetlands system are considered access points for both mining and pastoral interests. True to its "wise use" nomenclature, there are zero no-take areas. Not even the Coongie Lakes Control Zone (CLCZ), comprising just 1% of the entire area of Santos' petroleum exploration leases, is deemed out of bounds. This particular zone had been mapped in the past as a crucial area of ecological significance by government, business and non-governmental researchers. Instead, Santos argues that its activities are not in opposition with the ecological values of this scientific control zone and, consequently, it will not countenance any restriction on its activities: 99% access is not enough for Santos.

EXCLUSIVENESS

The Coongie Lakes Wetlands-Ramsar Management Plan (RMP) roundtable shares some important similarities with the CCF at Roxby Downs. The stakeholders were defined similarly: pastoralists, mining interests, conservationists, traditional owners and water users. In addition, in the case of Coongie, the tourism industry was granted stakeholder status. As with the CCF, there was no labour stakeholder. The roundtable was again constructed as a pie, with conflicting "stakeholders" depicted as constituting a confined segment.

There are also significant differences. The Coongie roundtable only existed on paper: the stakeholders never actually met. This is the low cost, low maintenance version of "wise use" decision making. Once the State government had been awarded $100,000 to implement the RMP it farmed out the responsibility to the various sectors aforementioned to actually provide the appropriate information to be included in the final plan. None of the stakeholders received money or support for this time and resource consuming task.

The Conservation Council of South Australia coordinated the preparation of an "Issues Paper" for the Conservation Stakeholder Working Group. This process was difficult as the diverse ideological and tactical positions of seven different environment organisations had to be reconciled and presented as a single and confined conservation position. The depiction of conservation interests as constituting a separate segment of the pie under the "wise use" model further limited their definition. To imagine a situation where our polity is a symbolic "Arthurian" *round table*, with clearly defined sectors denoting different stakeholders is not only simplistic or devious, but anti-ecological. Ecological concerns cross borders of other sectors and involve issues relating to tourism, indigenous peoples, mining, pastoralism and water usage. In this narrow sectoral view, the environment is merely seen as an external, instrumental reality. "Conservation", as a symbol, eventually emerged from this process in a very narrow manner, largely to do with birds, frogs and aesthetically pleasing places.

Two stakeholders did not submit position papers: the pastoralists and the traditional owners. In one meeting, it was communicated to the CCSA that the SA Government had "been unable to find any traditional owners to consult with". This is a nonsense, and only points to further exclusion of indigenous peoples from resource decision making. The pastoralists, although identified, could not see any gains to be made from participating. Instead, they pursued other avenues to exert their power, usually behind closed doors.

The only active rôle which the State Government had in this process was to provide access to one bureaucrat — Jenny Bourne — who met with the participating stakeholders once or twice. The endpoint of this process was the creation of a document which, reputedly, would compromise and reconcile all of the conflicting position papers, leading to another "win-win" outcome synonymous with the non-conflictual goals of "wise use". Bourne was placed in an unenviable position with no real power and few resources. Although Bourne still symbolised the central but minimal rôle of the state, in reality the state had abdicated its rôle as mediator. It became obvious to all who participated that this process had made a mockery of "public participation".

This exclusion of genuine public participation as shown in the preparation of the RMP was also evident in other decision making contexts surrounding Coongie Lakes. When Santos applied for its Petroleum Exploration Licenses 5 and 6 (which includes the CLCZ) environmentalists argued that it was essential for an EIS to be prepared, providing a mechanism which would include adequate public input. The government decided that it was unnecessary for Santos to prepare an EIS for mining exploration, even though this was within the Innamincka Regional Reserve occurring in an area classified by the Ramsar Convention as a wetland of international importance.

TERMS OF REFERENCE

Another key distinction between the roundtables at Roxby and Coongie relates to the terms of reference. Whereas the former was rigid in its constricting ToRs, the latter provided ToRs within a "Stakeholder Plan Structure" — which were nebulous, to say the least. In the case of Coongie, the document provided to approved RMP stakeholders only listed broad goals, objectives and mission statements. As the entire process was rarely taken seriously by the SA Government, the initial terms of reference for the RMP were flawed and eternally flexible.

At the conclusion of the process, in the "Summary of Key Recommendations", the Conservation Stakeholder Working Group argued for the "exclusion of grazing and mining activities from the Coongie Lakes Control Zone and the riparian frontages of the North-West branch of Cooper Creek".[30] This recommendation was made despite the fact that neither the SA Government or Santos would take it seriously.

It was the broader political picture which provides a better understanding of the authentic limitations to the terms of reference. As was evidenced by the unwillingness of the SA Government to demand that Santos prepare an EIS, the entire RMP was completed with the full knowledge that no matter what the outcome of the combined stakeholders' reports, there would be no restrictions placed on the Company. David Noonan, the Australian Conservation Foundation (ACF) Campaigner Officer for South Australia, wrote the following:

> Santos' "consultation process", where the outcome of mining in Coongie Lakes is predetermined is a farce. The Minister for Environment claims that approvals have already been given to Santos, that there is no decision to be made. Yet he also claims that conservation groups have been invited to "provide some very real input". If he has already decided, what is he offering to discuss? If the Government refuses to conduct an Environment Impact Statement on the Santos proposal, there will be no public process in place, there is no opportunity for real input.[31]

At a meeting of various representatives of the PIRSA and the CCSA (held 21 August 1998), it was suggested that exclusive ecological "no-take zones" in the Coongie Lakes could only really be achieved after Santos had deemed the area "surplus to its requirements": this is sequential use in its most blatant form.

INFORMATION RESTRICTION

The SA Government granted Santos monopoly mining rights in the Cooper Basin until February 1999. This lack of market competition promotes overly close relationships between the state and the corporation in question. These exclusive rights provide a situation which is nearly identical to uranium mining at Roxby, where no information is released to the public if either State government or corporation deems it inappropriate.

Unlike the more heavily choreographed and expensive round-table experience at Roxby, where stakeholders receive ecological data generated largely by the Corporation, stakeholders in the Ramsar process have to generate their own data. They do not see the position papers of the other stakeholders until they have been finally presented to the government. This latter version of "wise use" decision making is just as insidious as the first; but for different reasons. In the case of the former, base line data is produced by the Company; in the latter there is no collective knowledge base, however corrupted, upon which to make informed, shared decisions.

This cheaper model of "wise use" information provision, as evidenced at Coongie, unfortunately, is achieving greater prominence in the management of other arid lands in Australia. In the Simpson Desert Regional Reserve Ten Year Review, the SA Government has outsourced the Review to a private consultant, Resource Monitoring and Planning Pty Ltd. The consultant has requested any "information regarding relevant activities of the numerous stakeholders in the area over the last 10 years, and some basic descriptive background material".[32] In a response to this management/public relations company, Vera Hughes, State Coordinator of The Wilderness Society, writes:

> The ecological quality of the Simpson Desert Regional Reserve over the past ten years is impossible to assess given the lack of scientific data currently available. We simply have no credible means of measuring the impact of exploitation. From your letter, it is clear the focus of your concern is on gathering this data any way you can. Basing studies on data provided by vested interests may be better than nothing. Or, it may not. If the attempt to assess the viability of the regional reserve for conservation is sincere, ongoing scientific data must be gathered and interpreted by independent parties. If this data has not been gathered on an on-going basis, a thorough and rigorous audit of the Reserve is not possible.[33]

When the state relinquishes the responsibility of providing or adequately funding the compilation of baseline scientific data upon which to establish a management régime, each stakeholder whistles in the dark.

CONCLUSIONS

The problems with "wise use" decision-making processes are many. At a symbolic level, "they remain a corporatist exercise designed for quieting opposition and coopting more radical, non-governmental strategies".[34] They deliberately ignore power differentials between stakeholders, whilst "manufacturing nature" in economic rationalist terms. "Wise use" and sustainable development work hand in hand with free market economics. As the market is deemed "natural", the ecology of the ecosphere becomes "the market". All inputs and outputs are given value in monetary terms and then, so it is argued, the "natural", "real" and "essentialist" economy of ecology shall emerge, unfettered by the constraints of science and governmentality. The trickle-down effect will benefit those species living on the lower rungs of the natural hierarchy, promoting widespread ecological health and doing away for ever with any notions of science-generated ecological safety nets thrown over the most disadvantaged species and habitats — the very resources most at risk. Nothing is irreversible; everyone and everything will win: the chocolate ration has been increased.

In the South Australian context, particularly with reference to arid zones, this ideology has led to pressure being placed on ecological safety zones to produce economic profits. Along these lines, ex-Minister for Mines and Energy in SA, Stephen Baker, has repeatedly declared that "parks must pay". This logic is similar to that shown in the development of overseas aid programmes for the less affluent world which must show profitable returns for the donor country. In both the Roxby and Coongie cases, the State has argued that "wise use" of resources will lead to mining royalties which can be used to manage nature in an environmentally appropriate way. The real point here is that the State will no longer fund, provide and support its own management régimes.

These case studies provide strong evidence that the State is retreating from past responsibilities; it is no longer the hub of the round table. There is no doubt that there is a close collusion between the State and big business. Furthermore, and of more importance, is the fact that the State now imagines itself as a corporation. Recently in SA, both the Department of Primary Industry and the Department of Environment, Housing and Aboriginal Affairs have undergone a structural transition to a purchaser/provider model which has been echoed in numerous other bureaucracies under free market governments. The purchaser/provider model dictates that the purchaser, or client, is no longer the public. Each bureaucratic division's client is now its own departmental director. The director purchases the services from its own employees. When these services can be more efficiently and effectively purchased outside the bureaucracy, the director outsources these tasks. Where once the public would demand the public service to act in its interests, now the bureaucracy must satisfy its own CEOs who, in SA, are largely political appointees of a party whose interests are often inseparable from those of big business. The bureaucracy must now provide the "correct" information which will lead to profitable outcomes. In this manner, business becomes the client and government becomes its service provider.

One critical impact of this situation is the profound loss of the public input which once led to the State acting on the citizens' behalf in the processes of mediation, data generation, monitoring, legislation and regulation. Santos now produces its own Declaration of Environmental Factors for Coongie Lakes. This is a lower level, non-public process; instead of the government instigating an EIS, WMC largely monitors itself, producing its own base data when and if it wants to.

Non-government organisations like the CCSA are now often

forced to bypass the State and attempt to negotiate directly with companies like Santos and WMC. In correspondence with Santos on the Coongie issue the CCSA asked to meet with the company CEO Ross Adler.[35] Although the CCSA represents a combined membership of 60,000 South Australians, the letter did not even elicit a reply. Whereas once the government was forced to listen to pressure groups, the company, ultimately, only has responsibility to its shareholders.

There is also some need in this conclusion to comment on the inadequacy of several public policy textbooks in their analysis of resource conflicts under conservative Australian governments. Many of these texts, such as Bridgman and Davis' recently published *Australian Policy Handbook*, still articulate the central and separate rôle of the state in resource decision making, almost ignoring the power of business, whilst providing an ideological framework where wise-use style, win-win roundtables derive substantial credence and justification.[36] These outdated, rational comprehensive style texts operate on the widely accepted but unquestioned premise that the "model of society underlying the contemporary rationality project is the market".[37] Stone critiques this position as follows:

> Society is viewed as a collection of autonomous, rational decision makers who have no community life. Their interactions consist entirely of trading with one another to maximise their individual well-being. They each have objectives and preferences, they each compare alternative ways of attaining their objectives, and they each choose the way that yields the most satisfaction. The market model and the rational decision-making model are thus very closely related.[38]

Laissez-faire ecology is a non-science. Within it, there is no understanding of the reality of relationships within and between societies and ecosystems. Imagining nature exclusively as an ecological free market will lead to massive species extinction and habitat degradation, and extend inequities between human beings. Unrestrained commodification of the planet Earth will not lead to win-win games; but will, in the short term, lead to very few, but extremely large wins for a powerful minority, and in the long term, will lead to massive losses for all forms of life on the planet.

TOURISM AND COASTAL ZONE MANAGEMENT: THE UNEASY PARTNERSHIP

D. Mercer

Coastal zone tourism and recreation in Australia faces substantial problems but has great potential.

However, both the terrestrial and marine sections of the coastal zone in the settled parts of the country have been consistently under-valued in terms of their ecological, "public service" functions and have been subjected to the "tyranny" of countless, localised and ill-coordinated decisions that have combined to create a seriously degraded environment in many places. Traditionally, the state has placed relatively weak regulatory controls on the private sector in the Australian coastal zone, and — notwithstanding the rhetoric of the Commonwealth-sponsored 1995 "Coastal Action Plan"[1] — it is not possible to speak of anything remotely resembling a "national coastal zone management policy".

A belated understanding of the serious planning mistakes that have been made in past coastal zone management is sparking a small effort to develop new institutional structures and "ecological health" measures to ensure that the same errors are not repeated in the future. But this is happening at a time when, under the banner of "national competition policy", both the States and local government authorities are competing to attract the tourist dollar in the context of an increasingly globalised economy, when the Commonwealth Government is divesting itself of many of its environmental responsibilities, and when "privatisation" and "corporatisation" are the leading policy ideas in public administration. Ultimately these are much more powerful forces.

TOURISM: THE INDUSTRY OF THE FUTURE?

By any measure tourism is now a major sector of the Australian economy, its value recently estimated at around $16 billion, and employing 1 million people.[2] Though international tourism is considered important, 80% of demand is domestic, predominantly intrastate and central to this discussion.[3]

Naisbitt suggests that three main "paradigm industries" (one being tourism) will be the driving forces of the global economic system in the twenty-first century. In view of recent, dramatic plunges in Australian commodity prices, continuing thought needs to be given to a radical reshaping of the Australian economy, away from its historical dependence on the export of a limited range of unprocessed agricultural and mineral products in an increasingly competitive global marketplace.[4] Currently attracting over 4.2 million overseas visitors annually to these shores — and having increased four-fold in the decade prior to 1996 — tourism is often cited as offering an obvious and environmentally acceptable alternative, especially in regional Australia.[5]

Accordingly, governments of all political persuasions have for years been generous in their financing of promotional campaigns, particularly in Japan and North America. Indeed, the express purpose of the *Australian Tourist Commission Act 1987* is the marketing of the country internationally as a travel destination through the promotional activities of the Australian Tourist Commission (ATC), to which the Federal Government's May 1998 budget allocated $58 million over four years. Critical examination of this strategy is rare, as the public debate is dominated by such agencies as the ATC, the Committee for the Economic Development of Australia (CEDA)[6] and the Tourism Council of Australia (TCA). A major outcry greeted a suggestion by the Mayor of Noosa in 1995 that his town should cap its population at 60,000. At the present time Noosa's population is doubling approximately every 12 years and will reach around 43,000 inhabitants by the year 2000.[7] Tourism's importance is not reflected in the allocation of R&D funding; agriculture and mining gain approximately 14% and 7% respectively, but tourism is allocated a mere 0.3%.[8]

Nor have desirable visitor numbers been actively discussed, for instance in relation to the controversy concerning Australia's population "carrying capacity". Increasing visitor numbers potentially have extensive environmental consequences through airport, road and resort expansion programmes, as well as impacting on resource use generally (water, energy, land and so on). Resident opposition to aircraft flight paths, new runways and airport locations is not restricted to Sydney; ongoing conflict can be anticipated. For example, for some years Cairns has been one of Australia's fastest growing airports in terms of annual traffic flows. In 1997–98 its passenger traffic was around 3 million people, and in 1993 forward estimates suggested a doubling of both domestic and international visitor numbers to the Cairns region between 1993 and 2001.[9] Yet there has been no serious debate about the desirability of such a rate of growth or detailed analyses concerning water supply and waste disposal consequences, the assimilative capacity of the Cairns bioregion, or the likely impacts on nearby World Heritage areas. Between 1976 and 1989, a 37% increase in the total number of island resorts on the Great Barrier Reef, plus a steady increase in their size, led to more people, buildings, boats, harbours and associated environmental impacts. Growth has been so rapid in the Cairns section of the Great Barrier Reef Marine Park (GBRMP) that a moratorium on the issuing of new tourism operator permits was instituted in 1995.[10] What is more, some projections of growth in tourist numbers by the tourism industry have simply extrapolated past trends, leading to exaggerated claims which are then used to justify lavish expenditure on new resort and infrastructure developments, with associated environmental impacts. The end result is that accommodation over-capacity or project non-completion are not uncommon. These issues are of current concern given the sudden dramatic decline in visits from such countries as South Korea, Indonesia and Japan as a consequence of the financial crisis that engulfed those countries from 1997 onwards. In 1997–98 international traffic through Cairns airport fell by almost 3% (to 1.12 million) by comparison with the previous year. In a notoriously volatile industry, Japan is, after Europe, the second-largest market for overseas tourists in far north Queensland. Yet in the year ended May 1998, Japanese tourist arrivals through Cairns airport were down 15% and Korean levels 28%.

Another related though under-researched aspect of the promotion of Australia as a tourism destination is the linkage with foreign direct investment and the globalisation of capital. Like all economic sectors, international tourism increasingly is becoming dominated by a small number of vertically integrated corporations owning and controlling all, or major portions of the industry, from airlines through to travel agencies, hotel chains and resort complexes. For such conglomerates, countries, regions and individual resorts represent "products" or "commodities" that compete for market share. The real danger is that environmental regulations then come to be seen as an unproductive restraint on investment in mass tourism and that in a federation like Australia the individual States engage in a competitive and ongoing relaxation of environmental controls — a "race to the bottom".[11] In a survey published in 1990 the Bureau of Industry Economics ranked environmental assessment procedures ahead of such constraints as exchange rate volatility, company tax and overseas trade barriers as an impediment to major project development.[12]

A major resort project at Yeppoon, near Rockhampton, proposed by the Japanese magnate Iwasaki, was never completed for financial reasons. But it was one of a number of classic cases of political favouritism on the part of the Queensland Government (assisted, in this case, by the Foreign Investment Review Board) towards specific developers and "fast-track" projects since the 1970s. At the very least, these have always involved fundamental property rights changes from leasehold to freehold, and often a range of extraordinarily generous financial, legal and regulatory inducements, including the bypassing of environmental assessment procedures. Though not involving foreign capital, the Hamilton Island and Sanctuary Cove developments are examples, as was the bungled Lindeman Island sale.[13] More recently, in 1990, the Japanese woodchip-processing company, Narui Norin, purchased 900 hectares of prime coastal real estate near Kingscliffe in Tweed Shire. Considerable assistance has been given by both the Queensland Government and the local shire and — similar in concept to the Iwasaki development — the current vision includes residential construction for 20,000 people, a 300-room beachfront resort and an 18-hole golf course. The serious financial crisis in Japan lends particular interest to the evolution of this highly publicised "hi-tech resort city".[14]

"HIGH IMPACT" AND "LOW IMPACT" TOURISM

The "natural environment", in the form of climate, land and water resources and scenic amenity, is the central "resource" for the tourism sector, even in those highly urbanised resort settings where artificial structures such as theme parks dominate the landscape. However, from the outset, two quite distinct varieties of tourism need to be recognised and kept constantly in mind. The first is highly concentrated, resort, or "mass" tourism, represented by such places as the Gold Coast and Noosa in Queensland, or Lorne and Phillip Island, in Victoria, where the environmental impacts can be, and often are, profound. The second is the generalised category of "low impact", or "ecotourism", which, in its "purest" form, pays careful attention to the minimisation of environmental impacts and, indeed, sees natural capital like wildlife, forests and reefs and so on as the major resource base for long-term, sustainable tourism. The importance of the latter to the sustainability of the Australian tourism industry — both economically and ecologically — was highlighted in the Tourism Working Group's Final Report to the Prime Minister as part of the Ecologically Sustainable Development (ESD) policy discussions in 1991 and three years later in the Commonwealth Department of Tourism's National Ecotourism Strategy.[15] In many ways, apart from the lack of indigenous representation, the 1990 Tourism ESD Working Group "round table" was the most frank and revealing expression of alternative views about tourism on the part of industry, government and environmental interests that had ever taken place in Australia. For this reason it will be revisited at various points in this chapter.

The two categories of tourism outlined are "ideal types" representing the two ends of a continuum. The ongoing academic debate as to whether strictly defined "ecotourism" should ever include any activity that takes place outside protected areas such as national or marine parks does not take account of the argument that even in relatively densely populated resort settings it is possible to design settlements that have minimal environmental and scenic impact, provided that strong planning and regulatory controls are in place, that there are appropriate and effective sanctions for non-compliance, and that strict limits are set on population and spatial expansion. Already, around Australia more and more low impact, "green" architectural design principles are being used both for individual buildings and resort complexes. The challenge is a dual one: to "retro-fit" existing resorts (for example by redesigning waste management and zoning schemes) and to bring about a situation where such practices, in new resorts and old, are seen as "normal" and "mainstream", rather than merely "interesting" or "novel".

With over 500,000 unique flora and fauna species, Australia is the world's only affluent "megadiverse" country, and if managed properly, this richness of biodiversity offers significant economic opportunities that are available nowhere else. As international travellers become increasingly sensitive to environmental issues, they are likely to be very discerning in their choice of future travel destinations; a country's policies and record in relation to such things as pollution control and wildlife preservation will count. As Agardy puts it: "Ecotourists will be more inclined to visit a well-managed protected area where species diversity is high, water quality is good, and the landscapes/seascapes are kept intact, than an area where management failures are rampant".[16] The ESD Tourism Working Group recognised this; one of its key recommendations was the establishment of a national, representative system of protected areas. Kenya and Costa Rica have already discovered the dollar-earning potential of "nature tourism" based around their unique wildlife and botanical resources, and in Australia there is no shortage of local success stories that point to an alternative development path. The small town of Albany, in WA, has responded to the demise of whaling by "reinventing" itself as a whale-watching base, generating far more revenue than whaling; and at Monkey Mia, in the same State, over 100,000 visitors each year spend some $10 million to watch dolphins in the wild. Similarly, Driml and Common highlight the enormous economic value of World Heritage listing in Queensland when they estimate gross tourist expenditure by the 1.5 million visitors to the Great Barrier Reef World Heritage Area at almost $800 million per year and for the Wet Tropics World Heritage Area at $377 million per year.[17] For comparison, the earnings from commercial fishing in 1995/96 were estimated at $143 million. On a less optimistic note, the dugong population in the Barrier Reef region has fallen by between 50% and 80% in many parts of the Marine Park.

DEMOGRAPHIC SHIFTS

The overwhelming significance of domestic tourism to pressures on the coastal zone is linked fundamentally to the distribution of the population. If the terrestrial part of the coastal zone is defined in terms of local government areas that abut the coast, then about 17% of the country's land area is "coastal". Moreover, paralleling a common demographic trend worldwide, almost 90% of Australia's population now live in this narrow belt, and that proportion is rising with each successive census.[18] Out of every six Australians, five now live within 50 km of the coast. Southern Queensland, central and northern NSW and suburban Melbourne and Perth have seen particularly rapid coastal zone population growth in recent years. While Australia's overall population growth rate between 1971 and 1991 was 32%, the equivalent for non-metropolitan coastal settlements was 95%.[19] Between the 1991 and 1996 censuses the most rapidly growing settlements were all located on the Indian and Pacific Oceans. Moreover, Victoria lost 107,832 people to other States (two-thirds to the Gold Coast and other coastal parts of Queensland, but excluding Brisbane). If the present demographic shifts continue, Queensland will replace Victoria as the second most populous State by about 2030.[20]

A recent paper analysed in detail all 115 tourism developments that were proposed in Australia in the seven-year period 1987–93, and subjected to an environmental impact assessment. All but 16 were proposed by the private sector, and five in every six of the projects were in coastal locations such as Cairns, the Peel-Harvey Inlet in WA and near the Gippsland Lakes in Victoria. Sites adjacent to marine or national parks were especially favoured and 34% of the total — including many of the fashionable "canal estates" — were deemed to be potentially damaging to coastal wetlands. Developments such as "resort-residential villages" have voracious space requirements, covering 1500 ha and catering for the accommodation needs of 10,000 people. Marina berths and golf-course developments were not unusual accompaniments and the combined total for all 115 projects was 233 sq km. The conclusion points to a real need for a coordinated approach and much stronger regulation of property developments in the coastal zone, warning that such projects "… may act as a catalyst for urban development in and around rural and conservation areas with little previous development".[21] This particular study focussed on large projects but in an earlier paper the same authors also highlighted what, potentially, may be a far more serious problem in terms of coastal environmental impacts: the cumulative impacts of a number of smaller-scale projects which, individually, are not deemed large enough to warrant an environmental impact assessment procedure.[22]

THE "CULTURAL ECOLOGY" OF THE COASTAL ZONE

The coastal management system can be conceptualised as an interacting system of relationships between three broad stakeholder groups:

1 policy makers and management agencies of various kinds;
2 members of the scientific community, both social and natural scientists, with an interest in the coastal zone; and
3 those people who either live on or near the coast or who otherwise have an interest in what happens in the coastal zone.

Orbach has referred to this system as the "cultural ecology of coastal public policy making".[23] For any given management controversy in Australia, the sheer number of involved groups and agencies can be formidable. The (eventually abandoned) Port Hacking artificial tombolo issue which spanned a decade from the late 1970s involved, for example, no less than 12 relevant public authorities, a range of residents' organisations, three major activity-based groups, two key local environmental protection groups and three environmental lobby groups beyond Port Hacking.[24] Similarly, Goldin and Sann found 34 public authorities involved in decision making along the 1800 km stretch of southern Tasmanian coastline that they studied in detail.[25]

In Australia the rôle of the scientific community in coastal management has never been strong, though increasingly in recent times its advice has been sought on a range of issues when commercial interests have been directly threatened. Beach re-nourishment, fisheries decline, offshore pollution, marine exotic pests and the likely impacts of sea-level rise or cyclonic activity are obvious examples. Path-breaking work on seagrasses in WA is discovering enormous variations in the diversity and resilience of seagrass meadows within fairly short distances. This has major significance for decisions regarding the siting of new infrastructure facilities that will disturb the seagrasses, for some sites are far more potentially devastating from an environmental perspective than others.[26] Needless to add, in such cases as the Port Hacking tombolo proposal, much of the controversy surrounded the way in which different environmental professionals "constructed" the problem and identified simplistic technical "solutions".

As has already been noted, of the stakeholder groups the private sector has had the most significant influence on current patterns of land and water use in the Australian coastal zone, frequently supported by the developmentalist state and the courts. In Victoria, in the 1960s, through a series of generous Acts of Parliament, such as the *Westernport (Oil Refinery) Act 1963*, the Bolte Government transferred large tracts of public, foreshore title alongside the then largely "undeveloped", Westernport Bay to a number of major companies like BHP, BP and John Lysaght Australia, and also provided equally generous financial assistance for these companies. The bay, once a prime recreational and wildlife site rich in fish and bird life close to Melbourne, is today a highly industrialised and polluted inlet virtually devoid of fish.[27] The wholesale destruction of seagrass beds (18,000 ha, or 85% of the total biomass) and fringing mangroves wreaked havoc on fish-breeding grounds. Ironically, as these actions begin to impact negatively on one of Victoria's premier international tourism drawcards, Westernport is being vigorously promoted by a 1990s State government equally intent on assisting private enterprise to "develop" Victoria's natural assets. At the Penguin Parade on

Phillip Island, at the mouth of Westernport — an attraction that in the past has earned in excess of $100 million for Victoria — penguin numbers have dropped dramatically over the years because of the drastic decline in their staple diet of fish.

Following the High Court's landmark rulings in *Mabo* (1992) and *Wik* (1996), growing indigenous claims to a voice in Australian coastal zone and marine management can also be safely predicted. Outcomes are likely to vary considerably, depending upon local circumstances. Fairly widespread adoption of the kind of co-management arrangements that have been developed already at Kakadu and Uluru National Parks can be anticipated. Additional, drawn-out legal and political wrangles such as that triggered by the proposed Hindmarsh Island Bridge and Marina Project in SA are unfortunately also likely. In this case the Ngarrindjeri plaintiffs opposed the building of the bridge on the grounds that it would desecrate their traditions and culture.[28] A successful land rights claim at Crescent Head on the NSW north coast was finalised in October 1996. A year later, a royalty agreement was negotiated between a Japanese-Australian pearling company and the traditional owners of Croker Island in the Northern Territory. There are currently approximately 140 native title claims with a marine or coastal component awaiting a determination by the National Native Title Tribunal.

Aside from the two notable Commonwealth/State negotiated agreements — the 1980 Offshore Constitutional Settlement and the establishment, in 1975, of the Great Barrier Reef Marine Park and associated Authority (GBRMPA) — the Commonwealth Government's rôle largely has been to concentrate on the preparation of one major "coastal inquiry" after another.[29] These have played their part in the accumulation of an important body of useful information about the coastal zone and its ongoing environmental and management problems. Invariably, as in the recent (1997) Inquiry into Marine and Coastal Pollution, a key recommendation has been the proposal that a central, national authority be established to coordinate research, as well as coastal and marine policies — but, for political reasons, this has never been acted upon. Theoretically, the 1992 Intergovernmental Agreement on the Environment (IGAE) did represent an important and historical advance in terms of forging much closer institutional linkages between the various State and Territory governments and the Australian Local Government Association. However, as the Resource Assessment Commission Coastal Inquiry recognised, it does have major deficiencies with respect to the complex area of coastal zone management and, as Gilbert rightly emphasises, it "is no more than a political compact with no legally binding force ... [it] is hostage to the first participating government ... that decides to renege on the arrangements contained in it".[30]

MULTIPLE INTERACTIONS

While it is possible to categorise all relevant coastal zone activities/values (including non-consumption and climate regulation factors) under ten different headings, definitional problems mean that it is not possible to discuss topics such as "Tourism and Recreation" in isolation from the many other uses. Multiple pressures, and the complexity of the numerous overlapping interactions involved, often make "tourism" indistinguishable from the broader question of "coastal residential/resort infrastructure and related transport developments". Moreover, growing pressure in Australia — often from environmentalists — for the wider application of wind power as an alternative to the burning of fossil fuels for electricity production follows similar developments in such countries as Denmark and Britain. However, the "best" wind power sites are frequently high on headlands in scenic coastal locations, such as in south-western WA, along the south-east coast of SA and at Capes Nelson and Bridgewater, near Portland in Victoria, and "unsightly" wind farm proposals invariably are bitterly opposed by tourism interests. Similar conflicts are arising in Tasmania between tourism and aquaculture enterprises.

Also, as population levels rise around the Australian coast, so too do the problems associated with sewage treatment and disposal. In 1960, with a population of around 25,000, the sprawling seaside suburb of Frankston, some 40 km to the south of the Melbourne central business district, was completely unsewered. This created the kind of pollution and health-related problems that are all too common today around the Australian coastline offshore from settlements that have grown much faster than the capacity to deal effectively with the waste treatment problem.[31] Two additional examples of the coastal zone being treated as an appropriate site for land uses deemed "undesirable" elsewhere come from Victoria and NSW. In both cases, the projects were eventually abandoned because of public outrage at the suggestions. The first was the 1997 proposal to relocate the Coode Island chemical storage facility from its existing site close to the Melbourne central business district to an internationally recognised wetland at Point Lillias, near Geelong. Notwithstanding Australia's ratification of the Ramsar Convention, the Federal Government, in March 1997, acceded to the Victorian Government's request that 20 ha of the wetlands should be exempted from the conditions of the

Convention "in the national interest". The second plan, to build an Armaments Complex at Jervis Bay (Booderee), south of Sydney was the most recent in a long line of suggested land-use changes which, in the past, had included a steel mill, a naval base and a nuclear power station. National and Marine Park status was eventually granted in 1997.

THE COASTAL RESOURCE BASE: ENVIRONMENT UNDER PRESSURE

Totalling approximately 37,000 km, Australia's coastline is one of the most extensive in the world. Accordingly, generalisations about environmental quality, or level of development, have to be treated with the utmost caution. While many different geomorphological types (mangroves, cliffs, estuaries and so on) are represented, 56% of the length (around 20,000 km) "consists of long, gently curving sandy beaches, typically backed by dunes or dune sandstones".[32] Scientific understanding of coastal processes and ecosystems in Australia is extremely patchy, both geographically and in relation to particular kinds of shoreline. A detailed analysis of scientific papers published between 1980 and 1987 highlights the pre-eminence of research activity in Queensland, NSW and WA by comparison with the other States and the Northern Territory. It concludes that of all Australia's benthic marine habitats, tidal flats are by far the least studied and scientifically understood.[33] This, in turn, should act as a salutary reminder of Dorothy Nelkin's insight that in all disputes over new technologies and environmental issues limited knowledge is "a resource exploited by all parties to justify their political and economic views".[34]

Photographic images of beach settings, as well as scenic coastal roads like Victoria's Great Ocean Road, are routinely used to "sell" Australia as a tourist destination, both for domestic and international travellers, and as a profitable country for overseas tourism and related infrastructure investment. Given that at least 64% of all Australian tourist accommodation is in the coastal zone, this is not surprising.[35] Unfortunately, however, the quality of many of these amenity environments is not always as high as it may appear from glossy tourism brochures. A recent attitude survey found that 42% of respondents perceived the natural condition of the Great Barrier Reef is currently poor and likely to either remain that way or deteriorate further.[36] Interestingly, in the lead-up to its victory in the 1998 Queensland State Election, the Australian Labor Party's policy platform included a commitment to banning further canal estate developments on the grounds of their damage to the coastal environment.

THE LEGACY OF THE PAST

Because of the small population base, much of Australia's coastline is virtually untouched by "development". But, at the same time, people have long assumed the right of free public access, and coastal areas within or close to the major metropolitan centres experience usage levels and pressures comparable to those in the more densely settled parts of Europe and North America, and for a longer period each year. Recreational pressures on Port Phillip Bay beaches and Sydney Harbour boat mooring infrastructure are intense, and exist as well in other States.[37]

Fortunately for the people of Australia — and in marked contrast to the situation in many other nations — only a relatively small proportion of Australia's beaches are currently in private ownership, for over a hundred years ago all the State governments gazetted continuous, crown land coastal reserves for the public's use. These linear spaces are rarely less than 30 m in width and, taken as a whole, are an invaluable part of the national estate. But they are continually under threat from erosion, alienation by the state and from the ongoing "tyranny" of thousands of small decisions which, each year, allow more or less inappropriate developments to occur. These individual, and uncoordinated actions are often taken by local government officials, or even by local "committees of management" to whom foreshore management has been delegated. They include access "improvements" in the form of roads and car parks, marinas, sewage outfalls and infrastructure of various kinds.

In what can now be seen as a fundamental design fault on the part of the state in areas of flat topography in Australia, coastal roads and railway lines were in the past frequently positioned much too close to the shoreline. Universally, this has encouraged real estate speculation and the kind of low-density, linear, urban sprawl along the transport corridors adjacent to the sea so familiar in all our major coastal cities and provincial towns. A much more appropriate strategy from the environmental perspective would have been to have sited the transport arteries a considerable distance from the coast, with large, protected "natural areas" between limited feeder routes to the coast. Interestingly, if we exclude "high profile" sites such as Hinchinbrook Island and the Great Barrier Reef Marine Park, coastal and marine national parks are a relatively uncommon feature of the 37,000 km coastline, especially close to the major urban centres. Altogether, only 3.5% of Australia's marine environment is in "no-take", Marine Protected Areas and 80% of this total lies within the Great Barrier Reef Marine Park. With one-third of Australia's coastline, WA has only seven marine parks. Further, national parks such as Wilsons

Promontory and Croajingolong in Victoria, D'Entrecasteaux in WA and Royal National Park in NSW are noteworthy for their rarity and invariably are testimony to the tenacity of environmental groups in pressing for preservation status over private commercial interests, often over many decades. In the 1880s, the Victorian Field Naturalists Club, a landmark player in the early Australian environmental movement, was instrumental in lobbying for Wilsons Promontory to be accorded national park status (the status was successfully legislated in 1898, with further additions in 1908).

Australian coastal ecosystems are very poorly represented in national parks or equivalent reserves. To take one example, the Perth-Bunbury region has already lost 85% of its wetlands and the WA Government has only just (in mid-1998) released its first draft marine environmental protection policy for that State. Moreover, the "entrepreneurial state" is also posing a renewed threat to national parks and the coastline in general in places like Victoria and WA in the form of a strong push to develop energy resources immediately adjacent to reserves, to privatise park management, and capitalise on what is seen as the underdeveloped dollar-earning capacity of park resources through tourism.[38] In mid-1998 the World Wide Fund for Nature's third report on marine protected areas in Australia gave the best ratings to Tasmania, WA and Queensland, and the lowest to SA, NSW and Victoria. The latter State was ranked last because of no new protected areas being declared and for its lack of indigenous involvement in marine reserve management.[39]

At the time of writing, a highly publicised development conflict is being played out near Cardwell in north Queensland. Keith Williams' proposed 1500-bed, 250-berth marina/resort/residential complex on his land at Oyster Point, adjacent to the World Heritage-listed Hinchinbrook Channel, has provoked one of the strongest reactions from environmental activists seen in Australia in recent times. The mega-project, which involves the removal of 4.5 ha of mangroves, has been given the green light by both the Queensland and Federal Governments as well as the full bench of the Federal Court in 1996, the latter ruling that the Federal Environment Minister had followed legitimate procedures in allowing the stalled project to continue. Notwithstanding this "technical legality", the charge that such an extensive development alongside prime dugong and seagrass habitats in a World Heritage Area is totally inappropriate has the backing of a coalition of green groups, as well as international environmental luminaries such as David Bellamy and David Attenborough. As earthworks have proceeded, the main criticism has been that the developer has consistently breached the conditions of his "deed of agreement" and that the Federal Government should consequently withdraw permission for work to continue. In view of the newly elected Queensland Government's stated policy position on coastal "canal estates", it will be interesting to see the final outcome of the current Senate Environment, Recreation, Communications and the Arts References Committee inquiry into the Port Hinchinbrook controversy.

Davis has made a plausible case for focussing more closely on State-by-State comparisons of environmental management in Australia rather than merely on the dynamics of Commonwealth-State relations.[40] Indeed, in addition to the variations already alluded to in the World Wide Fund for Nature report, glaring inter-State variations in environmental policy and regulations also featured strongly in the key findings of the recently released OECD Environmental Performance Review of Australia.[41] It could well be argued that, historically, climate and the physical nature of the coastline in different places have played a not insignificant rôle in the levels of development, coastal alienation and degradation that we see today. Viewed in this "environmentally determinist" way, much of Victoria's rugged coastline, facing a climatically inhospitable Bass Strait, has deterred the scale of rapid private resort development that has eaten up — and continues to devour — much of the coast of NSW and Queensland.

As noted earlier, a longstanding engineering practice in the Australian coastal zone has been to dump partially treated effluents into the sea. Apart from being wasteful of water, there are health effects associated with the release of pathogens. Well-tried, on land effluent disposal technologies that can also yield irrigation benefits now exist. The radical redesign of effluent disposal systems in coastal settlements should now be rapidly implemented, with allotment densities being matched against local biophysical constraints, and with developers being required by local authorities to adhere to strict on-site waste treatment and nutrient control standards.[42]

CHALLENGING THE DEVELOPMENTALIST PARADIGM

Australia's Surfrider Foundation was formed in the early 1990s as an environmental watchdog body in response to mounting concerns among surfers about declining water quality, health effects and degraded beach environments. At different times the health warnings of the Foundation have been endorsed by the Australian Medical Association, especially with respect to the numerous harmful viruses associated with the country's 700 sewage outfalls.[43] The Surfrider Foundation's most recent survey of 1600 representative beaches valued by the surfing fraternity found that:

- 72% have property and/or infrastructure developments within 250 m of the high tide mark;
- 1 in 20 had completely lost their dunes to beachfront development;
- 1 in 5 were within 5 km of a public sewerage outfall; and
- 141 public sewerage outfalls contributed more than 3 billion litres of sewerage effluent into the sea each day.[44]

Such issues are not of direct concern only to boardsurfers. Right around Australia's coast local lobby groups, "Dunecare" organisations and regional planning strategies are focussing with renewed energy on issues of coastal amenity. These bodies not only are attempting to reverse serious planning "mistakes" from the past (especially ocean outfalls), but also are involved in grassroots coastal refurbishment and rehabilitation projects, as well as campaigns to halt what are perceived as "inappropriate" new developments in the form of coastal subdivisions, catchment vegetation clearance and the like.[45] Not uncommonly, such groups find themselves in opposition to decisions being "handed down" by entrepreneurial state and local governments and to outmoded planning regulations that privilege private property rights over the public interest and encourage ecologically inappropriate developments to proceed.[46] Equally, the contemporary power of the idea of "competition policy" should not be underestimated, and environmentalists await with interest the outcome of the current Senate Select Committee Inquiry into the Socio-economic Consequences of the National Competition Policy, which also is addressing environmental impacts.

Occasionally, large developments, like the proposed Sellicks Beach, Jubilee Point and Glenelg Harbour marinas in SA, are abandoned, largely because of strong public opposition.[47] Sometimes, too, decisions taken by local councils are challenged in the courts, but with mixed success. In March 1993, for example, Richmond River Council in NSW granted a residential subdivision permit for 110 allotments to Irongate Developments Pty Ltd at Evans Head. There was substantial evidence that the area was of considerable environmental significance and an environmentalist — Mr Oshlack — challenged the validity of the permit under s 123 of that State's *Environmental Planning and Assessment Act 1979* in the Land and Environment Court in the same year. Stein J. subsequently ruled against Oshlack but argued that the appellant should not be required to pay the legal costs of the Shire and the developer because he had nothing to gain personally and the case was "in the public interest". An appeal against the costs ruling went to the NSW Court of Appeal in 1996 and then to the High Court where, in February 1998, by a 3 to 2 majority the Court ruled in favour of Stein J.'s initial decision. Environmentalists welcomed this apparent support for a trend towards taking "public interest" issues into account when determining cost liabilities, but it is worth noting in passing that three of the High Court judges were also of the view that, in future, local government authorities should be much more cautious about entering into litigation involving developers and environmentalists.[48] In some ways this issue resembled an earlier conflict involving a proposed new ocean outfall for the Coffs Harbour region first suggested in the early 1980s. The Look-At-Me-Now Headland proposal was strongly opposed in the NSW Land and Environment Court by the Coffs Harbour Environment Centre Inc. The dispute lasted for over a decade and involved two major Commissions of Inquiry. It was finally resolved when the newly elected State Government overruled the local authority in March 1995, and disallowed the outfall option for waste disposal.[49]

COASTAL AND MARINE INQUIRIES

The Surfrider Foundation survey mentioned above came three years after the appearance of Australia's first ever *State of the Marine Environment Report* (SOMER),[50] and followed no less than 29 other inquiries relevant to the coastal zone published between 1980 and 1992. One of these, published in 1991, was tellingly entitled *The Injured Coastline*.[51] Most recently, October 1997 saw the release of the report from the Senate Environment, Recreation, Communications and the Arts References Committee outlining the findings relating to *Marine and Coastal Pollution*.[52] The coastal zone — its "health" and management — appears then to be one of those perennial "problems" deserving of official — and often very expensive — study in Australia. But whether "investigating and reporting" on the issue, as in the wide-ranging Resource Assessment Commission inquiry of 1993, necessarily has translated into more ecologically sustainable and better coordinated policies is doubtful at best.[53] Indeed, the Keating Government's closing down of the Resource Assessment Commission in 1993, after only four years, can be seen as one of the clearest indications yet of a lack of political commitment on the part of the Commonwealth government to resolving issues of scientific uncertainty and addressing environmental issues of national significance. At the State level this action had its parallel in Victoria with the abolition, in 1997, of that State's independent arbiter on land-use decision making, the Land Conservation Council and its replacement by the Environment Conservation Council.

The SOMER study highlighted the significant changes that have taken place since the time of European settlement. For Queensland, it estimated that the sediment quantities, as well as phosphorus and nitrogen entering the sea, have all increased fourfold over the last two hundred years. The report also identified enormous variability in terms of environmental conditions around the country, ranging from "almost pristine" to "locally poor". In general, the latter areas were close to major population centres or adjacent to intensively used agricultural catchments. Overall, the top five concerns were:

- declining marine and coastal water/sediment quality, particularly as a result of inappropriate catchment land-use practices;
- loss of marine and coastal habitat;
- unsustainable use of marine and coastal resources;
- lack of marine science policy and lack of long term research and monitoring of the marine environment; and
- lack of strategic, integrated planning in the marine and coastal environments.

Australia's 783 estuaries and enclosed waters were a particular focus of SOMER. Of these, it was concluded that 188 are experiencing a "real" or "potential" threat to fisheries values, and 178 a "real" or "potential" threat to their conservation values. Most of the threatened estuaries are located in Queensland and NSW. The Commonwealth Government's recently released "Oceans Policy" discussion paper has called for the National Environmental Protection Council to develop a national environmental protection measure (NEPM) for estuarine and marine water quality. The paper also urges the adoption of mandatory national standards for ambient water quality, guidelines for achieving the standards and the adoption of a monitoring protocol. However, these suggestions have to be seen in the light of the current low level of political commitment to national approaches to environmental protection and policy.

THE COSTS OF COASTAL DAMAGE: NATURAL AND HUMAN-INDUCED

Historically, the sea level around Australia has risen and fallen substantially; 18,000 years ago it was considerably lower than at present, and 3500 years ago it was slightly higher than today. However, the current coastal configuration has been reasonably stable for the past 10,000 years or so. But natural processes of quite rapid coastal retreat in some areas and accretion in others continue; the former being much more common. For example, along the Ninety Mile Beach in

SA there has been considerable "natural" coastal erosion since the mid-1800s. Also, as a consequence of inappropriate coastal developments and the cutting-off of beach sediment supply, coastal erosion problems first started becoming serious in certain places in the 1920s and 1930s, but were especially problematic in areas like south-western WA, the Gold Coast and the Adelaide region in the 1960s, often following devastating storms. In both the latter two areas new legislation in the form of the Queensland *Beach Protection Act 1968* and SA's *Coastal Protection Act 1972* represented the favoured policy response to property loss and diminished public amenity.[54] Even a glimpse of these issues suggests the range and complexity of coastal zone public policy issues. For example: (1) Who should pay for costly coastal protection and/or refurbishment programmes? (2) What are the issues surrounding legal liability if and when it can be proven that artificial structures of various kinds have completely altered "natural" coastal processes and exacerbated subsequent erosion or accretion problems locally, or elsewhere? (3) What are the most appropriate institutional arrangements for "managing" the coastal zone, including the "mix" of private and public responsibilities?

Cost has always been controversial. With cut-backs in public expenditure, recent years have seen steadily mounting calls for a "user-pays" approach to coastal zone management.[55] For example, federal funding to the Great Barrier Reef Marine Park Authority (GBRMPA) fell by $1.5 million between 1996–97 and 1997–98 and is projected to fall another $3.1 million in 1998–99. Initially, in July 1993, the Authority's response was to institute a $2 Environment Management Charge (EMC or "reef tax") on all passengers taking boat excursions to the Great Barrier Reef, to defray some of the costs of environmental management. In April 1998, in the face of opposition from many tourism operators, this was increased to $4, and may well be increased again in the future. But in December 1997, some 17,000 fewer tourists took reef trips than in the previous December, a drop in revenue of $34,000.[56] Quite clearly, the federal government has forced the GBRMPA to accept the "logical" — but potentially environmentally damaging — connection between tourist visitation levels and revenues for conservation and environmental management purposes, a link that is also commonly being made now by most of the State governments.

As we have come to learn more about the peculiarities of the Australian physical environment it has become increasingly clear that one of the "sleeping giant" environmental problems in the coastal zone relates to the widespread presence of acid sulphate soils. One estimate is that over 2 million ha of these soils (containing an estimated 1 billion tonnes of iron pyrite) occur in areas, like the Tweed River catchment, where mangroves once grew at a time when the sea level was much higher than today. These soils can extend down to depths of 10 metres or more, and when left in their natural state they are not a problem. But if they are disturbed for the purposes of drainage, agricultural development or marina or resort construction, the sulphuric acid leaches out from the iron pyrite to pollute rivers and estuaries. In effect, these are "natural toxic waste dumps" where each tonne of pyrite can yield up to 1.5 tonnes of sulphuric acid, and their disturbance by human activity can have eventually disastrous consequences for aquaculture, commercial and recreational fishing, as well as for tourism in general. Marine and estuarine waters become seriously contaminated and the high acidity levels corrode building structures. The widespread presence of these soils, alone, points to the need for enormous care when it comes to choosing sites for coastal resort or marina developments.[57]

While there is no doubt that the present Commonwealth Government is resolved to devolve much of its existing responsibilities for environmental regulation to the States, in mid-1997 it gave an indication of its willingness to accept some responsibility for improving the condition of the coastal zone when it allocated $125 million over five years for this purpose from the $1.2 billion Natural Heritage Trust. This is called the "Coasts and Clean Seas" programme, and almost half of the total has been earmarked for water quality improvement projects, many in areas damaged by unplanned resort expansion in the past. One targeted project — at Hervey Bay in Queensland — is to develop a management plan to deal with the environmental problems resulting from rapid growth in accommodation and visitation. In another case $1 million has — belatedly — been allocated to tackle pollution problems in the Wallis Lake region of the central NSW coast. In 1996 this multi-purpose use region (tourism, recreation, farming and aquaculture) was identified as the source of oysters contaminated with sewerage effluent resulting in a serious Hepatitis A outbreak and the collapse of a major oyster farm industry. Subsequently, the identified polluter — Charles Gardner — received the harshest penalty ever handed down by an Australian court for an environmental crime. The Land and Environment Court fined Gardner $250,000 and sentenced him to 12 months imprisonment for illegally pumping 17 million litres of raw sewage into the Karuah River over a two-and-a-half year period. This case highlighted problems associated with unplanned and poorly regulated waste management practices in a high amenity, but environmentally stressed, coastal region, and follows the Codd Inquiry's finding in

NSW that the "failure rate" for septic tanks could be as high as 90%. Subsequently, in 1998, through the *Local Government (Approvals) (Amendment) (Sewage Management) Regulation* the NSW Government has significantly tightened the regulations relating to the approval and operation of the septic tank systems common in coastal settlements.[58] More recently, the same State government has introduced path-breaking new laws requiring local councils to produce management plans including details about which of their activities will promote the principles of ecologically sustainable development (ESD).[59]

Recently, many scientists have predicted a gradual sea-level rise as a consequence of human-induced atmospheric global warming and thermal expansion of the oceans. This would have a potentially disastrous impact on much of Australia's densely settled, low-lying coastline, especially if — as many climate experts suggest — it were also to be accompanied by an increased incidence of extreme weather events in the form of severe tropical and temperate storm activity.[60] As a brief reminder of what can happen along the Australian coastline, in March 1899 a tropical cyclone passed over Bathurst Bay in north Queensland. An anchored pearling fleet was destroyed with the loss of 300 lives, and the associated 13-metre storm surge carried sharks inland for some 30 km.[61] Enormous damage was wrought by tropical cyclone Tracy to Darwin in 1974 and tropical cyclones Joy (1990) and Justin (1997) to the coast of Queensland. Justin's damage bill in Queensland alone was in excess of $150 million, and included the destruction of a $5 million marina in Cairns. The extent of recent and continuing population shifts to the north (comparable with the rise in popularity of Florida as a residential and tourist locale in the United States of America) makes such natural disasters of mounting concern to insurance companies, State governments and private commercial interests. Such events should advance the cause of those advocating a precautionary approach to the settlement and development of Australia's coastal zone, especially in the coastal tropics and northern NSW. While hazards such as severe wind storms cannot be prevented, loss mitigation through such mechanisms as restrictive zoning and enforced building codes is something that can be controlled.[62]

The precautionary principle is yet to be widely adopted and accepted in Australia. But as early as 1975 it was incorporated into the *Great Barrier Reef Marine Park Act* and more recently it was included in the 1992 Intergovernmental Agreement on the Environment as one of the principles that the various State parties agreed would "inform" their environmental decision making.

Needless to add, the IGAE does not mandate the principle and, indeed, in a recent Federal Court case (*Friends of Hinchinbrook Society Inc v Minister for Environment* (1997) 142 ALR 632) Sackville J. argued that the principle is not a relevant consideration that the Minister must take into account under the *World Heritage Properties Conservation Act 1983*.[63]

SCIENTIFIC UNCERTAINTY

Coastal environments are enormously complex, four-dimensional systems which are constantly evolving in space and time, which can sometimes change dramatically as a consequence of sudden and dramatic climatic or other events, and which also are impacted by a broad range of human activities, both on land and offshore. Knowledge of the interactions in the various "nested hierarchical systems" involved is steadily improving, but there is still a high degree of uncertainty and, in many cases, full understanding has come far too late.[64] The recency of scientific knowledge concerning the ecological significance of such "unaesthetic" ecosystems as mangroves is one such example (there are 39 species along 6000 km of shoreline) and the conclusions still have not been as well communicated as they might have been outside the professional scientific community. Indeed, the "Estuaries and the sea" section of the 1996 national *State of the Environment Report* repeatedly used such phrases as "we have few data on ...", or "we do not have enough information to assess ...".[65]

This level of uncertainty creates considerable management problems, especially in situations where specific user groups feel themselves unfairly disadvantaged. In 1994, for example, after an exhaustive, $5 million study, the NSW State Government drew up a draft management plan for a large Aquatic Reserve at Jervis Bay (mentioned earlier in this chapter). "Protected areas" were a key feature of this plan but these were contested by both recreational and commercial fishing interests on the grounds that:

- restricting fishing in one area places higher pressure on adjacent areas;
- there was limited scientific evidence to justify either the locations or sizes of the protected zones; and
- inadequate attention was paid to costing issues having to do with compliance and monitoring.[66]

Because of the scientific uncertainties involved, environmental impact assessment procedures really should conclude with much greater frequency that resort and related developments should not be allowed to proceed. Yet in their recent appraisal of the quality of the scientific information contained in a number of recent, tourism-related Environmental Impact Assessment (EIA) studies in Australia, Warnken and Buckley lend added weight to the proposition that EIA is often little more than a ritual exercise in "rubber-stamping" development decisions that have already been made and that are frequently quite advanced in terms of the financial and other commitments made. This was the substance of an unsuccessful legal challenge mounted by the Australian Conservation Foundation against the Commonwealth Government in 1978 when, in its enthusiasm to encourage direct foreign investment, the government gave the go-ahead to the Iwasaki resort project prior to the release of the Environmental Impact Statement. Warnken and Buckley conclude that "... the overall quality of EIA and monitoring for tourism development in Australia during the past 15 years has not been high", and that, further, "As an exercise in applied science ... EIA falls a very long way short of the most basic standards."[67]

INTEGRATED COASTAL ZONE MANAGEMENT

It should now be abundantly clear that that problematic geographical entity, "the coastal zone", or "the shoreline", sandwiched between two quite different physical worlds, poses unique and considerable problems for policy makers and managers. As Clark has emphasised, "Most countries have conservation programmes that address land resources or that address water resources, but too few countries treat them together in a unified framework."[68] Aspiring towards this goal is known as "integrated coastal zone management" (ICZM), or "integrated coastal management" (ICM) and — like the companion concept, "ecologically sustainable development" — is a topic about which there is now a vast body of literature, both in Australia and internationally.[69] ICZM involves balancing the various competing demands on coastal resources, but there is heated debate about precisely how to accomplish this, and what should be the appropriate regulatory régime. Often, as already noted, policy is implemented in a context of poor or non-existent ecological understanding.

Following the ambitious and highly publicised involvement of over 60 organisations in the formulation of the 25-year, Great Barrier Reef World Heritage Area Strategic Plan, which started in 1991, the Great Barrier Reef is often cited as a world-class example of ICZM. However, a major shortcoming has been the lack of involvement of onshore commercial interests such as the banana and sugar industries. The latter industry is worth around $5 billion per year to the

Australian economy and is particularly important in coastal northern Queensland where there is still much uncleared coastal land. The enormous (and irrational) economic pressure to expand the industry for export purposes conflicts with growing evidence that land clearing for plantations in coastal catchments is generating a total of around 15 million tonnes of sediment, loaded with phosphorous and nitrogen, which is being trapped between the reef and the shore. Preliminary evidence suggests that fish populations and coral health are both being affected. In the long term, this will impact significantly on the tourism-earning potential of the World Heritage area. The Cooperative Research Centre for Sustainable Sugar Production is currently undertaking scientific measurements, but already the sugar industry has pointed out that cane growing uses less than 10% of the reef catchment area, that there are also "natural" processes of coral decline at work, and that there are other, contributing land uses such as grazing and tourism resort development that also need to be investigated.[70] What is becoming increasingly clear is that the build-up of greenhouse gases in the atmosphere now appears to be significantly reducing calcification rates in coral reefs through a kind of underwater "acid rain" effect and that this, in turn, saps coral strength.[71] A combination of nutrient accumulation, cyclonic storm damage, floods, increased sedimentation and weakened coral could have a disastrous long-term impact on one of Australia's most prized tourist drawcards, and is a further indictment of the short-sightedness of the Howard Government's negotiated policy response at the Third Conference of the Parties to the United Nations Framework Convention on Climate Change, held in Kyoto in December 1997.[72]

Mention has already been made briefly of national competition policy. The link between this and integrated coastal zone management became clear in 1998 when a coalition of commercial fishing organisations, the Australian Conservation Foundation, the GBRMPA and the Rockhampton City Council, pressured the National Competition Council to take environmental damage into account before handing over "competition payments" to the Queensland Government to help pay for the Nathan Dam in the Fitzroy basin. This latest dam proposal is largely to provide irrigation water for cotton growing, but the green coalition has voiced serious concerns about the offshore environmental effects on tourism, ecosystem health and commercial fishing, as well as about the "uncompetitive" subsidisation of inappropriate new irrigation schemes.[73]

Making progress towards ICZM is even more complicated in a federated state such as Australia because of the different administrative "layers" and the changes in their interrelationships and powers over time.[74] While local government, through planning and development powers, has traditionally played, and often continues to play, arguably the most significant rôle in coastal zone land-use decision making, State governments in recent times, not least in Queensland and Victoria, have begun to enforce considerable "external" control over the activities of local government. The States also hold title to an area extending to three nautical miles offshore and, since the 1983 "Off-shore Constitutional Settlement", share management of the territorial sea beyond that with the Commonwealth government in relation to such things as hydrocarbon resources, fisheries and marine parks. The Commonwealth government, in turn, administers about fifty Acts of direct relevance to the coastal area and also has responsibilities flowing from Australia's ratification of a number of international conventions such as the Ramsar (Wetlands), Biodiversity and World Heritage Conventions.[75]

It has largely been left up to the individual States to develop their own coastal management strategies, more or less independently. Current developments have been called at best "embryonic with much more effort needed to fully integrate activities across the various sectors in order to achieve truly integrated coastal zone management".[76] What is desperately needed in Australia at the present time is for the Commonwealth Government to play a much stronger lead rôle in terms of the national integration of coastal zone management and for agreed national criteria and conditions for such things as commercial developments in or near ecologically sensitive sites such as estuaries. This points simultaneously to a need for greater emphasis on regional planning as a key policy instrument. Moreover, regional delimitation should be based upon ecological criteria, and regional plans should be subject to robust EIA procedures. These are by no means new suggestions, but as with so many aspects of environmental policy in Australia in recent times, they run directly counter to the existing economic orthodoxy and to the continuing power of the States' rights agenda.[77]

SYDNEY: SUSTAINABLE CITY?

R.E. Taplin

The medium to long term quality of life for Sydney's residents — ten, twenty and fifty years hence — is being determined by critical decisions being made now, and those which will be made over the next few years. Choices are now being made for the Sydney region in planning and urban design, transport, air pollution and greenhouse. All have economic, social, environmental and demographic ramifications. They will not only shape the type of city that Sydney will be, they will determine whether it develops sustainably.

This chapter discusses the concept of sustainable development and reviews suggested practice elsewhere. It reports on a "stakeholder" survey conducted in Sydney during 1998, which tends to show that awareness of sustainability as a city planning problem is not yet widespread. It concludes with some suggestions for the direction of urban planning in Sydney.[1]

SUSTAINABLE DEVELOPMENT AND CITIES

The special problems affecting cities make the definition of sustainable development, as it applies to them, very complex. Choices about urban sustainability are currently being made in other urban centres in Australia, as well as in many cities worldwide. During the 1990s some cities have changed their approaches to sustainability issues. Best-practice award programmes for city sustainability have been instituted by the United Nations Centre for Housing and Settlements (UNCHS) and the International Council for Local Environmental Initiatives and recognition has been given via these awards to cities that have visibly improved the quality of their living environments.

SUSTAINABLE DEVELOPMENT

Sustainable development, as a concept, has been accused of meaning all things to all people; many definitions have been put forward. It has been widely supported for over a decade by politicians, bureaucrats and business people as well as those concerned about environmental protection because it accommodates economic as well as environmental concerns. Milbrath argues that thinking environmentally is urgently needed in public discourse if we are to take a sustainable pathway to the future. He says sustainable development means "… learning better ways of enjoying life without injuring the life systems that sustain us and other creatures". Milbrath also maintains that "A society trying to be sustainable must maintain the integrity of life systems. A contemplated action is right when it tends to maintain the ecological diversity, integrity and sustainability of Earth's life systems, and wrong when it tends otherwise."[2] Lowe says that the best short definition of sustainable development is along the lines of that given in the mid-1980s World Commission on Environment and Development's Brundtland report: "a pattern of activity which meets the needs of the present generation without reducing the opportunities to future generations".[3] The United Nations Development Programme (UNDP) has adopted the concept of sustainable human development and defines it as "… development that not only generates economic growth, but distributes its benefits equitably; that regenerates the environment rather than destroys it; and that empowers people rather than marginalises them".[4] The term "ecologically sustainable development" (ESD) has been widely used in Australia; the word "ecologically" is included to emphasise the natural environment aspects of sustainable development.

In 1992, the federal government suggested, in the National Strategy for Ecologically Sustainable Development, the following simple working definition for ecologically sustainable development in Australia:

> Ecologically Sustainable Development is development which aims to meet the needs of Australia today, while conserving its ecosystems for the benefit of future generations.[5]

The National Strategy maintains that there are two main features that distinguish sustainable development from development:

1 the need to consider, in an integrated way, the wider economic, social and environmental implications of our decisions and actions for Australia, the international community and the biosphere; and
2 the need to take a long-term rather than a short-term view when taking those decisions and actions.[6]

The NSW *Protection of the Environment Administration Act 1991* defines ecologically sustainable development as "… the effective integration of economic and environmental considerations in decision making processes". The 1997 Amendment to the NSW *Local Government Act*, which requires councils to adopt a "strategic whole of council approach" to ESD and to respond positively to environmental problems in their areas came into force on 1 January 1998. The Act defines ESD as involving the following principles:

• the Precautionary Principle;
• intergenerational equity;
• conservation of biological and ecological integrity; and
• improved valuation, pricing and incentive mechanisms incorporating the Polluter Pays Principle and accounting for full life cycle costs recovery.

THE GREENHOUSE POLICY CONTEXT: FROM GLOBAL TO LOCAL

The United Nations Framework Convention on Climate Change (FCCC) was opened for signature at the UN Conference on Environment and Development in Rio de Janeiro in June 1992. The Convention came into force in March 1994, and by November 1998 had been ratified by 176 countries. Australia was one of the earliest to ratify the Convention, in late 1992. Additionally, in the same year the Australian government released a National Greenhouse Response Strategy.[7] However, in the years since then, Australia's progress in reducing its greenhouse gas emissions has been slow.

The Third Conference of the Parties (COP-3) to the FCCC was held in December 1997 in Kyoto, Japan. Intense negotiations in the months leading up to the meeting and at COP-3, led to parties to the FCCC adopting the Kyoto Protocol on 11 December 1997. In the Kyoto Protocol's Annex I, parties to the FCCC agreed to commitments with a view to reducing their overall emissions of six greenhouse gases by at least 5% below 1990 levels between 2008 and 2012. As of 13 November 1998, 60 countries have signed the Kyoto Protocol including Australia. While agreement was reached to cut emissions globally via the Kyoto Protocol, Australia was permitted to increase output of greenhouse gases by 8% above 1990 levels by 2008–12. This was due to Australia's persistence in pushing for recognition of its "unique" circumstances with regard to climate change. Australia argued that its trade and competitive profile and economic dependence on fossil fuel made many specific greenhouse policies and measures inappropriate for Australia to adopt and implement. Meg McDonald, Australian Ambassador for the Environment who led Australia's delegation to Kyoto said: "It's a major achievement that we ... got much more significant cuts than anyone believed possible".[8]

In late 1998, the Australian government released a new National Greenhouse Strategy, a cooperative effort of the Commonwealth, State and Territory governments. The strategy includes policies to promote efficient transport and sustainable urban planning. As noted in the strategy, "Transport was responsible for 17% of Australia's net greenhouse gas emissions and 24% of emissions produced through activities involving the use of energy in 1996."[9]

Additional greenhouse policy measures relating to urban sustainability in the 1998 National Greenhouse Strategy include:

- integrating urban land use and transport planning;
- promoting best practice in transport and land-use planning;
- developing greenhouse performance indicators for all urban centres with populations greater than 40,000;
- developing and applying an "integrated investment framework" for funding of urban transport that takes into account economic, social, environmental and greenhouse costs and benefits;
- promoting telecommuting and ride sharing;
- optimising greenhouse outcomes in traffic management;
- improving public transport services and investigation of new public transport modes and technologies;
- encouraging greater use of walking and cycling.

This suite of policies builds on the urban planning and transport goals of the 1992 National Greenhouse Response Strategy and, if seriously pursued, could result in considerable improvement in greenhouse policy implementation in Australian cities.

WHAT IS URBAN SUSTAINABLE DEVELOPMENT?

The concept of a sustainable city and formulation and implementation of policy to enable urban environmental transformation to sustainability has been the focus of many reports, papers, books and conference declarations. The Newcastle Declaration is a recent example. It was endorsed in June 1997 at the Pathways to Sustainability: Local Initiatives for Cities and Towns international conference held in Newcastle, NSW. The declaration emphasises active community participation and partnerships in enhancing local sustainability together with participatory mechanisms for monitoring, feedback and accountability. Two reports released by the federal government before the release of the National Strategy for Ecologically Sustainable Development in December 1992 focus on interpreting the principles of ESD for cities in the Australian context.[10] They suggest that the Australian cities of the future will be consistent with ESD principles if they:

- contribute to material wellbeing by not imposing economic costs on society through the inefficiencies that arise from current urban problems;
- contribute to non-material wellbeing through positive contribution to quality of life and high-quality urban living, making the most of advantages that urban life can bring;
- contribute to intergenerational equity through providing urban infrastructure keyed to the long-term needs of the city, so that future generations can reap the benefits of far-sighted decisions made now;
- contribute to intragenerational equity through removing locational disadvantages and other urban-related inequities so that cities will be fairer;
- contribute to maintaining natural ecosystems through reductions in emissions of greenhouse and ozone-depleting gases from urban energy use; and
- contribute to maintaining "social ecosystems" — that is, social and cultural habitats and environments that work to the benefit of present and future inhabitants.

Frecker, discussing the rôle of local government in urban sustainable development and in combating the greenhouse effect, focusses on citizens' perceptions of their local community environments, saying "... we need to determine the nature of the sustainable environment and the sustainable society in which we all want to live".[11] A United Nations Development Programme report on effective practices in urban management identifies some of the obstacles to the vision of sustainable development in relation to urban transformation. It nominates: hopelessness and despair (that paralyses policy makers and general public alike); outmoded assumptions of policy makers; isolation among sectors, disciplines and cities; counterproductive incentives; resistance to change; entrenched bureaucracy; corruption; and selfishness.[12]

METHODS FOR ASCERTAINING THE SUSTAINABILITY OF CITIES

There are several approaches that are used to assess the sustainability of cities. These utilise different approaches, including:

- state of the environment reporting[13]
- urban metabolism analysis[14]
- ecological footprint assessment[15]
- environmental costing[16]
- best practices assessment[17]

Two sets of criteria associated with best practices assessment are worthy of note. Firstly, best practice in relation to urban sustainability has been defined by UNCHS as "a project that visibly improves the quality of the living environment and that can serve as a model for others". Best practices are expected to have three attributes:

1 "They must have an impact, i.e., provide tangible improvements in people's lives";
2 "They must be characterized by partnerships between local and national governments, community organizations, the private sector and international agencies"; and
3 "They must demonstrate sustainability through changed legislation, policies and long-term, rather than one-off, funding methods."[18]

Secondly, the European Sustainable Cities Reports of 1992 and 1996 provide a framework for evaluation of local sustainable development.[19] The Final Report identifies the following four principles as the basis of city sustainability:

1 the principle of urban management;
2 the principle of policy integration — horizontal and vertical integration of social, environmental and economic dimensions;
3 the principle of ecosystems thinking — based on a dual network approach of an energy, natural resources and waste production

network and an infrastructure (for example, regulation of traffic)
network; and
4 the principle of cooperation and partnership — between levels,
   organisations and interests.[20]

Five main groups of tools for sustainable development implementation are advocated:

1 collaboration and partnership;
2 policy integration;
3 market mechanisms;
4 information management; and
5 measuring and monitoring.[21]

MOBILITY AND ACCESS

Chapter 7 of *European Sustainable Cities: First Report* addresses key
sustainability issues for mobility and access in the urban environment.
It suggests actions to reduce the use of private cars but also comments that "it is important to recognise that the car is difficult to
replace for certain journeys".[22] In relation to urban transport systems, it advocates a number of measures. The land-use planning
strategies should reduce the need for mobility and allow for the
development of alternatives to road transport. "Urban transport systems which give priority to public transport, pedestrians and cyclists
and provision of adequate link-ups between the different stages of
the journey" should be promoted. Use of the private car should be
"more environmentally rational" and "changes in driving rules and
habits" should be encouraged. Reduction of urban traffic should
accord with "specific and measurable targets" to "provide a focus for
action and also provide a basis against which to measure progress and
make any necessary policy adjustments". The Report also suggests
that policy makers should question whether a better quality of life
results from ever more rapid transport, and hence of the relationship
between accessibility and sustainability. Funding priorities should be
established.

In a series of recommendations, the Report suggests the development of "… intermodal transport systems where complementarity
rather than competition between modes is promoted". For public
transport, it sees a need for attention to service levels, presentation
and safety. Accessibility for the handicapped is also important. Use of
"park and ride" schemes can be encouraged if siting is good, pricing
is attractive and security extends to cars parked and to their drivers.
Reduction of parking space in city centres may be coupled with

"other dissuasive measures for cars". Trams, trolleybuses or light rail systems could be "revived" or reintroduced. Specialist vehicles or unusual fuels can be explored.

To accompany these measures, the Report also recommends good publicity, and harnessing the "large majorities in favour of preferential treatment of the more environment friendly mode of transport".[23]

SUSTAINABLE CITIES: INTERNATIONAL BEST PRACTICE CASES

Some cities are internationally recognised as having implemented very successful sustainability programmes and many of them have received best practice awards. They are not the only cities that are active in the field, but each has made landmark progress. Table 9.1 lists each city and its programme.[24]

Table 9.1: Best practice cities

Curitiba, Brazil	Sustainable Urban Development and a Mass Transit System that Works
Hamilton-Wentworth, Canada	Creating a Sustainable Community: Hamilton's VISION 2000
Toronto, Canada	Strategy to Reduce CO_2 Emissions
Aalborg, Denmark	Municipality of Aalborg: Environmental Management Agreements
Tampere, Finland	Combating Climate Change in Tampere
Solingen, Germany	Masterplan of Solingen in the Spirit of Sustainable Development
Gothenburg, Sweden	Improving Living Environments through Comprehensive Local Policy
Leicester, UK	"Blueprint" for Leicester
Chattanooga, USA	Chattanooga, the Sustainable City
Portland, USA	Sustainable Programmes in Portland

Curitiba, Hamilton-Wentworth, Leicester, Chattanooga and Portland have introduced comprehensive frameworks for city sustainability policy. Two criteria appear to be required for the "policy space" for a comprehensive approach to city sustainability to develop: (1) institutional or administrative flexibility (that is, willingness of local authorities to adopt a philosophy of sustainable development) and (2) community involvement and ownership in the concept of local sustainability.

SUSTAINABLE DEVELOPMENT FOR SYDNEY: STAKEHOLDERS' VIEWS

Policy processes are far from transparent, and may be quite invisible. Furthermore, it is often difficult and can even be counterproductive to attempt to trace policy "blow by blow". Where policy is still in flux, most common methodologies are less than adequate. Consequently, a survey of persons engaged in, or having major concerns about policy, was conducted, to ascertain perceptions both of Sydney's progress toward sustainability and the trends for the future.

THE PROBLEMATIC

There are several key questions about progress with, and barriers to, formulation and implementation of sustainability policy for Sydney that need to be examined. Sustainable development requires definition for specific cities, in this case Sydney. The framework of economic activity and its effect on Sydney's settlement patterns, transport use and the daily life of citizens must be understood, especially as it affects likely success of sustainability policies. Quality of life for ordinary citizens in Sydney requires evaluation, and the possible contributions ecological sustainability can make to it explored. And, lastly, the question of power: who actually builds and shapes Sydney? In considering these questions, Wilheim's words are pertinent:

> In addition to planners and governments, real estate, business, land owners, private transport companies, corporate lobbies, social movements, homeless ... they are all stakeholders and very active in the shaping of cities.[25]

To obtain the views and perceptions of people close to, or with interests in, the policy-making process, in order to evaluate current thinking about sustainable development for the Sydney Basin, stakeholder representatives were interviewed from local government, regional organisations of councils, State government and business and industry. Interviewees totalled 44, 18 female and 26 male. All were selected professionals who come into contact with sustainability issues in their day-to-day working lives. Twenty-four were from 13 local government authorities, 4 from 3 regional organisations of councils, 8 from 7 State government agencies and 8 from 6 companies and organisations in the business and industry sector. Interviews were face-to-face, open-ended and semi-structured; all questions were of a qualitative nature. Each interview required between 40 and 70 minutes. The questions posed to the interviewees were:

1 What type of actions/activities being undertaken or being planned to be taken in the Sydney Region are you aware of that you believe are sustainable?

2 What actions/activities being undertaken or planned are not sustainable?

3 What rôle does sustainable development play in your own work?

4 How do you think sustainable development issues in Sydney rate in relation to economic issues? For example, are there contradictions between policies for economic development versus environmental sustainability?

5 What is your opinion of how sustainable development is being addressed in current planning for the Sydney Region?

6 Are stakeholders and citizens given adequate opportunity to engage in the policy process in relation to Sydney's sustainability?

7 Is the private sector in Sydney sufficiently involved in the sustainable development process?

8 How do you think that business and industry can best be involved in the sustainable development of Sydney?

9 What do you think are the foremost issues that need to be addressed for Sydney to move towards becoming a sustainable city?

10 Do you have any other comments regarding the potential for Sydney to move towards becoming a sustainable city?

FINDINGS

Almost all of the stakeholders interviewed indicated that activities are being undertaken in Sydney that contribute to sustainable development. But the comments and degree of enthusiasm regarding progress being made varied, showing that in many ways sustainability initiatives in Sydney are undeveloped or have not developed nearly as far as they might.

> There is potential rather than actual at the moment. A number of councils are working on it. A few councils are working gently to link with strategic planning. It is looking at fairly massive social change.

In a number of responses, the Olympics was raised as a prime example of sustainable development implementation in Sydney. Complimentary comments commending the positive example set in the approach that has been implemented for the Olympic site development came from business and local and State government sources. One of the stakeholders said:

> The Olympics is a symbol. It is showcase stuff and will set a lot of precedents. Sustainability problems are being addressed that would not have been touched if the Olympics hadn't happened.

Although these comments were supportive, some negative aspects were also raised.

> The Olympics was going to be serious attempt at ESD but there's been quite a bit of watering down and outcomes are not as good as they should be. The construction industry has provided obstacles.

State of the Environment (SoE) reporting was cited as a sustainable activity and clearly seen as a tool to assist in providing regular assessments of sustainability indicators such as air quality. One respondent aptly characterised it:

> SoE reporting provides a feedback loop. As a process it will improve over time. Not all councils are using it.

The ESD Amendment to the NSW *Local Government Act* came into force on 1 January 1998. It requires local government in NSW to take a "whole of council" approach in implementing ESD. Comments by those interviewed with regard to the concept embodied in, and the potential impact of, the ESD Amendment were broadly favourable. However, several concerns were raised about implementation of the ESD Amendment and the lack of specific guidelines available.

Some respondents also identified problems with the term ESD; for example, one said that the "E" is seen as "deep green" while another saw the "D" as promoting too much of a "development premise". Concerns were also raised about the marked lack of availability of both human and financial resources for implementation within local government. Comparisons were drawn with the State government which is seen to have greater resources than councils and yet to be less actively implementing ESD.

Transport and Sydney's air quality were linked in responses on transport sustainability. Integrated planning was one theme that respondents emphasised as important and starting to occur:

> ESD Principles are the principal objective of the new Transport Plan ... it is an integrated strategy and a plan for the next twenty years. It includes regional action plans relevant for particular areas.

> The integrated transport plan is a "sea change" document. It will have a big impact if it comes about.

With reference to energy and greenhouse, NSW's Sustainable Energy Development Authority (SEDA) activities were the most commonly cited examples of sustainable development initiatives. Many of the respondents mentioned specific SEDA programmes, such as the Greenlight Consortium, Energy Smart Homes, Energy

Smart Business and programmes with industry dealing with energy consumption. By contrast only two respondents mentioned the federal government's Greenhouse Challenge programme and no one mentioned the new Federal Greenhouse Allies programme for small and medium enterprises.

Though these opinions were positive, strong criticisms were also made and many examples were given of unsustainable activities by respondents from business and industry, local government and regional organisations of councils:

> I think most development at the moment isn't sustainable. There are piecemeal initiatives but a lot don't do them.

Areas cited by all respondents as unsustainable included current urban planning and design, urban fringe development and expansion, Sydney's population expansion, economic forces and market activity in the city, social inequity, Sydney's housing stock and transport in Sydney. Concerns about transport included the issues of air pollution and the relationship between employment location and journey to work.

Further revealing responses on unsustainable activities focussed on the topic of implementation of ESD policy at the federal, state and local levels as a barrier to sustainability. Several reasons were given:

> There is no link up the chain; State Government do not transparently have a "whole of government" approach. Federal and State Government need to demonstrate a high level of support [to local government].

> Local governments are doing their bit but not the feds. Success at the local level hinges on state and federal commitment.

> The NSW State Government and the Department of Local Government's perception of ESD is very narrow. There is a lack of state government backup at the policy level: i.e., no leadership. The State Government response is reflective of the Federal Government approach — it is trying to devolve to local government.

> The Federal Government gives lipservice to sustainability. Their own actions are not consistent with what they say.

Answers from State government respondents were much more optimistic than those of other respondents and focussed on issues relating to working towards sustainability and monitoring progress.

> The biggest issue we face is that the sorts of [sustainability] issues we've talked about are not being dealt with in a uniform way. We are dealing with 42 councils [in Sydney]. Some local councils have been very

innovative and have probably done more than a greater metropolitan area plan or ESD would have required but others have done less. It will take quite an extended period to get to where the total outcome [for Sydney] is affected. For air, it will take ten years to stop growth in per capita VKT [vehicle kilometres travelled] and twenty years to stop growth in overall VKT and this is an ambitious vision.

We really don't have the models or the data to get a high degree of progress and monitor this. We are not able to monitor this. We are not able to quantify where we relate to a sustainable city. We don't have the data to commission the research to get a good understanding of the structure of the population and the structure of the economy that are leading us to adverse environmental impacts. Also increasing size of GNP now may not have the same adverse impact on the environment as in the past.

Most responses on the relationship between sustainable development issues and economic issues in Sydney pointed to conflicts and contradictions between sustainable development policies and economic policies. Some, however, decried the perception of conflict, stressing the interdependence of economic development and environmental sustainability. One representative from business and industry pertinently emphasised that "Sustainable development itself is triple bottom line: economic, social and environmental and we shouldn't lose sight of this." Several respondents commented that they believed that there are deficiencies in mainstream economics and accounting perspectives as compared with environmental economics and accounting approaches, since only the latter could detect sustainability improvements.

The types of comments made about the rôle of sustainable development in current planning for Sydney indicate considerable dissatisfaction. Statements included: "We need to be doing more …", "We are early in the process …", "There isn't a coherent strategy …", and "We don't have an overall framework …".

Nevertheless positive views expressed about current urban planning and its impact on sustainability included this comment:

The new metro urban development programme of DUAP [NSW Department of Urban Affairs and Planning] is beginning to come to terms with the criteria needed for new urban development needs ie dealing with environmental factors and public transport factors. It's quite important that has happened.

Also, in a further group of responses from business and industry, local and State government, policies directed towards urban consolidation and creating a compact city were commended as moving towards sustainability:

Urban consolidation policy did not target sustainability originally but it's quite adaptable and quite useful in discouraging developing on the fringe. The City of Sydney and South Sydney City Councils have definitely taken this up. There is a huge boom in inner city development, market forces have allowed residential redevelopment along sustainability lines.

Urban development planning for where greenfield sites will be in the future is using criteria such as the degree that areas can be served by public transport and regional air quality. It's the first time that we have tried to do urban planning in quite this way.

However, several of the respondents despaired of the fact that Sydney does not have a comprehensive plan based on sustainability principles. Many of the respondents focussed on structural factors as being obstacles to better planning for Sydney. Problems with coordination due to fragmentation of decision making both at the State government level between agencies and at the council level due to the large number of local government areas in Sydney, were highlighted. The need for integration of decision making and for local government to be as fully involved as possible, when strategies or plans for the Greater Sydney Metropolitan Region are devised, was emphasised.

Transport and urban consolidation were the two biggest areas of contention that respondents emphasised. The population size of Sydney was also raised: "Questions such as what are reasonable population expectations for the Cumberland Basin and what form of living space should that population dwell in are not being answered."

Comments on the availability of opportunities for stakeholders and ordinary citizens to engage in the sustainability policy process pointed to extreme differences in attitudes; they ranged from the perception that there is too much stakeholder and community involvement to the feeling that there is not enough involvement. One council official said: "Consultation processes are extensive. We consult till the cows come home!" Some comments were critical of public participation procedures as only paying lipservice to community involvement.

Consultation is not truly participatory. We are not workshopping and developing plans but saying "this is what we are going to do, do you have any problems?"

One respondent from the business and industry group said "I don't think people [in general] understand sustainable development."

Most of the respondents said that they felt that the private sector could be far more involved in the sustainable development process. Compliance with environmental regulations was cited as an obvious area of involvement for business and industry. A need for education of members of the private sector with regard to the principles of sustainable development was expressed, as a lack of sustainability literacy was perceived as a problem. One industry respondent said:

> The most active are large enterprises; small and medium enterprises don't understand [sustainable development] and are not involved. They are locked into economic motivation. Sustainable development is a 25-year vision and is not related to their timeframe.

Several apt suggestions were made about ways for business and industry to be best involved in Sydney's sustainable development:

- look at their own operations in terms of improving practices along sustainability lines;
- involve themselves in sustainable development via market and economic involvement;
- ensure that they comply with regulation as a minimum and aim for best practice;
- educate employees about sustainable development;
- engage in environmental reporting.

Suggestions were also made about how government could foster business and industry involvement in sustainable development, via:

- partnerships with, or incentives from government;
- awards for best practice which have public relations returns for business and industry.

Use by industry of the sustainability legacy of the Olympics was also discussed:

> I'd like to see the information that has been learnt with the Olympics to be made available as a central database of information. There needs to be a progressive new agency to be more responsive to industry needs [with regard to] sustainable development that is industry led with government support. Sydney needs to have a life after September 2000. Industry needs to tell other industry how they did it. There is, of course, the question of the competitive advantage of the knowledge. It's the double edged sword in the "business" of the environment.

Eight well-defined areas for sustainability improvement were raised by respondents:

1 Transport;
2 Population;
3 Planning (vision);
4 Decision-making knowledge;
5 Changing human behaviour and consumer demand via community education;
6 Energy use;
7 ESD — finding a balance between social, environmental and economic factors; and
8 Coordination, leadership and authority for implementation.

Examples of comments made by the interviewees include:

> We need to determine what does being a sustainable city mean for Sydney and a description of what is sustainable as possible ie what is a reasonable target for us to look at and can we identify the milestones that can be ticked off.

> In many senses NSW has shown great leadership in setting up legislation but it now needs to be made to work.

But the respondents mentioned a host of other issues that need to be addressed, including transport infrastructure, the journey to work, targets for VKT (vehicle kilometres travelled), modal split in the movement of freight (road versus rail), road congestion, traffic noise, freeways, lack of planning for a second airport, air quality, compact city issues, population, waste and its long distance haulage, sewerage, pollution by nitrous oxides and carbon dioxide, air pollution generally, Australia's Kyoto commitments and their impact on greenhouse, energy use both domestic and commercial, and especially dependence on coal, sensible management of water, recycling water, stormwater runoff, sustainable use of agricultural land, urban encroachment on rural land, availability of industrial land, social justice, quality of life, crime, homelessness and residential and rural heritage.

One of the less optimistic interviewees said:

> I'm not sure that it's really possible. A city of this size with its demand for business activity going on can't really be sustainable. Maybe this will be possible in 150 years. Now it's too much of a cost commitment.

Perceptions from local government and regional organisations of councils about the potential for Sydney to become a sustainable city revealed that considerable effort needs to be put into sustainable development policy formulation and implementation:

> It would certainly need a big effort from the three tiers of government

involving: resources from federal government, directives from state government, and cooperation of local government. It would also need to involve a change in mindset of people involved.

It's going to take some bold steps to pull it all together. One organisation needs to take responsibility. Sustainable development is still not mainstream policy. If NSW produced a sustainable strategy for NSW or Sydney, it would make it easier for councils. State government could have a bigger rôle in providing coordination.

I think the biggest issue is when you say "No". I think we should have done that already in Sydney. As Australia's premium global city, the demand for people to live here will grow. You can't look at Sydney in isolation of the development of regional centres. They need to be made attractive so the demand for people to live in Sydney is lessened. We need to decide on a population size and limit it.

The Olympics project ESD messages should be distributed. It could be the foundation stone for ESD policy for the State.

We do need better alliances between public and private in Sydney.

One State government respondent said: "Closeknit coordination between agencies is needed on sustainable development views within government organisations. This is not being practised as well as it could be."

Finally, some of the comments made by those interviewed from business and industry were:

There is a need for better planning, management, and practical solutions which involve all levels of government.

I'm fairly pessimistic. It requires a strong sense of vision and a capacity to communicate that vision to make it happen. It needs to be a vision that recognises that prosperity and sustainability are interlinked and have economic, social and environmental dimensions.

All of the issues arising from the interviews with stakeholders about progress with sustainable development in Sydney indicate that tackling Sydney's sustainability is not an easy endeavour. Some progress has been made to date but many obstacles need to be overcome before further progress is made.

COMPARING SYDNEY WITH INTERNATIONAL BEST PRACTICE

The comments made by the interviewees highlight both achievements in and barriers to implementation of sustainable development in Sydney. Benchmarking Sydney's progress with sustainable development with international best practice is a complex task. The best practice criteria referred to earlier in this chapter are demanding, but nevertheless some cities internationally are satisfying them. Currently, sustainable development policy formulation and implementation for the Sydney region as a whole does not accord with all of these guidelines. Aspects of best practice criteria are conformed with, for example, NSW legislation embodying ESD, including the 1997 Ecologically Sustainable Development Amendment to the *Local Government Act*. And while there is no coordinated strategy that aims to move the Sydney region towards international best practice, a few forward-thinking councils are approaching sustainability with a best practice approach.

This study's stakeholder interviews reveal that the NSW government and local government authorities are implementing numerous disconnected policies which tend to work towards sustainability in the Sydney region. However, a coordinated sustainable development strategy embodying collaboration and partnerships, vertical and horizontal policy integration, market mechanisms, information management and measuring and monitoring has not been formulated, let alone commenced, in the Sydney region.

Also, comparison of Sydney's transport related policies with actions advocated in the European Sustainable Cities reports, as discussed earlier, does not place Sydney in a good position with regard to the key sustainability issues of mobility and access in the urban environment. Apart from implementation of specific and measurable targets in relation to the reduction of urban traffic which are incorporated in the new Transport Plan, interviewees' comments reveal that actions are "poor" or "working towards" sustainability goals. It is clear that Sydney is not measuring up well with approaches to transport sustainability adopted as best practice internationally.

CONCLUSIONS

This chapter has shown that sustainable development and the quality of life for Sydney's residents in the medium to long term is not a mainstream concern in Sydney. In fact, the concept of sustainable development appears not to be well understood by many in the elected and bureaucratic spheres of local and State government, business and industry and by members of the Sydney community in general. Nevertheless, critical decisions are being made now and over the next few years which will determine the social, economic, environmental and demographic future of Sydney. Planning and urban design and transport choices in particular will not only shape the type of city that Sydney will be, but will determine whether it develops as a livable city for its residents.

Local government is the only level of government where active implementation and involvement has occurred in sustainable development to date. Overall, it appears that those working at the local government level on sustainable development implementation are very critical of the lack of state and federal government involvement in sustainable development. They feel that there is a marked lack of support for local government efforts which is manifested in an absence of financial support. This is notwithstanding the existence of State legislation requiring that a whole of government approach for implementation of ESD should be undertaken by councils.

Activity at the federal and NSW government levels has focussed on policy formulation and legislation. These have important symbolic ramifications but more than symbolic policy is required for Sydney's future sustainability. The most viable of the NSW Government efforts to date have been activities of the Sustainable Energy Development Authority and the sustainable development approach implemented in the Olympics site development. Federal government appears to be backing away from sustainable development policy by handing responsibilities to state and local government without allocating funding resources to the very state and local levels they are devolving to, for ESD purposes. Also, although the new National Greenhouse Strategy includes commendable policies that promote urban sustainability and greenhouse gas emissions reduction from cities, it remains to be seen whether these will be effectively resourced and implemented.

Thus a whole of government approach to urban sustainable development is not being implemented currently at federal and state levels and local government authorities are struggling with the expectation that they should do so. The important arenas of public-private partnerships and partnerships between community organisations and government for sustainable development are being little considered.

The fact that Sydney needs to address its pressing urban management problems, such as air pollution, transport, energy, water, waste, among others, is not unique in Australia or internationally. Some councils in the Sydney region are trying hard to achieve best practice in local sustainability, but they are being impeded in their aspirations. To redress the situation in Sydney, considerably more action needs to be taken at both the state and federal levels. Other Australian cities are facing similar problems. In the case of air pollution, the Inquiry by the Australian Academy of Technological Sciences and Engineering in 1997 found that:

> ... while Australian urban ambient air quality is good in world terms, there is no room for complacency. Per capita, Australians are among the

world's highest pollutant emitters although fortunately emissions per unit area are low by world standards due to the relatively low population density of our cities.[26]

Sydney's sustainability status, in fact, is a warning to other Australian cities, especially if they have similar lackadaisical policies. If choices are not made about urban sustainability and incremental decisions continue to prevail, current and future urban quality of life will be compromised.

OPPORTUNITIES FOR POLICY CHANGE

Suggestions for policy improvements that may help Sydney move further towards sustainability arise from the issues raised by the stakeholder interviewees and lessons from cities where best practice has been implemented. Further action towards implementing sustainable development policy for Sydney may be achieved via:

- improved horizontal and vertical coordination between state and local government agencies on sustainable development;
- the formulation of a strategic sustainability plan for the greater Sydney metropolitan area where prosperity and sustainability goals are interlinked, and implementation of this strategy with vision and leadership;
- community education about sustainability;
- sustainable development partnerships or alliances between government, business and industry and community organisations;
- detailed guidelines for local government for implementation of the ESD Amendment to the *Local Government Act*;
- motivation or incentives for business and industry to be involved in sustainable development;
- one transport agency being designated as overall provider and coordinator;
- improvement of the sustainability knowledge base available to decision-makers in government, industry and the community, including knowledge gained through the Olympics developments.

Thus there are numerous viable lines of policy development for sustainability in Sydney.

The exact mix is likely to be determined by the evolving policy process, and is difficult to predict in advance. However, as the survey results make plain, one of the most intractable difficulties remains the general lack of awareness, both of the meaning and of the possibilities, of sustainable development in Sydney.

10

LOCAL ENVIRONMENTAL POLICY MAKING IN AUSTRALIA

G. Adams & M. Hine

The authors are professional practitioners in the arena of environmental management and policy, and have been integrally involved throughout almost the entire period of the 1990s in its development and implementation at the local level in SA. During that time their publications have mostly addressed issues related to environmental management practice on the part of local authorities and the communities which they represent. Therefore, this chapter is a first-hand account of how the formulation and delivery of local environmental policy in Australia generally, and SA specifically, have been influenced by the policy tensions in the Australian intergovernmental environmental policy arena in the 1990s. In this context, the emergence of Local Agenda 21 (LA21) is discussed and identified as an increasingly utilised and important local environmental policy framework which now places local government at the forefront of environmental policy in Australia. In the authors' view this situation mirrors environmental policy developments in most industrialised capitalist countries.

INTRODUCTION

The general subject of Australian environmental policy in the 1990s offers the student of politics little in terms of consistent and clearly defined paradigms or processes. However, the one policy area which has maintained enough consistency to progress from being almost totally disregarded to a point where it now constitutes an imperative in its own right is that of local environment policy. This has been an evolutionary process, central to the thesis presented here and heartening for those who have put in the long hours at the local coalface. This is because it has occurred despite the apparent lack of genuine commitment to local environmental policy processes by the makers of strategic policy frameworks at the national level. Furthermore, it has occurred in the face of the continued predominance, amongst many political scientists, of the conventional wisdom that policy and practice originating at the local level cannot have any implications for state, national or even global considerations, and can therefore be safely ignored. On the latter point, the indexes of the standard reference texts speak for themselves; but the former matter is one that is fundamental to the content of this chapter.

Despite this background, environmental management practice, implemented under the auspices of deliberate policies defined by local government authorities, has had a few readily identifiable champions operating at a national level in recent years. Outside of local government itself (individual councils, regional and state associations and the peak body, the Australian Local Government Association) the most durable and interactive champions have been those involved in the work done under the National Local Government Environmental Resource Network (NLGERN) banner, led by Dr Val Brown at the Australian National University, and by the Melbourne based national non-government organisation Environs Australia, formerly the Municipal Conservation Association.

The authors have spent almost the entire period of the 1990s directly involved in environmental policy and management processes centred on local government. Consequently they are acutely aware of the extent to which local government has emerged as an increasingly important player in the development and delivery of environmental policy in Australia.[1] Furthermore, through participation in interstate and international networks during this time, they have also been made aware that this is not a phenomenon unique to the politics of this country. Rather, it reflects a global trend that has seen the nature of governance generally, and environmental policy making specifically, in many industrial, capitalist countries change dramatically.[2]

Nationwide deregulation, decentralisation and devolution of traditional national or state level functions, including environmental management, to local government have significantly influenced these changes in governance, especially in Australia. This situation can be seen to have arisen as a result of fiscal constraints at a national level. The outcome has been to underscore a general shift from centralised policy-making towards local governments and communities playing an increasingly formative rôle in the development and delivery of environmental policy. Consequently, this trend towards devolution of responsibilities regarding environmental issues has contributed to local government being described as the "sleeping giant" of environmental politics.[3]

While these changes are clearly symptomatic of the recent general trend away from state interventionist strategies and policies at a national level, Farthing suggests there are also other societal issues and spatial factors which have led to local government's pivotal rôle in environmental policy. Firstly, despite the significance of macro trends such as global warming and loss of biodiversity, many of the specific issues that derive from these trends are local in nature, and therefore spatially restricted in an environmental and social sense. This has led to a strengthening of the connection between global imperatives and local action that was embodied in the catchcry, extensively used in the authors' line of work, "Think globally, act locally". This has more recently been termed "glocalisation".[4]

Secondly, there is the recognition that how people live their daily lives within a locality can have a significant impact on the environment. Therefore, if the environment is to be protected and human health and quality of life maintained there need to be fundamental changes in the lifestyle and local social processes, as opposed to national or international processes, that help to produce and reproduce the routines of daily life. In the authors' experience this view is clearly echoed across the whole gamut of local government approaches to environment policy and management, whether it be driven, for example, by strategic commitments to ecologically sustainable development on one side or by more narrowly focussed natural resources/catchment management issues on the other.

Thirdly, there is the point that policy and practice at the level of local government is itself an important determinant of environmental outcomes. This can be seen not only in terms of local government's traditional environmental regulation rôles but also through recognition of the fact that the very process of providing local government services can have its own significant environmental impacts.

THE EMERGENCE OF LOCAL AGENDA 21 AS A PUBLIC POLICY-MAKING PROCESS: AN INTERNATIONAL PERSPECTIVE

Having acknowledged the underlying dimension to local environment policy outlined above, we now turn our attention to the emergence of what we see as the centre piece of this framework, Local Agenda 21 (LA21).

LA21 has emerged as an increasingly important public policy process for addressing environmental and sustainability issues at a local level. It represents a local manifestation of Agenda 21, which was adopted at the Rio Earth Summit[5] in 1992 as a strategy to address global environmental problems, in the form of a blueprint for a sustainable world in the twenty-first century. Chapter 28 of Agenda 21 specifically identified the pivotal rôle that local governments should play in implementing Agenda 21 and its companion international environmental conventions.[6] Since 1992, more than 2000 local governments in 64 countries have established LA21 planning processes to implement Agenda 21 at a local level, and the number is growing.[7] In Britain, 170 local governments have commenced work on LA21s as part of a nationally supported programme.[8] By 1996, 40 Australian councils had commenced LA21s and a total of 120 were undertaking initiatives that sought to promote the principles of sustainable development.[9]

Agenda 21 did not set down a prescribed process for developing a LA21 and at that time there was very little information or direction for local governments to proceed with LA21s,[10] which has led to some LA21 practitioners describing the LA21 process as "like trying to sculpture fog". Therefore, since 1992 there has been a great deal of diversity in the approaches to LA21 taken by local governments both within Australia and overseas.

At an international level, the International Council for Local Environmental Initiatives (ICLEI) recommended a process for implementing LA21[11] and then produced a planning framework in 1996 derived from the experiences of Local Agenda 21 programmes developed since 1992 throughout the world. These latter guidelines identify the following elements as being central to any LA21 programme:

- establishing a multi-sectoral planning body responsible for guiding the LA21 programme;
- assessing existing social, economic and environmental conditions at a local level;

- committing to a participatory process to identify local priorities for action in both the short and long term;
- developing and implementing a multi-sectoral action plan; and
- establishing procedures for monitoring and reporting which hold local government, business and residents accountable to the LA21 programme.[12]

Examples of LA21 planning used by ICLEI to devise this model included increasing local government activity in establishing their own programmes and initiatives to address global environmental issues; for example, the coalition of over 160 cities in 34 countries that have joined ICLEI's Cities for Climate Protection (CCP) campaign to reduce greenhouse emissions at a local level by as much as 20%.[13]

The above model for LA21 planning represents a marked departure from conservation and single issue focussed environmental policy processes that preceded the emergence of LA21. In fact what we see with these guidelines, in policy terms, is that they propose a process which is as much about participatory decision making and local democracy as it is about sustainable development and environmental issues.

Clearly, a commitment to a LA21 policy process presents fundamental challenges to the "centralised" policy-making and "elitist" decision-making paradigms that have typified public policy formulation and delivery in modern industrialised countries. In this context, it has been claimed that LA21 activity "has helped to open up town and country halls to the public and to assist in the democratic deficit".[14] It is also this aspect of LA21, along with its powerful identification with the principles of sustainable development, that cements it as a key plank in the policy frameworks and processes that have been used to address environmental and sustainability issues in Australia since the mid-1990s.

LOCAL AGENDA 21 — THE AUSTRALIAN EXPERIENCE

It is one of the several ironies associated with our thesis of local government occupying the centre spotlight on the environmental policy stage that when the curtain first went up in 1992 all three spheres of Australian government had lead rôles in the script.

The 1980s and early 1990s can be characterised by the appearance of a series of global and national strategies that embraced the concept of "sustainable development" as a means of addressing the resource management and conservation issues with which the world was seen to be faced. In chronological order these strategies were:

- The World Conservation Strategy, 1980[15]
- The Australian National Conservation Strategy, 1984[16]
- The Brundtland Report (*Our Common Future*), 1987[17]
- The Hawke Government Statement (*Our Country, Our Future*), 1989[18]
- The Second World Conservation Strategy (*Caring for the Earth*), 1991[19]

The central notion of sustainability common to all these strategies is that a sustainable world is one in which future generations will have the same or better choices about their quality of life because of environmental policy decisions made and implemented in the present. Clearly a global outcome of this nature would represent the sum of public policy implementation to this end by national governments. Equally, the achievement of sustainable development at a national level would represent the sum of changed human practices regionally and locally.

However, even in Australia, as we entered the 1990s, progress on moving these strategies from government showpieces to agents for local level change had been slow. The National Landcare Programme, and its affiliated strategies, had emerged from Hawke's 1989 Prime Ministerial Statement but as far as we were aware only the State of Victoria had followed his Government's earlier lead and developed a State Conservation Strategy. Under the auspices of the latter the Victorian Ministry for Planning and Environment then made funds available in 1987–89 to support two pilot projects in the development of Local Conservation Strategies (LCS).[20]

By the turn of the decade this had been expanded to the provision of salary subsidies for LCS Project Officers in a significant number of local authorities. We understand that in the face of the Victorian financial crisis which ultimately swept the Kennett Government to power the salary subsidies were withdrawn and most of the LCS projects collapsed as a result.

Meanwhile, overseas in 1991 and early 1992 the infant ICLEI was laying the basis of its future reputation by tenaciously clinging to the heels of the architects of Agenda 21, as they met in a series of drafting sessions in Switzerland,[21] until it was agreed to incorporate a chapter on local authorities in the document. This, as we later came to realise, was in fact the origin of Chapter 28 and LA21.

Against this background events were unfolding that would make 1992 a landmark year in terms of environmental policy in Australia. Alongside the global strategies that came out of the Rio Earth Summit there was a newly emerging Australian strategic framework for environment policy, founded in a National Strategy for Ecologically Sustainable Development (NSESD).[22] What seemed at the time to make these latter developments unique was their inclusivity — they represented a form of partnership for sustainability with all three spheres of Australian government as signatories.

From down at the water's edge it seemed, although nobody articulated the view at the time, that these developments of 1992 had the effect of completing the apotheosis of sustainability. The authors certainly responded as if that was indeed the case. With the twin icons of ESD and LA21 in their back pockets the capacity to facilitate environment policy and management through local government acquired a newfound leverage — especially by the empowering of community groups and representatives with the credibility and legitimacy of universally endorsed principles and strategies. To assist this process, guidelines for the development of local environmental policy based upon the concepts of ecologically sustainable development and in response to Agenda 21 began to emerge in Australia. The most notable of these were those produced in 1992 for the South Australian Department for Environment and Natural Resources.[23]

Like ICLEI's Local Agenda 21 model, the LA21/Local Environmental Policy models promoted in these guidelines extended the "conservation" or "nature" focussed model used in the development of Local Conservation Strategies to address broader sustainability issues through a participatory decision-making process. For example, urban sustainability and environmental issues such as air pollution, public transport, traffic management, urban design and form, stormwater management and energy efficiency all became significant matters for attention.

In 1997 the United Nations General Assembly met in Special Session (UNGASS) to receive reports on the implementation of the Rio Declaration and Agenda 21, the two principal outcomes of the 1992 Earth Summit. In its findings UNGASS was forced to note the discrepancy between the positive achievements of local authorities and communities in that period, in contrast to the relative lack of progress on the Agenda 21 commitments at regional (state/provincial) and national level. In his report to the UN, the Secretary General concluded that:

> Some of the most promising developments have taken place at the local level of cities and municipalities, where Local Agenda 21 initiatives have predominated ... Local level strategy and plans have proved far more successful than those at the national level in terms of making a direct impact.[24]

From the perspective of our involvement at both local and State level during that five-year period, we would have to agree that overall this observation was as applicable to Australia as it was to anywhere else. In terms of the development and implementation of environmental policy by the respective spheres of government, that represents a particular irony: in the face of increasing national government conservatism with regard to environmental legislation and policy, especially in the latter part of the period since 1992, local government has emerged as a key player in the formulation and delivery of environmental policy. What makes this development so notable is that it has occurred despite local government being disadvantaged and marginalised by the "economic rationalisation" of the overall intergovernmental policy framework in Australia.

THE RISE AND FALL OF AN INTERGOVERNMENTAL ENVIRONMENT POLICY FRAMEWORK

So how realistic was it for us to believe that the essential elements of a conventional, bureaucratically structured and comprehensive environmental policy framework were put in place for the first time in 1992?

The 1992 Earth Summit and Agenda 21 were planned as a watershed in the cause of sustainable development, and the acceptance of the importance of local environmental policy was one of the indicators of that. In Australia, the finalisation of an Intergovernmental Agreement on the Environment (IGAE),[25] with all three spheres of government as signatories and the release of the NSESD in the same year had the potential to reinforce that acceptance, although the NSESD has been criticised for not adequately reflecting local government' s interests.[26]

As strategic policy frameworks both the IGAE and NSESD were the outcome of considerable (if not completely harmonious) negotiation and consultation, as well as reflecting the personal influence of the then Prime Minister, Bob Hawke, in the environment policy arena. A complementary regulatory framework also began to emerge from 1992 with the establishment of the Commonwealth Environment Protection Agency and a period of legislative review and amendment in the States leading by 1995 to a comprehensive nationwide network of companion statutory authorities. Furthermore, notwithstanding the fact that Hawke's successor did not share the same enthusiasm for environment policy, these frameworks remained fundamental, at least to the federal government's position, until Keating Labor was tumbled out of office by the Howard-led Coalition in March 1996. Since that time the Commonwealth has orchestrated a withdrawal from the strategic environmental policy process that would rival the December 1915 ANZAC evacuation of Gallipoli for stealth.

The irony of having had this strategic framework in place lies in the fact we can now see it not only failed to reflect pre-1992 developments at the local level[27] but then failed to ensure the incorporation of this local dimension in the implementation of environmental policy in the following years. This situation can be substantially attributed to the Council of Australian Governments (COAG) having a key rôle in the process. Under COAG an Intergovernmental Committee on Ecologically Sustainable Development (ICESD) was established and assumed responsibility for monitoring and reporting on the implementation of the NSESD. Other reporting processes included the Foreign Affairs portfolio providing the required returns to the United Nations Commission on Sustainable Development regarding Australia's meeting of the Agenda 21 commitments that it made at the Earth Summit in 1992.

This is not to suggest that local level policy developments were ignored. On the contrary, one of the additional ironies, as it looked to us, was that LA21 achievements were amongst the few trump cards that Australia had to play in reporting to the UN, not withstanding the dearth of Commonwealth and State resources committed to supporting outcomes in that arena.

To further compound this situation, throughout this post-1992 period State Ministers chose to ignore the spirit of the IGAE and steadfastly refused to contemplate admission of local government as a full member of the Australian and New Zealand Environment and Conservation Council (ANZECC). This was made all the more bizarre by the fact that whilst the IGAE and NSESD were being finalised in 1991–92, the Conference of Local Government Ministers commissioned and received a report on the *Rôle Of Local Government in Environmental Management*.[28] Given what is now confirmed in our view as the elitist approach adopted by the national and State governments with regard to environmental policy, it is little wonder that the Local Government Ministers showed no enthusiasm for implementing the report's recommendations for local authorities to play an active part in achieving sustainability goals.

For ICESD the swan song came with the belated publication in July 1996 of the second report on implementation of the NSESD, covering the period 1993–95.[29] With 33 chapters in 200 pages, and drawing on information from the Commonwealth, State and Territory and local governments it was never going to be anything but superficial. If this and the post-Federal Election delay in publishing the report were not a sufficient signal of the demise of any semblance of a strategic framework for environmental policy then the document's virtual silence on Agenda 21 and Australia's commitments certainly was.

In reality therefore what was seen to occur with the 1992 strategic framework was that, while it offered the potential for a comprehensive approach, in fact it served to maintain the 1980s status quo of excluding local government from the environment policy process. The framework became a stage on which ministers, collectively at least, played out the charade of a tripartite approach, without having to contemplate substantial change in the environment policy process in real terms. Individually of course there were exceptions, the most notable being Deputy Prime Minister Brian Howe who, as Federal Minister for Housing, Local Government and Community Services, established a short-lived Local Government Ministerial Environmental Advisory Group in 1993.[30]

The underlying power dynamics of intergovernmental relationships in Australia have long been recognised as an impediment to the development of an integrated and strategic approach to environmental policy. Fundamental to this dynamic is the fact that local government is effectively a state instrumentality. Local governments are not recognised in the Australian Constitution, rather they are created by state legislation that defines their responsibilities and therefore their power to effect environmental change through a policy process.

In defining the implications of concurrent federalism in Australia, Doyle and Kellow[31] argue that where overlapping jurisdictions occur, the Commonwealth government may not actively seek out or exercise jurisdiction over environmental matters, but rather can engage in "blame avoidance" where the responsibility is left to the States. Given that the concurrent nature of governance in terms of environmental policy extends to local government, this process of "blame avoidance" also typified state and local government relations throughout the late 1980s and 1990s. For instance, increasingly in each State, environmental protection powers and responsibilities, in terms of regulation and policy, are being devolved from State to local government. The increase in environmental rôles and responsibilities of local government is not however coupled with any increase in revenue raising powers. As local government takes on more responsibility for environmental protection the cost burden shifts from "progressive Commonwealth taxation and broad based state duties to narrowly based, regressive Council rates".[32] Recent State-driven local government reforms, amalgamations and rate capping have compounded this situation.

Fiscal constraints at both national and State level have undoubtedly had a significant influence on the trend to devolve functions to local government. As ever, financial constraints at a local level are restricting the latter sphere's ability to effect the cultural, operational and structural changes necessary to meet the increasing environmental demands being placed on it — a regulatory rôle from above and a management one from below. A stalemate has in many cases resulted, with state and local governments alike accusing each other of dragging their feet in terms of environmental management. In some instances the States have used their legislative powers to impose new rôles and responsibilities on local government, such as the requirement in NSW for annual State of the Environment Reporting.

Research undertaken in Britain has shown that similar changes in the nature of governance and fiscal constraints are occurring there, with an associated outsourcing of services and functions to the private sector. This situation has resulted in "a fragmentation of the local environmental policy making process".[33] The research also found that this institutional breakdown has been coupled with both a breakdown in the ability of local governments to undertake LA21 programmes and a greater centralisation of power as councils are forced to contract out many traditional local authority functions. Nevertheless, one interesting conclusion of the research is that despite the inequities in power between national, supranational and local government "the lack of power can encourage action towards greater self determination".[34]

Whether Australian councils are ready or willing to harness the "power of resistance" is yet to be determined, but there are signs that councils are organising and mobilising in the absence of national and state government policy direction and coordination. Councils are demonstrating a growing "willingness and ability" to address sustainability and environmental issues.[35]

The emerging demand at community level for enhanced environmental performance by local authorities has in many ways generated its own inclusivity imperative. Initially this was seen in a variety of guises, and represented a classic local version of the Pressure-State-Response model as groups demanded action and received support on a variety of issues. From our own direct and network experience these included:

- recycling and waste minimisation (for example, South Sydney, NSW);
- energy conservation (for example, Brunswick, Victoria);
- restoration of urban bushland (for example, Brisbane, Queensland);

- coast care (for example, Sydney and Adelaide Coastal Councils); and
- stormwater management (for example, Noarlunga, SA).

In many of these instances there were additional drivers such as the annual Ian Kiernan inspired "Clean Up Australia" campaign and the negative motivation for urban groups of not being able, in the main, to access Landcare funds during the first five years of that programme (1989–94).

Until the mid-1990s these developments emerged in the context of, but (it would seem) disconnected from, the strategic policy framework offered by Agenda 21 and NSESD. As *ad hoc* as it might seem in retrospect, what was happening nevertheless was that a demand for local outcomes was shaping a local environment policy approach. By 1995, as the Localinks Conference in Melbourne revealed,[36] councils were increasingly utilising the LA21 policy framework to address local environmental and sustainability issues. The growing commitment to LA21 since then has occurred despite the lack of any national government support that we have been aware of. This situation is even more noteworthy when taking into account the fact that on a global level the uptake of LA21 has been most successful in countries where there is in fact well-established support of that nature.[37]

Evidence of this upsurge in local environmental or sustainability initiatives has been demonstrated at a number of recent national and international conferences held in Australia. One of the most important of these was the Pathways to Sustainability Conference that was held in Newcastle, NSW in June 1997. The conference was attended by 1000 delegates from around the world and showcased local sustainability initiatives from a number of countries. It culminated with the signing off of the Newcastle Declaration which called for LA21 to be utilised by local government and recognised by all spheres of government as a fundamental framework for local environmental policy and a means to implement the NSESD and Agenda 21. The signatories, including the President of the Australian Local Government Association (ALGA) and the Federal Minister for the Environment, gave an undertaking to support local government in its efforts to achieve this.

Clearly, environmental politics and policy-making processes are becoming increasingly more localised. This has placed extreme pressure on local government to change its structure and operational culture. On an international scale these changes have been mostly facilitated through the LA21 process and have been most notable in the areas of institutional development, public participation and improved management systems.[38] In Australia a series of national studies have shown that these pressures on local government have necessitated reforms to both intra-council structures and operations and intergovernmental relationships to allow for more inclusive and integrated decision making and delivery of services.[39] The TASQUE report[40] identified these structural and operational reforms as being prerequisites of effective environmental management by local government. Consequently, it could be argued that an increasing number of local governments are engaging in LA21 programmes for two primary reasons. Firstly, they are a means of building their skills base and overall capacity to fulfil their increasing environmental responsibilities. Secondly, they provide a strategic planning framework that addresses environmental and sustainability issues and, if done effectively, ensures community participation in local governance and the integration of environmental, economic and social factors in the associated decision-making process.

INTERGOVERNMENTAL COOPERATION: THE SOUTH AUSTRALIAN PARTNERSHIP FOR LA21

In the light of the *ad hoc* dimension of the emergence of local environment policy that we have posited above, the 1995 establishment in our home State of South Australia of a Partnership for Local Agenda 21, under the auspices of a wider Sustainability Programme, is an example of "the exception proving the rule".

This intergovernmental and cooperative partnership had its strategic roots in the developments of 1992 and the subsequent delineation of a local component in the South Australian Department of Environment and Natural Resources (DENR) Sustainability Programme. And if Agenda 21 (and specifically Chapter 28 on Local Authorities) and the NSESD provided the policy basis for a State Government Local Sustainability Programme, then through that Programme they also provided a formal framework that gave policy legitimacy and structure to the community and council Local Environment Policies (LEPs) that DENR had been promoting and facilitating since 1991.[41]

The Partnership itself was inspired by the then Minister for Environment and Natural Resources, David Wotton, in his response to reports on the 1994 Global Forum Conference at Manchester in Britain. The City of Adelaide had participated in this Conference, a biennial follow-up to the Earth Summit, as one of fifty cities from around the world that were invited to send formal delegations of local authority officials, community, business and trade union representatives. At the invitation of the Lord Mayor of Adelaide, responding positively to DENR's Local Sustainability Programme, the State government had been represented in the delegation by the Programme's coordinator.

Reacting to Global Forum's concern at the lack of progress in implementing the commitments to Chapter 28 of Agenda 21 (namely, the development of "Local Agendas 21"), Wotton urged DENR and the Local Government Association of South Australia (LGA) to find a way of accelerating the uptake of LEPs and LA21 by councils across the State. The result was a strategic partnership between the above two institutions and five disparate councils representing each of the categories of local authority recognised at that time by the peak body, the ALGA.

Officially and jointly launched in October 1995 by the Minister and the President of the LGA, the Partnership formally brought into the arena of local environment policy development and implementation the City of Adelaide (the central business district authority), the City of Marion (a suburban council), the City of Happy Valley (an outer urban-rural fringe council), the City of Whyalla (a regional centre) and the District Council of Streaky Bay (a rural council). All had accepted the invitation to join the Partnership on the basis of their existing commitment to and/or progress in enhancing environmental policy and performance at the local level. In so doing they also accepted responsibility for modelling and promoting LA21 to other councils in the State.

Since it was established in 1995 the Partnership has been instrumental in supporting the uptake and implementation of LA21 activity in South Australia. A total of 30 Councils, or over 40% of all Councils in the State, are now undertaking LA21 programmes including an array of local environmental and sustainability initiatives. A LA21 network for Council staff has been established and the programme is about to enter a new phase where the focus will be to develop mechanisms to integrate local and State policy outcomes and processes using LA21 as a medium. In policy terms this next phase in the Partnership is a litmus test of how effectively locally derived policies, priorities and outcomes can be used to inform and shape State policies, rather than LA21 just being a framework for delivering State-generated policies. As noted by ICLEI "few Local Agenda 21 initiatives are linked to national level strategies".[42] Therefore, this "closing of the policy loop" presents a quantum leap in terms of attempts to integrate and link multi-agency and government policy frameworks and processes in Australia.

The experiences and processes used by the Partnership Councils are presently being incorporated by the State government into a set of guidelines for Local Agenda 21. While each of the Council's programmes is very different, as LA21 has to reflect local needs and conditions, a number of common elements in these programmes have been identified.[43] These include the allocation of necessary resources to the programme, including staff, the establishment of a joint Council and community forum to guide the programme, a period of awareness-raising to "create a climate of support", the development of policies, strategies and action plans, and increasing regional and inter-government cooperation between groupings of Councils, their communities, regional Catchment Water Management Boards and State government agencies to address cross-boundary environmental and sustainability issues.

The achievements of the South Australian Partnership in producing an increased commitment to LA21 have been confirmed by a 1998 Environs Australia survey of 645 local authorities regarding the implementation of such programmes. Responses were received from 291 councils (45%) and, since the survey was self-selecting, it can be accepted that reporting was based on an understanding of what LA21 entails. Results showed that South Australia clearly leads the field in commitment to LA21, with 63% responding that such a programme was either in place or being developed. The response in WA, Victoria, NSW and the Northern Territory was in the 23–28% range, whilst Tasmania and Queensland scored 7% and 4% respectively. From an overall perspective, about 25% of the councils surveyed have committed to a LA21 programme — an increase from 17% in 1995.[44]

In terms of the development and implementation of environment policy at the local level the obvious indications are twofold.

Firstly, in South Australia, where the environment agency has maintained a statewide LA21 programme, the uptake by councils has continued to grow. This situation was acknowledged recently by one of the principal architects of the Partnership for Local Agenda 21, D.C. Wotton, formerly the State Minister for the Environment and Natural Resources. Wotton, in an address to the South Australian House of Assembly on 5 November 1998, on the subject of Local Agenda 21, made the following comments:

> Successful Local Agenda 21 programmes require a long term commitment to effect the behavioral, structural and operational changes to ensure that environmental considerations are factored into all decision making and that the community fully participates in that process. What has really impressed me, having been given the opportunity of visiting some of the councils, is how those councils have gone out of their way

to involve communities in the Local Agenda 21 process. The challenge for local communities is to get involved in the development and actioning of this programme. It is also a challenge for State Governments and for the Federal Government to support local initiatives to ensure that local strategies and policies, informed State and national policies and strategies are introduced.[45]

The above comments also reflect the fact that despite the collapse of a nominal strategic framework for environmental policy at the national level, there is an increasing trend for local government across the country to develop policies and programmes for the environment/sustainability imperative, in response to community expectation and demand.

ENVIRONMENTAL MANAGEMENT SYSTEMS: A CORPORATE POLICY FRAMEWORK

Finally, it is worth pointing out that eventually there will be an even higher level of irony in the whole saga of local environment policy, generated from the international arena. Since late 1995 Australia has adopted the International Standard for Environmental Management Systems (EMS) known as ISO 14001.[46] As with all Standards of this type, the notion of an EMS is nothing more than a management tool which, when fully implemented, provides an organisation with assurance that its operations and activities comply with its legal obligations and deliver any other sustainability targets that it sets for itself as part of its environmental policy commitment. Through external auditing an organisation can obtain certification that its EMS complies with ISO 14001; this process is regulated under the auspices of the Joint Accreditation System of Australia and New Zealand (JAS-ANZ).

It is interesting that ANZECC is represented on the technical committee that both prepared the International Standard for adoption in Australia and New Zealand and is responsible for its ongoing review. Despite this high level association, there is no indication (especially in the absence of a strategic environmental policy framework) that public sector agencies have been encouraged to use an EMS as a means of enhancing their own performance in both policy advice and operational terms.

There is some potential for this situation to change, via a Productivity Commission inquiry into the implementation of the NSESD by Commonwealth departments and agencies. The inquiry was ordered by Federal Treasurer Peter Costello in August 1998 and followed by the release of a Commission Issues Paper[47] in September. Whilst the paper is silent on ISO 14001 it does open up the prospect of both a revival of a strategic environmental policy framework and a systematic approach to its implementation, specifically at federal level. Encouragingly the Commission has also left open the door of policy coordination in the arena of ecologically sustainable development across all spheres of government. At the time of writing, with the Federal Coalition government's majority substantially reduced and the Commission's report due in May 1999, the possibility of an enhanced and integrated approach to developing and delivering environmental policy should attract considerable interest. On the other hand, there are those who would undoubtedly find the prospect of direct Treasury involvement somewhat daunting.

In the meantime, local government on the other hand, was quick to respond to the adoption of ISO 14001 in Australia. Using Local Government Development Programme funds (LGDP — another federal Labor initiative that did not survive the Howard Government's first budget) the ALGA produced in 1996 a guidelines handbook for councils on EMS and the new standard.[48] Without assuming that the handbook had a direct and immediate impact, the Environs Australia survey referred to above also reported that 34% of councils either have or are developing an EMS.

The value of an EMS, which is recognised in the ALGA handbook, is that it provides councils with a systematic planning and management tool for implementing their LA21 programmes and achieving their sustainability goals. To the extent therefore that local authorities are committing to a joint EMS/LA21 approach, they would certainly appear to be providing a lead nationally, in terms of delivering on environmental outcomes within a deliberate policy framework, while at a national level this framework appears to be becoming more poorly defined and irrelevant.

CONCLUSION

Whether this increased uptake of LA21 planning and EMS processes has led to the necessary cultural changes for an environmental ethic to become fully embedded in local governance right across Australia has yet to be determined. Certainly the policy frameworks of each mechanism allow for greater integration of environmental issues in local decision making and practice. The distinguishing dimension of LA21 is that it sets down some fundamental challenges to local government in terms of how it operates and interacts with both the local community and other spheres of government. With little support from the latter, other than in South Australia, local government is seemingly trying to rise to this challenge in response to increased responsibilities and community demand.

There is no doubt that either way environmental issues are being integrated into local government operations and policy processes. This trend is intimately associated with the changing style of governance in Australia. Given this, any discussion regarding the changing rôle of local government in the nation's political processes needs to be grounded in the fact that the inequities in the power relationships between the spheres of government means that what constitutes "local government" in each State remains a very diverse and fragile institution. Consequently, as witnessed by the overnight transformation of councils in Victoria in 1993, and imposed reforms such as amalgamations and competition policy, it must be recognised that while the "sleeping giant" of environmental politics is waking from its slumber, by the same token it is walking on shaky ground. That this "ground" can be made more stable and supportive through the cooperation of other spheres of government has been demonstrated in the South Australian Partnership for LA21. While some semblance of the National Strategy for Ecologically Sustainable Development remains intact, even as it enters the jaws of the Productivity Commission, it is still possible that a fully integrated and strategic environmental policy framework can be realised in Australia. The growing acceptance of LA21 by local government and the increasing recognition of it as a mechanism to deliver State and national policy means that this locally derived policy framework could well be the catalyst for this to occur. If this potential is to be realised concerted action by all spheres of government needs to occur in terms of commitment to LA21.

The advantage of LA21 as a tool for the development and implementation of local environment policy is that it is not the creation of any one political party, and therefore vulnerable to banishment when its originators fall from grace. Instead it was born out of an international forum and evolved into a movement whereby global imperatives inform local action. This should ensure that LA21 has a life span that is considerably greater than that of most policy frameworks and planning models that are spawned in one political era, only to be deserted in another. From where we stand, LA21, as the cornerstone of a local environmental policy framework in Australia, is passing the acid test by demonstrating its capacity to sustain itself and survive the cycle of state and federal governments.

INSTITUTIONALISING ECOLOGICALLY SUSTAINABLE DEVELOPMENT: PROMISES, PROBLEMS AND PROSPECTS

S. Dovers

INTRODUCTION

The Australian Government's ecologically sustainable development (ESD) working parties sat between 1990 and 1992. The policy process is now too commonly perceived as over, but in fact it continues with the development and, to some extent implementation, of subsidiary policies. This chapter shows that ESD is an ongoing "metapolicy" theme and process, but one stumbling in implementation and lacking proper foundations, and explores the issue of how it might be entrenched and extended.[1] The ESD process is still remarked upon internationally, and remains the most broad-ranging and inclusive policy process engaged in by Australia on sustainability issues, but it has been insufficiently analysed in any official manner.[2] The Australian political and policy system does not often enough engage in policy evaluation and learning, thus — knowingly or not — choosing to reinvent unworkable wheels and repeat past mistakes. Policy learning is much conceptualised and advocated, but poorly understood or carried out.[3] Regarding Australian environmental policy, Walker notes that:

> Evaluation is also extensively neglected. There is very poor provision in democratic systems, and programmes with evaluative criteria built in have often failed. Bureaucracies tend to subvert evaluation or to fit it into their own frame of reference, thus distorting its original purpose.[4]

To some extent this chapter seeks to evaluate, but it is more concerned to advance arguments as to how an under-implemented and under-evaluated process might be rescued. Sustainability is a national and international imperative given great weight even in official policy (at least in principle), and the scientific underpinnings of concern — both theoretical and empirical — are strong. Thus the persistent and purposeful pursuit of sustainability in public policy should be evident to all by now, but this is not the case. While the ESD consultation process was worthwhile, albeit imperfect, its promise has not been fulfilled. The ESD "process" was geared to *making* policy, but it is only through subsequent institutionalisation that gains in implementation, outcomes and long-term capacity can be realised.[5] This is where ESD has disappointed. To explore the reasons, the nature of sustainability problems must first be considered.

THE FIRST PROBLEM: THE NATURE OF SUSTAINABILITY

Sustainability as an idea has deep and diverse roots, in classical economics, energy analysis, renewable resource management and elsewhere.[6] The modern idea of sustainability as a global problem of environment and development can be dated from around the time of Boulding's classic "spaceship earth" essay.[7] A related series of UN-inspired discussions and events — Stockholm 1972 and the related declaration, the Brandt and Palme commissions, the 1982 World Charter for Nature and so on — were particularly important in focussing growing concern over the magnitude of environmental problems and, more crucially, their linkages with issues of development, poverty and (in)security. In the wake of much intellectual and policy activity, sustainable development has been only a little too grandly described as the universally agreed goal of human progress.[8] Seeking to integrate concerns of human development, ecological integrity and security over the long term, sustainability presents a suite of interrelated policy problems of a complexity and magnitude sufficient to profoundly challenge existing modes of policy analysis and policy formulation. Larger policy problems in sustainability — such as greenhouse, land degradation, biodiversity or population-environment linkages — display a number of attributes found more often, and more often in combination, than problems in more traditional policy fields.[9] The attributes include:

- problematic spatial and temporal scales;
- possibly absolute ecological limits;
- irreversibility and urgency;
- connectivity and complexity;
- pervasive risk, uncertainty and ignorance;
- cumulative effects;
- new moral dimensions (future generations, other species);
- "systemic" problem causes (deeply embedded in patterns of production and consumption and governance);
- requirements (substantive and political) for community participation; and
- sheer novelty.

This is not to say that problems in other policy fields are easy, or to denigrate efforts in those fields. But longstanding institutional arrangements have grown up around such issues as improving public health, encouraging economic development or bettering service delivery, and whatever their shortcomings these are much more evolved and far more familiar as policy tasks and institutional settings than sustainability. There is a prima facie case that policy processes and modes of analysis not used to problems displaying the attributes listed above will have difficulty gaining purchase on such problems. To be fair, then, scepticism in viewing policy failure or disappointment should be seasoned by an acceptance that these problems are different in both kind and degree. And these are early days; sustainability has really only been on the international political and scientific agenda for a decade. Desires for instant policy gratification are unreasonable.

In the following sections of this chapter, features of policy responses before ESD, the international setting, the nature, limitations and strengths of the ESD process, some comparisons between it and another "metapolicy" field (marketisation), and finally the sorts of institutional measures capable of entrenching and extending ESD will be considered.

PROBLEMS, THEN PROMISES: THE ROOTS OF ADHOCERY AND AMNESIA

It is now widely accepted that Australian environmental policy has been too often characterised by "policy adhocery and amnesia", by discrete processes and episodes unconnected across time and space and lacking in consistency, learning and persistence.[10] ESD is the second attempt to impose a greater degree of problem construction and policy cohesion across the often fragmented realm of environmental concern, and this history deserves noting.

Even though there is a tendency to forget the fact, Australia's environment has been managed by humans for millennia. Resource and environmental management, in the modern sense of public policy and administration, began in Australia within a very few years of European occupation.[11] Australia's responses to the growing environmental concern of the 1960s were similar to those elsewhere, with some local peculiarities. New laws, agencies and so on were created, and, while this made things better than they might otherwise have been, the response was piecemeal, sectoral and unconnected, although it certainly evolved much over the decades.[12] But environmental degradation has continued to worsen.[13] Not only did analysts and agitators judge the response insufficient; government policy said as much. The 1983 "consensus-built" National Conservation Strategy for Australia (NCSA) — a response to the 1980 World Conservation Strategy (WCS) — entailed an acceptance that piecemeal approaches were insufficient, and attempted to bring the fuller range of issues together with wider input from stakeholders than had previously been the case.[14] In brief, the NCSA was a disappointment, although it left a legacy of heightened awareness and of some state and local strategies. Vagueness, discretion and above all a lack of measures for implementation and extension were the chief weaknesses.[15] It was five years before administrative guidelines on implementing the Strategy emerged in the Commonwealth bureaucracy, by which time there was little to implement.[16] The WCS had called for stronger national institutions, but in the main these were not forthcoming. The "sustainable development" called for by the NCSA (which did not much address equity or economic dimensions) remained very much at the margins of mainstream public policy and administration. Barely had the half-hearted implementation of the NCSA begun than Hawke's 1989 environment statement appeared, soon to be followed by and confused with a 1990 Commonwealth discussion paper dealing with ESD.[17] Australia had begun addressing the modern idea of sustainability.

The World Commission on Environment and Development (WCED) consolidated the agenda in the politically remarkable *Our Common Future*, establishing gross ecological and human unsustainability and giving us the standard definition, repeated here in more than the usually truncated form:

> Sustainable development is development that meets the needs of the present without compromising the ability of future generations to meet their own needs. It contains within it two key concepts:
>
> the concept of "needs", in particular the essential needs of the world's poor, to which overriding priority should be given; and

the idea of limitations imposed by the state of technology and social organization on the environment's ability to meet present and future needs.[18]

The WCED constructed a startling agenda linking environmental and resource concerns with those of the human condition; poverty, development, economic management, equity and security. This was translated at and after the United Nations Conference on Environment and Development (UNCED) in Rio de Janeiro in 1992 into the following central outcomes:[19]

- the Rio Declaration and related plan of action, Agenda 21;
- conventions on climate change, biodiversity and desertification;
- a Commission for Sustainable Development; and
- a department within the United Nations, and various cross-agency mechanisms.

Activity continues, encouraging in rhetoric but disappointing in vigour and implementation. Whatever criticisms one may have of the WCED-UNCED process,[20] given the constraints on international policy coordination the outcomes were impressive enough, and the UN itself set up believable institutional arrangements. Critics should recognise that in the absence of the UN far less would have happened, and nation-states are responsible for implementation.

PROMISES, THEN PROBLEMS: WHAT HAPPENED, WHAT DID NOT, AND WHY

The ESD process was Australia's response to the WCED-UNCED agenda. The process was far from perfect, but was the most comprehensive and inclusive attempt at policy formulation across the field up until then, and indeed since. Deficiencies in the process included: lack of comprehensive coverage of cross-sectoral issues; greater emphasis on production rather than consumption aspects; lack of questioning of economic growth and existing institutional arrangements; limited public discussion and biases in the representation of interest groups in the working group process; and above all a watering down of recommendations in formulating the ensuing strategy.[21] While these deficiencies certainly existed, for the purposes of this chapter they can be overlooked and attention turned more toward what can be done with the outcomes of the process.

The principal elements of the ESD process were:

- a 1990 Commonwealth discussion paper;

- nine sectoral working groups (non-government organisations (NGOs), government, unions, industry);
- nine working group and two chairs' reports;
- a draft strategy drawn from these;
- a final National Strategy for Ecologically Sustainable Development (NSESD), constructed by a State-Commonwealth bureaucratic committee and accepted by the Council of Australian Governments in December 1992.[22]

Associated were the National Greenhouse Response Strategy, and the 1992 Intergovernmental Agreement on the Environment (the IGAE forms a Schedule to the Commonwealth *National Environment Protection Council Act 1994*). The IGAE sets out basic principles and describes the respective responsibilities of the national and State/Territory governments. (Once again, matters were confused by another major Prime Ministerial statement on the environment in late 1992.)

This is the "metapolicy setting", but more pertinent here is what has happened post-1992 in development of subsidiary policies beneath the ESD banner. From 1992 on, national policies have been evolved or are evolving, or in some cases were co-opted, for a range of subsidiary problems and sectors. This is the "macro-policy setting" dealing with biodiversity, greenhouse, waste minimisation, forests, land care, recreational fisheries, oceans, energy, wetlands, rangelands and so on. These policies vary in their detail, strength and vigour of implementation, and are supported by (literally!) hundreds of subsidiary policies and programmes. To illustrate this setting, Table 11.1 sets out the major policies, with further detail given for biodiversity, illustrating the detailed policy development that has occurred.[23] Table 11.1 runs the risk of ascribing to this ESD-related policy setting a cohesiveness it does not really possess, but does underline the fact that a quite considerable phase of policy development has occurred, often involving input from non-government stakeholders. Major policies concerning biodiversity, rangelands, forests and the like were constructed adjacent to or following the ESD process, and expressly state ESD principles or refer to them. The intent of the ESD strategy and related policies are stated in the Strategy as:

Goal: Development that improves the total quality of life, both now and in the future, in a way that maintains the ecological processes on which life depends.

Core objectives: To enhance individual and community wellbeing and welfare by following a path of economic development that safeguards the welfare of future generation; to provide for equity within and between generations; to protect biological diversity and maintain essential ecological processes and life-support systems.

GUIDING PRINCIPLES:

- decision-making processes should effectively integrate both long term and short term economic, environmental, social and equity dimensions:
- where there are threats of serious or irreversible environmental damage, lack of full scientific certainty should not be used as a reason for postponing measures to prevent environmental degradation (the precautionary principle);
- the global dimension of environmental impacts of actions and policies should be recognised and considered:
- the need to develop a strong, growing and diversified economy which can enhance the capacity for environmental protection should be recognised;
- the need to maintain and enhance international competitiveness in an environmentally sound manner should be recognised;
- cost effective and flexible policy instruments should be adopted, such as improved valuation, pricing and incentive mechanisms;
- decisions and actions should provide for broad community involvement on issues which affect them.

Table 11.1: A national policy hierarchy? Circa 1997

Meta-policy (International policies and instruments arising from UNCED): National Strategy for Ecologically Sustainable Development — Intergovernmental Agreement on the Environment

Macro-policy (examples): National Environment Protection Council — Decade of Landcare — Murray-Darling arrangements — National Waste Minimisation Strategy — National Pollution Inventory — National Greenhouse Response Policy (plus reiterations) — National Forest Policy Statement (plus CRA—RFA process) — (draft) Rangelands Strategy — (status unclear, prospects unknown) conservation strategy for the Australian Antarctic Territory — (in formulation) oceans policy

National Strategy for the Conservation of Australia's Biological Diversity:

Meso-policy (biodiversity, examples only): Conservation of Australian Species and Ecological Communities Threatened with Extinction: a National Strategy — Endangered Species Programme — Feral Pests Programme — national reserves network Programme — Save the Bush and One Million Trees Programmes — Commonwealth Wetland Policy — (proposed) national long-term biodiversity monitoring Programme

Micro-policy (biodiversity, examples only): River Murray Corridor of Green Programme — Grasslands Ecology Programme — Marine Wildlife Programme — individual species or community recovery programmes — particular threat abatement programmes — and so on.

The emerging policy framework (Table 11.1) is a welcome and encouraging start and fleshes out the broader ESD policy field. It certainly gives the lie to the flippant "ESD is dead" line used by some people as a substitute for thinking about what happened, what did not, and why. More consensual (or at least corporatist) modes of policy formulation were found valuable. The incoming, conservative Commonwealth Government in 1996 largely accepted this policy setting, at least in its rhetoric. The most interesting question concerns what has or can be done to consolidate, implement and extend the policy setting, the bulk of which exists only as non-binding avowals of intent.

Implementation has been less encouraging, although it is rather too early in most cases for final judgements.[24] In keeping with a tradition of policy adhocery and policy amnesia in Australian environment policy, there has been reluctance to entrench these initiatives via robust, persistent institutional arrangements, or to support them with substantial financial, human or informational resources.[25] Recommendations made by the ESD process, such as for Offices of ESD in first ministers' departments, an ESD research advisory council, or further references to the Resource Assessment Commission (RAC), were not acted upon, nor was the widespread plea for the continuation of the ESD stakeholder discourse.[26] Similarly, the concurrent process considering population-environment issues by the National Population Council recommended various ongoing measures, but these were ignored or very reluctantly addressed.[27]

In terms of what did happen, institutionally, as a result of the ESD process, the list is short. Two arrangements stand out. The National Environment Protection Council (NEPC) is an encouraging and potentially important development, although its scope remains that of traditional environmental protection rather than ESD more broadly. The NEPC has not been a sparkling spectacle, but federalism does stand in the way. National State of the Environment Reporting (SoER) was recommended, and in 1996 came to initial fruition.[28] Whatever the weaknesses of the process and the first report, this is welcome.[29] However, national SoER lacks a statutory mandate, as did the short-lived and generally forgotten 1980s national SoER exercise. On the other hand, SoER in some States (and even at local government level in NSW) is so mandated.

More recently, the Natural Heritage Trust (NHT) was created by the incoming government in 1996 to expend privatisation proceeds on environment programmes, and does not clearly relate to ESD. The NHT is not a particularly valuable institutional development, however welcome the associated programme spending may be (though judgement on this must wait). The NHT was a splendid political wheeze to win environment votes and sweeten a privatisation, but it has a use-by date, and — dangerously in the medium term — removes much environment policy from the normal realm of Westminster public finance. The near-total focus of the Trust programmes on "on-ground" works unsupported by institutional development and monitoring is unfortunate, and the fact that the Trust is constituted by two government ministers instantly singles it out as a political target.

According ESD statutory expression is a prime indicator of how seriously it is taken. In the States and Territories, ESD principles (for example, the precautionary principle) have been codified as statutory objects in a number of pieces of legislation; a more fundamental institutionalisation than at Commonwealth level (for example, in NSW, *Protection of the Environment (Administration) Act 1991, Fisheries Management Act 1994*). The only real statutory expression of ESD principles in the Commonwealth sphere is in the legislative framework of the Australian Fisheries Management Authority, which incidentally is a source of potential lessons largely ignored by other sectors.[30] The statutory mandate of the now-defunct RAC was also an early expression of sustainability, instructing integration of ecological and economic dimensions in its inquiries. At the time of writing, the Commonwealth Environment Protection and Biodiversity Conservation Bill is before the Senate, and while this states ESD principles it does so weakly and further proposes a lessening of Commonwealth legal intervention in environmental matters despite clear constitutional bases for greater such involvement.[31]

Now to the question of why ESD has not been firmly institutionalised. This is complex, and relates to the position of environment and ESD in the landscape of public policy and administration relative to other concerns. Detailed analyses of the process have been published elsewhere, so some major factors can be just noted here. Some of the more important (and interrelated) reasons for weaknesses of the ESD process (and the policy field generally) include:[32]

- processes meant to deal with complex long-term issues but which compressed consideration within a short time period and superficial public consultation;
- the establishment of forums (for example, ESD working groups) with a preponderance of production and economic interests;
- a lack of intersectoral analysis and recommendations;[33]
- a downplaying of the avowed "global dimension" of ESD, diverting attention from global equity issues;
- relatedly, insufficient attention to high per capita consumption in Australia as an underlying cause of unsustainability;
- termination of the ESD consultative process, rather than establishing an ongoing dialogue;
- a lack of questioning of existing institutional arrangements, meaning that policy must be delivered through arrangements and portfolio divisions reflecting past rather than present or future imperatives;
- weakening of the working group reports by an intergovernmental committee in drafting the final strategy;
- a change in government attitude to both the environment and to participative policy formulation; and
- overall, a reluctance by most participants in the process to consider changes other than at the margins of selected production sectors.

Significantly, it was not only environmental groups that voiced disappointment over failure to vigorously pursue and implement the ESD process outcomes; some industry and professional groups did also, suggesting that government had fallen behind the rest of society in its attitude to sustainable development. It can be asked whether, with some other process in place, the fate of ESD would have been different. Other countries sought to implement the global sustainable development agenda in different ways, consistent with their own political traditions and imperatives at the time.[34] Canada, for example, created consultative "roundtables" on economy and environment at different political levels, not unlike ESD working groups but longer-lasting.[35] Britain formulated a sustainable development strategy,[36] whereas New Zealand relied on a new core statute, the *Resource Management Act.*[37]

Which was and is better? Problems of resourcing and implementation

214 . AUSTRALIAN ENVIRONMENTAL POLICY 2

have not just been evident in Australia. In the absence of research and analysis beyond the scope of this chapter, it is hard to discern any sharply different performance, attributable to these initiatives, between countries in terms of positive change in the environment, human use of it, or the human condition. At a comparative sustainable development symposium at the 1992 Association for Canadian Studies in Australia and New Zealand Conference held at the University of Wellington, New Zealand, the three countries' processes were discussed. It was notable that most people involved thought that another country's process was better, and were somewhat disappointed to find that participants from that country had less positive views. Certainly, for a person from a federal system, a core statute, well designed and implemented, is attractive, but not constitutionally possible in Australia at the national level. An interesting question for legal research would be whether a great deal more could be achieved under New Zealand's *Resource Management Act* than could be under the NSW *Environmental Planning and Assessment Act 1979*, should the latter have been supported by political and community will. This issue is more one of success or failure in implementing whatever it is that has been done — the theme of this chapter.

The Resource Assessment Commission (1989–93) serves as another case to explore the reasons behind institutional weakness, or "short-livedness" in this case.[38] The RAC was a bold institutional experiment — globally unprecedented, even — and, despite less than well-thought-out briefs, attracted reasonably strong support and indicated an encouraging way forward. Its most impressive features were careful research matched with reasonably wide consultation during inquiries, an explicit statutory mandate to integrate ecological and economic aspects, and reporting directly to the Prime Minister. In a general policy sense it has been identified as a positive example, and was an explicit response to adhocery.[39] Yet it was cut down well before its prime. The following range of reasons were evident:

- a change of Prime Minister, with different priorities and style;
- bureaucratic jealousies on the part of existing, non-environmental agencies;
- frustration at the lack of clear yes/no answers, especially with the Coronation Hill inquiry, contrary to the inevitably political nature of decisions in such matters;
- impatience with detailed and careful deliberation, and a related desire for instant policy gratification;
- a sense that some players could gain greater advantage from a return to conflict;

- unease at the exposure of political decisions;
- ill-advised promotion and/or expectations of some techniques implemented, such as contingent valuation and multi-criteria analysis;
- lack of active support by some players, even if supportive in principle;
- exposure of the systemic tensions between environment and (simply defined) development, and thus the obstacles to policy reform; and
- simple cost cutting.[40]

All these factors and others lie behind the more general failure and reluctance to institutionalise ESD. And, as ever, there is simply the bothersome nature of change. This is not, of course, a problem only in Australia; witness the sombre embarrassment so evident at the 23–27 June 1997 United Nations General Assembly Special Session ("Rio+5"), where widespread failure to move forward was admitted. Most significantly of all is the fact that seriously pursuing sustainability will involve addressing deep, structural inconsistencies between human and natural systems. The problem attribute of systemic causes is a supremely difficult one: the roots of unsustainability are embedded firmly in our systems of production and consumption and patterns of governance and settlement. A good example is the ongoing farce of Australia's greenhouse policy, where doing anything real involves addressing the fundamental issue of energy.[41] Australia's generous allowance post-Kyoto to continue to increase greenhouse gas emissions is hardly a spur to either policy or technological reform.

At every turn where real change might be achieved, sustainability policy runs into entrenched barriers and opposition. To explore this further, ESD must be considered in the broader landscape of public policy and administration.

ANOTHER PROBLEM: ESD ON THE "LEVEL PLAYING FIELD"

Anyone who has played junior football can impart the invaluable lesson that a level playing field, set rules and fixed goal posts — the stuff of healthy competition — matter little when someone twice your size charges at you. Just as big firms can (and do) run over and flatten small firms in a "fair and competitive" market, so it is that weakly institutionalised policy considerations can be easily outweighed by strongly institutionalised ones. Thus it is for ESD, and the lack of institutionalisation is evidenced in comparison to other public policy fields. Even official sustainability policy states that environmental, social and economic policy should be balanced and integrated, and this means that there should be some degree of parity in policy processes. Yet the underpinnings of much social and especially economic policy are vastly more substantial than environmental concerns. Where are the ecological equivalents of the Australian Bureau of Statistics, National Accounts, Census, input-output tables, monthly population surveys, or Productivity Commission? Where is the implementation that would make ESD — a weak statement of ecological rationality — comparable to its counterpart from economic rationality, the pervasive National Competition Policy (NCP)? NCP makes for an interesting comparison.[42]

ESD and NCP should be, in theory, comparable, but they are not.[43] Both are products of extra-parliamentary processes (especially the Council of Australian Governments, an opaque and unaccountable aberration in our Westminster system), and both are domestic manifestations of broader, international "metapolicy" concerns. Yet ESD has been kept to the margins of public policy and administration, and implemented weakly. As the State of Environment Advisory Council put it regarding the impact of ESD strategies, "there is little evidence that these strategies affect decision making in any but the most perfunctory way".[44] On the other hand, NCP is having a profound impact across all policy fields, and is being implemented with vigour and relish. One part of NCP is a legislative review of some 1800 Australian statutes (including many environmental laws), seeking out "anti-competitive elements". Suggesting such a wide review to find "unsustainable elements" in environmental laws would not be taken seriously. Yet as good or even a better case could be made. Much more Commonwealth money persuades the States to implement NCP than ESD. The intellectual bases of sustainability — theoretical and empirical — are stronger than those of the neo-liberal marketisation agenda of which competition policy is a manifestation. Sustainability as a metapolicy imperative has been accepted, in principle, as very important by the vast bulk of nation-states (170 of them at Rio de Janeiro, in fact). Marketisation as an unquestionable, overriding policy imperative has been, for the most part, confined to the English-speaking developed nations over the past couple of decades.[45] Furthermore, ESD policy developed in a reasonably open and consultative manner (it is seen as contestable), whereas the NCP process has been markedly exclusive and opaque (it is not seen as contestable). While equality of ESD with economic imperatives may be a fanciful hope, a greater degree of parity in institutional and policy terms is not an unreasonable one.

So much for what did happen, what did not happen, and why

not. The more positive discussion has to do with what could yet happen, should we still be serious about ESD.

HOPEFUL PROSPECTS: WHAT COULD YET HAPPEN

A range of institutional reforms can now be considered, designed to be achievable within existing political and constitutional parameters, address this lack of parity and entrench sustainability concerns more firmly in the landscape of public policy and administration in Australia. This is a stated goal avowed in national policy, in keeping with calls from the 1980 WCS, through UNCED at Rio in 1992 and constantly stated ever since, of building national institutions to support sustainable development.[46] In assessing institutional reform to entrench sustainability, policy imperatives reflecting the principles enunciated in policy internationally and in Australia, and the weaknesses of current arrangements, can be kept in mind. The following list is not exclusive or detailed, but it would be generally accepted that fulfilling these would markedly enhance policy and management capacities:[47]

- improve information capacities to support both the general sustainability policy discourse, and the formulation and implementation of policies and management régimes;
- improve coordination and integration, across sectors and problems, and between different governments and administrative scales, to address disjointed or conflicting policies;
- seek greater longevity and persistence in policy initiatives and processes, to allow monitoring and adaptation in the face of uncertainty;
- encourage enhanced policy learning over time, and across regions, portfolios, agencies and sectors;
- improve processes and techniques for policy instrument choice, involving an enlarged commitment to comparative policy analysis, to lessen the constricting influence of short term policy fashions;
- create clearer policy mandates for agencies and governments, and provide stronger institutional and statutory foundations for policy to reduce discretion and encourage persistence of efforts;
- encourage more consistent and sophisticated definition of policy problems in sustainability, to overcome poor or fragmented definition of problems and improve the matching of policy instruments to policy problems; and
- enhance and institutionalise processes for broader community inclusion and participation in sustainability policy, and make policy processes more transparent to the community.

There are many realistic institutional reforms that would address these imperatives, at least in part. The following treatment is not complete or detailed, but illustrative. It is not suggestive of instruments or outcomes, but concerns processes and institutions to promote more informed, sustained and inclusive policy deliberations; the achievement of greater parity in process. The following relate mostly to the national/continental scale, and concern sustainability generally and not particular "macro-policy problems" within the "meta-problem" of sustainability, such as land degradation, greenhouse or biodiversity. What follows is not a recipe, but a sample menu. A few together would more than fulfil UNCED's simplistic recipe of national councils for sustainable development. In many cases, an equivalent from another policy area is noted, to show that these measures are not fanciful, if we are serious about sustainability. This is important: the following menu of reforms shows that significant strengthening of ESD policy capacity can be achieved within existing political, constitutional and customary parameters.

Resurrect and institutionalise the broader ESD dialogue that took place with the ESD working groups, but lapsed after the groups finalised their Reports. This would engage major interests — three levels of government, industry, green and consumer groups, unions, research bodies — in an ongoing discourse, rather than only with respect to more particular policy episodes. The process would need to be reasonably informal, but guaranteed of some persistence. This would lessen the propensity for consultation to be used expediently and then discontinued.

Establish Offices of ESD in the Prime Minister's and Premiers' Departments, charged with overview and cross-portfolio coordination of sustainability policy (as per existing offices of the status of women or indigenous affairs).

Establish a ministerial council for ESD, as exists for many other areas, to engage the States, Territories and Commonwealth in policy coordination and development. In a departure from usual practice, local government should be represented. This council may or may not subsume existing ministerial councils covering environment and natural resources, and should, as with the Murray-Darling Basin Council and the NEPC, be provided with a statutory basis.

Establish an ESD research council, to identify, consolidate, communicate, encourage and in some cases fund or commission research, particularly cross-sectoral or interdisciplinary work, into ESD. This would be an equivalent to, in style if not scale, the National Health and Medical Research Council.

Establish an independent Commissioner for ESD at the Commonwealth level, with statutory office, to assess and report on progress with ESD policy. This could also provide a more independent statutory and institutional home for, among other things, national SoER.

Establish an ESD research and monitoring agency as a Commonwealth statutory authority, perhaps overseen by the suggested ESD research council or Commissioner, to substantially enhance the information base for sustainability policy. This would operate with an in-house research and collating capacity, commission work, and act as a national clearing house for ESD information. This would be equivalent to the rôle played by the impressive Australian Institute of Health and Welfare.

Where appropriate, codify ESD principles as statutory objects in Commonwealth law. If we are serious about obeying such instructions as the precautionary principle or the integration of social, environmental and economic dimensions, then such principles should be imposed upon at least instruct the actions of governments and their instrumentalities.[48] Some States (NSW, Tasmania, SA) have gone further down this path, and in NSW interesting and useful interpretations of, for example, the precautionary principle are emerging now through the courts.[49] An example of where this might apply would be the *Environmental Protection (Impact of Proposals) Act*.

Possibly, enact an overarching sustainability Act, providing the basis for several such arrangements as suggested here, and codifying ESD principles as statutory objects instructing the Commonwealth.

Undertake a comprehensive, independent review of Commonwealth legislation and administrative arrangements to identify provisions which discourage sustainability, or which could encourage it if recast (as per the NCP legislative review, but carried out in a more systematic and transparent fashion).

Resurrect the Resource Assessment Commission (1989–93). The RAC was an unprecedented informing and learning institution, yet was given the scandalously short institutional life of less than four years before being swept off the table in a fit of expedient pique. The enabling statute remains in place, and the only sizable amendment might be to allow Parliament rather than the Prime Minister alone to assign references. As for a future agenda of inquiries, the ESD Intersectoral Report made a number of recommendations, many of which are still relevant. A resurrected RAC would be an equivalent, smaller but less ideologically and methodologically constricted, to the Productivity (originally Industry) Commission.

Establish a national resource and environmental management "policy learning" institute. There are few processes whereby the status, trends and lessons of resource and environmental policy and management in Australia can be accessed in a timely and thorough fashion. This applies across jurisdictions, but also across portfolios and sectors within jurisdictions. This would not have a policy formulation rôle, but would seek to maximise linkages, communication and learning across the very fragmented range of groups, professions, agencies and stakeholders involved in resource and environmental management and the broader field of ESD. A precedent and starting model is the Commonwealth-funded and very impressive Australian Emergency Management Institute.

Resurrect the Inter-State Commission which has, strangely, only existed rarely and briefly, since the Australian Constitution in 1901 stated that there "shall be" such a body.[50] Many sustainability problems are complicated by federalism, and the Inter-State Commission would seem a suitable body to progress some of these.

Complete the "macro-policy setting" constructed in the six years post-ESD, and now including national or at least Commonwealth policies or strategies on such problems as greenhouse, recreational fisheries, biodiversity, waste minimisation, wetlands, rangelands and so on. While such strategies do not solve problems, they are minimum but necessary first steps in problem recognition and definition. Candidates for attention include water, rural lands, the minerals sector, population and settlement.

Finally, provide better statutory, institutional and organisational support for the emerging, large array of community-based environmental management and monitoring groups and programmes (Landcare, Dunecare, Frogwatch, Saltwatch and the like). Given that it now seems these are here to stay in environmental management and that such participation is a core principle in sustainability policy, it is time to provide solid and ongoing support and not leave them reliant on the whim of annual programme funding. Otherwise, they risk withering as the demands of voluntarism overwhelm people and the suspicion grows that "community-based" can be code for abrogation of state responsibility.[51]

Further, there is much scope for better coordination of the bewildering and growing array of community-based initiatives.

One workable mechanism would be local or regional scale "community environmental trusts", qualifying for administrative funding and support from a national fund for periods of, say, five years, given the meeting of basic criteria of accountability and representativeness. These would be in addition to specific programme funding, and the majority of trustees would represent community groups. The administrative basis would be in local government (local government Acts allow for such arrangements, either solo or in concert), thus providing a statutory, administrative and logistic home.

Elections for such trusts could even be held, in conjunction with council elections. Larger local government areas may have a single trust, or smaller LGAs might form joint bodies, providing a basis for many emerging regional endeavours. These trusts would operate in addition to specific programme funding (for example, land care, heritage, nature conservation and so on), and would provide strategic overview, coordination, organisational, educative and fund-raising support across the range of a local or regional community's ESD issues (varying according to the nature of the region and the concerns of the community). The scale of the enterprise would be in the order of, say, one professional and one administrative staff position and a modest administrative budget per trust. If we allow one trust per 100,000 people (more in densely, less in sparsely populated regions), the total direct annual cost might be in the order of $AU25 million; not much at all. Such a scheme would have four effects: provide a basis for regional programmes and processes; provide coordination of the myriad of local or community based initiatives in resource and environmental management; make an explicit commitment that such approaches are accepted as core to our response to sustainability; and enable and influence local government.

This menu could be expanded both in terms of number and detail. Questions of overlap and coordination between such arrangements are not dealt with here. In particular areas, similar agendas could be constructed, institutionalising the macro-policy setting. In the energy-greenhouse area, a sustainable energy authority as proposed in 1994 would be logical. A biodiversity research and development corporation has been suggested. In the difficult area of population policy, if a clear policy is beyond agreement, arrangements (currently absent) might at least be established to allow more informed and constructive debate concerning population-environment linkages and what a population policy might require and entail.[52]

CONCLUSION: POOR PROSPECTS?

In conclusion, some points are positive and some less so. First, these proposals are relatively modest. The comparable arrangements noted from other public policy fields show that, if government were indeed serious about ESD, these sorts of reforms would be quite natural things to do within its normal parameters. However, if a number of such institutional reforms were put in place, in the longer term at least, far more would be getting done, in a public policy sense, than at present. At the time of writing, the Productivity Commission was commencing an inquiry into the implementation by Commonwealth agencies of the National Strategy for ESD. Whatever the Commission's own findings (some find the tasking of this strange, the Commission being widely regarded as a "dry" economic organisation), the issue of implementation of ESD will come to some prominence again in the public debate, and institutional reform may rise on the agenda.

Less positively, there are signs that even such modest, pragmatic steps are unlikely. Building solid institutional foundations to inform and enable policy and management capacities has not been a feature of recent years. Indeed, useful or promising institutions have been mutilated — notably the RAC, the Bureau of Immigration, Multicultural and Population Research, the Energy Research and Development Corporation, or the National Population Council. Victoria's outstanding Land Conservation Council has recently been interfered with. Further, the statutory independence and future status of key (although not perfect) Commonwealth agencies such as the Great Barrier Reef Marine Park Authority and the Australian Heritage Commission — even, according to some whispers, the Murray-Darling Basin Commission — seem to be under a cloud. The building of such notable institutions was mostly done in the past, in response to a previous, narrower construction of the problem than ESD. Following a decade and a half of institutional and administrative change associated with marketisation and new managerialism, it is becoming apparent that the Westminster tradition of minister's office-department-statutory authority does not hold as it once did. While admitting the ossified and rigid nature of some statutory authorities in the past, the principle they embodied — that certain public functions require arm's-length independence from the politics of the moment — is an important one for many aspects of sustainability and should not slip away unnoticed.

There is a deep inconsistency between official sustainability policy — let alone more radical prescriptions — which says we need to do much more to enhance sustainability, and the dominant neo-liberal fashions of public policy and administration — marketisation, corporatisation, privatisation, downsizing, outsourcing, budget-cutting, and a general withdrawal of the state. Moreover, there is a trend of attacks on institutions independent of direct ministerial control. Attributes of sustainability problems — especially temporal scale, uncertainty and the imperative of inclusion — indicate that statutory authorities and other once-removed, independent but persistent mechanisms are attractive options, given that they are inclusive and participatory. On another note, the ability of marketised resource management agencies to advance sustainability principles such as precaution, cross-portfolio or cross-landscape integration and community participation (other than as reactive consumers) is questionable.

Can Australia downsize its way to comprehensive environmental management, or outsource its responsibilities to the future? Sustainability is inevitably a collective, public project — the biggest of our time — but the collective, public capability is being ever-reduced. This chapter implies a major rôle for the state, not in a strict regulatory fashion but an enabling one. As government takes its hands off the wheel, it may be in vain to hope that reasonable institutional dues be paid to sustainability. Perhaps sustainability is just unlucky, arising in an era when public projects are unfashionable and the state is timidly shrinking.

One cannot leave this issue without asking the question: is withdrawal of the state from managing the Australian environment as inevitable and logical as we are told? Is the state so terribly bloated? According to the International Monetary Fund (IMF), cited in *The Economist* (20 September 1997), the standard measure of the size of the state — government expenditure as a proportion of GDP — was 37% in Australia in 1996, roughly the same as Japan. In post-Thatcher Britain the figure was 42% and, in that paragon of the joys of downsizing, New Zealand, it was 47%. The average for developed nations was 45%. It would seem that Australia could on calmer reflection choose that it can indeed invest collectively in a sustainable future. And it might invest, not in general avowals of intent or in use-by-date throwaway programmes of dubious long-term benefit, but in the essential informational and institutional infrastructure required to lift ESD from the margin to the mainstream of public policy and administration.

CONCLUSION: ENVIRONMENTAL POLICY IN THE GLOOMY 1990s

K.J. Walker

The year 1998 and the first half of 1999 were marked by seemingly endless freak weather. 1998 was the hottest year since records began. There were floods and "natural disasters" everywhere. In China, the Yangtze flooded, displacing millions and killing unknown numbers. Immense floods in the Ganges and Brahmaputra river systems submerged *two-thirds* of Bangladesh and did extensive damage in neighbouring India. Serious droughts afflicted much of Africa. In Europe, severe flooding afflicted countries as far apart as Italy, Britain and Poland. Major hurricanes and devastating tornadoes hit the Caribbean and the south-east of the United States of America. Immense damage was done, including massive flooding, mudslides and crop destruction in four countries. In Australia, some regions went direct from drought to flood, with no change in their "natural disaster" relief status, which in some cases had already lasted several years.

In October, the *Living Planet Report* documented the extent of environmental destruction in the last 30 years. In November, at a meeting in Buenos Aires, the Hadley Centre for Climate Change presented their findings that global warming was worse and was developing more rapidly than predicted. Desertification, crop failures, water shortages and flooding affecting millions were predicted. Global warming could be expected to "run away" uncontrollably after 2050.[1] Though controversial, these reports spelt out widespread fears. Was this string of disasters "natural"? Was all this due to neglect of ecological constraints? Or were these merely "freak" conditions just a little outside the norm, but within the statistical probabilities? If so, why were they so widespread? Either way, government and communities were caught flat-footed, the problems unforeseen.

But the Greenhouse Effect is man-made: global warming is a human problem. If 1998 was the leading edge of climatic change, it is early and unwelcome. With uncharacteristic candour, the Chinese government admitted that the Yangtze floods had been aggravated, if not actually caused, by extensive deforestation in the catchment areas. Similar admissions from nominally more "democratic" governments have not been forthcoming.

And that is at the core of the problem. For the "democratic bargain" has relied on an uneasy truce between rich and poor, based on the distributionism of the mass market. This has built a "growth imperative" into modern political systems. Structurally, it is difficult to break out of. Political parties geared to short-term electoral success have been reluctant to try. Corporations, more than ever worried about short-term share price fluctuations and their "bottom line", have not encouraged them. But the massive slowing down of the global economy, in what could be the end of the post-1945 boom, confronts them. Simultaneous ecological and economic crisis is a nightmare for which "liberal" democracy is not equipped.

Australia, home of the "cultural cringe", has reflected these trends in its own distorting mirror. As Economou notes, the pendulum has swung from a situation in which, during the early 1980s, environmentalists were defining some of the terms of the debate, to one in which by the late 1990s, they have been effectively excluded. As Doyle points out, one powerful mechanism for this has been the development of a doctrine of "market environmentalism", in which ecosystems are treated as infinitely renewable and infinitely substitutable, after the manner of neoclassical economics.

These changes have transformed the study of environmental policy in two ways. Firstly, there is presently very little point in developing or applying sophisticated models of the policy process, since the process itself is far from sophisticated. Secondly, the policy of devolving Commonwealth responsibilities focusses attention on the state and local levels of government. While the States have always been important, the emergence of local government as a major player is an interesting, and largely unpredicted, development. As Adams and Hine observe, the question of the survival of local government initiative in the face of rate-capping and other restrictive measures is of some importance.

Dissonance between public concern and political neglect persists. Especially on the Right, ideologically driven developmentalism has surged, ignoring virtually all of the long-running debate about ecological constraint and collective goods. Furthermore, as Carden points out, there is every reason to suppose that environmental concern, far from being an outcome of "postmaterialist" values, as suggested by some survey researchers, is driven predominantly by *utilitarian* values. As Doyle suggests, this delegitimises the notion that environmentalism reflects only the concerns of a tiny minority. This fact is reflected in the general rise in concern about environmental issues, which has continued with only minor fluctuations.[2] And if general concern about environmental issues is utilitarian, it is likely, firstly, to be responsive to rational argument, secondly, to be persistent, and thirdly, to culminate in demands for change in institutions and policies.

However, both the major political parties and the mass media now take environment to be a minority concern, and consequently not news, nor are the relevant issues widely debated. It appears, as Economou notes, as if there has been an "issue-attention" cycle; but the waning of interest is only in the ruling camp. This dissonance between public concern and élite lack of attention is symptomatic of Australia's drift towards the North American model of plebiscitary plutocracy.

Two consequences arise. The first is that policy must be understood at the level of political economy before it can be pursued at a more detailed level. The second, and interesting, consequence is that environmental policy processes are now considerably more diffused, tending to increase the probability of uncoordinated, *ad hoc* and reactive decision making.

POLITICAL ECONOMY: GLOBAL PERSPECTIVE

Ecological processes are the most fundamental, from the point of view of all living beings. Animal life depends on photosynthesis, and with it a vast range of other ecological interactions. Nearly all of the productive processes on which humans depend for their basic sustenance are natural, not human. Human productive systems *harness* natural processes, but they do not replace them. It is very doubtful that they could ever do so.

Policy processes therefore should begin with natural processes, and build up from there. But they do not, building down instead from human societies and their dynamics. Stranger still, they frequently rely on bodies of theory that assume natural goods to be inexhaustible, infinitely replaceable and eternally resilient. In short, there is a fundamental dissonance between traditional statecraft and ecology.

This is understandable, if undesirable. For most of human history, natural resources of all kinds have been abundant. Shortages have typically been local; in consequence, while ecological stress has been a powerful agent of social and technological change, it has not been an explicit policy problem until very recent times.[3] Instead, social dynamics, and in particular interstate competition, have been the dominant evolutionary forces.

THE EVOLUTION OF NATION-STATES

The evolution of the nation-state, with its distinct hierarchy of priorities, focussed statecraft firstly on survival in competition with other states. Survival *of the ruling élite* is the issue. The importance of non-rulers lies in their ability to support the rulers, not in their essential humanity or their god-given human rights.

Rose's division of modern nation-state policies into the three broad classes of "defining", "resource mobilising" and "social welfare" remains influential. "Defining" policies include territorial defence, maintenance of internal order, and "securing resources" via taxation and the issue of currency. They are handled by ministries of war, legal affairs, police and finance. The second class includes "... building canals, roads and railways, or creating a postal and telegraph service"; the third pensions, health services, education and so on. States attend first to their defining functions, then to resource mobilisation, and finally to social welfare, with considerable divergence in levels of provision. Only 20 of 32 states in Rose's study had "at least one ministry concerned with questions of land use and/or with the protection or exploitation of natural resources".[4]

As the modern state's "defining" activities become increasingly dependent on technology, its survival depends more and more on resource mobilisation, inclusive of economic management. The "defining" and "resource mobilising" policy categories become inextricably intertwined. Because, since the Industrial Revolution, social harmony in the wealthier countries at least has been bought by a steadily rising material standard of living, élites are under continual pressure to keep the goods flowing.

Consequently, the political élites of modern nation-states

unavoidably accept substantial responsibilities for economic management. Pressure for "economic transformation" is maintained by popular aspirations for economic wellbeing and improvement, plus interstate competition.[5] In the competitive multi-state system which emerged from the Industrial Revolution, this required an emphasis on "national" capital, state support of capital and a close relationship between capital and military.[6] Super-power arms races and competition in military technologies generate pressure for innovation in "hard" technologies and economic growth. Under these conditions, "military-industrial complexes" reflect the powerful convergence of state and corporate interests.[7] Rose contends that states never give up activities: realignments of priorities may lead to massive transfers of resources between functions, but none are relinquished.

Even during the present wave of ideologically driven retreat from the functions of government, regulation, social welfare and distributive justice are being cut back, though not relinquished. But military expenditure is not reduced, nor are massive subsidies to politically powerful groups such as farmers or the road lobby. The application of right-wing libertarian mythology to public policy stops short at the interests of the military-industrial complex and corporate power.

The primacy of "defining" functions has meant that states tend to relegate ecological and other long-term issues to a place behind even social welfare. As doctrines of "smaller government" gain a hold, such issues are pushed even further into the background.

However, one devastating implication of environmental crisis is that this set of priorities is no longer appropriate; mere survival requires that it be radically transformed. If ecological stability must be given priority, then failure to accord it the importance it deserves is likely to lead to collapse of the most basic life-support systems.[8] States which simply pursue their traditional "defining" functions may be headed for the same fate as the Minoan, Sumerian or Mayan civilisations .

THE DEMOCRATIC DILEMMA

This poses a particularly acute dilemma for democratic régimes, or more accurately, those which depend to some extent on popular voting mechanisms to manage transitions between governments.[9]

In "democratic" countries, once economic management becomes a political goal, politics revolves about distribution, because political parties gain and maintain support by offering handouts to favoured groups. This is particularly easy in the "frontier" stage of political history, because resources are abundant and waste apparently insignificant. (Though the near-extinction of the North American bison and the wiping out of the passenger pigeon should never be forgotten.)

The advent of Keynesian economics, with its stress on the use of government expenditure to stimulate the economy, offered a utilitarian justification for distributionism. But Keynes' model of economic management is counter-cyclical, requiring governments running deficits during a slump to budget for a surplus in boom time, thus dampening the boom-and-bust cycle. During the post-1945 economic boom, enthusiasm for economic growth prompted abandonment of such budgetary restraint; political resistance made the distributive expenditures of depression difficult to eliminate. The outcome was a semi-Keynesian pattern of deficit expenditure at all times, with inflationary consequences: the "Keynesian ratchet".[10] Government attempts to "grow" their way out of this problem generally worsened it. "Stagflation" was one important result.

The "Keynesian ratchet" is a serious trap once resources become scarcer. "Growth", especially of the cruder, indiscriminate kind, requires resources which are increasingly unavailable or suffering from abuse. Pursuit of growth-oriented policies consequently creates increasing conflict, not merely with alternative resource uses, but with socially, aesthetically or ecologically desirable goals. Carried to extremes, it can be socially and ecologically destructive. Worse, the most telling and electorally convincing symptoms often appear *after* irreversible harm has been done.

A double paradox thus results. "Growth" measures which were once electorally popular become an increasing liability; yet rulers cannot perceive alternatives. At least three factors contribute: slow public realisation of the problems; ideological and intellectual rigidity in political parties unable to revise their problem definitions; and the effects of the mass media, which in addition to their profoundly conservative and seriously trivialising effects, are often even less capable than the political parties of sniffing change in the air, and adjusting their thinking.

The second leg of the paradox results from the state's close intertwining with corporate interests, as well as the structural consequences of its own economic management strategies. The dominant policy mechanisms geared to "economic transformation" — primarily by promoting capital accumulation — are not designed to accommodate radical structural change. Instead, they promote tunnel vision, clinging to the distributionist status quo. In response to the "failure of Keynesianism" the Right in particular have emphasised a programme of retreat to defining and resource mobilising functions, shifting public resources to private hands in the hope of promoting economic growth.

GLOBALISED DISHONESTY: THE MARCH OF CAPITALISM

One outcome of the collapse of the Soviet Union was a perception that the doctrines of the Left had failed. This was certainly true, at least as regards Leninism, which was more properly a kind of forced-draught *state capitalism* enforced by totalistic state control. But, in a classic example of muddled thinking, the conclusion was drawn that *therefore* the doctrines of the opposing political trend were valid. Some went so far as to claim that the great ideological disputes were over, and that all the world's affairs could now be solved in a mild Lockean liberal manner.

Naturally, the most powerful capitalist nations used the ensuing power vacuum in a most un-liberal fashion. They succeeded in engineering a rapid "transition" to market capitalism in Russia, provoking social and economic breakdown, a massive explosion of criminality, and extended misery for ordinary, decent people. Internationally, they used the power of the World Bank and the International Monetary Fund to demand the application of economic "rationalist" policies on Asian nations, provoking the 1998 collapse of the parasitic "tiger" régimes. And they sought the imposition of an international treaty régime that blatantly favoured the interests of major multinationals, the bulk of them based in the United States of America.

These recent modifications to the global treaty régime have attempted to institutionalise tenets of neoclassical economic dogma which not merely erode national political sovereignty, but have profoundly anti-ecological implications as well. The issue of patents in genetic material profoundly disturbed countries with a large subsistence sector to their economies, because multinational firms could patent DNA from plants used in traditional agriculture and then demand payment for its use. The setting up of the World Trade Organisation, under the auspices of GATT (the General Agreement on Trade and Tariffs), with sweeping powers to disallow discrimination in the name of "free trade", turns out to have dire implications for origin labelling, discrimination against repressive régimes, and even the consumer's right to know what is being purchased.[11] The proposed, but at the time of writing not yet concluded Multilateral Investment Agreement (MIA) would even allow giant corporations to sue governments for alleged loss of profits if denied access to markets or investment opportunities. This has excited such grave concerns that the treaty may never come to fruition.

With the emergence of global policy régimes, the less powerful nations are increasingly strait-jacketed, their policy options restricted. Where they are heavily dependent on one or two crops, or where the "commanding heights" of their economy are occupied by multinational corporations with significant bargaining power of their own, the pressures are considerable. As smaller nations often have better records of innovation and lateral thinking than larger ones, this may fatally inhibit needed change.

THE EMPIRE OF FUDGE: OUTDATED IDEOLOGIES

Major political parties all espouse political ideas which were formulated during the eighteenth and nineteenth centuries. Not only do they fail to deal adequately with the many changes, technological and social, which have occurred since then, but all are built around sociogenic first principles. Not even Marx, who saw further into the millstone than most, appreciated the profundity of the connection between human society and its biophysical environment.[12]

In general, the Left has responded poorly to the environmental challenge. The "hard" Left has been bewildered by the breakdown of its favoured developmentalist policy model — Stalinist forced-draught industrialisation — and the collapse of those political systems which embodied it. The "soft" Left, in less repressive countries, has similar difficulties with "blue-collar developmentalism". With occasional exceptions, flirtations with the Greens have not led to harmonious policy development: the conflict between Greens' social and industrial policies and the older Left positions has been quite intractable. Many attempts to popularise "Red-Green" and "Green Left" positions mask attempted hijackings, generally of the Greens by the Left. Some traditional Leftists have concluded that the Greens have nothing to offer, rejecting Green policies as "poison". Tasmanian Labor, having earlier sabotaged its Accord with the Greens, colluded with the Liberals to reduce the size of the Tasmanian Parliament, thus diminishing minority party access. Such knee-jerk reactions show that the old Trades Hall machine politics methods are still alive, well, and kicking heads.

CRITIQUE OF THE RIGHT

The attempt to avert change — and the necessity of constructive thought — is also the response of the Right. As Economou and Doyle show, it has been quite explicit and ideological. Given their near-monopoly control of press and media, it is hardly surprising to find that the Right position is better-articulated, more structured, and far more pervasive than any competing viewpoint.

Yet the right-wing position is not simply hostile to ecological thinking; it also embodies some serious and crippling inconsistencies.

The Right depend heavily on a selective reading of the "social choice" school of political economy, predictably stopping short of some of its more socially responsible findings.[13] This view denies the existence of common interests and reduces government to a "night watchman state", fending off a Hobbesian "war of all men against all men". Public policy space is to be minimised to "expand" that for private investment and "enterprise": essentially a charter for wealth and greed, to the detriment of the less well off. Yet this view marks a mere stage in the development of social choice theory, pre-dating the work of Axelrod, Ostrom and others, which shows that individuals can and do perceive cooperation as serving their self-interest, and behave accordingly.[14] Similarly, Olson suggested that particular groups within democratic political systems could gain a stranglehold on the system and reduce its efficiency by excessive demands.[15] But Olson's ideas were quickly subjected to a biased and blinkered interpretation. He had suggested that the high tariff régimes of Australia and New Zealand in the post-1945 period had led to the entrenchment of local business interests enjoying virtual monopolies, matched by entrenched trades unions. These had contributed to the ongoing decline in standard of living relative to the rest of the world. But the Right used this argument — which has been heavily criticised — highly selectively, to justify the application of "economic rationalism" to Australia. It hit small domestic manufacturing and trade unions exceptionally hard, but failed to tackle other, politically more difficult, irrationalities. In the period since the 1960s, social inequalities greatly increased and unemployment rose to unprecedented levels. The Right's policies aggravated these trends.

The theories — political and economic — on which the Right base their dogmas are notable for their ignoring of power. Yet in practice, most economic exchanges, and, by definition, all political ones, occur between participants of unequal power. The most serious of all criticisms of Adam Smith's model of exchange was simply that once an element of power entered the relationship, it was neither free nor uncoerced, and consequently would no longer *necessarily* result in a gain in welfare. This objection was so important that Smith himself recognised it, though his followers have been more reluctant. Thus the biggest failure of the "libertarian" Right view that small government is always good is simply that huge concentrations of economic power — such as giant multinational corporations — are responsible to no one. Some regulation and control of these institutions is unavoidably necessary, and government is the only even marginally responsible institution to hand.[16] The emergence of various supranational institutions, especially in Europe, underlines this need, especially when the tensions between traditional "defining" functions and the needs of ecological sustainability remain unresolved, and require policy, decision and institution-building.

POLITICAL ECONOMY: AUSTRALIA

Australia's place as a supplier of unprocessed and semiprocessed raw materials to the industrialised world has always placed it in a precarious position, vulnerable in particular to global market price fluctuations. A small population and consequent limited market have made industrialisation difficult; poor communications have made the problem worse. The risk was always of a slide into Argentinian chaos, unable to break out from a status as mere farm, woodlot and quarry. The retrograde economic policies of the 1980s and 1990s have worsened this problem, especially the irresponsible commitment to a level of "free" trade — or more accurately tariff abolition — far beyond that of most of Australia's trading partners. Worsening economic vulnerability has not only increased unemployment, expanded crime and pauperised a growing underclass. It has also led to attacks on environmental standards, justified by "necessity".

But the "necessity" is always short-term, and the neglect of the long-term consequences is both damaging and scandalous. Furthermore, it is often *economically* irrational in the medium term, and sometimes even the short.

The rapid growth of "quarry Australia" is one such example. Low current mineral prices suggest a short-term oversupply, and the wisdom of holding off on mineral development until prices are more favourable. But instead, state and federal governments push ahead with new and bigger projects, reducing the promoters' costs by transferring them to the public purse or indigenous inhabitants. The McArthur River case in this collection is illustrative; and it may be seen as a "dry run" for the Jabiluka uranium mine in the Kakadu national park, approved and doggedly backed by the Howard Government despite widespread disquiet. Uranium mining is particularly controversial on environmental grounds, and its economics is highly suspect. As with nuclear power, project estimates rarely if ever include the cost of "cleaning up" the site after closure, nor do they make allowance for accidents. Yet radioactive spills have occurred from Australian mines, and their long-term impact is unknown. The health hazards of uranium mining have been known since the Middle Ages. They include carcinogenic effects due to dust inhalation and the release of radon gas . Tailings dumps, larger in volume than the original ore body, may remain radioactive for 100,000 years; their fine dust is easily spread by wind and water.[17] The taxpayer will eventually subsidise the clean-up and bear the health and environmental costs; it is quite probable that the net gain to Australia will be negative.

Woodchipping of native and especially old-growth forests is another example. The newly elected Labor government of Tasmania celebrated its accession to office in August 1998 by doubling the rate of woodchipping in Tasmania. This is particularly damaging in Tasmania given the enormous importance of tourism to its economy, and the centrality of pristine forest environments as a tourist "draw". Nor is woodchipping rational even in forestry terms: the scarcity of quality cabinet timbers means that many of the trees being chipped at knockdown (and even subsidised) prices could be sold, in smaller volume, for many times the price. In the process, many more jobs could be created, and, in the current jargon, the timber sold "value-added".

If ecological irrationalities are added, the list becomes longer: Australia had an excellent opportunity — 20 years ago — to put itself in the forefront of research and development in solar energy in particular. Abundantly endowed with sunlight, Australia's opportunities were great. Interest was high in the universities, too. Instead, Australians were humiliated in 1997 to see envoys of "their" government claiming at Kyoto that Australia was "critically dependent" on fossil fuels. A Minister of that same government had earlier responded to a question about renewable energy sources by saying that the changeover to gas was well advanced!

Australia's present system, in short, does not deliver economically *or* ecologically rational policies. Structural rigidities are one reason.

DEPENDENT DEVELOPMENTALISM

Structural rigidity in the Australian system arises both from its position in the global system, and from its governmental and intergovernmental arrangements. Dependence on overseas resources for "development" has imposed a specific policy régime and limited government options, while the imbalance of resources and responsibilities between levels of government has sharply inhibited responsible policy making. The sectoral dissonance of Australian policy is in part traceable to these causes.

Australia's economy was and remains "dominion capitalist", like those of Canada, New Zealand and Brazil. It depends on exports of primary or minimally processed products, is dominated by foreign capital in manufacturing investment, and has a large service sector. Economic growth, mythologised as "development", is a continuing pressure on governments.[18] Financial dependence also means technological dependence and a "branch-plant" economy controlled by remote overseas owners. To attract industry and investment in competition with other nations, governments offer direct subsidies as well as the "infrastructure" which distinguishes colonial developmentalism. Chronic balance of payments problems are typical.[19]

As Carden notes, this dependence can be deep indeed. The London market's blockade of loan finance for Queensland in the early 1920s was far more than a dispute over credit ratings. It was an intervention, by foreign capital, in the domestic affairs of Queensland, in support of a particular interest group, in this case the graziers. Its effect was to cripple the industrial policy of Queensland's Government. This event eerily foreshadowed the difficulties encountered by the Whitlam Government of 1972–75, in its attempts to "buy back the farm". Dependence on foreign capital inevitably means a restriction on policy opportunities, beyond the mere desire of the capital source to control its application. Political "propriety" may be as important as fiscal.

Dependent development by its nature creates links between domestic and foreign capital of the kind revealed in the 1920s and 1970s. Given the sectoral dissonance of the Australian policy system, this can result in severe mismatches of power between different sectors.

The traditional Australian system of statist developmentalism masks this dissonance. "Development" is identified as a goal for both business and government, bringing the concerns of business onto the agenda of government, at the same time setting the terms of debate.[20] Deliberately left vague, its rhetoric conceals what goes on behind it, from handouts of public money to outright corruption. Historically, it was fostered by colonial developmentalism.

Government participation in the economy, even though extensive, was nearly always aimed at "creating conditions" for profitable private economic activity. Differences in emphasis between the major political parties were less important than the broad strategy. Government control of "natural monopolies", such as rail transport, communications and energy supply, for a time generated profits which could be used to cross-subsidise uneconomic services, or reinvested in further infrastructure. From the late 1920s onwards, the supplanting and decay of "natural monopolies" in transport and urban services paralleled a shift in fiscal dominance to the federal government.

The growing imbalance of resources between federal and state spheres led both to constraints on policy and distortions in the process. The Financial Agreement of 1927 is generally considered to have been the first major shift in power toward the centre; and the Commonwealth's assumption and retention of the income tax power during the 1940s was the second.

This made the States dependent on the Commonwealth for a high proportion of their revenue. Since the States have large fixed budgets due to their responsibilities in education, policing and many other routine tasks, their tax revenues fell in concert with the fall in revenues from trading. Bound to the distributionist "Keynesian ratchet", and faced after 1945 with massive demands for expanded services, their options narrowed. The single area under their control with potential for substantial expansion was (and is) natural resources. A commitment to their exploitation easily generates hostility to conservation and even to ecological sensitivity in exploitation. Conflict often arises between principle and expediency, as the Labor Party has shown over uranium mining.[21] The temptation to maximise short-term throughput is ever-present; often there is no attempt at all to consider long-term implications. A direct result is a strong, at times authoritarian, commitment to "development" at any cost.[22]

Because States are not responsible for fiscal management, the federal system tempts them to overspend in the knowledge that the Commonwealth can be blamed for inflationary consequences.[23]

There is likely to be little change if the Howard Government manages to implement its proposed tax changes. The promise to turn over the revenue from a GST to the States has not been translated into legislation, as more than one State government complained on seeing the Bills in question in November 1998. The effect is to leave fiscal *control* in federal hands, even though more resources appear to be offered to the States. Limiting resources available to lower levels of government was one of the more draconian measures imposed by the Thatcher Government in Britain.

Adams and Hine further warn that the implementation of Agenda 21 at local level may be affected by rate-capping — another Thatcher trick. State governments labouring under additional loads of transferred responsibility, short of resources, and given to conservative ideology, might well be so tempted.

The changes in policy at the federal level have therefore not affected the broad framework of Australian political economy as much as might be expected. Statist developmentalism continues. The effect of "handing back" responsibilities to the States is not merely to evade and in some cases abandon the national government's responsibilities under international agreements and a reasonable expectation of national government performance. It also diminishes government power vis-á-vis the private sector, given the relative weakness and lack of resources of state and local government. That in turn leads, not merely to *ad hoc* and inadequate assessment and policy formulation, but to a virtual collapse of regulation.

POLICY PROCESSES

In the previous edition of this book, considerable space was devoted to an analysis of meso-level policy processes, of the kind that might be found within single government departments, or at Cabinet level. Given the extent to which ideology has intruded into policy during the 1990s, the importance of political economy has grown in relative terms, and that of established policy process proportionately diminished.

In assessing the impact of the advice offered by planners to government, it has long been appreciated that a planning process in which the final say lies with the politicians is as much subject to corruption as it is to popular input. The planners' careful, tidily interlocked proposals can be mutilated or destroyed by a single corrupt, self-interested or populist decision at the political level. The seriousness, and the likely extent of such decisional vandalism is already being demonstrated. Not merely, as Economou suggests, is it "back to the 1980s", but the effects of anti-green backlash and right-wing "biological Spencerism" have to be accounted for.

The most marked effect, documented throughout this collection, is the virtual abandonment of evaluation of policy prior to its implementation. This is particularly noticeable with large projects of various kinds, such as mines. Furthermore, established techniques, such as environmental impact assessment, are neglected, abused or distorted. Given their inherent weaknesses in the first place, this is a serious development.

The second effect, and perhaps the more pervasive, is greatly to increase the impact of sectoral dissonance. It is this that underlies the piecemeal, *ad hoc*, reactive policy trends so universally observed. Overlaid by the ideological commitment to devolution, the policy process becomes positively fragmented. Governments deliberately weakened become less able to regulate, let alone direct, policy, and the relative power of the private sector is increased.

Within the constraints sketched under political economy, policy processes therefore still require examination detail, bearing firmly in mind that in Australia they are generally fragmented, *ad hoc* and reactive.

BYPASSING TECHNIQUE

For many years a significant debate centred about the choice of tools for the evaluation of environmental policy. Two issues were of exceptional importance: firstly, on what model of decision making evaluative tools should be based, and, secondly, what techniques should be adopted. True debate, however, was stillborn. The technique universally adopted was Environmental Impact Assessment (EIA), embodied in the Environmental Impact Statement (EIS); legislative provision made the EIS universal, if not mandatory.

But the EIA technique was always ill-adapted to environmental decisions. It was a **synoptic**, or **rational-comprehensive** approach, making no allowances for scientific uncertainty or even for changing knowledge. It assumed implicitly that all the necessary data was available, and that it would be sufficient for a final decision.

The rational-comprehensive decision model is extremely influential. It is taught in schools, and many decision makers genuinely believe that they make use of it. Basically, it assumes that the would-be decision maker first gathers together all the relevant data, then evaluates it, and finally comes to a decision which is the "best" choice.[24] Economists are particularly fond of this model, since it underpins the whole "welfare economics" approach, out of which social choice theory grew. In their hands, the notion of "optimality", which may crudely be defined as a formula which offers the best outcome, over time, for all, is particularly powerful.

But rational-comprehensive decision making has been sharply criticised both on technical and on normative grounds. Technically, it is paralysed if full data is not available; in that case, any decision reached must be incomplete and in all probability suboptimal. Data, of course, is costly, and imposes costs for gathering and evaluation. But worse, environmental data can never be final, because of scientific uncertainty. Thus no rational-comprehensive decision dependent on it can be final, nor is there any guarantee that it is optimal. And that is not all. Most decisions having a social impact involve making a choice between one group and another, and environmental decisions may involve choices between humans and other species. The rational-comprehensive model gives no guidance for such choices.

During the 1960s and 1970s, the economists refined the rational-comprehensive approach into a technique known as **cost-benefit analysis**, or CBA. This technique essentially tots up the economic benefits and the economic losses that may be ascribed to a particular proposal, and attempts to quantify them. If the benefits outweigh the disadvantages, preferably by a healthy margin to allow for miscalculation, the proposal is judged worthwhile. The technique, although useful, tends systematically to undervalue long-term goods and socially beneficial considerations. Pearce has shown that conventional cost-benefit analysis will always result in lower allocations of resources than the long run welfare optimum, and that blindness to deficiencies in CBA techniques when dealing with environmental goods leads to their over-exploitation.[25]

EIA is an extension of CBA to environmental decision making. It originated in the United States of America, and is markedly less quantitative. It requires the *proponent* of a particular proposal to conduct the survey, including all relevant information, and draw from that an evaluation of the worth and likely impact of the proposal. In practice, EIA has tended to ignore limitations on information availability, and to distort the implications. This is in part a consequence of cost considerations, and in part a result of having the proponent conduct the investigation. In practice, of course, EIA is carried out by specialist consultants, who are not anxious to upset potential future customers. The requirement that the proponent conduct the evaluation resembles the "polluter pays" formula, with the attraction that government can then avoid the costs. Unfortunately, experience shows that there is no real substitute for independent oversight of project evaluation based on a broader view of the problems and drawing on a wider experience of the environmental conditions. This really requires regulatory agencies with independent investigative and data gathering powers.

Regrettably, the alternatives are not much better. The chief competitor to the rational-comprehensive approach is **disjointed incrementalism**, a decision strategy used far more frequently in the "real world". It makes decisions by a process of approximation, limiting data gathering to what seems relevant to the decisional options at hand. This runs a risk of omitting data which may be relevant to alternative policy lines which have not been identified as options. The name "incrementalism" derives from a habit of building on previous decisions, and making marginal changes. For this reason it has been accused of conservatism. It is adapted to poor information and uncertainty, but by its nature it is less than adequate for any decision requiring a degree of comprehensiveness.[26]

Absolute benchmarks from which decisions can be made *a priori* do not exist, and the search for them is doomed to failure; humans operate by making a series of comparisons, and refining them as they go. Thus good decision strategies need to be **iterative** (that is, geared to repetition), **reversible**, so that damage done in ignorance may be mitigated (if not fully repaired) and **cautious**, aware of scientific uncertainty, the fallibility of human knowledge and the accident-prone nature of human arrangements.

The evidence suggests that much decision making in Australia is quite crudely incremental, and highly disjointed as well. Governments are notoriously reluctant to iterate or even to re-examine decisions; often they are not at all reversible, and developmentalism is not well acquainted with caution. Paradoxically, Australian incrementalism operates within the statist developmentalism policy régime, which means that it is also imperfectly comprehensive. This mixing of decision strategies, especially where one belongs to metapolicy and one to practice, is by no means uncommon. In Australia, it is closely associated with sectoral dissonance and the diffusion of responsibility integral to the federal political system. The changes of the 1990s mean a much more extensive use of *ad hoc*, reactive, incrementalist policy strategies, especially at the more localised levels of the system to which responsibility — but not power — is being devolved.

SECTORAL DISSONANCE

Sectoral dissonance is essential to understanding policy processes in Australia. It has not one, but several implications. Firstly, both Commonwealth and State governments are more competent in some areas than others; policy successes therefore tend to cluster in the areas of competence. Secondly, policy processes are fragmented. Lateral communication between government departments remains poor; cooperation between the different levels of government is desultory and prone to breakdown. On a given issue, relevant policies may be decided at more than one location, and at different times.

Sectoral dissonance arises in part because government leaves some policy areas predominantly to private "enterprise"; and in part for historical reasons, due to concentration on certain sectors of the economy. Experience in organising major single-purpose statutory authorities, geared to delivering a single service, was once thought to be a major strength of Australian government. Frequently there is a body of competence in a particular area, as a result of government's rôle in promoting or regulating a specific activity. But in other areas, competence is lacking. Certain recent events, such as the disastrous results attendant on the utilisation of State banks to support speculative industrial investment, suggest that such lacunae are serious.

For coordinated environmental management, of course, sectoral dissonance goes with diffusion of responsibility as a prime cause of *ad hoc*, disjointed, reactive policy making.

CORRUPTION

Corruption is in many ways the joker in the pack of policy analysis. It is capable of subverting the most sophisticated explanations, simply by changing outcomes unpredictably. It is the antithesis of openness in the policy process. This is of particular importance for environmental policy, insofar as it requires important inputs from those outside the main channels of policy, such as scientists and those affected by policy decisions.

In the last two decades it has been generally recognised that corruption has long existed in Australian politics, and that it has been particularly rife in two States, NSW and Queensland, that have established anti-corruption watchdog bodies during that period.

However, most people think of corruption in terms of pay-offs, bought politicians and crooked deals. Certainly there has been no lack of this. The sale of honours under certain governments became scandalous. Land rezoning is a perennial source of corruption allegations at municipal level. Petty bribery in relation to the enforcement of standards is by no means unheard of. State and federal politicians have been known to accept shares from firms whose profitability might be affected by their decisions; to "rort" travel allowances and other benefits; and to mislead their colleagues and the public.

However, there are other forms of corruption, much of it including behaviour which would not necessarily be regarded as corrupt by everyone. Most political parties, when in power, lean to one side rather than another, "helping their mates" where possible. But there is a narrow line between being helpful and positively disadvantaging other members of the community. Australian political history is littered with examples of public money being used to underpin private profit; never regarded as scandalous because of the statist bias in colonial developmentalism, it has nonetheless transferred from public purse to private pocket sums which, in cumulative terms, are very large indeed.

Corrupt political techniques are also rife. One of the most common is the partial or complete bypassing of deliberative bodies. Backroom deals — proper or not — are "stitched up", then presented to the legislators as a fait accompli, not so much for approval as for rubber-stamping. Few who have served on committees can have failed to experience this technique.

Corruption poses quite specific threats to democratic politics. In particular, its lack of transparency subverts open debate and is likely to exclude informed opinion in favour of short-term self-interest. Its persistence is in part due to the partiality of ruling élites for secrecy, and their anxiety to avoid scrutiny. Under those conditions, well-meant confidentiality may well prove extraordinarily difficult to disentangle from blatant dishonesty.

Of course there is no guarantee whatsoever that democratic decisions will be ecologically rational. In fact, given the drastic restriction of information available to the average citizen, voters may even be unable to choose according to their own best interests. But with the observed widespread concern about environmental issues, grounded firmly in utilitarian considerations, sane environmental policy is probably better served by democratic openness than hole-and-corner bargaining.

RE-ESTABLISHING HEGEMONY

As Economou notes, Commonwealth government policy from Hawke onwards aimed at re-establishing political and administrative control over a policy process in which the environmental movement had achieved partial success in defining the terms of debate. This openness was undoubtedly a shock to government, used to defining and confining public discussion. It was probably no accident that the development of metapolicy worked so as to restrict access to government for the environmental movement. Such devices as insisting on a single environment representative, the use of the "roundtable" approach criticised by Doyle, and the "institutionalisation" — or co-opting — of the process all tended in the same direction. The goal was the re-establishment of hegemony.

Ruling élites desire to maintain and extend their power, both for reasons of patronage and the maintenance of their "defining" functions.[27] Under conditions in which orthodoxy is threatened, their instinctive response is to close ranks. The ability to do so effectively depends in part on the capability to continue the promotion and maintenance of characteristic myths — such as those about "development" — and the ability of those in power to "block" dissenting viewpoints. Control of the political agenda is central to maintaining existing institutional arrangements and promoting élite consensus on their efficacy. Serious consideration of viable alternative strategies may thereby be throttled, delayed or entirely prevented. This is "non-decision making", characteristic of régimes under which significant sectors of the community are excluded, or significant viewpoints repressed.[28] Such restrictions of the political agenda may make even the hegemonists themselves vulnerable to the threat of electoral backlash, if they attempt novel policies.

But a much deeper constraint exists: historically, hegemony has been built on exploitation, both of natural resources and of human beings. In modern mass-market societies it is maintained by distributionism. Threats to that undermine not merely hegemony, but the whole nineteenth century "smokestack" approach to industry and development.

ESCAPE ROUTES: POSITIVE POLICY OPTIONS

There are, as the preceding chapters emphasise, many escape routes open. Most, if not all, offer a challenge to "business as usual". For that reason, they are more demanding, if potentially more rewarding.

COOPERATION AND COORDINATION

The most frequently emphasised theme throughout this book is the need for cooperation and coordination in policy making. Mercer instances the pressures on the coastal strip; Carden notes the disjunctions in Queensland development policy; Adams and Hine find local policy development inhibited by attitudes at state and federal levels; Taplin's findings stress the lack of mutuality in the Sydney region; and Dovers points to persisting lack of integration among the relics of the ESD "process".

Coordination in particular is inescapable, since connectivity guarantees that policies will have ramifications outside their immediate focus. Policy moves under the Hawke Government appear to have recognised this need, and to have been groping towards a more comprehensive approach, involving both metapolicy and institution-building.

It is less clear that a clearly defined regulatory régime was ever explored in any depth, or even sketched in outline. This is particularly unfortunate, as it set to one side much valuable work that has been done on responsive regulation, involving cooperation between government and industry. It also scouted the thorny but important issue of effective enforcement. Since this, in turn, involves effective evaluation, and no serious attempt has been made to set up powerful and competent evaluative bodies at state or federal levels, this must be counted a major gap.

IMAGINATION AND NOVELTY

Carden's focus on the general lack of viability of European-style farming in the tropics carries with it a series of corollaries, and not only for farming.[29] In general, the trend in environmental metapolicy has been to stress the advantages — economic as well as ecological — of working *with* the biophysical environment, rather than attempting to force it into a predetermined mould. Irrigation in Australia's inland, for example, suffers from very high evaporative losses, directly affecting the design and desirability of storages. Conflict over upriver irrigation proposals, often sparked by downriver objectors, is becoming very common. Such projects often disrupt delicately balanced ecosystems as well as farmers. Resources such as coal and gas are exploited at rates far beyond the optimum, with short-term effects such as inadequate returns and major disruptions to the landscape; in the longer run, they may become both expensive and excessively scarce.

But alternatives do exist. In WA, after the collapse of cotton production on the Ord River scheme, and the later withdrawal of subsidies, farms were kept afloat by sophisticated crop diversification, exploiting the long growing season to access markets at times when prices were high, and by adoption of varied, high-value crops for domestic and foreign markets.[30] Other regions copying the technique would not be hamstrung by remoteness and high costs as the Ord was; especially along the Queensland coast, no major engineering works would be required, as water is abundant. Arid zones might well be targeted for novel productive techniques compatible with or even exploiting the low rainfall régime. In the energy field, *capture* rather than *generation* is central to sustainability, especially in semi-tropical Australia, where sunlight abounds. In other words, solar and wind energy, not gas or coal, and certainly not nuclear, are the keys.

Such techniques are compatible with a range of policy "settings" in Canberra and the States, except possibly total *laissez-faire*. High labour costs, a consequence of decent living standards for workers, mean that Australia has always to think in terms of exporting products with a high added value, or trading in skills and knowledge. The implications include the need for policies directed at discovering and channelling suitable technologies, effective education, and an entrepreneurial class able to seize and exploit the consequent opportunities. Despite massive subsidies to the wealthy, such a class does not seem to exist in Australia.

SUSTAINABILITY AND INSTITUTION-BUILDING

The development of a truly sustainable policy régime, as Dovers points out, depends quite critically on sustained institution-building at all levels. By this is not meant *institutionalisation* in McCall's sense, in which problems are "taken over" and passed back to existing bureaucracies — with other preoccupations — for routinisation. Nor does it embrace *co-optation*, in which environmental groups and the public are minority participants in "round table" processes dominated by powerful vested interests.

As Dovers demonstrates, the aftermath of the ESD process left Australia with "literally hundreds" of developing institutions, which, given coordination, could have formed a powerful and important policy network. This would have permitted exchange of information and experience, as well as direct collaboration over policy formulation. But some institutions were abolished early; others limped on, and others still have been starved or thwarted. Ironically, the rapid progress of Agenda 21 at the municipal level has actually meant an increase in the number of institutions competent to join a coordinated national policy régime.

Yet, despite the advertised "retreat" from many functions, especially at the federal level, the will to innovate is not dead.

Interestingly, "state-assisted marketisation" has given rise to novel regulatory bodies such as the Productivity Commission and the competition watchdog, both endowed with sweeping powers and the teeth to enforce them. To repeat, statist developmentalism is not dead in Australia; it has merely undergone a sea change.

CONCLUSION: POLICY PERSPECTIVES

In global, historical, perspective, human societies have tended to use increases in productivity to support larger populations; enhanced living standards are a mere by-product. Paradoxically, this results in a long-term increase in the sum total of misery, rather than its alleviation: the classic Malthusian dead end. In Australia's case, culture, political attitudes and social organisation since European settlement have been derivative. The desire to "catch up" has led to the attitude that resources must be developed at all costs, and that bigger is better: more population, more exports and imports, expansion of cultivation, all should be sought without limit. The global ecological crisis is not the first challenge to that wisdom, but it is by far the most significant. It suggests that nothing less than radical changes in attitude and policy are needed.

One of the characteristics of exponential growth is that, because the rate of growth itself increases, crises tend to develop rapidly. This has been very evident during the last half of the twentieth century in Australia. From being a country in which many mineral resources were unmapped and unknown, and in which the "outback" was genuinely untouched, Australia now finds foreign multinational mining companies opposing indigenous land rights because they might "lock up" underpriced mineral resources, while would-be cotton farmers propose to irrigate plains in the Cooper Creek catchment. Bitter interstate and intercommunal disputes arise over water use in the Murray-Darling Basin, while urban congestion and recreational pressures threaten hundreds of miles of coastline. The abruptness of these changes is very marked: suddenly, the continent is shrinking alarmingly.

Mere conservation becomes urgent under such conditions; ecologically responsible management metamorphoses from pleasant pipe-dream to pressing imperative. Australia's unique fauna and flora represent a reservoir of biological resources of enormous potential, quite apart from their considerable non-utilitarian value. But the opportunities they present for novel approaches to "development" have so far been almost completely ignored. State governments and the major political parties, for example, still construct the environmental problem in terms of "jobs versus conservation". There has been little awareness of the employment and other economic benefits of sustainable yield technologies, nutrient cycling, alternative energy and numerous other ecologically benign activities essential to maintain future agriculture, industry and urban living standards. Even the impacts of the "greenhouse effect" and global warming were — and still are — apprehended only dimly. Opportunities for genuinely constructive change are repeatedly missed, and the environmental impact of accelerating high-volume, low-employment activities grows steadily.

It is therefore rather striking that some of the most important contemporary changes linking conservation with production — such as the new emphasis on sustainable agriculture — continue to occur through cooperation between voluntary and producer groups, such as the Australian Conservation Foundation and the National Farmers' Federation, and even between indigenous and producer groups. If not in despite of government, these developments are at least in advance of it. Farmer participation may be especially significant, given that some at least subscribe to values opposed to "economic rationality", such as stewardship of the land, and its preservation for the benefit of future generations. The extended involvement of local government, one of the most important changes of the 1990s, also transforms the scope of potential change. However, as Dovers notes, such initiatives require institutional support and policy nurture.

This is important, because the fundamental conflict, at all levels of public decision making, remains that between the rationalities of neoclassical economics and administration on the one hand, and that of ecology on the other. It is unlikely that environmental management will be effective unless this conflict is resolved, and the implications permeate all levels of government and administration. Among the prerequisites are the revaluation of natural resources, the adoption of a "steady state" approach to materials and emphasis on energy conservation in the economy, and the redefinition of growth to emphasise ecological and social utility. Practical policy implications include emphasis on conservation and recycling of materials and energy; emphasis on energy "capture" rather than creation or generation; a conservative, stewardship-oriented approach to environmental exploitation. The probability that this would create unforeseen economic opportunities, rather than stagnation, has been widely canvassed elsewhere.

The major challenge for Australia in the future remains the development of an ecologically sensitive society, in which European attitudes to nature and to human society have been thoroughly re-examined. A genuine "stationary state", a novel, stable community with high but sustainable standards of living within a stable, sensitively managed natural environment, is an attractive prospect. The exciting possibilities of enlightened and intelligent public policy making which this raises urgently need further exploration, academic and practical.

NOTES

CHAPTER 1: INTRODUCTION

1. IUCN/UNEP/WWF, *Living Planet Report 1998*. Gland, Switzerland: WWF International, 1998.
2. See, e.g., Ehrlich, P.R. & Holdren, J.P. (eds), *Human Ecology*; Birch, C.A., *Confronting the Future*.
3. Dubos, R., *So Human an Animal*, or Martin, A., *The Last Generation* for a passionate argument that it is already too late.
4. To the puzzlement of many children, Blake's "dark satanic mills" and Cobbett's *Rural Rides*, so remote from Australian concerns, remained on Australian state school curricula through the 1950s; on Marx, see Walker, K.J., "Ecological Limits and Marxian Thought", *Politics*, Vol. XIV, No. 1, May 1979, pp. 29–46.
5. Fairfield Osborne published *Our Plundered Planet* in 1948, and *The Limits of the Earth* in 1953; Harrison Brown's *The Challenge of Man's Future* appeared the following year; Rachel Carson's *Silent Spring* in 1962, and Barry Commoner's *The Closing Circle* in 1971. McMichael, A.J., *Planetary Overload*, is one of the latest and most cogent.
6. Some of the best include Dubos, R., *So Human an Animal*, Birch, op. cit., and the WCED's *Our Common Future* (the Brundtland report).
7. Revelle, R., Khosla, A. & Vinovskis, M. (eds), *The Survival Equation*; Ehrlich,

P., *The Population Bomb*; Meadows, D.H., et al., *The Limits to Growth*.

8. Union of Concerned Scientists, *The World Scientists' Warning to Humanity*, quoted in Suzuki, D., "The Super Species", *Island Magazine*, No 66, Autumn 1996, p. 104.

9. Martin, op. cit.; Ehrlich, P.R., *The Machinery of Nature*, esp. Introduction and Epilogue.

10. This view is taken, for example, by the anthropologist Marvin Harris: *Culture, People, Nature*, esp. Ch. 12.

11. Hughes, J.D., *Ecology in Ancient Civilisations*; Walker, K.J., "The State in Environmental Management: The Ecological Dimension", *Political Studies*, Vol. XXXVII, March 1989, pp. 26–39.

12. See, e.g., M'Gonigle, R.M., "The 'Economising' of Ecology: Why Big, Rare Whales Still Die", *Ecology Law Quarterly*, Vol. 9, (1980) No. 1, pp. 120–237.

13. See, in Australia's case, Birch, op. cit.; Serventy, V., *Saving Australia: a Blueprint for Our Survival*.

14. Roddewig, R.J., *Green Bans: The Birth of Australian Environmental Politics*.

15. See, e.g., Head, B., "Introduction: Intellectuals in Australian Society", Ch. 1 in Head, B. & Walter, J. (eds), *Intellectual Movements and Australian Society*, pp. 21–22.

16. Formby, J., "Environmental Policies in Australia — Climbing the Down Escalator", Ch. 6 in Park, C.C.(ed), *Environmental Policies, an International Review*, pp. 183–221; esp. pp. 206–207.; Doyle, Ch. 7 and McCall, Ch. 6, in this collection.

17. Beder, S., "Science and the Control of Information: An Australian Case Study", *The Ecologist*, Vol. 20, No. 4, July/August 1990, pp. 136–140, and *Toxic Fish and Sewer Surfing: How Deceit and Collusion are Destroying our Great Beaches*; Doyle, T. & Kellow, A.J., *Australian Environmental Politics and Policy*; Eckersley, R., *Environmentalism and Political Theory: Toward an Ecocentric Approach*; Formby, J., "Environmental Policies in Australia — Climbing the Down Escalator", Ch. 6 in Park, C.C. (ed), *Environmental Policies: an International Review*, pp. 187–198; Hay, P., Eckersley, R. & Holloway, G., *Environmental Politics in Australia and New Zealand*; Hay, P. & Eckersley, R., *Ecopolitical Theory*; Taplin, R.E., "Adversary Procedures and Expertise: the Terania Creek Inquiry", Ch. 8 in Walker, K.J. (ed), *Australian Environmental Policy*.

18. Stretton, H., *Capitalism, Socialism, and the Environment*, p. 5; Kellow, A.J. & Moon, J., "Governing the Environment: Problems and Possibilities", in Marsh, I. (ed), *Governing in the 1990s: an Agenda for the Decade*, pp. 228–255.

19. Commoner, op. cit., pp. 33–39.

20. It was eating such contaminated shellfish that caused the notorious Minamata disaster in Japan. Tsubaki, T. & Irukayami, K. (eds), *Minamata Disease: Methylmercury Poisoning in Minamata and Niigata, Japan*. Cattle grazing on pastures contaminated with pesticides may concentrate them to harmful levels — as happened in Australia during the 1970s and 1980s. Human mothers' milk concentrates the radioactive isotope strontium-90, which mimics the chemical characteristics of calcium and is contained in nuclear fallout, exposing babies to serious risks.

21. See, e.g., Meadows, D.H., et al., *The Limits to Growth*; Brown, L., *The Twenty-Ninth Day*.

22. Catton, W.R., Jr., *Overshoot: The Ecological Basis of Revolutionary Change*, esp. Chs 2 & 3.

23. See Bilsky, L.J. (ed), *Historical Ecology*; Harris, M., *Cultural Materialism*, Ch. 4; Hughes, J.D., op. cit.

24. Hempel, L.C., *Environmental Governance*, p. 122.

25. Ibid., p. 21.
26. Rothman, H., *Murderous Providence*, esp. Ch. 9.
27. Patterson, W.C., *Nuclear Power*; Jeffery, J., "The Unique Dangers of Nuclear Power: An Overview", *The Ecologist*, Vol. 16, No. 4/5, 1986, pp. 147–163.
28. Fischer, D.W. & Kerton, R.R., "Perception of Environmental Diseconomies: Technical vs. Economic Invisibility", *Social Science Information*, Vol 14, No. 1, March 1975, pp. 81–90; Daly, H.E. (ed.), *Toward a Steady-State Economy*.
29. For more comprehensive overviews, see Walker, K.J., *The Political Economy of Environmental Policy: An Australian Introduction*, and Doyle, T. & McEachern, D., *Environment and Politics*.
30. The general problem of amorphous, widespread social needs as against highly focussed vested interests is well known. It has received a stimulating formal treatment at the hands of Mancur Olson: *The Logic of Collective Action*.
31. This is formalised as the "Mutual Pollution" game in Hamburger, H., *Games as Models of Social Phenomena*, pp. 187–188.
32. See the claims of Hardin, e.g. in *Exploring New Ethics for Survival*, and compare with Walker, K.J., "The Environmental Crisis: A Critique of Neo-Hobbesian Responses", *Polity*, Vol. XXI, No. 1, Fall 1988, pp. 67–81.
33. McLean, I., *Public Choice: An Introduction*, Chs 1, 7–9.
34. Ibid., pp. 179–180.
35. Estimates by the Institute of Ecological Economics in the University of Maryland; *Nature*, Vol. 387, 17/5/97, p. 253. Holmes, R., "Don't ignore nature's bottom line", *New Scientist*, Vol. 154, No. 2082, 17 May 1997, p. 11.
36. See, e.g., Daly, op. cit.; Pearce, D.W., *Environmental Economics*.
37. Grabosky, P. & Braithwaite, J. (eds), *Business Regulation and Australia's Future*.
38. State of the Environment Advisory Council, *State of the Australian Environment*.
39. Lines, W.J., *Taming the Great South Land: A History of the Conquest of Nature in Australia*, p. 12.
40. State of the Environment Advisory Council, *State of the Australian Environment*, 1996, p. ES-8.
41. Smith, D., *Saving a Continent: Towards a Sustainable Future*, Sydney: UNSW Press, 1994; Toyne, P. *Reluctant Nation: Environment, Law and Politics in Australia*, Sydney: ABC Books, 1994.
42. Fisher, T., "Managing Threats to Biodiversity", in "ACF: Protecting the Environment for 30 Years", supplement to *Habitat Australia*, Vol. 24, No. 6, June 1996, p. 27.
43. Blainey, G., *The Tyranny of Distance*; Griffiths, T. & Robin, L., *Ecology and Empire*.
44. Bolton, G., *Spoils and Spoilers*, Chs 1–5, 8–9; Marshall, A.J. (ed.), *The Great Extermination*; Rolls, E.C., *They All Ran Wild*.
45. Breckwoldt, R., *The Last Stand*, p. 11.
46. See, e.g., Day, L.H. & Rowland, D.T. (eds), *How Many More Australians?*, Part 3; Boyden, et al., op. cit.; Serventy, op. cit., esp. Chs 1 & 2; and more generally, McMichael, A.J., *Planetary Overload*.
47. Fowler, R.J., "Vegetation Clearance Controls in South Australia — A Change of Course", *Environmental and Planning Law Journal*, Vol. 3, No. 1, March 1986, pp. 48–66.
48. Dovers, S., "Sustainability: Demands on Policy", *Journal of Public Policy*, Vol 3, No 16, 1997, pp. 303–318; and see Ch. 11 of this collection.
49. Lafferty, W.M., "The Politics of Sustainable Development: Global Norms for

National Implementation", *Environmental Politics*, Vol. 5, No. 2., Summer 1996, pp. 185–208.
50. Walker, K.J., "Methodologies for Social Aspects of Environmental Research", *Social Science Information*, Vol. 26, No. 4, December 1987, pp. 759–782.

CHAPTER 2: STATIST DEVELOPMENTALISM IN AUSTRALIA

1. See, e.g., Birch, C., *Confronting the Future*; Bolton, G.C., *Spoils and Spoilers*; Boyden, S., Dovers, S. & Shirlow, M., *Our Biosphere Under Threat*; Lines, W.J., *Taming the Great South Land*; Pyne, S.J., *Burning Bush*; Smith, D., *Continent in Crisis*.
2. E.g. Blainey, G., *The Tyranny of Distance*.
3. Crosby, A.W., *Ecological Imperialism*.
4. Lines, op. cit.
5. Blainey, op. cit.
6. For illuminating and informative outlines of many of these issues, see Smith, op. cit.; Boyden, et al., op. cit.; Bolton, op. cit.
7. Head, B. (ed), *The Politics of Development in Australia*, p. 11.
8. Head., B. (ed), *State and Economy in Australia*, p. 6.
9. Davidson, B.R., *Australia Wet or Dry?* p. 93.
10. Lines, op. cit., p. 96; Powell, J.M., *Environmental Management in Australia*, pp. 26–32.
11. Bolton, op. cit., Chs 8, 9 & 12.
12. Russell, J.S. & Isbell, R.F. (eds), *Australian Soils*.
13. Butlin, N.G., Barnard, A. & Pincus, J.J., *Government and Capitalism*, pp. 13–18; Blainey, op. cit., Chs 6 & 11.
14. Davies, A.F., *Australian Democracy*, p. 4.
15. Frawley, K., "Evolving visions: environmental management and nature conservation in Australia", Ch. 4 in Dovers, S. (ed), *Australian Environmental History*, pp. 55–78; p. 61.
16. Bolton, op. cit., Ch. 2.
17. Ibid., pp. 84–85.
18. Blainey, op. cit., pp. 124-137, 261–262.
19. See Boyden, et al., op. cit., Chs 4 & 10; Cocks, D., *Use With Care*, Ch. 4; and, more radically, Lines, op. cit.
20. Mann, M., "Capitalism and Militarism", Ch. 1 in Shaw, M. (ed), *War, State & Society*, pp. 25–46; pp. 35–36; Rueschemeyer, D. & Evans, P.B., "The State and Economic Transformation: Toward an Analysis of the Conditions Underlying Effective Intervention", in Evans, P.B., Rueschemeyer, D. & Skocpol, T. (eds), *Bringing the State Back In*, pp. 44–77; see Hancock, W.H., *Australia*, and Eggleston, F.W., *State Socialism in Victoria* for early Australian comment.
21. Butlin, Barnard & Pincus, op. cit., p. 13.
22. See, e.g., Pope, op. cit.; Wotherspoon, G., "The Determinants of the Pattern and Pace of Railway Development in New South Wales, 1850–1914", *Australian Journal of Politics and History*, Vol. XXV, No. 1, April 1979, pp. 51–65; Kerr, J., *Triumph of the Narrow Gauge*, passim.
23. Powell, J.M., op. cit., Ch. 10, and *Watering the Garden State*, esp. Chs 4 & 5.
24. Powell, *Environmental Management in Australia*; Bolton, op. cit., Chs 4, 5, 8 & 12.
25. Butlin, N.G., "Colonial Socialism in Australia, 1860–1900", Ch. 2 in Aitken, H.G.J., *The State and Economic Growth*, p. 27. See also Eggleston, op. cit.

26. Reeves, W. Pember, *State Experiments in Australia and New Zealand.*
27. Patmore, G., *Australian Labour History*, p. 51; McQueen, H., *A New Britannia*, p. 195.
28. Compare, e.g., Castles, F.G., *The Working Class and Welfare*, Chs 2 & 3, with Patmore, op. cit., esp. pp. 65–68.
29. Op. cit., pp. 188–202.
30. Pope, D., "Australia's Development Strategy in the Early Twentieth Century: Semantics and Politics", *Australian Journal of Politics and History*, Vol. 31, No. 2, 1985, pp. 218–229.
31. Pusey, M., *Economic Rationalism in Canberra*, p. 214.
32. Kellow, A.J., *Saline Solutions*, p. 68.
33. Butlin, Barnard & Pincus, op. cit., pp. 322–323.
34. Kellow, A.J., "The Environment, Federalism, and Development: Overstated Conflicts?", Ch. 10 in Walker, K.J. (ed.), *Australian Environmental Policy*, pp. 206–210.
35. Oliphant, J. & Morley, P., "Goss backs zinc giant", *The Courier-Mail* (Brisbane), 7 March 1991, p. 1.
36. Bonyhady, T., *Places Worth Keeping*, Chs 4 & 5, esp. p. 78.
37. James, P. (ed.), *Technocratic Dreaming.*
38. Tighe, P.J., "Hydroindustrialisation and Conservation Policy in Tasmania", Ch. 7 in Walker, K.J. (ed.), *Australian Environmental Policy*, pp. 124–156: p. 127; and Blakers, A., "Hydro-Electricity in Tasmania Revisited", *Australian Journal of Environmental Management*, Vol. 1, No. 2, September 1994, pp. 110–120.
39. Crowley, K., "Accommodating Industry in Tasmania: Eco-Political Factors Behind the Electrona Silicon Smelter Dispute", in Hay, P., Eckersley, R. & Holloway, G., *Environmental Politics in Australia and New Zealand*, pp. 45–58; Crowley, K., "Tasmania Greening? Ecopolitics from Pedder to Wesley Vale".
40. Davidson, B.R., *The Northern Myth*, p. 201.
41. Bolton, G.C., "From Cinderella to Charles Court: The Making of a State of Excitement", in Harman, E.J. & Head, B.W., *State, Capital, and Resources in the North and West of Australia*, pp. 27–42; Walker, K.J., "The Neglect of Ecology: The Case of the Ord River Scheme", Ch. 9 in Walker, K.J. (ed.), *Australian Environmental Policy*.
42. Lowe, I., "The Political Rôle of Energy Forecasting Mythology", in Hay, Eckersley & Holloway, op. cit., pp. 33–43.
43. Kellow, *Saline Solutions*, loc. cit.; Walker, K.J. (ed.), *Australian Environmental Policy*, pp. 237–251; Wiltshire, K., *Planning and Federalism: Australian and Canadian Experience*, Ch. 2.
44. Bell, S.R., "State Strength and State Weakness: Manufacturing Industry and the Post-War Australian State", Ch. 10 in Bell, S.R. & Head, B. (eds), *State, Economy, and Public Policy in Australia*, pp. 250–268; p. 263.
45. Ibid.
46. Bell, S.R. & Head, B., "Australia's Political Economy: Critical Themes and Issues", Ch. 1 in Bell & Head, op. cit., pp. 1–21; Bell, S.R. & Wanna, J. (eds), *Business-Government Relations in Australia*, Parts IV and V.
47. Lowi, T., "American Business, Public Policy, Case-Studies, and Political Theory", (review article), *World Politics*, Vol. XVI, 1964, pp. 677–715.
48. Walker, K.J., "Business, Government and the Environment: Unresolved Dilemmas", Ch. 23 in Bell & Wanna, op. cit., pp. 243–254.
49. Walker, "The Neglect of Ecology".
50. Kellow, A.J., "The Environment, Federalism, and Development", pp. 206–208; Hoysted, P.A., Kellow, A.J. & McCuaig, M.A., "Woodchipping in

Tasmania; an Estimate of Social Costs and Benefits", in Kellow, A.J. (ed.), *Perspectives on Forest Policy in Tasmania*; Watson, I., *Fighting Over the Forests*, esp. Ch. 1.

51. Kellow, "The Environment, Federalism, and Development", p. 208.
52. Davis, B.W., "Tasmania: the Political Economy of a Peripheral State", Ch.9 in Head, *The Politics of Development in Australia*, pp. 209–225; Davis, B.W., "The Political Economy of Expediency: Tasmania's Bell Bay Railway Project", in McMaster, J.C. & Webb, G.R. (eds), *Australian Project Evaluation*, pp. 206–223.
53. Grant, op. cit; James, op. cit.; Hill, S. & Johnson, R. (eds), *Future Tense?*; Davidson, *Australia Wet or Dry?*.
54. Kellow, A.J., "Managing an Ecological System: The Politics and Administration", *Australian Quarterly*, Vol. 57, 1985, pp. 107–127; p. 117.
55. This is not to say, of course, that sporting and other groups should not have facilities: the point is that all such facilities compete with each other, and with less defined activities such as recreational walking or casual bird watching, and can erode opportunities for their exercise.
56. Ehrlich, P., *The Machinery of Nature*. New York: Simon & Schuster, 1986.
57. See Walker, K.J., *The Political Economy of Environmental Policy*, Ch. 15, for a discussion, and Formby, J., "Where has EIA Gone Wrong?: Lessons from the Tasmanian Woodchips Controversy", in Hay, Eckersley & Holloway, op. cit., pp. 3–17.
58. Bonyhady, op. cit.
59. Walker, D., "State's Air Deal Under Attack," *Age* (Melbourne), 23 March 1994, p. 1; and "Controversy over grant threatens airline plan", ibid., 25 March 1994, p. 3.
60. Crough, G. & Wheelwright, T., *Australia: A Client State*, esp. Chs 1, 7 & 8.
61. Grant, P., "Technological Sovereignty: Forgotten Factor in the 'Hi-Tech' Razzamattazz", *Prometheus*, Vol. 1, No. 2, December 1983, pp. 239–270; p. 258.
62. For an accessible historical overview, see Bolton, *Spoils and Spoilers*; also Powell, *Environmental Management in Australia*; and most passionately, Lines, op. cit.; more partial pictures are in Ratcliffe, F., *Flying Fox and Drifting Sand*; Marshall, A.J. (ed.), *The Great Extermination*.
63. Bolton, *Spoils and Spoilers*, pp. 30–31.
64. Pope, D., "Australia's Development Strategy in the Early Twentieth Century: Semantics and Politics", *Australian Journal of Politics and History*, Vol. 31, No. 2, 1985, pp. 218–229.
65. Ratcliffe's 1948 warning was ignored, as were earlier ones dating back to the 1860s (Powell, *Environmental Management in Australia*, Ch. 5); Charles Birch's *Confronting the Future* appeared in 1975; more recent reviews of Australia's environmental predicament are Serventy's *Saving Australia* and Smith, op. cit.
66. Lowe, I., "Towards a Green Tasmania: Developing the 'Greenprint'", *Habitat Australia*, August 1991, pp. 12–14.
67. See, e.g., Wells, D., "Green Politics and Environmental Ethics: A Defence of Human Welfare Ecology", *Australian Journal of Political Science*, Vol. 28, No. 3, November 1993, pp. 515–527.

CHAPTER 3: EXPLAINING ENVIRONMENTAL POLICY: CHALLENGES, CONSTRAINTS AND CAPACITY

1. Earlier versions of this paper were presented as a guest contribution to the graduate Seminar in Resource Policy, NR 604, at Cornell University, 11

September 1995, Ithaca, NY, and as a paper, "Ecopolitics and Environmental Governance", at the *Ecopolitics X* Conference in September 1996, at the Australian National University in Canberra. I would like to acknowledge the supportive feedback I received at these presentations, as well as Nicole Tyson's assistance in editing both this chapter's footnotes and bibliographic references.

2.   Leiss, W. (ed.), *Ecology Versus Politics in Canada*, p. 259.
3.   Pybus, C. & Flanagan, R., *The Rest of the World Is Watching*, pp. 34–36.
4.   These are discussed at length in Ch. 1 of this collection.
5.   Agenda 21 objectives of "not compromising the environment and resource base of future generations; recognising the interdependency of environment, development and security; actively integrating ecological, economic and social policies; preserving ecological integrity; and employing precautionary approaches in the face of uncertainty": Dovers, S.R. & Lindenmayer, D.B., "Managing the Environment: Rhetoric, Policy and Reality", *Australian Journal of Public Administration*, Vol. 56, No. 2, 1997, p. 65.
6.   Weale, A., *The New Politics of Pollution*, p. 210.
7.   Dryzek, J., "Ecology and Discursive Democracy: Beyond Liberal Capitalism and the Administrative State", *Capitalism, Nature and Socialism*, Vol. 3, No. 2, 1992, pp. 18–42.
8.   Janicke, M., "Democracy as a Condition for Environmental Policy Success", in Lafferty, W.M. & Meadowcroft, J., *Democracy and the Environment: Problems and Prospects*.
9.   Christoff, P., "Environmental Challenges for Public Policy: The Search for Ecological Governance", in Bonyhady, T. (ed.), *Ecological Discourses*.
10. Christoff, P., "Degreening Government in the Garden State: Environment Policy under the Kennett Government", *Environmental Planning and Law Journal*, Vol. 15, No. 1, February 1998, pp. 10–32; Dovers & Lindenmayer, op. cit.; Davis, B., "Achieving Sustainable Development: Scientific Uncertainty and Policy Innovation in Tasmanian Regional Development", *Australian Journal of Public Administration*, Vol. 55, No. 4, 1996.
11. Weale, op. cit.
12. Weale, op. cit.; Vig, N.J., "Toward Common Learning? Trends in US and EU Environmental Policy", Lecture for Summer Symposium "The Innovation of Environmental Policy", Bologna, Italy, 22 July 1997; Lafferty & Meadowcroft, op. cit.; Dovers, S., Ch. 11 of this collection.
13. Weale, op. cit.
14. Walker, K.J. (ed.), *Australian Environmental Policy*, p. 14.
15. Toyne, P., *The Reluctant Nation*, p. 3.
16. Walker, op. cit., p. 2.
17. Federal government, that is; see Economou, N., Ch. 4 of this collection.
18. Horstman, M., "New law fails the leadership test", *Habitat Australia*, Vol. 26, No. 4, 1998, p. 21; "'Reform' of Commonwealth Environmental Law", NSW Environment Defender's Office, *http://www.edo.org.au/cthlrev.htm*, current at 29 March 1999.
19. Hill, R., *Investing in Our Natural Heritage: The Commonwealth's Environment Expenditure 1998–99*, Statement by the Honourable Robert Hill, Minister for the Environment, 12 May 1998.
20. Downey, T.J., "Understanding Policy-making A Necessary First Step for Environmentalists", in *Alternatives*, Vol. 14, No. 2, May/June 1987; Weale, op. cit.; Bartlett, R. & Buhrs, T., *Environmental Policy in New Zealand*.
21. The traditional "conveyor belt" model focusses upon initiation, formulation, selection, budgeting, implementation and evaluation. Hempel, L.C., *Environmental Governance: The Global Challenge*, p. 121.

22. Simeon's categories include: context, power, ideas, institutions and process. Downey, op. cit.; Simeon, R., "Studying Public Policy", *Canadian Journal of Political Science*, Vol. 9, No. 4, 1976, pp. 548–580; p. 555.
23. Weale, op. cit., p. 37–8.
24. Ibid., p. 38.
25. Cockfield, G., "Complexity Theory: the New Policy 'Science'", unpublished paper presented to the Public Policy Network Conference, Department of Political Science, University of Tasmania, Hobart, 1–2 February 1996.
26. Howlett, M. & Ramesh, M., *Studying Public Policy*, p. 201.
27. Ibid., p. 40; p. 200.
28. Such as Considine's "structure of policy systems"; Considine, M., *Public Policy: A Critical Approach*, p. 9.
29. Fiorino, D.J., *Making Environmental Policy*.
30. Simeon, op. cit., p. 555; Weale, op. cit., p. 214; Bartlett & Buhrs, op. cit., p. 14; Weir, M., "Ideas And The Politics of Bounded Innovation", in Steinmo, S., Thelen, K. & Longstreth, F., *Structuring Politics*, pp. 188–216.
31. Fischer, F., *Evaluating Public Policy*, p. 168; see also Amy, D.J., "Toward a Post-Positivist Analysis", *Policy Studies Journal*, Vol. 13, No. 1, September 1984, pp. 207–212; p. 207.
32. Worster, D., "The Ecology of Order and Chaos", in Pierce, C. & Van De Veer, D. (eds), *People, Penguins, and Plastic Trees*, pp. 280–286.
33. Weir, op. cit.; used by Vig, op. cit.; and used in the Australian public policy context by Stephen Bell to explain economic policy in Bell, S., *Ungoverning the Economy*, pp. 41–59.
34. See, e.g., Fenna, A., "Explaining public policy: Theoretical Perspectives", in Fenna, A., *Introduction to Australian Public Policy*, pp. 61–88.
35. Ham, C. & Hill, M., *The Policy Process in the Modern Capitalist State*, pp. 17–18.
36. Davis, G., Wanna, J., Warhurst, J. & Weller, P., *Public Policy in Australia*.
37. See, e.g., Dryzek, J.S., *The Politics of the Earth: Environmental Discourses*.
38. Weale, op. cit., p. 57.
39. Paehlke, R., "Environmental Values and Public Policy", in Lafferty & Meadowcroft, op. cit., pp. 75–94; p. 75.
40. Sabatier, P.A., "Toward Better Theories of the Policy Process", in *PS: Political Science & Politics*, June 1991, pp. 151–153.
41. Bell, op. cit., p. 57.
42. Davis, et al., op. cit., p. 32.
43. Downey, op. cit., p. 30.
44. Bell, op. cit., p. 25.
45. Vig, op. cit.; Fiorino, op. cit.
46. See Walker, K.J., Ch. 2 in this collection.
47. See, e.g., Drengson, A.R., "Shifting Paradigms: from the Technocratic to the Person-Planetary", *Environmental Ethics*, Vol 3, pp. 221–225; Cotgrove, S. & Duff, A., "Environmentalism, Middle Class Radicalism & Politics", *Sociological Review*, Vol. 28, No. 2, 1980, pp. 333–351; p. 345.
48. Drengson, op. cit.; Cotgrove & Duff, op. cit.
49. See, for example, Hempel, who talks of "the struggle to protect the biosphere and the public policies and the institutions involved in that struggle": Hempel, op. cit., p. xii.
50. Cotgrove & Duff, op. cit., p. 345.
51. Downs, A., "Up & Down with Ecology — The 'Issue-Attention' Cycle", *The Public Interest*, Vol. 28, 1972, pp. 38–50.
52. Downs' own misgivings about his "attention cycle" are never cited. He himself conceded in his oft-quoted article that, unlike many other social issues,

environmental issues may well endure despite the vagaries of his attention cycle. Indeed Downs expected that environmental concern could well linger rather than disappear, given the broad nature of environmental problems and the potential for public concern. He also conceded that the key cost realisation hurdle for issue persistence may be straddled where blame for an environmental problem is easily attributed, to industry for instance, and its costs covered. Downs, op. cit., pp. 46–50.

53. Such as: 1) Where did I and my society come from? 2) Who am I and what is my society? 3) Where am I and my society heading? 4) What is right and what is wrong? (Satterfield, D.R., "A Change in Academic Environmental Thought: From Paradigms to Ideology", *Sociological Inquiry*, Vol. 53, No. 2–3, Spring/Summer, 1983, pp. 136–149; p. 138).

54. Caldwell, L., "Environmental Policy as a Catalyst of Institutional Change", in Milbraith, L. & Inscho, F.R., *The Politics of Environmental Policy*, pp. 95–104; pp. 98–100.

55. Hempel, op. cit., p. 120.

56. Victor, P.A., "Economics & the Challenge of Environmental Issues", in Leiss, op. cit., pp. 34–55; p. 48.

57. Walker K.J., "Economic Growth & Environmental Management: The Dilemma of the State", paper delivered at the 27th Conference of the Australasian Political Studies Association, Adelaide, 28–30 August 1985, p. 2.

58. Lane, M. & Corbett, T., "World Heritage: Which Way from Here?", *Habitat Australia*, Vol. 24, No. 5, 1996, pp. 10–13, 15; Crowley, K., "Nature, Culture & The Green State: Policy Challenges & Complications in Australia", in Low, N. (ed.), *Selected Electronic Proceedings presented to the Environmental Justice: Global Ethics for the 21st Century Conference*, 1–3 October 1997, University of Melbourne, *http://www.arbld.unimelb.edu.au/envjust/papers/allpapers/crowley/home.htm*.

59. When the Australian Constitution was framed in 1901, with its various powers set out in Section 51 and elsewhere, it was silent on environment. In order to exert power over the States on an environmental issue, the federal government must therefore "hang" its intervention on an existing power, which is invariably challenged and subject to interpretation by the High Court. In response, the High Court has generally expanded the environmental powers of the Commonwealth: Toyne, op.cit. For the separation of environmental powers between federal, state and local government in Australia, see Dent, G., "Environmental Controls in Australia: The Environment and Development – in Search of Balance", in Marsh, I. (ed.), *The Environmental Challenge*, pp. 212–242; also Gilpin, G.A., *Australians and their Environment*, pp. 156–183.

60. Bell, S., "Socialism & Ecology: Will Ever the Twain Meet?", *Social Alternatives*, Vol. 6, No. 3, pp. 5–12.

61. See Eckersley, R., "Greening the Modern State: Managing the Environment", in James, P. (ed.), *The State in Question*, pp. 74–108.

62. See also Walker, K.J., "The State in Environmental Management: the Ecological Dimension", *Political Studies*, Vol. XXXVII, March 1989, pp. 25–38.

63. Vig, op. cit., who describes (after Hall, in Steinmo, Thelen & Longstreth, op. cit.) 1) first order change — of policy instruments; 2) second order change — of instruments and their settings; and 3) the highest third order change in "the hierarchy of goals behind policy".

64. Walker, K.J., "The State in Environmental Management", p. 38.

65. Identified by Neo-Marxists: see, for example, Habermas, J., *Legitimation Crisis*.

66. Dryzek, J., *Democracy in Capitalist Times: Ideals, Limits & Struggles*, p. 44.
67. See Economou, N., Ch. 4 of this collection.
68. Whitlam's was the only Australian federal Government to be dismissed at both levels by the Governor-General following an impasse between the Houses of Parliament over the passing of twenty-one government Bills: Parkin, A.J., Summers, J. & Woodward, D., *Government, Politics and Power in Australia*, p. 16.
69. Cass, M., "Gough said, 'Stay out of Tassie'", in Green, R., *Battle for the Franklin*, pp. 69–82; p. 71.
70. Boardman, R., *Global Régimes and Nation States*, p. 9.
71. Although Whitlam was responsible for initiating "cornerstone", expansionist environmental legislation, the federal government's response to environmental concern did not begin with him and neither was it at its most ecologically innovative under him: Christoff, P., "Environmental Politics", in Brett, J., Gillespie, J. & Goot, M. (eds), *Developments in Australian Politics*, pp. 348–421; p. 350; Boardman, op. cit., p. 97–9; Papadakis, E., "Environmental Policy", in Parkin, et al., op. cit., p. 120.
72. Between 1975 and 1983, for instance, Fraser, the then Prime Minister, stopped sandmining on Fraser Island, banned oil drilling on the Great Barrier Reef and declared Kakadu National Park Stage 1. He then endorsed each place, as well as Willandra Lakes, Lord Howe Island and South West Tasmania, for World Heritage listing; consulted broadly on the implementation of the World Conservation Strategy, and placed a moratorium on commercial whaling: Mosley, G., "Thirty Years of ACF Achievements", in "ACF Protecting the Environment for 30 Years", supplement in *Habitat Australia*, Vol. 24, No. 6, 1996; Boardman, op. cit., pp. 108–111; Papadakis, op. cit., p. 120.
73. For discussion of this at length, see Economou, N., Ch. 4 of this collection.
74. Boardman, op. cit., p. 102.
75. The significance of McCall's contribution to this collection (Ch. 6) is that it demonstrates how the Keating Labor Government acted in this way over the approval of the contentious McArthur River mine, well before the current devolutionary trend.
76. A 1997 Council of Australian Governments agreement defined these to include world heritage, wetlands, endangered species and ecological communities, migratory species, nuclear activities, Commonwealth waters and heritage places of significance: Hill, op. cit., p. xii.
77. Langmore, J. & Quiggan, J., *Work for All: Full Employment in the Nineties*.
78. Walker, K.J. (ed.), *Australian Environmental Policy*; Stewart, R. & Ward, I., *Politics One*; Dovers & Lindenmayer, op. cit.
79. See, e.g., Davis, op. cit.; Economou's institutional analysis in general; and Dovers' critique of the ecologically sustainable development process, Ch. 11 in this collection.
80. State of the Environment Advisory Council, *State of the Australian Environment*, p. ES-9.
81. Dovers & Lindenmayer, op. cit., p. 73.
82. Eckersley, op. cit., p. 91.
83. Davis, B., "Federal-State Tensions in Australian Environmental Management: The World Heritage Issue", Ch. 11 in Walker, K.J. (ed.), *Australian Environmental Policy*, pp. 215–232.
84. Horstman, M., "Why Keith Williams Must Not Resort to Hinchinbrook" *Habitat Australia*, Vol. 24, No. 6, December 1996, p. 9.
85. Alexander, J. & Fisher, T., "Running Out of Time", *Habitat*, Vol. 23, No. 1, pp. 11–18.

86. Economou, N., "Australian Environmental Policy Making in Transition: the Rise & Fall of the Resource Assessment Commission", *Australian Journal of Public Administration*, Vol. 55, No. 1, 1996a, pp. 12–22.

87. Keating blamed the hip pocket nerve for Labor's loss, and the press corps mindlessly bleated the same story, neglecting the massive defection to Green candidate, James Warden, who had campaigned against raising of the national woodchip export quota: see Economou, N., Ch. 4 in this collection.

88. See McCall, T., Ch. 6 in this collection.

89. Christoff, "Environmental Politics", in Brett, Groot & Gillespie, op. cit., p. 364.

90. That is, establishing an environmental policy programme (to be administered by a newly established Natural Heritage Trust) funded by the part privatisation of the state-owned Telstra telecommunication service: Hill, op. cit.

91. Crowley, 1997, op. cit.

92. That is, in terms of OECD nations: OECD, *OECD Environmental Performance Reviews, Australia: Conclusions and Recommendations*, OECD Group on Environmental Performance, November 1997, *http://www.erin.gov.au/portfolio/esd/intergovtunit/OECD/oecd.pdf*.

CHAPTER 4: BACKWARDS INTO THE FUTURE: NATIONAL POLICY MAKING, DEVOLUTION AND THE RISE AND FALL OF THE ENVIRONMENT

1. For the legal text of the Tasmanian Dams Case, see Coper, M., *The Franklin Dam Case*. A legal-political commentary can be found in Saunders, C., "The Federal System", in Galligan, B. (ed.), *Australian State Politics*, pp. 159–160.

2. Crook, S. & Pakulski, J., "Shades of Green: Public Opinion on Environmental Issues in Australia", *Australian Journal of Political Science*, Vol. 30, No. 1, March 1995, pp. 39–55; McAllister, I., "Dimensions of Environmentalism: Public Opinion, Political Activism and Party Support in Australia", *Environmental Politics*, Vol. 3, No. 1, Spring 1994, pp. 22–42.

3. See Dror, Y., *Public Policymaking Rexamined* and *Design for Policy Sciences*.

4. Papadakis, E., *Politics and the Environment: the Australian Experience*, pp. 124–128, and see also Richardson, G., *Whatever it Takes*.

5. Papadakis, op. cit.

6. McEachern, D., *Business Mates*, pp. 108–133.

7. For a theoretical discussion on the dynamics of Labor-environmental relations, see Seigmann, H., *The Conflicts Between Labour and Environmentalism in the FDR and USA*, and see also Watson, I., *Fighting Over the Forests*, pp. 104–118.

8. See Papadakis op. cit. and also see a discussion of postmaterialism in Gow, D., "Economic Voting and Post Materialist Values", in Bean, C., et al. (eds), *The Greening of Australian Politics*, pp. 54–72.

9. Ibid.; Crook & Pakulski, op. cit.; see Christoff, P., "The 1993 Elections — A Fading Green Politics?", *Environmental Politics*, Vol. 3, No. 1, Spring 1994, pp. 130–158, and compare with Warhurst, J., "Single Issue Politics: the Impact of Conservation and Anti Abortion Groups", *Current Affairs Bulletin*, Vol. 60, No. 2, 1983, pp. 19–31.

10. See Pusey, M., *Economic Rationalism in Canberra*; Gruen, F. & Grattan, M., *Managing Government*; Hughes, O., *Australian Politics*, pp. 7–17.

11. Ibid., and pp. 124–128; Jaensch, D., *The Hawke-Keating Hijack*; Stutchbury, M., "Macroeconomic Policy", in Jennett, C. & Stewart, R. (eds), *Hawke and Australian Public Policy*, pp. 54–78.

12. For a discussion, see Dryzek, J., "Ecological Rationality", *International Journal of Environmental Studies*, Vol. 21, 1983, pp. 5–10; and Dryzek, J., *Rational Ecology*.
13. See also Eckersley, R., *Environmentalism and Political Theory*.
14. This is outlined in a paper by the (Commonwealth) Department of Primary Industry and Energy: *Ecologically Sustainable Development: A Commonwealth Discussion Paper*.
15. Economou, N., "Reconciling the Irreconcilable? The Resource Assessment Commission, Resource Policy-making and the Environment", *Australian Journal of Public Administration*, Vol. 51, No. 4, 1992, pp. 461–475.
16. Economou, N., "Australian Environmental Policy-making in Transition: the Rise and Fall of the Resource Assessment Commission", *Australian Journal of Public Administration*, Vol. 55, No. 1, June 1996, pp. 12–22.
17. Australia. Government. Department of Arts, Sport, Environment, Tourism and Territories. *Intergovernmental Agreement on the Environment*.
18. An extensive study of this may be found in Rosauer, D., *Conservation of Natural Forests*.
19. See this critique in a speech made by Paul Keating entitled "The Commonwealth and the States and the November Special Premiers Conference", National Press Club, Canberra 22 October 1992, and see also a discussion of Hawke's "New Federalism" in Galligan, B., "Australian Federalism: Rethinking and Restructuring", *Australian Journal of Political Science*, Vol. 27, Special Issue on Federalism, 1992, pp. 1–6.
20. This incident is discussed in greater detail in Economou, N., "The 'greening' of the Coalition's Environment Policy", in Prasser, S. & Starr, G. (eds), *Policy and Change: the Howard Mandate*, pp. 122–181.
21. *Australian*, 27 March 1995.
22. *The Weekend Australian*, 3–4 February 1996.
23. McAllister, I. & Bean, C., "Long Term Electoral Trends and the 1996 Election", in Bean, C., et al. (eds), *The Politics of Retribution*, pp. 173–189.
24. For a fuller discussion of this argument with particular reference to the environment issue, see Economou, N., "Accordism and the Environment: the Resource Assessment Commission and National Environmental Policy-Making", *Australian Journal of Political Science*, Vol. 28, No. 3, November 1993, pp. 399–412, and Downes, D., "Neo-Corporatism and Environmental Policy", *Australian Journal of Political Science*, Vol. 31, No. 2, June 1996, pp. 175–190.
25. *NAFI News*, Special Edition, November 1996.
26. For a discussion of these approaches, see Fenna, A., *An Introduction to Australian Public Policy*, pp. 23–60; Emy, H. & Hughes, O., *Australian Politics: Realities in Conflict*, pp. 552–555.
27. Kemp, D., *Foundations for Australian Political Analysis*, pp. 181ff.
28. Puplick, C. & Southey, R., *Liberal Thinking*, pp. 88–117; Hughes, op. cit., p. 266.
29. Fenna, A. & Economou, N., "Green Politics and Environmental Policy in Australia", in Fenna, op. cit., p. 354.
30. National Forest Plan — see *http://www.nafi.com.au/issues/forest-plan.html* and also *Age* (Melbourne), 10 November 1997.
31. See Anderson, J. (Minister for Primary Industries and Energy), "Clear Cut Way to Save the Forests", *Age* (Melbourne), 10 February 1997.
32. See Mosley, G., "The Triumph of the Woodchip Mentality", *Age* (Melbourne), 10 February 1997.
33. *Age* (Melbourne), 14 June 1997.
34. Downs, A., "Up and Down with Ecology — the 'Issue-Attention Cycle'", *The Public Interest*, No. 28, Summer 1972, pp. 38–50.

CHAPTER 5: UNSUSTAINABLE DEVELOPMENT IN QUEENSLAND

1. See Walker, K.J., Ch. 2 in this collection.
2. Scholarly studies of Queensland's environmental problems and their policy implications are few. But see Mercer, D., Ch. 8 in this collection, and Carden, M.F., "Land Degradation on the Darling Downs", Ch. 4 in Walker, K.J. (ed.), *Australian Environmental Policy*, pp. 58–83.
3. Carden, M.F., "Reformulating Political Ecology: Towards an Intelligent Pragmatism", Ecopolitics XI Conference Proceedings, pp. 57–71.
4. Tighe, P. J, "Hydroindustrialisation and conservation policy in Tasmania", in Walker, op. cit., pp. 124–155.
5. Ibid., and Blakers, A., "Hydro-Electricity in Tasmania Revisited", *Australian Journal of Environmental Management*, Vol. 1, No. 2, September 1994, pp. 110–120.
6. Ibid.
7. There is another reason for attempting to evaluate the ecological and economic rationality of development policies. Adherents of the postmaterialist explanation for the modern ecological movement argue that there is something unique, almost irrational, about modern environmentalists and their associated movement. This might be true if environmental conflict merely involved a clash of values regarding economic development and lifestyles: modernism/materialism versus postmodernism/postmaterialism. However, if development policies potentially threaten the future provision of material welfare, then postmaterialist explanations are inadequate. If, as environmentalists argue, current development policies ignore fundamental biophysical constraints, threatening the material basis of society, then environmental critiques of existing economic development policies are *ipso facto* utilitarian and materialist, irrespective of arbitrary "lifestyle" categories assigned by researchers.
8. Davidson B.R., *The Northern Myth, Australia Wet or Dry?* and *European Farming in Australia*.
9. Australia. Government. Department of the Environment, Sport, and Territories. State of the Environment Advisory Council. *Australia; State of the Environment 1996*, Ch. 3.
10. Davidson, *Australia Wet or Dry*, pp. 26–61; Kelleher F.M., "Climate and Crop Distribution", in Prately, J.E., *Principles of Field Crop Production*, pp. 24–39.
11. Davidson, *The Northern Myth*, p. 73.
12. Ibid.
13. Holmes, J.H., "The Future of Remote Pastoral Towns in Western Queensland", in *Urban Australia*; Holmes, J.H. (ed.), *Queensland*.
14. The intention was to slowly increase the population and its density. Pastoralism was supposed to be an interim economic activity. Eventually, pastoral leases were to be retired and the land given over to intensive agriculture to feed towns or provide produce for export. In the process the population densities were to rise, hence the term "closer settlement".
15. May, D., "The North Queensland Beef Cattle Industry: An Historical Overview", in Dalton, B.J. (ed.), *Lectures On North Queensland History*, No. 4, p. 121.
16. Refrigeration had not yet been developed and would not become a truly economic proposition until the early twentieth century.
17. Kerr, J., *Triumph of Narrow Gauge*, pp. 23, 27–29, 32–33, 35, 43.
18. Johnston, W.R., *The Call of the Land*, p. 80.
19. Fitzgerald, R., *From the Dreaming to 1915*, p. 266.

20. For a full historical review of the Queensland gold industry see Blainey G., *Gold and Paper.*
21. Gough, M., et al., *Queensland: Industrial Enigma*, p. 2.
22. Ibid.
23. Bolton, G.C., *A Thousand Miles Away*, pp. 260–262.
24. Harris, S., *Regional Economic Development in Queensland*, p. 92.
25. Carden, M.F., *The Queensland Development and Environment Policy Process*, p. 109.
26. Bolton, op. cit., p. 260–266.
27. Ibid.
28. Fitzgerald, op. cit., p. 169.
29. Bolton, op. cit., p. 271.
30. Carden, *The Queensland Development and Environment Policy Process*, p. 173.
31. Davidson, *European Farming in Australia*, p. 152.
32. Ibid., pp. 152–153.
33. Ibid., p. 152.
34. Ibid.
35. Significantly, by the late 1980s the sugar industry had still not generated sufficient surplus wealth to compensate the Queensland and Australian economies for the opportunity cost of the subsidies paid to it since its inception. Carden, *The Queensland Development and Environment Policy Process*, pp. 182–184, 332–338.
36. Davidson, *European Farming in Australia*, pp. 273, 276.
37. The Kanaka trade was slowly being recognised as the slave trade it was.
38. Queensland. Government. *The Queen State*, p. 25.
39. One way of determining the impact is to compare the number of factories per capita in each State to that in NSW. By normalising in this way, comparisons between the States are enabled. Measures such as Gross Manufacturing Product were not calculated at that time and are unavailable. It is impossible to make direct comparisons of the size of the States' manufacturing sectors as each had a different sized population, and therefore varying levels of intrinsic demand. This is especially true for the Australian States at the turn of the century as they had only small volumes of manufactured exports and relied heavily on primary products for export income. Fortunately, travel between the States was difficult and freight costs high, so each State was still relatively isolated protecting local manufacturing from much competition. Before federation NSW favoured free trading policies, so it is reasonable to assume that the lowering of trade barriers had fewer adverse effects on this State. At the same time NSW gained the same benefits of Commonwealth protection as the other States, placing all on an equal footing in this regard. These facts make NSW ideal for basing comparisons of this type as the impact of federation on manufacturing in that State should have been minimal, whereas the others either greatly benefited or suffered.
40. This finding also conforms to that of Gough, et al., who identified this period as the beginning of the permanent stagnation of manufacturing in Queensland: Gough, et al., op. cit., p. 8.
41. Carden, *The Queensland Development and Environment Policy Process*, p. 114.
42. The following data is derived from Commonwealth Bureau of Census and Statistics: *Production Bulletins*, various issues; *Manufacturing Establishments Summary of Operations by Industry Class: Australia*, various issues.
43. Carden, *The Queensland Development and Environment Policy Process*, p. 115.
44. Gough, et al., p. 12.
45. Ibid., pp. 7, 13.
46. Bolton, op. cit., p. 271.

47. Murphy, D.J., "Organization, Structure and Finance", in Murphy, D.J., Joyce, R.B. & Hughes, C.A. (eds), *Labor in Power*, pp. 3–60.
48. Bolton, op. cit., p. 305.
49. Ibid., p. 307.
50. Shogren, D., "Agriculture: 1915–29", in Murphy, et al., op. cit., p. 181.
51. Ibid.; Hughes, C.A., "Labor in the Electorates", in ibid., p. 62.
52. Ibid.
53. Ibid.
54. Ibid.
55. Kennedy, K.H., *The Mungana Affair*, p. 1.
56. Ibid., p. 6.
57. Bolton, op. cit., p. 295.
58. For a thorough review of these events see, Kennedy, op. cit.
59. Ibid., pp. 23–31.
60. Ibid., pp. 39–52.
61. Ibid., pp. 40–41.
62. For a full review of this period of Queensland's history see Cochrane, T., *Blockade*.
63. Shogren, op. cit., p. 178.
64. Ibid., p. 190.
65. *The Queen State*, p. 25.
66. Fitzgerald R., *From 1915 to the Early 1980s*, p. 74.
67. Ibid., p. 76.
68. Ibid.
69. Bradfield, J.J.C., *Queensland, The Conservation and Utilization of Her Water Resources, 1938*.
70. "Water Diversion Schemes", *The Australian Encylopaedia*, pp. 187–191; Idriess, I.L., *The Great Boomerang*.
71. Queensland. Parliament. Papers. *Annual Report* of the Bureau of Investigation for the year 1946, QPP, Vol. 2, 1947/48, pp. 654–662; Australia. Government. The Rural Reconstruction Commission, *Irrigation, Water Conservation and Land Drainage*. Eighth Report.
72. Carden, *The Queensland Development and Environment Policy Process*, pp. 211–250.
73. Giblin L.F., "A Note on Taxable Capacity", *Economic Record*, Vol. 5, 1929, p. 345; Commonwealth Grants Commission, *Second Report*, p. 120.
74. Giblin, loc. cit., p. 342.
75. Commonwealth Grants Commission, *Second Report*, p. 114; Australian Bureau of Statistics, *Commonwealth Government Year Book*, various issues, 1925–50.
76. Fitzgerald, op. cit., p. 171.
77. Australian Bureau of Statistics, *Commonwealth Year Book*, No. 18, 1925, pp. 576–577.
78. Commonwealth Bureau of Census and Statistics, *Commonwealth Year Book*, various issues; Australian Bureau of Statistics, *Queensland Year Book*, various issues.
79. Murphy, D.J., "Abolition of the Legislative Council", in Murphy, et al., op. cit., p. 97–98.
80. Coaldrake, P., *Working the System*, p. 30.
81. Fitzgerald, op. cit., pp. 291–292.
82. Gough, et al., op. cit.
83. Bolton, op. cit., p. 324.
84. Queensland Cane Growers' Council, *Submission to the Sugar Industry Inquiry 1978*, Submission No. 1, 1978; Courtenay, P.P., "Agriculture, Development and the Burdekin".

85. Queensland Cane Growers' Council, op. cit.
86. Ibid.
87. Courtenay, op. cit.
88. Ibid., p. 325.
89. Australian Bureau of Statistics, *Australian National Accounts*, various issues.
90. Carden, *The Queensland Development and Environment Policy Process*, pp. 136, 320–326; Harman E.J., "Resource Development and Personal Income Levels", in Harman E.J. & Head B.W. (eds), *State, Capital and Resources in the north and west of Australia*, pp. 359–376.
91. Carden, *The Queensland Development and Environment Policy Process*, pp. 321–331; Australian Bureau of Statistics, *Australian National Accounts*, various issues; Australian Bureau of Statistics, *Demography Bulletin*, No. 87; Australian Bureau of Statistics, *Commonwealth Government Year Book*, various issues.
92. Carden, *The Queensland Development and Environment Policy Process*, pp. 321–331; Australian Bureau of Statistics, *Australian National Accounts*, various issues.
93. New South Wales was fourth and, as always, Tasmania came last.
94. Later renamed the National Party.
95. Coaldrake, op. cit., p. 172.
96. Cribb, M.B., "The National Party campaign: justifying a strategy", in Cribb, M.B. & Boyce, P.J. (eds), *Politics in Queensland*, pp. 180–202; Coaldrake, P., "The Coalition Crisis and the Queensland Election of 1983", *Politics*, Vol. 19, No. 1, May 1984, p. 87.
97. Mullins, P., "Queensland: Populist politics and development", in Head, B. (ed.), *The Politics of Development in Australia*, p. 152.
98. See Carden, M.F., "Land Degradation on the Darling Downs", Ch. 4 in Walker, K.J. (ed.), *Australian Environmental Policy*, pp. 58–83.
99. Suppression of dissent has been a constant tool of government in Queensland, irrespective of the political persuasion of the government. See Coaldrake, *Working the System*, pp. 89–103.
100. Carden, "Land Degradation on the Darling Downs".
101 Criticism of the government, and especially the National Party, was generally met with a swift and bitter response. Dissent within the public service was rewarded with harsh treatment. In contrast, those favoured by the government, or the National Party, were offered rapid advancement within the service. This process helped create a public service that saw its interests as lying with the conservative government. The police force received similar treatment and they in turn responded favourably. Opposition members and other government critics were sued at the taxpayers' expense. Street marching was banned and protestors arrested, fined and jailed. The media was increasingly pacified as the government became a major employer of journalists, offering high salaries and quick promotions. Most intellectuals suffered ridicule, and their advice was rarely incorporated into the policy process.
102. High level corruption has always been a problem in Queensland. As noted earlier, it brought down the Labor government in the 1920s, but it was also endemic during the nineteenth century. Indeed, it nearly crippled the State's finances in the 1890s, when the Queensland National Bank collapsed. This was the biggest financial institution in the State and the manager of the government's funds. Significantly most of the State Cabinet were either directors or large shareholders in the bank. Part of the collapse was due to rampant embezzlement of funds by the Bank's Manager and the State Premier, who was also State Treasurer. This crisis occurred at the same time as the economic depression that struck Europe and the other Australian States. As with the rest

of the European world, Queensland fell deep into depression. Complicating this was the drought of the 1890s. For a full review see Gough, T., "Tom McIlwraith, Ted Dury, Hugh Nelson and The Queensland National Bank 1896–1897", *Queensland Heritage*, Vol. 3, No. 8, 1978, pp. 3–13.

103. Indeed, their material interests are well served by their radical political position and actions.

104. Of course, this region is already rapidly developing, but at present it is not proceeding in a planned or particularly ecologically and humanely sensitive fashion. The consequent tensions produced played a large part in the downfall of the Goss Labor Government, and the electoral success of the One Nation Party in the peri-urban regions of the State.

CHAPTER 6: DEVOLUTION IN EMBRYO: THE MCARTHUR RIVER MINE

1. The author wishes to acknowledge the substantial assistance given by the editors in the writing of this chapter, and the editorial suggestions provided by Prue Cameron in its preparation. The usual disclaimers apply. For the detail of the mine project, Toyne's essay in Chapter 9 of *The Reluctant Nation* is highly recommended.

2. Mount Isa Mines (MIM) Holdings web site: *http://www.mimholdings.com.au/3McArinfo.html*, 8 September 1998.

3. For an account of Keating's response to the focus on ESD within his own department, Prime Minister and Cabinet, see Edwards, P., *Keating: the inside story*, pp. 469–470.

4. ABC Radio, *PM*, Thursday, 21 January 1993. Australia. Parliament. Department of the Parliamentary Library, online transcript 86–4252.

5. Economou, N., "Problems in Environmental Policy Creation: Tasmania's Wesley Vale Pulp Mill Dispute", Ch. 3 in Walker, K.J., *Australian Environmental Policy*, pp. 41–42. See also Chapman, R.J.K., *Setting Agendas and Defining Problems — The Wesley Vale Pulp Mill Proposal*.

6. Galligan, B. & Lynch, C., *Integrating Conservation and Development*.

7. The first policy response of import was from the then Prime Minister, Hawke, in 1989: *Our Country, Our Future: Statement on the Environment*.

8. Stone, D., *Policy Paradox*, pp. 156–162.

9. Dryzek, J.S., "Democracy and Environmental Policy Instruments", in Eckersley, R., *Markets, the State and the Environment*, pp. 295–296.

10. Commonwealth of Australia, *National Strategy for Ecologically Sustainable Development*, p. 14.

11. Commonwealth of Australia, *Compendium of Ecologically Sustainable Development Recommendations*, Section 9.

12. Toyne, op. cit., p. 160.

13. Australia. Government. Department of Arts, Sport, Environment, Tourism and Territories. *Intergovernmental Agreement on the Environment*, pp. 154–156.

14. Ibid.

15. Ibid.

16. Quoted in ibid., p. 157.

17. Ibid., p. 159.

18. Ibid., p. 161.

19. Ibid., p. 162.

20. Ibid.

21. ABC Radio, *PM*, Thursday, 21 January 1993. Australia. Parliament. Parliamentary Library, online transcript, 86–4252.

22. Ibid.
23. Ibid.
24. Toyne, op. cit., p. 163.
25. Ibid., p. 167.
26. ABC Radio, *PM*, Thursday, 21 January 1993.
27. Toyne, op. cit., p. 174.
28. Ibid., p. 155.
29. Ibid., p. 169.
30. ABC Radio, *AM*, Tuesday, 1 June 1993. Australia. Parliament. Department of the Parliamentary Library, online transcript 87–1424.
31. ABC Radio, *Daybreak*, Monday, 31 May 1993. Australia. Parliament. Department of the Parliamentary Library, online transcript, 87–1416.
32. Toyne, op. cit., p. 170.
33. ABC TV, *Lateline*, Thursday, 24 June 1993. Australia. Parliament. Department of the Parliamentary Library, online transcript, 87-2415.
34. Toyne, op. cit., p. 170.
35. Ibid., p. 171.
36. Jackson, S. & Cooper, D., "Coronation Hill Pay-back, the Case of McArthur River", *Arena*, October–November 1993, p. 20.
37. Toyne, op. cit., p. 172.
38. Krockenberger, loc. cit.
39. Hill, R., *Reform of Commonwealth Environment Legislation*, p. 1.
40. Outlined in Prest, J. & Downing, S., "Shades of Green? Proposals to Change Commonwealth Environmental Laws", Laws and Bills Digest Group, Research Paper 16, 1997–98. Australia. Parliament. Parliamentary Library, under section headed: "Background to the Process".
41. Hill, R., op. cit., p. 4.

CHAPTER 7: ROUNDTABLE DECISION MAKING IN ARID LANDS UNDER CONSERVATIVE GOVERNMENTS: THE EMERGENCE OF "WISE USE"

1. Along with the works by Dowie and Rowell, mentioned below, other excellent "wise use" critiques are found in Helvarg, D., *The War Against the Greens: The "Wise Use" Movement, the New Right, and Anti-Environmental Violence*. In Australia, some of the strategies of the "wise use" movement have been ably monitored and published in a number of articles by Bob Burton — for example, "Right Wing Think Tanks", in *Chain Reaction*, special edn, "Corporations, Power and the Environment", Doyle, T. (ed.), No. 73–74, 1995.
2. Dowie, M., *Losing Ground: American Environmentalism at the Close of the Twentieth Century*, p. 93.
3. Morgan, H., quoted in McEachern, D., *Business Mates: The Power and Politics of the Hawke Era*, p. 110.
4. Dowie, op. cit., p. 95.
5. Rowell, A., *Green Backlash: Global Subversion of the Environmental Movement*, p. 190.
6. Dowie, op. cit., p. 94.
7. Helvarg, loc. cit., p. 76.
8. Prideaux, M., Horstman, M. & Emmett, J., "Sustainable Use or Multiple Abuse", *Habitat*, Vol. 26, No. 2, April 1998, p. 15.
9. Hill, R., quoted in ABC Radio Interview, Port Lincoln. ABC Radio, *News*, Monday 14 September 1998.
10. Sierra Club, "'Local Control' a Smokescreen for Logging", *The Planet*: The

Sierra Club Activist Resource (on line at *http://www.sierraclub.org/planet/199711/delbert.html*), p. 1.

11. McCloskey M., quoted in Mazza, P., "Cooptation or Constructive Engagement?: Quincy Library Group's Efforts to Bring Together Loggers and Environmentalists Under fire", *Cascadia Planet* (on line at *http://www.cascadia@tnews.com*), August 1997, p. 3.

12. Strong, G., "The Green Game", *Age* (Melbourne), 17 August 1998 (on line at *http://www.theage.com.au/daily/980717/news/news22.html*), p. 3.

13. Moore, P., "Consensus", *Greenspirit* (on line at *http://www.pmoore@rogers.wave.ca*), p. 3.

14. Doyle, T. & McEachern, D., *Environment and Politics.*

15. Britell, J., "Partnerships, Roundtables and Quincy-Type Groups are Bad Ideas that Cannot Resolve Environmental Conflicts" (on line at *http://www.harbourside.com/home/j/jbritell/welcome.htm*), 1997, p. 6.

16. Select Panel of the Public Inquiry into Uranium, *The Report of the Public Enquiry into Uranium*, pp. 1–40.

17. Olympic Dam Community Consultative Forum, "Terms of Reference and Membership for the Olympic Dam Community Consultative Forum", p. 1.

18. Select Panel of the Public Inquiry into Uranium, loc. cit.

19. Hagan, R., quoted in Rosewarne, C., "Undermining Aboriginal Interests: A Case Study of Western Mining Corporation", *Chain Reaction*, special edn, "Corporations, Power and the Environment", Doyle, T (ed.), No. 73–74, pp. 38–41.

20. Hine, M., "Native Title Claim Puts Roxby in Fluid Situation", *Chain Reaction*, No. 69, pp. 23–25.

21. Kerin, R. to Doyle, T., correspondence, 24 April 1998, p. 1.

22. Canberra Movement Against Uranium Mining, quoted in Select Panel of the Public Inquiry into Uranium, loc. cit., p. 27.

23. Olympic Dam Community Consultative Forum, loc. cit., p. 1.

24. Yeeles, R. to Doyle, T., correspondence, 20 July 1998.

25. Olympic Dam Environment Consultative Committee, "Summary Record", Primary Industries, Natural Resources and Regional Development (PIRSA), 24 March 1998, p. 3.

26. Beder, S., *Global Spin*, p. 43.

27. Grady, M. to Colliver, A., correspondence, 29 September 1997, p. 4.

28. Noonan, D., ACF Campaign Officer for South Australia, strategy memo to Doyle, T., August 1998.

29. Australian Nature Conservation Agency, "The Ramsar Convention", brochure, 1997.

30. Conservation Stakeholder Woking Group, "Ramsar Management Plan for Coongie Lakes Wetlands; an Issues Paper", April 1998, p. 1.

31. Noonan, D., "SA Government Excludes the Australian Public From a rôle in the Future of Coongie Lakes", ACF Media Release, 16 January 1997.

32. Resource Monitoring and Planning Pty Ltd, correspondence to Doyle, T., 17 August 1998.

33. Hughes, V., correspondence to Playfair, R., 17 September 1998.

34. Doyle, T., "Sustainable Development and Agenda 21: The Secular Bible of Global Free Markets and Pluralist Democracy", *Third World Quarterly*, Vol. 19, No. 4, 1998.

35. Doyle, T. to R. Adler, personal correspondence, August 1998.

36. Bridgeman, P. & Davis, G., *Australian Policy Handbook.*

37. Stone, D., *Policy Paradox.*

38. Ibid., p. 9.

CHAPTER 8: TOURISM AND COASTAL ZONE MANAGEMENT: THE UNEASY PARTNERSHIP

1. Australia. Government. Department of the Environment, Sport and Territories, *Living on the Coast: The Commonwealth Coastal Policy.*
2. Estimate of the Tourism Council of Australia, *The Weekend Australian*, 15–16 August 1998.
3. For example, in the year 1996–97, 63 million trips involving an overnight stay were undertaken by Australian residents aged 14 years and over, and 41% of these were for the purpose of pleasure or holiday. Moreover, intrastate travel dominates so that the propensity to travel tends roughly to parallel State populations. (Bureau of Tourism Research, *Domestic Tourism Monitor 1996–97.*)
4. The other two are telecommunications and information technology. See Naisbitt, J., *Megatrends 2000.*
5. Hall, C.M., Jenkins, J. & Kearsley, G. (eds), *Tourism Planning and Policy in Australia and New Zealand: Cases, Issues and Practice*, p. 1.
6. See, for example, Baird, B. "Tourism: The Industry of the Future", in Marsh, I. (ed.), *Australia's Emerging Industries. Achieving Our Potential. Growth 45*, pp. 45–55.
7. *The Weekend Australian*, 16–17 September 1995.
8. "CSIRO Probes Booming Tourism", *The Weekend Australian*, 15–16 March 1997.
9. Driml, S. & Common, M., "Ecological Economics Criteria for Sustainable Tourism: Application to the Great Barrier Reef and Wet Tropics World Heritage Areas, Australia", *Journal of Sustainable Tourism*, Vol. 4, 1996, p. 7.
10. See Zajacek, R., "The Development of Measures to Protect the Marine Environment from Land-based Pollution: The Effectiveness of the Great Barrier Reef Marine Park Authority in Managing the Effects of Tourism on the Marine Environment", *James Cook University Law Review*, Vol. 3, 1996, pp. 64–92.
11. See, for example, Clancy, M., "Commodity Chains, Services and Development: Theory and Preliminary Evidence from the Tourism Industry", *Review of International Political Economy*, Vol. 5, 1998, pp. 122–148; Clark, G.L., "Global Competition and Environmental Regulation: Is the 'Race to the Bottom' Inevitable?", in Eckersley, R. (ed.), *Markets, The State and the Environment. Towards Integration*, pp. 229–257.
12. Hawkins, B., "Environmental Approval Processes for Major Industrial Projects", paper presented at Twelfth National Environmental Law Association Conference, Canberra, 4–6 July 1993, pp. 3–4. The paper drew upon: Bureau of Industry Economics, *Environmental Assessment — Impact on Major Projects.*
13. See Viviani, N. & Selby, J., *The Iwasaki Tourist Development at Yeppoon*; Doyle, T., "Freeholding, Resorts and Barrier Reef Islands", *Legal Service Bulletin*, Vol. 13, 1988, pp. 6–9; Doyle, T., "Lindeman Island: Environmental Politics in Queensland", *Journal of the Royal Historical Society of Queensland*, Vol. 13, 1989, pp. 462–472; Craik, J., *Resorting to Tourism. Cultural Policies for Tourist Development in Australia.*
14. "Japan Firm Plans $2.5b Resort City", *The Sunday Herald-Sun* (Melbourne), 10 May 1998.
15. Commonwealth of Australia, Ecologically Sustainable Development Working Group, *Final Report: Tourism*; Commonwealth Department of Tourism, *National Ecotourism Strategy.*
16. Agardy, M.T., "Accomodating Ecotourism in Multiple Use Planning of Coastal and Marine Protected Areas", *Ocean & Coastal Management*, Vol. 20, 1993, pp. 219–239.

17. Driml, S. & Common, M., "Ecological Economics Criteria for Sustainable Tourism: Application to the Great Barrier Reef and Wet Tropics World Heritage Areas, Australia", *Journal of Sustainable Tourism*, Vol. 4, 1996, pp. 3–16.

18. Resource Assessment Commission, *Coastal Zone Inquiry, Final Report*, November 1993. On the global scale, approximately 60% of the world's population (around 3.8 billion people) live within 140 km of the sea. This is projected to rise to 75% of the population (about 6.15 billion people) within three decades (see Hinrichsen, D., "Humanity and the World's Coasts: A Status Report", *Amicus Journal*, Winter 1997, p. 1).

19. Australia. Government. Department of the Environment, Sport, and Territories. State of the Environment Advisory Council. *Australia; State of the Environment*, 1996, pp. 3–11.

20. See "Australians Moving North", *Sunday Age* (Melbourne), 19 July 1998.

21. Warnken, J. & Buckley, R., "Major 1987–93 Tourism Proposals in Australia", *Annals of Tourism Research*, Vol. 24, 1997, p. 977.

22. Warnken, J. & Buckley, R., "Coastal Tourism Development as a Testbed for EIA Triggers: Outcomes Under Mandatory and Discretionary EIA Frameworks", *Environmental & Planning Law Journal*, Vol. 13, 1996, pp. 239–245.

23. Orbach, M., "Social Scientific Contributions to Coastal Policy Making", in *Improving Interactions between Coastal Science and Policy: Proceedings of the California Symposium*, pp. 49–59.

24. Harding, R., "The Port Hacking Tombolo: A Controversy in Estuary Management", in Harding, R. (ed.), *Environmental Decision-making. The rôles of Scientists, Engineers and the Public*, pp. 264–280.

25. Goldin, P. & Sann, A., "South East Tasmania Case Study, Australia", in *Coastal Zone Management: Selected Case Studies*, pp. 201–226.

26. ABC, Radio National, "New Seagrass Discoveries", *Earthbeat*, 29 August 1998. See also Silberman, J. & Klock, M., "The Recreation Benefits of Beach Renourishment", *Ocean & Shoreline Management*, Vol. 11, 1988, pp. 73–90.

27. See, Timlin, J., "Megacorp and Westernport Bay", in Dempsey, R. (ed.), *The Politics of Finding Out*, pp. 62–67.

28. See the High Court of Australia judgment in *Kartinyeri v The Commonwealth* (1998: the "*Hindmarsh Island* case"). See also Harris, M., "The Narrative of Law in the Hindmarsh Island Royal Commission", in Chanock, M. & Simpson, C. (eds), *Law and Cultural Heritage*, pp. 115–139.

29. Cicin-Sain, B. & Knecht, R.W., *Integrated Coastal and Ocean Management: Concepts and Practices*, p. 350.

30. Gilbert, C.D., "Future Directions in Commonwealth Environmental Law", in Duncan, W.D. (ed.), *Planning and Environment Law in Queensland*, p. 74.

31. Jones, M.A., *Frankston: Resort to City*. See also Beder, S., *Toxic Fish and Sewer Surfing*; and Brunton, N., "Holidays by the Sewer: Coastal Water Pollution and Ecological Sustainability", paper presented at National Environmental Law Association Conference, Coolum, 8–12 May 1996.

32. Bird, E., "The Future of the Beaches", in R.L. Heathcote (ed.), *The Australian Experience. Essays in Australian Land Settlement and Resource Management*, pp. 163–177.

33. Fairweather, P.G. & Quinn, G.P., "Marine Ecosystems: Hard and Soft Shores", in Zann, L.P. & Kailola, P. (eds), *The Marine Environment; Technical Annex 1. State of the Marine Environment Report for Australia*, pp. 25–36.

34. Nelkin, D., "Science, Technology, and Political Conflict: Analyzing the Issues", in Nelkin, D. (ed.), *Controversy*, p. 16.

35. See Table 8.1 in Australia. Government. Department of the Environment,

Sport, and Territories. State of the Environment Advisory Council. *Australia; State of the Environment*, 1996.

36. Greenwood, T., "Australians Divided About Reef's Future", *Reef Research*, June 1998, pp. 19–20.

37. For analysis in detail, see Mercer, D., "Beach Usage in the Melbourne Region", *Australian Geographer*, Vol. 12, 1972, pp. 123–139, and Sant, M., "Accomodating Recreational Demand: Boating in Sydney Harbour, Australia", *Geoforum*, Vol. 21, 1990, pp. 97–109.

38. Charters, T., Gabriel, M. & Prasser, S., *National Parks. Private Sector's rôle.*

39. "Marine Parks Rated Worst", *The Herald-Sun* (Melbourne), 8 June 1998.

40. Davis, B., "Environmental Management", in Galligan, B., Hughes, O. & Walsh, C. (eds), *Intergovernmental Relations and Public Policy*, pp. 146–162.

41. OECD, *Environmental Performance Review of Australia*. Paris: OECD, 1998. See also Kay, R. & Lester, C., "Benchmarking the Future Direction for Coastal Management in Australia", *Coastal Management*, Vol. 25, pp. 265–292.

42. See Gardner, T., Geary, P. & Gordon, I., "Ecological Sustainability and Effluent Treatment Systems", *Australian Journal of Environmental Management*, Vol. 4, 1997, pp. 144–156.

43. See "Cesspool Alert on Oceans", *The Herald Sun* (Melbourne), 27 December 1995; "AMA's Call to Close Ocean Sewer Outfalls Dismissed as Impractical", *Age* (Melbourne), 28 December 1995.

44. Walker, M.L., *Human Impact on Australian Beaches.*

45. Dutton, I.M., Boyd, W.E., Luckie, K., Knox, S. & R. Derrett, "Measuring Coastal Landscape and Lifestyle Values: An Interpretive Approach", *Australian Journal of Environmental Management*, Vol. 2, 1995, pp. 245–256.

46. See Sperling, K., "Subdivision versus Sustainability: The Conflict between Private Rights and Public Interest in Land Use Decision Making", in C. Star (ed.), *Proceedings of the Ecopolitics XI Conference*, Melbourne, 1998.

47. Harvey, N., "Public Involvement in EIA", *Australian Planner*, Vol. 33, 1996, pp. 39–46.

48. See unreported decision of the High Court in *Oshlack v Richmond River Council*, 25 February 1998; Baird, R., "Public Interest Groups and Costs — Have the Flood Gates been Opened?", *Environmental and Planning Law Journal*, Vol. 15, 1998, pp. 294–299.

49. Pearson, L., "Planning and Land Use Decision-Making at State and Local Level: The Look-At-Me-Now Headland Ocean Outfall", *Environmental and Planning Law Journal*, Vol. 12, pp. 221–230.

50. Zann, L.P., *Our Sea, Our Future. Major Findings of the State of the Marine Environment Report for Australia.*

51. Australia. Parliament. House of Representatives Standing Committee on Environment, Recreation and the Arts, *The Injured Coastline: Protection of the Coastal Environment.*

52. Australia. Paliament. Senate. *Inquiry into Marine and Coastal Pollution.*

53. Resource Assessment Commission, *Coastal Zone Inquiry, Final Report.* For a "minority", dissenting view on the RAC Final Report see R.J. Graham's "Making the Connections: An Introduction to the Alternative to the RAC Proposals for Coastal Zone Management" (unpublished). Graham was a Special Commissioner with the Coastal Zone Inquiry and his major criticism was that the final report was too general and did not go far enough in terms of spelling out specific mechanisms for dealing with the ongoing environmental problems in the coastal zone.

54. See Gourlay, M.R., " History of Coastal Engineering in Australia", in Kraus, N.C. (ed.), *History and Heritage of Coastal Engineering*, pp. 1–79.

55.   See "Use of Publicly Owned Natural Attractions for Recreation and Tourism", in *Subsidies to the Use of Natural Resources*, pp. 106–115.
56.   "Downturn Hits Reef", *Australian*, 22 April 1998.
57.   White, M.E., *Listen … Our Land is Crying. Australia's Environment: Problems and Solutions*.
58.   *Environmental Manager*, No. 195, 31 March 1998, p. 2.
59.   See, Mobbs, M., "Fear and Loathing on the ESD Trail", *Australian*, 18 September 1998.
60.   See, e.g., Warrick, R.A. & Rahman, A.A., "Future Sea-level Rise: Environmental and Socio-Political Considerations", in Mintzer, I.M. (ed.), *Confronting Climate Change: Risks, Implications and Responses*; Fankhauser, S., "Protection versus Retreat: The Economic Costs of Sea-level Rise", *Environment and Planning A*, Vol. 27, 1995, pp. 299–319; Bryant, E., "CO_2 Warming, Rising Sea-level and Retreating Coasts: Review and Critique", *Australian Geographer*, Vol. 18, 1987, pp. 101–113; Reed, D.J., "Sea Level", *Progress in Physical Geography*, Vol. 20, pp. 482–486.
61.   Whittingham, H.E., "The Bathurst Bay Hurricane and Associated Storm Surge", *Australian Meteorological Magazine*, Vol. 23, 1958, pp. 14–36.
62.   See Feldhaus, W.R., "The Physical Environment for Risk and Insurance", in Skipper, H.D. (ed.), *International Risk and Insurance. An Environmental-Managerial Approach*, pp. 416–442; Berz, G.A., "Global Warming and the Insurance Industry", in Toth, F.L. (ed.), *Cost-Benefit Analyses of Climate Change. The Broader Perspectives*, pp. 41–56.
63.   See Gullett, W., "Environmental Impact Assessment and the Precautionary Principle: Legislating Caution in Environmental Protection", *Environmental & Planning Law Journal*, Vol. 14, pp. 52–69; Deville, A. & Harding, R., *Applying the Precautionary Principle*.
64.   See, for example, Hotta, K. & Dutton, I.M. (eds), *Coastal Management in the Asia-Pacific Region: Issues and Approaches*.
65.   Morrison, J. & West, R., "Chapter 8 — Estuaries and the Sea", *Australian Journal of Environmental Management*, Vol. 4, 1997, pp. 175–177.
66.   Smith, A.K. & Pollard, D.A., "The Best Available Information — Some Case Studies from NSW, Australia, of Conservation-related Management Responses which Impact on Recreational Fishers", *Marine Policy*, 20, 1996, pp. 261–267.
67.   Warnken, J. & Buckley, R., "Scientific Quality of Tourism Environmental Impact Assessment", *Journal of Applied Ecology*, Vol. 35, 1998, p. 5.
68.   Clark, J.R., "Coastal Zone Management for the New Century", *Ocean & Coastal Management*, Vol. 37, 1997, pp. 191–216.
69.   See, for example, Cicin-Sain & Knecht, op. cit.; Bower, B.T. & Turner, R.K., "Characterising and Analysing Benefits from Integrated Coastal Management (ICM)", *Ocean & Coastal Management*, Vol. 38, 1998, pp. 41–66; *Integrated Resource Management in Australia*, Information Paper No. 6 for Coastal Zone Inquiry; Kenchington, R. & Crawford, D., "On the Meaning of Integration in Coastal Zone Management", *Ocean & Coastal Management*, Vol. 21, 1993, pp. 109–127.
70.   *Age* (Melbourne), 18 August 1998; Raymond, K., "The Long-term Future of the Great Barrier Reef", *Futures*, Vol. 28, 1996, pp. 947–970.
71.   See *Age* (Melbourne), 17 March 1998 and 2 May 1998.
72.   Christoff, P., "From Global Citizen to Renegade State: Australia at Kyoto", *Arena Journal*, No. 19, 1998, pp. 113–127.
73.   "When the Levy [sic] Breaks", *Australian Financial Review*, 25 March 1998.
74.   See Scheberle, D., *Federalism and Environmental Policy: Trust and the Politics of Implementation*.

75. See Holm, M.C., *An Overview of Legal Issues Relevant to Coastal Zone Management in Australia.*
76. Wescott, G., "Reforming Coastal Management to Improve Community Participation and Integration in Victoria, Australia", *Coastal Management*, Vol. 26, 1998, pp. 3–15; Kay, R. & Lester, C., "Benchmarking the Future Direction for Coastal Management in Australia", *Coastal Management*, Vol. 25, 1997, p. 286.
77. See, for example, Taberner, J., "Management for the Protection of the Coastal Zone", paper prepared for the 13th Annual National Conference of the National Environmental Law Association, Melbourne, 6–8 October 1994; Australia. Government. Ecologically Sustainable Working Groups. *Final Report: Tourism*; Brown, V.A., *Turning the Tide. Integrated Local Area Management for Australia's Coastal Zone.*

CHAPTER 9: SYDNEY: SUSTAINABLE CITY?

1. The author gratefully acknowledges the contribution to this research made by the financial support of the NRMA Ltd. The author is also appreciative of the advice given by Bronwen O'Dwyer and Mark McKenzie, Transport and Environment Department, NRMA Ltd. The opinions expressed in the chapter, however, are the author's.
2. Milbrath, L., *Learning to Think Environmentally While There is Still Time.*
3. Lowe, I., *Shaping a Sustainable Future: Science, Technology and Society.*
4. United Nations Development Programme (UNDP) Monograph, *Inter-Regional Exchange and Transfer of Effective Practices on Urban Management.*
5. Australia. Government. *National Strategy for Ecologically Sustainable Development.*
6. Ibid.
7. Australia. Government. *National Greenhouse Response Strategy.*
8. Gillies, F., "Career Path: Meg McDonald, Australian Ambassador for the Environment", *Business Class* (Qantas in-flight magazine), March 1998, p. 16.
9. Australia. Government. *National Greenhouse Strategy.*
10. Green, R., Harris, S. & Throsby, D. (Ecologically Sustainable Development Working Group Chairs), *Intersectoral Issues Report*; Caldicott, R. & Komidar, P., *Urban Issues Background Paper.*
11. G. Frecker "Think globally, act locally", in Coghill, K. (ed.), *Greenhouse: What's to be Done?.*
12. UNDP, op. cit.
13. Brown, V., *Measuring Local Sustainability: Linking Rhetoric to Reality*; Brown, V. & Greene, D., *Local Government State of the Environment Reports: A Review of the First Year.*
14. Gum, K.C., Manicaros, M.A., Lanarch, A.L., Stimson, R.J., Taylor, S.P. & Western, J.S., *A Social Atlas of Brisbane and the South-East Queensland Region*; Kemp, D., Manicaros, M., Mullins, P., Simpson, R., Stimson, R. & Western, J., *Urban Metabolism: A Framework for Evaluating the Viability, Livability and Sustainability of South-East Queensland*; Newton, P.W. (ed.), *Re-Shaping Cities for a More Sustainable Future: Exploring the Link Between Urban Form, Air Quality, Energy and Greenhouse Gas Emissions*; Roberts, B.H., Stimson, R.J. & Taylor, S.P., *Monitoring a Sun-Belt Metropolis 1996: Evaluating the Performance of the Brisbane and South East Queensland Economy.*
15. Rees, W.E., "Achieving Sustainability: Reform or Transformation?", *Journal of Planning Literature*, Vol. 9, No. 4, 1995, pp. 341–361; Wackernagel, M. & Rees, W., *Our Ecological Footprint.*

16. Leitman, J., *Energy-Environment Linkages in the Urban Sector*; Maddison, D., Pearce, D., et al., *Blueprint 5: The True Costs of Road Transport.*

17. Blowers, A., *Planning for a Sustainable Environment*; Edelman, D.J. & Procee, P., "The rôle of Best Practices in Capacity Building for Urban Environmental Management", in *Pathways to Sustainability: Local Initiatives for Cities and Towns*; Edwards, K., "UNEP Perspectives on How We Are Travelling Along the Road to Sustainability", in ibid.; European Commission, *European Sustainable Cities: First Report*; European Commission, *European Sustainable Cities: Final Report*; Habitat II Secretariat, *A Guide to Nominating and Learning from Best Practices in Improving Living Environment*; N'Dow, W., Keynote Address presented to the Dubai International Conference on Best Practices in Improving the Living Environment, Dubai, 1995, cited in Edelman, D.J. & Procee, P., "The rôle of Best Practices in Capacity Building for Urban Environmental Management", in *Pathways to Sustainability: Local Initiatives for Cities and Towns*; Nijkamp, P. & Perrels, A., *Sustainable Cities in Europe*; World Resources Institute, *World Resources 1996–97: A Guide to the Global Environment — The Urban Environment.*

18. N'Dow, op. cit.

19. European Commission, *European Sustainable Cities: First Report*; European Commission, *European Sustainable Cities: Final Report.*

20. European Commission, *European Sustainable Cities: Final Report.*

21. Ibid.

22. European Commission, *European Sustainable Cities: First Report.*

23. Ibid.

24. Euronet/ICLEI Consortium, *Local Sustainability European Good Practice Information Service*, http://www.iclei.org/coldfus/citylist.dbm; ICLEI, *Case Studies on the Local Agenda 21 Process*, http://ww.iceli.org/csdcases; ICLEI, *Cities for Climate Protection*, http:www.iceli.org/cases; Together Foundation, *Best Practices Database*, http://www.1001.together.com; Pfeiff, M., "The Mayor Who Built Brazil's City of the Future", *Reader's Digest*, March 1998, pp. 26–31; Rabinovitch, J., "Curitiba: Towards Sustainable Urban Development", *Environment and Urbanization*, Vol. 4, No. 2, 1992, pp. 62–73; Rabinovitch, J. & Hoehn, J., *A Sustainable Urban Transportation System: the "Surface Metro" in Curitiba, Brazil*; Rabinovitch, J. & Leitman, J., "Urban Planning in Curitiba", *Scientific American*, March 1996, pp. 26–33; Together Foundation 1996, *Best Practices Database*, 1996 [http://www.1001.together.com]; Together Foundation/UNCHS, *Best Practices Database*, 1996–98 [http://www.1001.together.com].

25. Discussant remark by Jorge Wilheim (Deputy Secretary General, 1996 Habitat II Conference and former Secretary of Planning, Sao Paulo State, Brazil), at the Second Annual Conference on Environmentally Sustainable Development: The Human Face of the Urban Environment, National Academy of Sciences, Washington DC, 19–23 September 1994, cited in Serageldin, I. & Cohen, M.A. (eds), *The Human Face of the Urban Environment, Environmentally Sustainable Development Proceedings Series No. 5.*

26. Australian Academy of Technological Sciences and Engineering, *Urban Air Pollution in Australia.*

CHAPTER 10: LOCAL ENVIRONMENTAL POLICY MAKING IN AUSTRALIA

1. In addition to the NLGERN/Environs Australia connection, at least eight major conferences with a major focus on the rôle of local government in

environmental management and sustainable development have been held in Australia during the 1990s, viz.: Adelaide and Melbourne 1991, Surfers Paradise 1992, Sydney 1994, Melbourne 1995, Sydney 1996, Newcastle 1997, City of Mandurah, 1998. The "Pathways to Sustainability" conference hosted by the City of Newcastle was really the indicative milestone of local government's increasingly significant rôle in environmental policy and management, as were the "Important rôle to Play" and "Localinks" conferences in Melbourne in 1991 and 1995 respectively.

2.   The driving force in terms of a global connection and networking has been the International Council for Local Environmental Initiatives (ICLEI) which was established in 1991 after an international Local Authorities conference in the United States of America.It has been our experience that networks such as those encouraged by: ICLEI at a global level; the Local Government Management Board (LGMB) in Britain and Environs Australia at a national level; and the South Australian LA21 Network at a state and local level have been vital mechanisms in progressing the recognition, uptake and implementation of LA21 both overseas and in Australia. ICLEI, *Local Government Implementation of Agenda 21*, 1997; Gilbert, et al., *Making Cities Work*, 1996.

3.   Doyle, T. & Kellow, A., *Environmental Politics and Policy Making in Australia*, p. 179.

4.   Crowley, K., "'Glocalisation' and Ecological Modernity".

5.   The Earth Summit is also referred to as UNCED, the United Nations Conference on the Environment and Development.

6.   Brown, V., Orr L., & Smith, D., *Acting Locally*, p. 7.

7.   ICLEI, *Local Government Implementation...*, p. 1.

8.   LGMB, *Five Years On*, p. 2.

9.   Whittaker, S., *Local Agenda 21 Survey 1996*.

10.   ICLEI, *Local Agenda 21 Planning Guide*.

11.   ICLEI, *The Local Agenda 21 Initiative*.

12.   Pattenden, M., "A Global Perspective on Local Agenda 21", p. 8.

13.   ICLEI, *Local Government Implementation*. The CCP campaign has been extended to Australia with over 30 councils now involved in this programme.

14.   Hams, T., "Local Agenda 21 — A view from the United Kingdom", p. 10.

15.   IUCN/UNEP/WWF, *World Conservation Strategy*.

16.   Australia. Government. Department of Home Affairs and Environment (DHAE), *A National Conservation Strategy for Australia*.

17.   WCED, *Our Common Future*, 1987.

18.   Hawke, R., *Our Country Our Future: A Statement on the Environment*.

19.   IUCN/UNEP/WWF, *Caring for the Earth*.

20.   McGregor, *Looking Forward*, p. 3.

21.   Officers of the then South Australian Department of Environment and Planning who participated in this process and subsequently supported the State's Environment Minister at the Earth Summit, witnessed this phenomenon.

22.   Australia, Government. *National Strategy for Ecologically Sustainable Development*, and an Intergovernmental Agreement on the Environment (IGAE); COAG, *Intergovernmental Agreement on the Environment*.

23.   Adams, G., *Guidelines for the Development of a Local Environment Policy*, (1992) and, in 1994, by Environs Australia on behalf of the Commonwealth Department of Environment, Sport and Territories: Cotter, et al., *Managing for the Future*. At the time of going to press both these guidelines, in response to the increasing interest in and uptake of LA21, were in the process of being updated and due for release in either late 1998 or early 1999.

24.   United Nations General Assembly Special Session (UNGASS), *Program for the Further Implementation of Local Agenda 21*.

25. This agreement recognised the shared responsibility of all three spheres of government in Australia for the formulation and implementation of environmental policy within their own areas of jurisdiction: see Brown, Orr & Smith, op. cit.

26. Whittaker, S., "A Study of Local Government in Australia and Local Agenda 21".

27. Outside the Landcare programme these were best represented by the Victorian model of Local Conservation Strategies, referred to above, which came at the end of a chain of similarly named World, national and State strategies.

28. TASQUE, *The rôle of Local Government in Environmental Management*.

29. ICESD, *Report on the Implementation of the National Strategy for Ecologically Sustainable Development*.

30. Given the perennially frail nature of federal-state relations on the question of support for local government it was hardly surprising that Howe's Advisory Group only had one representative for all the state environment and local government agencies. Given the support that South Australia already had in place for LA21 by 1993, it was hardly surprising that the representative came from that State.

31. Doyle & Kellow, op. cit., p. 26.

32. Conservation Council of South Australia (CCSA), *Strategy for Local Government Reform*, p. 3.

33. Voisey, et al., "The Political Significance of Agenda 21", p. 46.

34. Ibid.

35. Brown, V., *Turning the Tide: Integrated Local Area Management for Australia's Coastal Zone*; Maher and Associates, *An Approach to Environmental Management Systems for Local Government*; Whittaker, op. cit.

36. Victoria. Government. Department of Conservation and Natural Resources (DCNR), "Localinks".

37. Pattenden, op. cit. Especially since 1995, Environs Australia, which has become established as the national, non-government peak body for local government environmental management initiatives, has filled some of this vacuum by playing a vital networking and information provider rôle. In particular it has promoted Local Agenda 21 and sustainability concepts and principles by undertaking a number of training and awareness-raising programmes and producing assorted educational and information products for use by Councils.

38. ICLEI, *Local Government Implementation ...*, p. 1.

39. Brown, *Turning the Tide*; Whittaker, "A Study of Local Government".

40. TASQUE, op. cit.

41. Adams, *Guidelines....*

42. Pattenden, op. cit., p. 9.

43. Hine, "Local Agenda 21 — Turning Policy into Practice".

44. *Environment Business*, Local Agenda 21 Survey, 1998.

45. South Australia. *Hansard*, House of Assembly, pp. 234–235.

46. ISO stands for International Standards Organisation and since 14001 has been jointly adopted as both an Australian Standard (AS) and a New Zealand Standard (NZS) its correct, abbreviated title is ISO AS/NZS 14001.

47. Australia. Productivity Commission, *Implementation of Ecologically Sustainable Development*.

48. ALGA, *Managing the Environment*.

CHAPTER 11: INSTITUTIONALISING ECOLOGICALLY SUSTAINABLE DEVELOPMENT: PROMISES, PROBLEMS AND PROSPECTS

1.   This chapter is drawn from a paper prepared for a symposium organised by the Academy of the Social Sciences and the Public Policy Program of the Australian National University.
2.   A broad-ranging evaluation is provided in Hamilton, C. & Throsby, D. (eds), *The Ecologically Sustainable Development Process: Evaluating a Policy Process.*
3.   May, P., "Policy learning and policy failure", in *Journal of Public Policy*, Vol. 12, 1992, pp. 331–345; Dovers, S. & Mobbs, C., "An alluring prospect? Ecology, and the requirements of adaptive management", in Klomp, N. & Lunt, I., *Frontiers in Ecology*, pp. 39–52.
4.   Walker, K.J., "Conclusion: The Politics of Environmental Policy", Ch. 12 in Walker, K.J., *Australian Environmental Policy*, p. 251.
5.   The terms "institution" and "institutionalisation" are used broadly here. The difference between institutions and organisations is ignored for simplicity. Institutionalisation is taken to refer to arrangements (statutory, organisational, customary and so on) that entrench a matter such as ESD in public policy and administration so as to guarantee a reasonable degree of visibility, persistence and longevity (the opposite to policy adhocery and amnesia).
6.   Dovers, S., "Sustainability in context: an Australian perspective", in *Environmental Management*, Vol 14, 1990, pp. 297–305; Common, M., *Sustainability and Policy.* The distinction between sustainability (a system property or probably impossible end state) and sustainable development (a variable process of enhancing that property or moving somewhat closer to that state) will be ignored here, with the terms used interchangeably. The Australian version, ecologically sustainable development, equates in this sense with sustainable development, not sustainability. See Dovers, S. & Handmer, J., "Uncertainty, sustainability and change", in *Global Environmental Change*, Vol. 2, 1992, pp. 262–276.
7.   Boulding, K., "The economics of the coming spaceship earth", in Jarratt, H., *Environmental Quality in a Growing Economy.*
8.   Harrison, P., *The Third Revolution.*
9.   Dovers, S., "Sustainability: demands on policy", in *Journal of Public Policy*, Vol. 16, 1997, pp. 303–318; see also Beck, U., "From industrial society to risk society: questions of survival, social structure, and ecological enlightenment", in *Theory, Culture and Society*, Vol. 9, 1992, pp. 97–123; Walker, K.J., *The Political Economy of Environmental Policy*; Adam, B., "Running out of time: global crisis and human engagement", in Redclift, M. & Benton, T., *Social Theory and the Global Environment*; Common, op. cit.
10.   The phrase and evidence is from Dovers, S., "Information, sustainability and policy", *Australian Journal of Environmental Management*, Vol. 2, 1995, pp. 142–156; but see also Toyne, P., *The Reluctant Nation*; Walker, *The Political Economy of Environmental Policy.*
11.   Powell, J.M., *Environmental Management in Australia*, 1788–1914.
12.   Frawley, K., "Evolving visions: environmental management and nature conservation in Australia", in Dovers, S., *Australian Environmental History.*
13.   For example, Australia. Government. Department of the Environment, Sport and Territories. State of the Environment Advisory Council (SEAC), *State of the Environment: Australia 1996.*
14.   The author recalls from the final drafting conference in 1983 that the Prime Ministerial instruction to reach consensus between government, industry and

conservation interests over the Strategy was tested severely (particularly over issues of legal standing) but prevailed. The lowest common denominator nature of many problem descriptions and recommendations in the document was the price of this, a price not unusually extracted in the name of consensus.

15. Erskine, J.M., *Integration of Conservation and Development*; McEachern, D., "Environmental policy in Australia 1981–1991: a form of corporatism?", *Australian Journal of Public Administration*, Vol. 52, 1993, pp. 173–186.
16. Emmery, M., *Ecologically Sustainable Development Processes in Australia 1990–1992*.
17. Hawke, R., *Our Country, Our Future: A Statement on the Environment*; Commonwealth of Australia, *Ecologically Sustainable Development: a Commonwealth Discussion Paper*, June 1990.
18. World Commission on Environment and Development (WCED), *Our Common Future*, p. 43.
19. United Nations, *Agenda 21: the UN Program of Action From Rio*.
20. Sachs, W., *Global Ecology*.
21. Dovers, et al., *Population Growth and Australian Regional Environments*, Ch. 3; Kinrade, P., "Towards ecologically sustainable development: the rôle and shortcomings of markets", in Eckersley, R., *Markets, The State and the Environment*, pp. 86–109; Diesendorf, M. & Hamilton, C., "The ecologically sustainable development process in Australia", in Diesendorf & Hamilton, *Human Ecology, Human Economy*, pp. 285–301; Hamilton & Throsby, op. cit.
22. Australia. Government. *National Strategy for Ecologically Sustainable Development*.
23. The micro-meso-macro scaling terminology is presented in Dovers, S., "A framework for scaling and framing policy problems in sustainability", *Ecological Economics*, Vol. 12, 1995, pp. 93–106.
24. For an assessment of the biodiversity strategy, see Dovers, S. & Williams, J., "Implementing the CBD: the Australian experience", in *Ambio*, (forthcoming).
25. For a commentary on tried-and-forgotten policy, see Dovers, "Information, sustainability and policy", loc. cit.
26. Australia. Government. Ecologically Sustainable Development Working Groups. ESD Chairs, *Intersectoral Issues Report*.
27. National Population Council, "Population Issues and Australia's Future"; Dovers, S., "Dimensions of the Australian population-environment debate", in *Development Bulletin*, Vol. 41, 1997, pp. 50–53.
28. State of the Environment Advisory Council, op. cit.
29. For a detailed review of the national SoE report, see Anderson, E., et al., "Review of national state of the environment report", in *Australian Journal of Environmental Management*, Vol. 4, 1997, pp. 157–184.
30. See Raynes, N., "Partnerships in Australian Commonwealth fisheries management", in Klomp & Lunt, op. cit.
31. Bates, G., *Environmental Law in Australia*. Regarding the Bill, see NSW. Government. Environmental Defender's Office, *Brief commentary on the Commonwealth Environment Protection and Biodiversity Conservation Bill*.
32. Downes, D., "Neo-corporatism and environmental policy", in *Australian Journal of Political Science*, Vol. 31, 1996, pp. 175–190; Dovers, et al., *Population Growth and Australian Regional Environments*; Kinrade, op. cit.; Diesendorf & Hamilton, op. cit.
33. The addition of intersectoral issues was belated, and although the ESD Chairs delivered an intersectoral report, much more should have been done in this regard.

34. For a review of policy styles in different countries, see Janicke, M., "Conditions for environmental policy success: an international comparison", in *The Environmentalist*, Vol. 12, 1992, pp. 47–58.

35. Doering, R.L., *Canadian Round Tables on the Environment and the Economy*.

36. Christie, I., "Britain's sustainable development strategy: environmental quality and policy change", in *Policy Studies*, Vol. 15, 1994, pp. 4–20.

37. For an analysis of the New Zealand arrangement, see Gleeson, B.J. & Grundy, K.J., "New Zealand's planning revolution five years on: a preliminary assessment", in *Journal of Environmental Planning and Management*, Vol. 40, 1997, pp. 293–313.

38. Stewart, D. & McColl, G., "The Resource Assessment Commission: An Inside Assessment", in *Australian Journal of Environmental Management*, Vol. 1, No. 1, June 1994, pp. 12–23; Economou, N., "Australian Environmental Policy-making in Transition: the rise and fall of the Resource Assessment Commission", in *Australian Journal of Public Administration*, Vol. 55, No. 1, June 1996, pp. 12–22.

39. Considine, M., *Public Policy*.

40. Dovers, S. & Lindenmayer, D., "Managing the environment: rhetoric, policy and reality", in *Australian Journal of Public Administration*, Vol. 55, 1997, pp. 65–80.

41. Dovers, S., *Sustainable Energy Systems*.

42. See, generally, House of Representatives Standing Committee on Financial Institutions and Public Administration, *Cultivating Competition: Inquiry Into Aspects of the National Competition Policy Reform Package*. For the record, the author is not anti-competition, but is sceptical of any widespread display of policy zealotry, and has respect for other "c" words, such as cooperation, coordination, cohesion and complementarity.

43. Dovers, S., "ESD and NCP: parity or primacy?", in Cater, M., *Public Interest in National Competition Policy*, pp. 75–92.

44. SEAC, op. cit., p. 10/28.

45. Castles, F., "The dynamics of policy change: what happened in the English-speaking nations in the 1980s", in *European Journal of Political Research*, Vol. 18, 1990, pp. 491–513; Bell, S., "Globalisation, neoliberalism and the transformation of the Australian state", in *Australian Journal of Political Science*, Vol. 32, 1997, pp. 345–367; Orchard, L., "Managerialism, economic rationalism and public sector reform in Australia: connections, divergences, alternatives", in *Australian Journal of Public Administration*, Vol. 57, 1998, pp. 19–32.

46. More radical prescriptions of what might constitute a "green state" exist, but are not dealt with here.

47. See also the heuristic model in Dovers, "Information, sustainability and policy".

48. The proposed new national environmental law does not offer real codification of ESD principles. Further, there is a clear intent to diminish Commonwealth power over key areas of environmental policy and weaken the environmental impact assessment process. Disturbingly for community involvement, there is also ominous intent as to the Register of the National Estate, comprising 11,000 places respected, researched and nominated over more than twenty years by a diverse range of community groups; see Hill, R., *Reform of Commonwealth Environment Legislation: Consultation Paper*.

49. Gullett, W., "Environmental protection and the precautionary principle", in *Environmental and Planning Law Journal*, Vol. 14, 1997, pp. 52–69.

50. Coper, M., "The untold story of the Inter-State Commission", in *Canberra Bulletin of Public Administration*, Vol. 75, 1993, pp. 131–133.

278 • Australian Environmental Policy 2

51. Martin, P. & Woodhill, J., "Landcare in the balance: government rôles and policy issues in sustaining rural environments", in *Australian Journal of Environmental Management*, Vol. 2, 1995: pp. 173–183; Woodhill, J., "Natural resources decision making: beyond the landcare paradox", in *Australasian Journal of Natural Resources Law and Policy*, Vol. 3, 1996, pp. 91–114; Dovers, S., "Community involvement in environmental management: thoughts for emergency management", in *Australian Journal of Emergency Management*, Vol. 12, 1998, pp. 6–11.
52. Dovers, "Dimensions of the Australian population-environment debate", op. cit.

CHAPTER 12: CONCLUSION: ENVIRONMENTAL POLICY IN THE GLOOMY 1990s

1. Brown, P., "Greenhouse effect worse than feared", *The Guardian Weekly*, week ending 8 November 1998, p. 1; Pearce, F., "Can't stand the heat", *New Scientist*, Vol. 180, Nos 2165/6/7, 19/26 December 1998–2 January 1999, pp. 32–33.
2. Australian Bureau of Statistics (ABS), *Environmental Issues: People's Views and Practices*.
3. See especially Walker, K.J., "The State in Environmental Management: the Ecological Dimension", *Political Studies*, Vol. XXXVII, March 1989, pp. 25–39.
4. Rose, R., "On the Priorities of Government: a Developmental Analysis of Public Policies", *European Journal of Political Research*, Vol. 4, 1976, pp. 247–289.
5. Rueschemeyer, D. & Evans, P.B., "The State and Economic Transformation: Toward an Analysis of the Conditions Underlying Effective Intervention", in Evans, P.B., Rueschemeyer, D. & Skocpol, T. (eds), *Bringing the State Back In*, pp. 44–77; Walker, K.J., "The State in Environmental Management: the Ecological Dimension", *Political Studies*, Vol. XXXVII, March 1989, pp. 25–39.
6. Mann, M., "Capitalism and Militarism", Ch. 1 in Shaw, M. (ed.), *War, State & Society*, pp. 25–46; pp. 35–36.
7. Smith, D. & Smith, R., *The Economics of Militarism*, pp. 91–92; Kidron, M., *Western Capitalism Since the War*, esp. Ch. 3.
8. See Dryzek, J., *Rational Ecology*, pp. 58–60, for the argument that ecological rationality must have "near-lexical" priority.
9. Some countries, such as the United States of America, have permanent underclasses of the poor who never participate in politics; such countries are more properly plutocracies. Their often-remarked dependence on élite adherence to "democratic" norms is a consequence. See, notably, Dye, T.R. & Ziegler, L.H., *The Irony of Democracy*; Parenti, M., *Democracy for the Few*.
10. Crouch, C., "The State, Capital and Liberal Democracy", Ch. 1 in Crouch, C. (ed.), *State and Economy in Contemporary Capitalism*, p. 15.
11. See, e.g., Purdue, D., "Hegemonic Trips: World Trade, Intellectual Property and Biodiversity", *Environmental Politics*, Vol. 4, No. 1, Spring 1995, pp. 88–107; "Food Law and Food Policy", Ch. 9 in Tansey, G. & Worsley, T., *The Food System: A Guide*.
12. Walker, K.J., "Ecological Limits and Marxian Thought", *Politics*, Vol. XIV, No. 1, May 1979, pp. 29–46; Benton, T., "Marxism and Natural Limits", *New Left Review*, No. 178, November–December 1989.
13. Beginning with the work of pioneers such as C.L. Dodgson, M. Ostrogorski, V. Pareto and D. Black, the subject was taken up by economists such as Arrow and Sen, and by political scientists such as Riker, Ordeshooke and others.

Most influential on the Right have been Tulloch and Buchanan, especially the latter. Scholars with a less social Darwinist worldview, such as Taylor, has have received markedly less attention. Taylor, M., *Anarchy and Cooperation; Community, Anarchy and Liberty.*

14. Axelrod, R., *The Evolution of Co-operation*; Ostrom, E., *Governing the Commons.*

15. Olson, M., *The Rise and Decline of Nations.*

16. Self, P., *Government by the Market?* offers an extended and critical examination of this problem.

17. See Patterson, W., *Nuclear Power*, for a chilling account of the industry's history; Jeffery, J., "The Unique Dangers of Nuclear Power: An Overview", *The Ecologist*, Vol. 16, No. 4/5, 1986, pp. 147–163; Caufield, C., *Multiple Exposures*, on the hazards; and Cawte, A., *Atomic Australia*, for the history of Australian nuclear policy up to 1990.

18. Head., B. (ed.), *State and Economy in Australia*, p. 6.

19. Crough, G. & Wheelwright, T., *Australia: A Client State*, esp. Chs 1, 7 & 8.

20. Head, B. (ed.), op. cit., p. 54.

21. Falk, J., *Global Fission*, Ch. 11.

22. See, e.g., Harman, E. & Head, B. (eds), *State, Capital and Resources in the North and West of Australia*; Stuart, R., "Resources Development Policy: the Case of Queensland's Export Coal Industry", Ch. 4 in Patience, A. (ed.), *The Bjelke-Petersen Premiership*, pp. 53–80.

23. Kellow, A., "Electricity Planning in Tasmania and New Zealand: Political Processes and the Technological Imperative", *Australian Journal of Public Administration*, Vol. XLV, No. 1, March 1986, pp. 2–17; esp. p. 13.

24. For a sketch of this and competing models, see Walker, K.J., *The Political Economy of Environmental Policy*, pp. 186–196.

25. Pearce, D., "The Limits of Cost-Benefit Analysis as a Guide to Environmental Policy", *KYKLOS*, Vol. 29, 1976, Fasc. 1, pp. 97–112. Elliott, D. & Yarrow, G., "Cost-Benefit Analysis and Environmental Policy: A Comment", ibid., Vol. 30, 1977, Fasc. 2, pp. 300–309. Smith, V.K., "Cost-Benefit Analysis and Environmental Policy: A Comment", ibid., pp. 310–313. Pearce, D., "Cost-Benefit Analysis and Environmental Policy: A Reply to Elliott and Yarrow and to Smith", ibid., pp. 314–318.

26. See especially Goodin's comprehensive critique of the varieties of incrementalism in *Political Theory and Public Policy*, Ch. 2.

27. Connell, R.W., *Ruling Class, Ruling Culture*; Encel, S., *Equality and Authority*; for an overview, see Parkin, A., "Power in Australia: an Introduction", Ch. 21 in Parkin, A., Summers, J. & Woodward, D., *Government, Politics and Power in Australia*, pp. 263–284.

28. Bachrach, P. & Baratz, M.S., *Power and Poverty.*

29. This point is not new: Ratcliffe was critical of sheepraising during the 1930s. Op. cit., and Dunlap, T.R., "Ecology and environmentalism in the Anglo settler colonies", Ch. 5 in Griffiths, T. & Robin, L., *Ecology & Empire*, p. 79.

30. Walker, K.J., "The Neglect of Ecology: The Case of the Ord River Scheme", Ch. 9 in Walker, K.J. (ed.), *Australian Environmental Policy*, pp. 183–202.

BIBLIOGRAPHY

ABC Radio, *AM*, Tuesday, 1 June 1993, Department of the Parliamentary Library, online transcript, 87–1424.

ABC Radio, *Daybreak*, Monday, 31 May 1993, Department of the Parliamentary Library, online transcript, 87–1416.

ABC Radio, *Earthbeat*, "New Seagrass Discoveries", 29 August 1998.

ABC Radio, *News* (South Australia — Port Lincoln) Monday, 14 September 1998.

ABC Radio, *PM*, Thursday 21 January 1993, Department of Parliamentary Library, online transcript, 86–4252.

ABC TV, *Lateline*, Thursday 24 June 1993, Department of the Parliamentary Library, online transcript, 87–2415.

Adams, G., *Guidelines for the Development of a Local Environment Policy by Local Government*. Adelaide: Department of Environment and Land Management, 1992.

Adams, G., "Towards Sustainability", *Seminar Proceedings: Indicators for Better Environmental Management*. Adelaide: Department of Environment and Natural Resources, 1996.

Agardy, M.T., "Accommodating Ecotourism in Multiple Use Planning of Coastal and Marine Protected Areas", *Ocean & Coastal Management*, Vol. 20, 1993, pp. 219–239.

Age (Melbourne), "AMA's Call to Close Ocean Sewer Outfalls Dismissed as Impractical", 28 December 1995.

Age (Melbourne), 14 June 1997; 10 November 1997; 17 March 1998; 2 May 1998; 18 August 1998.

Aitken, H.G.J., *The State and Economic Growth*. New York: Social Science Research Council, 1959.

Alexander, J. & Fisher, T., "Running Out of Time", *Habitat*, Vol. 23, No. 1, pp. 11–18.

Amy, D.J., "Toward a Post-Positivist Analysis," *Policy Studies Journal*, Vol. 13, No. 1, September 1984, pp. 207–212.

Anderson, E., et al., "Review of national state of the environment report", *Australian Journal of Environmental Management*, Vol. 4, 1997, pp. 157–184.

Anon, "Water Diversion Schemes", *The Australian Encyclopaedia*, Vol. 9, 1963, pp. 187–191. Sydney: The Grolier Society of Australia.

Australia. Consultancy report commissioned by Coastal Zone Inquiry. Canberra: Resource Assessment Commission, 1993.

Australia. Government. *Compendium of Ecologically Sustainable Development Recommendations*. Canberra: AGPS, 1992.

Australia. Government. Department of Arts, Sport, Environment, Tourism and Territories. *Intergovernmental Agreement on the Environment*. Canberra: AGPS, 1992.

Australia. Government. Department of Home Affairs and Environment (DHAE), *A National Conservation Strategy for Australia* (2nd edn). Canberra: AGPS, 1984.

Australia. Government. Department of Primary Industry and Energy. *Ecologically Sustainable Development: a Commonwealth Discussion Paper*, June 1990. Canberra: AGPS, 1990.

Australia. Government. Department of the Environment, Sport and Territories. *Living on the Coast: The Commonwealth Coastal Policy*. Canberra: AGPS, 1995.

Australia. Government. Department of the Environment, Sport and Territories. State of the Environment Advisory Council, *Australia; State of the Environment 1996*. Collingwood, Victoria: CSIRO Publishing, 1996.

Australia. Government. Department of the Environment, Sport and Territories, *Subsidies to the Use of Natural Resources*. Canberra: Environmental Economics Research Paper No. 2 (n.d.).

Australia. Government. Department of Tourism, *National Ecotourism Strategy*. Canberra: AGPS, 1994.

Australia. Government. Ecologically Sustainable Development Working Group, *Final Report: Tourism*. Canberra: AGPS, 1991.

Australia. Government. Ecologically Sustainable Development Working Groups. ESD Chairs, *Intersectoral Issues Report*, Canberra: AGPS, 1992.

Australia. Government. Ecologically Sustainable Development Working Groups, *Final Report: Tourism*. Canberra: AGPS, 1991.

Australia. Government. *National Greenhouse Response Strategy*. Canberra: AGPS, 1992.

Australia. Government. *National Greenhouse Strategy: Strategic Framework for Advancing Australia's Greenhouse Response*. Canberra: AGPS, 1998 (*http://www.greenhouse.gov.au/pubs/ngs/index.html*).

Australia. Government. *National Strategy for Ecologically Sustainable Development*. Canberra: AGPS, 1992.

Australia. Government. Resource Assessment Commission, *Integrated Resource Management in Australia*, Information Paper No. 6 for Coastal Zone Inquiry. Canberra: RAC, 1993.

Australia. Government. Resource Assessment Commission. Coastal Zone Inquiry *Final Report*. Canberra: AGPS, November 1993.

Australia. Government. The Rural Reconstruction Commission, *Irrigation, Water Conservation and Land Drainage*. Eighth Report; Canberra: Commonwealth Government Printer, 1945.

Australia. Parliament. House of Representatives Standing Committee on Environment, Recreation and the Arts (HORSCERA), *The Injured Coastline: Protection of the Coastal Environment.* Canberra: AGPS, 1991.

Australia. Parliament. House of Representatives. Standing Committee on Financial Institutions and Public Administration, *Cultivating Competition: Inquiry Into Aspects of the National Competition Policy Reform Package.* Canberra: AGPS, 1997.

Australia. Parliament. Senate. *Inquiry into Marine and Coastal Pollution.* Report from the Senate Environment, Recreation, Communications and the Arts References Committee. Canberra: AGPS, 1997.

Australian, "Downturn Hits Reef", 22 April 1998.

Australian Academy of Technological Sciences and Engineering, *Urban Air Pollution in Australia: Community Summary.* Parkville, Victoria: AATSE, 1997 (*http://www.environment.gov.au/epg/pubs/urban_air_summary.html*).

Australian Bureau of Statistics, *Australian National Accounts: National Income and Expenditure,* Catalogue Number 5204.0. Canberra: AGPS, various issues.

Australian Bureau of Statistics, *Commonwealth Government Year Book,* various issues.

Australian Bureau of Statistics, *Demography Bulletin No. 87.* Canberra: AGPS, 1971.

Australian Bureau of Statistics, *Manufacturing Establishments Summary of Operations by Industry Class: Australia,* Catalogue Number 8202.0. Canberra: AGPS, various issues.

Australian Bureau of Statistics, *Queensland Year Book,* various issues.

Australian Bureau of Statistics (ABS), *Environmental Issues: People's Views and Practices.* Canberra: ABS.

Australian Financial Review, "When the Levy [sic] Breaks", 25 March 1998.

Australian Local Government Association (ALGA), *Managing the Environment — A Practical Guide for Local Government to Environmental Management Systems and ISO 14001.* Canberra: ALGA, 1996.

Australian Nature Conservation Agency, *The Ramsar Convention* (brochure), 1997.

Axelrod, R., *The Evolution of Co-operation.* New York: Basic Books, 1984; Harmondsworth: Penguin, 1990.

Ayres, I. & Braithwaite, J., *Responsive Regulation: Transcending the Deregulation Debate.* Oxford: OUP, 1992.

Bachrach, P. & Baratz, M.S., *Power and Poverty.* New York: Oxford University Press, 1970.

Baird, R., "Public Interest Groups and Costs — Have the Flood Gates been Opened?", *Environmental and Planning Law Journal,* Vol. 15, 1998, pp. 294–299.

Bartlett, R. & Buhrs, T., *Environmental Policy in New Zealand: The Politics of Clean and Green?* Auckland: Oxford University Press, 1993.

Bartone, C., Bernstein, J, Leitman, J. & Eigen, J., "Toward Environmental Strategies for Cities", *Urban Management Program Policy Paper No. 18.* Washington DC: The World Bank, 1994.

Bates, G., *Environmental Law in Australia* (4th edn). Sydney: Butterworths, 1994.

Bean, C., et al. (eds), *The Politics of Retribution: the 1996 Federal Election.* Sydney: Allen and Unwin, 1997.

Bean, C., McAllister, I. & Warhurst, J. (eds), *The Greening of Australian Politics.* Melbourne: Longman Cheshire, 1990.

Beck, U., "From industrial society to risk society: questions of survival, social structure, and ecological enlightenment", *Theory, Culture and Society,* Vol. 9, 1992, pp. 97–123.

Beder, S., "Science and the Control of Information: An Australian Case Study", *The Ecologist,* Vol. 20, No. 4, July/August 1990, pp. 136–140.

Beder, S., *Global Spin.* Melbourne: Scribe, 1997.

Beder, S., *Toxic Fish and Sewer Surfing: How Deceit and Collusion are Destroying our Great Beaches*. Sydney: Allen & Unwin, 1989.

Bell, S., "Globalisation, neoliberalism and the transformation of the Australian state", *Australian Journal of Political Science*, Vol. 32, 1997, pp. 345–367.

Bell, S., "Socialism & Ecology: Will Ever the Twain Meet?" *Social Alternatives*, Vol. 6, No. 3, pp. 5–12.

Bell, S., *Ungoverning the Economy: the Political Economy of Australian Economic Policy*. Melbourne: Oxford University Press, 1997.

Bell, S.R. & Head, B. (eds), *State, Economy, and Public Policy in Australia*. Melbourne: Oxford University Press, 1994.

Bell, S.R. & Wanna, J. (eds), *Business-Government Relations in Australia*. Sydney: Harcourt Brace Jovanovich, 1992.

Benton, T., "Marxism and Natural Limits", *New Left Review*, No. 178, November–December 1989.

Bilsky, L.J. (ed.), *Historical Ecology*. Port Washington, NY: Kennikat Press, 1980.

Birch, C., *Confronting the Future — Australia and the World: the Next Hundred Years* (new edn). Ringwood, Victoria: Penguin, 1993.

Blainey, G., *The Tyranny of Distance*. Melbourne: Sun Books, 1966.

Blainey G., *Gold and Paper*. Melbourne: Georgian House, 1958.

Blakers, A., "Hydro-Electricity in Tasmania Revisited", *Australian Journal of Environmental Management*, Vol. 1, No. 2, September 1994, pp. 110–120.

Blowers, A., *Planning for a Sustainable Environment*, London: Earthscan, 1993.

Boardman, R., *Global régimes and Nation States: Environmental Issues in Australian Politics*. Minnesota: Carleton University Press, 1990.

Bolton, G.C., *Spoils and Spoilers: a History of Australians Shaping Their Environment* (2nd edn). Sydney: Allen & Unwin, 1992.

Bolton G.C., *A Thousand Miles Away, A History of North Queensland to 1920*. Canberra: Australian National University Press, 1972.

Bonyhady, T., *Places Worth Keeping*, Sydney: Allen & Unwin, 1993.

Bonyhady, T. (ed.), *Ecological Discourses*. (forthcoming).

Bonyhady, T. (ed.), *Environmental Protection and Legal Change*. Sydney: The Federation Press, 1992.

Bower, B.T. & Turner, R.K., "Characterising and Analysing Benefits from Integrated Coastal Management (ICM)", *Ocean & Coastal Management*, Vol. 38, 1998, pp. 41–66.

Boyden, S., Dovers, S. & Shirlow, M., *Our Biosphere Under Threat: Ecological Realities and Australia's Opportunities*. Melbourne: Oxford University Press, 1989.

Bradfield, J.J.C., "Queensland, The Conservation and Utilization of Her Water Resources", unpublished MS, 1938.

Breckwoldt, R., *The Last Stand: Managing Australia's Remnant Forests and Woodlands*. Canberra: Department of Arts, Heritage and Environment, 1986.

Brett, J., Gillespie, J. & Goot, M. (eds), *Developments in Australian Politics*. Melbourne: Macmillan, 1996.

Bridgeman, P. & Davis, G., *Australian Policy Handbook*. Sydney: Allen and Unwin, 1998.

Britell, J., "Partnerships, Roundtables and Quincy-Type Groups are Bad Ideas that Cannot Resolve Environmental Conflicts", 1997(on line at *http://www.harbourside.com/home/j/jbritell/welcome.htm*).

Brown, H., *The Challenge of Man's Future*. New York: Viking Press, 1954.

Brown, L., *The Twenty-Ninth Day*. New York: Norton, 1978.

Brown, P., "Greenhouse effect worse than feared", *The Guardian Weekly*, week ending 8 November 1998, p. 1.

Brown, V., *Acting Globally: Supporting the Changing rôle of Local Government in*

Integrated Environmental Management. Canberra: Department for the Arts, Sport, Environment and Territories, 1994.

Brown, V., Orr, L. & Smith, D., *Acting Locally: Meeting the Environmental Research Needs of Local Government*. Canberra: Department of the Arts, Sport, and the Environment and Territories, 1992.

Brown, V. "Measuring Local Sustainability: Linking Rhetoric to Reality", Discussion Paper, Centre for Resource and Environmental Studies, Australian National University, Canberra, 1996.

Brown, V. (ed.), *Managing for Local Sustainability: Policy, Problem-solving, Practice and Place*. Canberra: Department for the Environment, Sports and Territories, 1997.

Brown, V. & Greene, D., *Local Government State of the Environment Reports: A Review of the First Year*. Sydney: NSW Department of Local Government and Cooperatives, 1994.

Brown, V.A., *Turning the Tide. Integrated Local Area Management for Australia's Coastal Zone*. Canberra: Department of the Environment, Sport and Territories, 1995.

Brunton, N., "Holidays by the Sewer: Coastal Water Pollution and Ecological Sustainability", Paper presented to National Environmental Law Association Conference, Coolum, 8–12 May 1996.

Bryant, E., "CO2 Warming, Rising Sea-level and Retreating Coasts: Review and Critique", *Australian Geographer*, Vol. 18, 1987, pp. 101–113.

Bureau of Industry Economics, *Environmental Assessment — Impact on Major Projects*. Research Report No. 35, Canberra: AGPS, 1990.

Bureau of Tourism Research, *Domestic Tourism Monitor 1996–97*. Canberra: Bureau of Tourism Research, 1997.

Burton, R., "Right Wing Think Tanks", in Doyle, T. (ed.), "Corporations, Power and the Environment", special edition of *Chain Reaction*, Nos 73–74, 1995.

Butlin, N.G., Barnard, A. & Pincus, J.J., *Government and Capitalism: Public and Private Choice in Twentieth Century Australia*. North Sydney: George Allen & Unwin, 1982.

Caldicott, R. & Komidar, P., *Urban Issues Background Paper*. Ecologically Sustainable Development Working Groups. Canberra: AGPS, 1991.

Carden, M.F., *The Queensland Development and Environment Policy Process: With Special Reference to Irrigation Development in the Burdekin Region*. Unpublished Ph.D. Thesis, Faculty of Environmental Science, Griffith University, (Brisbane) 1993.

Carden M. F, "Reformulating Political Ecology: Towards an Intelligent Pragmatism", *Conference Proceedings*, Ecopolitics XI, Hobart: Ecopolitics Association of Australasia, 1998, pp. 57–71.

Castles, F., "The dynamics of policy change: what happened in the English-speaking nations in the 1980s", *European Journal of Political Research*, Vol. 18, 1990, pp. 491–513.

Castles, F.G., *The Working Class and Welfare: Reflections on the Political Development of the Welfare State in Australia and New Zealand, 1890–1980*. Wellington: Allen & Unwin Port Nicholson Press, 1985.

Cater, M., *Public Interest in National Competition Policy: Implementation Issues*. Sydney: Public Sector Research Centre, University of NSW, 1997.

Catton, W.R., Jr., *Overshoot: The Ecological Basis of Revolutionary Change*. Urbana, Ill.: University of Illinois Press, 1980.

Caufield, C., *Multiple Exposures: Chronicles of the Radiation Age*. Harmondsworth: Penguin, 1990.

Cawte, A., *Atomic Australia, 1944–1990*. Kensington, NSW: UNSW Press, 1992.

Chanock, M. & Simpson, C. (eds), *Law and Cultural Heritage*. Bundoora: Latrobe University Press, 1996.

Chapman, R.J.K., *Setting Agendas and Defining Problems — The Wesley Vale Pulp Mill Proposal*, Deakin Series in Public Policy and Administration No. 3. Geelong, Victoria: Centre for Applied Social Research, Deakin University, 1992.

Charters, T., Gabriel, M. & Prasser, S., *National Parks. Private Sector's Rôle*. Toowoomba: University of Southern Queensland Press, 1996.

Christie, I., "Britain's sustainable development strategy: environmental quality and policy change", *Policy Studies*, Vol. 15, 1994, pp. 4–20.

Christoff, P., "Degreening Government in the Garden State: Environment Policy Under The Kennett Government", *Environmental Law and Planning Journal*, Vol. 15 No. 1, February 1998, pp. 10–32.

Christoff, P., "From Global Citizen to Renegade State: Australia at Kyoto", *Arena Journal*, No. 19, 1998, pp. 113–127.

Christoff, P., "The 1993 Elections — A Fading Green Politics?" *Environmental Politics*, Vol. 3, No. 1, Spring 1994, pp. 130–158.

Cicin-Sain, B. & Knecht, R.W., *Integrated Coastal and Ocean Management: Concepts and Practices*, Washington DC: Island Press, 1998.

City of Newcastle, "Pathways to Sustainability: Local Initiatives for Cities and Towns", Conference Proceedings, Newcastle, 1–5 June 1997.

Clancy, M., "Commodity Chains, Services and Development: Theory and Preliminary Evidence from the Tourism Industry", *Review of International Political Economy*, Vol. 5, 1998, pp. 122–148.

Clark, J.R., "Coastal Zone Management for the New Century", *Ocean & Coastal Management*, Vol. 37, 1997, pp. 191–216.

Coaldrake, P, *Working the System: Government in Queensland*. St. Lucia: University of Queensland Press, 1989.

Coaldrake, P., "The Coalition Crisis and the Queensland Election of 1983", *Politics*, Vol. 19, No. 1, May 1984, pp. 84–92.

Cochrane T., *Blockade: the Queensland Loans Affair 1920–1924*. St. Lucia: University of Queensland Press, 1989.

Cockfield, G., "Complexity Theory: the New Policy 'Science'", unpublished paper presented to the *Public Policy Network Conference*, Department of Political Science, University of Tasmania, Hobart, 1–2 February 1996.

Cocks, D., *Use With Care*. Kensington, NSW: UNSW Press, 1992.

Coghill, K. (ed.) *Greenhouse: What's to be Done?* Sydney: Pluto Press, 1990.

Common, M., *Sustainability and Policy: Limits to Economics*. Melbourne: Cambridge University Press, 1995.

Commoner, B., *The Closing Circle: Nature, Man, and Technology*. New York: Knopf, 1971.

Commonwealth Bureau of Census and Statistics, *Production Bulletins*, Catalogue Number 8200.0. Canberra: Commonwealth Government Printer, various issues.

Commonwealth Grants Commission, *Second Report*. Melbourne: Commonwealth Government Printing Service, 1935.

Connell, R.W., *Ruling Class, Ruling Culture*. Cambridge: Cambridge University Press, 1977.

Conservation Council of South Australia (CCSA), *Strategy for Local Government Reform* — Discussion Paper. Adelaide: CCSA, 1992.

Conservation Stakeholder Working Group, "Ramsar Management Plan for Coongie Lakes Wetlands; an Issues Paper", April 1998, p. 1.

Considine, M., *Public Policy: A Critical Approach*. Melbourne: Macmillan, 1994.

Coper, M., "The untold story of the Inter-State Commission", *Canberra Bulletin of Public Administration*, Vol. 75, 1993, pp. 131–133.

Coper, M., *The Franklin Dam Case*. Melbourne: Butterworths, 1983.

Cotgrove, S. & Duff, A., "Environmentalism, Middle Class Radicalism & Politics," *Sociological Review*, Vol. 28, No. 2, 1980, pp. 333–351.

Cotter, B., Wescott, W. & Williams, S. (eds), *Managing for the Future: A Local Government Guide*. Department of Environment, Sports and Territories, 1994.

Council of Australian Governments (COAG), *Intergovernmental Agreement on the Environment*, Canberra: Commonwealth of Australia, 1992.

Courtenay, P.P., "Agriculture, Development and the Burdekin — some socio-political considerations", paper presented to the annual conference of the Australian and New Zealand Association for the Advancement of Science (ANZAAS), 1987.

Craik, J., *Resorting to Tourism. Cultural Policies for Tourist Development in Australia*. North Sydney: Allen & Unwin, 1991.

Cribb M.B. & Boyce P.J. (eds), *Politics in Queensland: 1977 and beyond*. St. Lucia: University of Queensland Press, 1980.

Crook, S. & Pakulski, J., "Shades of Green: Public Opinion on Environmental Issues in Australia", *Australian Journal of Political Science*, Vol. 30, No. 1, March 1995, pp. 39–55.

Crosby, A.W., *Ecological Imperialism: the Biological Expansion of Europe, 900–1900*. Cambridge: Cambridge University Press, 1986.

Crouch, C. (ed.), *State and Economy in Contemporary Capitalism*. London: Croom Helm, 1979.

Crough, G. & Wheelwright, T., *Australia: A Client State*. Ringwood, Victoria: Penguin, 1982.

Crowley, K., "'Glocalisation' and Ecological Modernity: challenges for local environmental governance in Australia", *Local Environment*, Vol. 3, No. 1, pp. 91–97, 1998.

Dalton, B.J. (ed.), *Lectures On North Queensland History*, No. 4. Townsville: Department of History, James Cook University, 1984.

Daly, H.E. (ed.), *Toward a Steady-State Economy*. San Francisco: W.H. Freeman, 1973.

Davidson, B. R, *Australia Wet or Dry? The Physical and Economic Limits to the Expansion of Irrigation*. Carlton, Victoria: Melbourne University Press, 1969.

Davidson, B. R, *European Farming in Australia: An Economic History of Australian Farming*. Amsterdam: Elsevier, 1981.

Davidson B. R, *The Northern Myth: Limits to Agricultural and Pastoral Development in Tropical Australia*. Carlton, Victoria: Melbourne University Press, 1965.

Davies, A.F., *Australian Democracy* (2nd edn). Melbourne: Longmans, Green, 1964.

Davis, B., "Achieving Sustainable Development: Scientific Uncertainty and Policy Innovation in Tasmanian Regional Development", *Australian Journal of Public Administration*, Vol. 55, No. 4, 1996, pp. 100–108.

Davis, G., Wanna, J., Warhurst, J. & Weller, P., *Public Policy in Australia*. Sydney: Allen & Unwin, 1988.

Day, L.H. & Rowland, D.T. (eds), *How Many More Australians?* Melbourne: Longman Cheshire, 1988.

Deville, A. & Harding, R., *Applying the Precautionary Principle*. Annandale: The Federation Press, 1997.

Diesendorf, M. & Hamilton, C., *Human Ecology, Human Economy: Ideas for an Ecologically Sustainable Future*. Sydney: Allen and Unwin, 1997.

Doering, R.L., *Canadian Round Tables on the Environment and the Economy*. Ottawa: NRTEE, 1993.

Dovers, S., "A framework for scaling and framing policy problems in sustainability", *Ecological Economics*, Vol. 12, 1995, pp. 93–106.

Dovers, S., "Community involvement in environmental management: thoughts for emergency management", *Australian Journal of Emergency Management*, Vol. 12, 1998, pp. 6–11.

Dovers, S., "Dimensions of the Australian population-environment debate", *Development Bulletin*, Vol. 41, 1997, pp. 50–53.

Dovers, S., "Information, sustainability and policy", *Australian Journal of Environmental Management*, Vol. 2, 1995, pp. 142–156.

Dovers, S., "Sustainability: demands on policy", *Journal of Public Policy*, Vol. 16, 1997, pp. 303–318.

Dovers, S., "Sustainability in context: an Australian perspective", *Environmental Management*, Vol. 14, 1990, pp. 297–305.

Dovers, S. (ed.), *Australian Environmental History: Essays and Cases*. Melbourne: Oxford University Press, 1994.

Dovers, S. (ed.), *Sustainable Energy Systems: Pathways for Australian Energy Reform*. Melbourne: Cambridge University Press, 1994.

Dovers, S., Norton, T., Hughes, I. & Day, L., *Population Growth and Australian Regional Environments*. Canberra: AGPS, 1992.

Dovers, S. & Williams, J., "Implementing the CBD: the Australian experience", *Ambio*, (forthcoming).

Dovers, S. & Handmer, J., "Uncertainty, sustainability and change", *Global Environmental Change*, Vol. 2, 1992, pp. 262–276.

Dovers, S.R. & Lindenmayer, D.B., "Managing the Environment: Rhetoric, Policy and Reality", *Australian Journal of Public Administration*, Vol. 56, No. 2, 1997, pp. 65–80.

Dowie, M., *Losing Ground: American Environmentalism at the Close of the Twentieth Century*. Boston, MA: MIT Press, 1995.

Downes, D., "Neo-corporatism and environmental policy", *Australian Journal of Political Science*, Vol. 31, No. 2, July 1996, pp. 175–190.

Downey, T.J., "Understanding Policy-making A Necessary First Step for Environmentalists", in *Alternatives*, Vol. 14, No. 2, May/June 1987, pp. 30–34.

Downs, A., "Up & Down with Ecology — The 'Issue-Attention' Cycle", *The Public Interest*, Vol. 28, 1972, pp. 38–50.

Doyle, T., "Lindeman Island: Environmental Politics in Queensland", *Journal of the Royal Historical Society of Queensland*, Vol. 13, 1989, pp. 462–472.

Doyle, T. "Sustainable Development and Agenda 21: The Secular Bible of Global Free Markets and Pluralist Democracy", *Third World Quarterly*, Vol. 19, No. 4, 1998.

Doyle, T. & Kellow, A., *Environmental Politics and Policymaking in Australia*. South Melbourne: MacMillan, 1995.

Doyle, T. & McEachern, D., *Environment and Politics*. London and New York: Routledge, 1998.

Drengson, A.R., "Shifting Paradigms: From the Technocratic to the Person-Planetary", *Environmental Ethics*, Vol. 3, 1980, pp. 221–225.

Driml, S. & Common, M., "Ecological Economics Criteria for Sustainable Tourism: Application to the Great Barrier Reef and Wet Tropics World Heritage Areas, Australia", *Journal of Sustainable Tourism*, Vol. 4, 1996, pp. 3–16.

Dror, Y., *Design for Policy Sciences*. New York: Elsevier, 1971.

Dror, Y., *Public Policymaking Reexamined*. Scranton, PA: Chandler, 1968.

Dryzek, J., "Ecological Rationality", *International Journal of Environmental Studies*, Vol. 21, 1983, pp. 5–10.

Dryzek, J., "Ecology and Discursive Democracy: Beyond Liberal Capitalism and the Administrative State", *Capitalism, Nature and Socialism*, Vol. 3, No. 2, 1992, pp. 18–42.

Dryzek, J., *Democracy in Capitalist Times: Ideals, Limits & Struggles*. New York: Oxford University Press, 1996.

Dryzek, J., *Rational Ecology: Environment and Political Economy*. Oxford: Basil Blackwell, 1987.

Dryzek, J.S., *The Politics of the Earth: Environmental Discourses*. New York: Oxford University Press, 1997.

Dubos, R., *So Human an Animal*. London: Sphere Books, 1973; first published 1968.

Duncan, W.D. (ed.), *Planning and Environment Law in Queensland*. Annandale: The Federation Press, 1993.

Dutton, I.M., Boyd, W.E., Luckie, K., Knox, S. & Derrett, R., "Measuring Coastal Landscape and Lifestyle Values: An Interpretive Approach", *Australian Journal of Environmental Management*, Vol. 2, 1995, pp. 245–256.

Dye, T.R. & Ziegler, L.H., *The Irony of Democracy*. Belmont, CA: Duxbury Press, 1971.

Eckersley, R., *Environmentalism and Political Theory: Towards an Ecocentric Approach*. Albany: State University of New York Press, 1991.

Eckersley, R. (ed.), *Markets, The State and the Environment: Towards Integration*. South Melbourne: Macmillan, 1995.

Economou, N. "Accordism and the Environment: the Resource Assessment Commission and National Environmental Policy-Making", *Australian Journal of Political Science*, Vol. 28, No. 3, November 1993, pp. 399–412.

Economou, N., "Australian Environmental Policy-making in Transition: the rise and fall of the Resource Assessment Commission", *Australian Journal of Public Administration*, Vol. 55, No. 1, June 1996, pp. 12–22.

Economou, N., "Reconciling the Irreconcilable? The Resource Assessment Commission, Resource Policy-making and the Environment", *Australian Journal of Public Administration*, Vol. 51, No. 4, 1992, pp. 461–475.

Edelman, D.J. & Procee, P., "The rôle of Best Practices in Capacity Building for Urban Environmental Management", *Pathways to Sustainability: Local Initiatives for Cities and Towns*, International Conference Proceedings, City of Newcastle, 1–5 June 1997.

Edwards, K., "UNEP Perspectives on How We Are Travelling Along the Road to Sustainability", *Pathways to Sustainability: Local Initiatives for Cities and Towns*, International Conference Proceedings, City of Newcastle, 1–5 June 1997.

Edwards, P., *Keating: the inside story*. Melbourne: Viking, 1996.

Eggleston, F.W., *State Socialism in Victoria*. London: King, 1932.

Ehrlich, P., *The Machinery of Nature*. New York: Simon & Schuster, 1986.

Ehrlich, P., *The Population Bomb*. New York: Ballantine Books, 1968.

Ehrlich, P.R. & Holdren, J.P. (eds), *Human Ecology*. San Francisco: W.H. Freeman, 1973.

Elliott, D. & Yarrow, G., "Cost-Benefit Analysis and Environmental Policy: A Comment", *KYKLOS*, Vol. 30, 1977, Fasc. 2, pp. 300–309.

Emmery, M., *Ecologically Sustainable Development Processes in Australia 1990–1992*, Background Paper 3/93. Canberra: Parliamentary Research Service, 1993.

Emy, H. & Hughes, O., *Australian Politics: Realities in Conflict* (2nd edn). Melbourne: Macmillan, 1991.

Encel, S., *Equality and Authority*. Melbourne: Cheshire, 1970.

Environment Australia. *Oceans Policy — An Issues Paper*. Canberra: AGPS, 1998.

Environment Business, "Local Agenda 21 Survey", September 1998, p. 12.

Environmental Manager, No. 195, 31 March 1998.

Erskine, J.M., *Integration of Conservation and Development: Towards Implementing the National Conservation Strategy for Australia*, CRES Working Paper 87/19, Canberra: Centre for Resource and Environmental Studies, Australian National University, 1987.

European Commission, *European Sustainable Cities: Final Report*. Brussels: EC, 1996 (*http://europa.eu.int/comm/dg11/urban/*).

European Commission, *European Sustainable Cities: First Report*. Brussels: EC, 1992 (*http://europa.eu.int/comm/dg11/urban/*).

Evans, P.B., Rueschemeyer, D. & Skocpol, T. (eds), *Bringing the State Back In*. Cambridge: Cambridge University Press, 1985.

Falk, J., *Global Fission: The Battle Over Nuclear Power*. Melbourne: Oxford University Press, 1982.

Fankhauser, S., "Protection versus Retreat: The Economic Costs of Sea-level Rise", *Environment and Planning A*, Vol. 27, 1995, pp. 299–319.

Farthing, S., *Evaluating Local Environmental Policy*. Aldershot: Avebury, 1997.

Fenna, A., *Introduction to Australian Public Policy*. Melbourne: Addison Wesley Longman, 1998.

Fiorino, D.J., *Making Environmental Policy*. California: University of California Press, 1995.

Fischer, D.W. & Kerton, R.R., "Perception of Environmental Diseconomies: Technical vs. Economic Invisibility", *Social Science Information*, Vol 14, No. 1, March 1975, pp. 81–90.

Fischer, F., *Evaluating Public Policy*. Chicago: Nelson-Hall Publishers, 1995.

Fisher, T. "Managing Threats to Biodiversity", in "ACF: Protecting the Environment for 30 Years", supplement to *Habitat Australia*, Vol. 24, No. 6, 1996, p. 27.

Fitzgerald, R, *From the Dreaming to 1915: A History of Queensland*. St. Lucia: University of Queensland Press, 1982.

Fitzgerald R., *From 1915 to the Early 1980s: A History of Queensland*. St. Lucia: University of Queensland Press, 1984.

Fowler, R.J., "Vegetation Clearance Controls in South Australia — A Change of Course", *Environmental and Planning Law Journal*, Vol. 3, No. 1, March 1986, pp. 48–66.

Fry, A., *Strategies for Sustainable Development: Local Agendas for the Southern Hemisphere*. Chichester: Wiley, 1994.

Galligan, B., "Australian Federalism: Rethinking and Restructuring", *Australian Journal of Political Science*, Vol. 27, Special Issue on Federalism, 1992, pp. 1–6.

Galligan, B. & Lynch, C., *Integrating Conservation and Development — Australia's Resource Assessment Commission and the Testing Case of Coronation Hill*. Canberra: Federalism Research Centre, ANU, 1992.

Galligan, B. (ed.), *Australian State Politics*. Melbourne: Longman Cheshire, 1986.

Galligan, B., Hughes, O. & Walsh, C. (eds), *Intergovernmental Relations and Public Policy*. North Sydney: Allen & Unwin, 1991.

Gardner, T., Geary, P. & Gordon, I., "Ecological Sustainability and Effluent Treatment Systems", *Australian Journal of Environmental Management*, Vol. 4, 1997, pp. 144–156.

Giblin L.F., "A Note on Taxable Capacity", *Economic Record*, Vol. 5, 1929, pp. 339–345.

Gilbert, R., Stevenson, D., Girardet, H. & Stren, R., *Making Cities Work: The rôle of Local Authorities in the Urban Environment*. London: Earthscan, 1996.

Gilpin, G.A., *Australians and their Environment*. Melbourne: Oxford University Press, 1998.

Gleeson, B.J. & Grundy, K.J., "New Zealand's planning revolution five years on: a preliminary assessment", *Journal of Environmental Planning and Management*, Vol. 40, 1997, pp. 293–313.

Goldin, P. & Sann, A., "South East Tasmania Case Study, Australia", *Coastal Zone Management. Selected Case Studies*. Paris: OECD,1993, pp. 201–226.

Goodin, R.E., *Political Theory and Public Policy*. Chicago: University of Chicago Press, 1982.

Gough, M., Hughes, H., McFarlane, B.J. & Palmer, G.R., *Queensland: Industrial*

Enigma: manufacturing in the economic development of Queensland. Carlton: Melbourne University Press, 1964.

Gough T., "Tom McIlwraith, Ted Dury, Hugh Nelson and The Queensland National Bank 1896–1897", *Queensland Heritage*, Vol. 3, No. 9, 1978, pp. 3–13.

Grabosky, P. & Braithwaite, J. (eds), *Business Regulation and Australia's Future*. Canberra: AIC, 1993.

Graham, R.J., *Making the Connections: An Introduction to the Alternative to the RAC Proposals for Coastal Zone Management*. Unpublished MS, University of Tasmania, 1993.

Grant, P., "Technological Sovereignty: Forgotten Factor in the 'Hi-Tech' Razzamattazz", *Prometheus*, Vol. 1, No. 2, December 1983, pp. 239–270.

Green, R., *Battle for the Franklin*. Melbourne: Australian Conservation Foundation, 1981.

Green, R., Harris, S. & Throsby, D., *Ecologically Sustainable Development Working Group Chairs Intersectoral Issues Report*. Canberra: AGPS, 1992.

Greenwood, T., "Australians Divided About Reef's Future", *Reef Research*, June 1998, pp. 19–20.

Griffiths, T. & Robin, L., *Ecology & Empire*. Melbourne: Melbourne University Press, 1997.

Gruen, F. & Grattan, M., *Managing Government*. Melbourne: Longman Cheshire, 1993.

Gullett, W., "Environmental Impact Assessment and the Precautionary Principle: Legislating Caution in Environmental Protection", *Environmental & Planning Law Journal*, Vol. 14, 1997, pp. 52–69.

Gum, K.C., Manicaros, M.A., Lanarch, A.L., Stimson, R.J., Taylor, S.P. & Western, J.S., *A Social Atlas of Brisbane and the South-East Queensland Region*. Brisbane: Australian Housing and Urban Research Institute, Queensland University of Technology, 1997.

Haas, P.M., "Banning chlorofluorocarbons: epistemic community efforts to protect stratospheric ozone", *International Organization*, Vol. 46, No. 1, 1992, pp. 187–224.

Haas, P.M., "Do régimes matter? Epistemic communities and Mediterranean pollution control", *International Organization*, Vol. 43, No. 3, 1989, pp. 377–403.

Haas, P.M., *Saving The Mediterranean*. New York: Columbia University Press, 1990.

Habermas J., *Legitimation Crisis*. Boston: Beacon Press, 1975.

Habitat II Secretariat, *A Guide to Nominating and Learning from Best Practices in Improving Living Environment*. Nairobi: UNCED, 1995.

Hall, C.M., Jenkins, J. & Kearsley, G. (eds), *Tourism Planning and Policy in Australia and New Zealand: Cases, Issues and Practice*. Sydney: Irwin Publishers, 1997.

Ham, C. & Hill, M., *The Policy Making Process in the Modern Capitalist State*. Brighton: Wheatsheaf, 1984.

Hamburger, H., *Games as Models of Social Phenomena*. San Francisco: W.H. Freeman, 1979.

Hamilton, C. & Throsby, D. (eds), *The Ecologically Sustainable Development Process: Evaluating a Policy Process*. Canberra: Academy of Social Sciences and Public Policy Program, Australian National University, 1998.

Hams, T., "Local Agenda 21 — A view from the United Kingdom", *Environment South Australia*, Vol 6, No. 4., 1998, pp. 10–11.

Hancock, W.H., *Australia*. Melbourne: Ernest Benn Ltd, 1930.

Hardin, G., *Exploring New Ethics for Survival: The Voyage of the Spaceship Beagle*. New York: Viking Press, 1972.

Harding, R. (ed.), *Environmental Decision-making: The rôles of Scientists, Engineers and the Public*. Annandale: The Federation Press, 1998.

Harman, E.J. & Head, B.W., *State, Capital, and Resources in the North and West of Australia*. Nedlands, WA: University of Western Australia Press, 1982.

Harris, M., *Cultural Materialism*. New York: Random House, 1979.

Harris, M., *Culture, People, Nature: An Introduction to General Anthropology* (2nd edn). New York: Harper & Row/Thomas Y. Crowell, 1975.

Harris, S., *Regional Economic Development in Queensland, 1859 to 1981, with Particular Emphasis on North Queensland*. Canberra: Centre for Research on Federal Financial Relations, The Australian National University, 1984.

Harrison, P. *The Third Revolution: Population, Environment, and a Sustainable World*. Harmondsworth: Penguin, 1992.

Harvey, N., "Public Involvement in EIA", *Australian Planner*, Vol. 33, 1996, pp. 39–46.

Hawke, R., *Our Country, Our Future: A Statement on the Environment*. Canberra: AGPS, 1989.

Hawkins, B., "Environmental Approval Processes for Major Industrial Projects", paper presented at Twelfth National Environmental Law Association Conference, Canberra, 4–6 July 1993.

Hay, P. & Eckersley, R., *Ecopolitical Theory: Essays from Australia* (Occasional Paper 24, Centre for Environmental Studies, University of Tasmania). Hobart: Board of Environmental Studies, University of Tasmania, 1992.

Hay, P., Eckersley, R. & Holloway, G. (eds), *Environmental Politics in Australia and New Zealand* (Occasional Paper 23, Centre for Environmental Studies, University of Tasmania). Hobart: Board of Environmental Studies, University of Tasmania, 1989.

Head, B. & Walter, J. (eds), *Intellectual Movements and Australian Society*. Melbourne: Oxford University Press, 1988.

Head, B. (ed.), *State and Economy in Australia*. Melbourne: Oxford University Press, 1983.

Head B. (ed.), *The Politics of Development in Australia*. Sydney: Allen & Unwin, 1986.

Heathcote, R.L. (ed.), *The Australian Experience. Essays in Australian Land Settlement and Resource Management*. Melbourne: Longman Cheshire, 1988.

Helvarg, D., *The War Against the Greens: The "Wise Use" Movement, the New Right, and Anti-Environmental Violence*. San Francisco: Sierra Club Books, 1994.

Hempel, L.C., *Environmental Governance: The Global Challenge*. Washington, DC: Island Press, 1996.

The Herald-Sun (Melbourne), "Cesspool Alert on Oceans", 27 December 1995.

The Herald-Sun (Melbourne), "Marine Parks Rated Worst", 8 June 1998.

Hill, D. (ed.), *The Baked Apple: Metropolitan New York in the Greenhouse*. New York: The New York Academy of Sciences, 1996.

Hill, R., *Investing in Our Natural Heritage: The Commonwealth's Environment Expenditure 1998–99*, Statement by the Honourable Robert Hill, Minister for the Environment, 12 May 1998.

Hill, R., *Reform of Commonwealth Environment Legislation: Consultation Paper*. Canberra: Department of the Environment, 1998.

Hill, S. & Johnson, R. (eds), *Future Tense? Technology in Australia*. St.Lucia, Queensland: University of Queensland Press, 1983.

Hine, M., "Local Agenda 21 — Cooperation for Change", *Environment South Australia*, Vol 6, No. 4, 1998, p. 7.

Hine, M., "Local Agenda 21 — Turning Policy into Practice", paper presented at the Planning for Sustainable Futures Conference, City of Mandurah, WA, 14–16 September 1998.

Hine, M., "Native Title Claim Puts Roxby in Fluid Situation", *Chain Reaction*, No. 69, pp. 23–25.

Hine, M., "Some thoughts on Local Agenda 21", *Environment South Australia*, Vol. 6 No. 3, 1997, p. 34.

Hinrichsen, D., "Humanity and the World's Coasts: A Status Report", *Amicus Journal*, Winter 1997, pp. 1–5.

Holmes, J.H., "The Future of Remote Pastoral Towns in Western Queensland", *Urban Australia: Living in the next decade*; papers presented at the Symposium on the Macro-Economic and Social Trends in Australia held by AIUS in October 1983. Canberra: AIUS Publication No. 116, Australian Institute of Urban Studies, 1984, pp. 86–94.

Holmes, J.H. (ed.), *Queensland: a geographical interpretation*. Brisbane: Boolarong Publications, 1986.

Holmes, R., "Don't ignore nature's bottom line", *New Scientist*, Vol 154, No. 2082, 17 May 1997, p. 11.

Horstman, M., "New law fails the leadership test", *Habitat Australia*, Vol. 26, No. 4, 1998, p. 21.

Horstman, M., "Why Keith Williams Must Not Resort to Hinchinbrook", *Habitat Australia*, Vol. 24, No. 6, December 1996.

Hotta, K. & Dutton, I.M. (eds), *Coastal Management in the Asia-Pacific Region: Issues and Approaches*. Tokyo: Japan International Marine Science and Technology Federation, 1995.

Howlett, M. & Ramesh, M., *Studying Public Policy: Policy Cycles and Policy Subsystems*. New York: Oxford University Press, 1995.

Hughes, J.D., *Ecology in Ancient Civilisations*. Albuquerque, NM: University of New Mexico Press, 1975.

Hughes, O., *Australian Politics* (3rd edn). Melbourne: Macmillan, 1998.

Hutchinson, C., *Vitality and Renewal: A Manager's Guide for the 21st Century*. Westport: Praeger, 1995.

McAllister, I., "Dimensions of Environmentalism: Public Opinion, Political Activism and Party Support in Australia", *Environmental Politics*, Vol. 3, No. 1, Spring 1994.

Idriess, I.L., *The Great Boomerang*. Sydney: Angus and Robertson, 1944.

Intergovernmental Committee for Ecologically Sustainable Development (ICESD), *Report on the Implementation of the National Strategy for Ecologically Sustainable Development (1993–1995)*. Canberra: Commonwealth of Australia, 1996.

International Council for Local Environmental Initiatives (ICLEI), *The Local Agenda 21 Initiative — ICLEI Guidelines for Local and National Agenda 21 Campaigns*. Toronto: ICLEI, 1994.

International Council for Local Environmental Initiatives (ICLEI), *Local Government Implementation of Agenda 21*. Toronto: ICLEI World Secretariat, 1997.

International Council for Local Environmental Initiatives (ICLEI), *The Local Agenda 21 Planning Guide; An Introduction to Sustainable Development Planning*. Toronto: ICLEI World Secretariat, 1996.

IUCN/UNEP/WWF, *Caring for the Earth. A Strategy for Sustainable Living*. Gland, Switzerland: IUCN, 1991.

IUCN/UNEP/WWF, *World Conservation Strategy*. Gland, Switzerland: IUCN, 1980.

IUCN/UNEP/WWF, *Living Planet Report 1998*. Gland, Switzerland: WWF International, 1998.

Jackson, S. & Cooper, D., "Coronation Hill Pay-back, the Case of McArthur River", *Arena*, October–November 1993.

Jaensch, D., *The Hawke-Keating Hijack*. Sydney: Allen and Unwin, 1989.

James, P. (ed.), *Technocratic Dreaming: Of Very Fast Trains and Japanese Designer Cities.* Melbourne: Left Book Club, 1990.

James, P. (ed.), *The State in Question: Transformation of the Australian State.* St Leonards: Allen & Unwin, 1996.

Janicke, M., "Conditions for environmental policy success: an international comparison", *The Environmentalist*, Vol. 12, 1992, pp. 47–58.

Jarratt, H., *Environmental Quality in a Growing Economy.* Baltimore: Johns Hopkins University Press, 1966.

Jeffery, J., "The Unique Dangers of Nuclear Power: An Overview," *The Ecologist*, Vol. 16, No. 4/5, 1986, pp. 147–163.

Jennett, C. & Stewart, R. (eds), *Hawke and Australian Public Policy.* Melbourne: Macmillan, 1990.

Johnston, W.R., *The Call of the Land: A history of Queensland to the Present Day.* Brisbane: Jacaranda Press, 1982.

Jolly, B. & Holland, I., *Facing the Future: Ecopolitics VII Proceedings*, Brisbane: Imagecraft, 1993.

Jones, M.A., *Frankston: Resort to City.* Sydney: Allen & Unwin, 1989.

Kay, R. & Lester, C., "Benchmarking the Future Direction for Coastal Management in Australia", *Coastal Management*, Vol. 25, 1997, pp. 265–292.

Kellow, A., "Electricity Planning in Tasmania and New Zealand: Political Processes and the Technological Imperative", *Australian Journal of Public Administration*, Vol. XLV, No. 1, March 1986, pp. 2–17.

Kellow, A.J., "Managing an Ecological System: The Politics and Administration", *Australian Quarterly*, Vol. 57, 1985, pp. 107–127.

Kellow, A.J. (ed.), *Perspectives on Forest Policy in Tasmania.* Environmental Studies Working Paper No. 18. Hobart: Board of Environmental Studies, University of Tasmania, 1984.

Kellow, A.J., *Saline Solutions: Policy Dynamics in the Murray-Darling Basin.* Deakin Series in Public Policy and Administration No. 2. Geelong, Victoria: Centre for Applied Social Research, Deakin University, 1992.

Kemp, D., *Foundations for Australian Political Analysis.* Melbourne: Oxford University Press, 1987.

Kemp, D., Manicaros, M., Mullins, P., Simpson, R., Stimson, R. & Western, J., *Urban Metabolism: A Framework for Evaluating the Viability, Livability and Sustainability of South-East Queensland* (Research Monograph No. 2). Brisbane: Australian Housing and Urban Research Institute, 1997.

Kenchington, R. & Crawford, D., "On the Meaning of Integration in Coastal Zone Management", *Ocean & Coastal Management*, Vol. 21, 1993, pp. 109–127.

Kennedy, K.H., *The Mungana Affair: State Mining and Political Corruption in the 1920s.* St. Lucia: University of Queensland Press, 1978.

Kerr, J., *Triumph of Narrow Gauge: a history of Queensland Railways.* Brisbane: Boolarong Publications, 1990.

Kidron, M., *Western Capitalism Since the War* (revised edn). Harmondsworth: Penguin, 1970.

Klomp, N. & Lunt, I., *Frontiers in Ecology: Building the Links.* London: Elsevier, 1997.

Kraus, N.C. (ed.), *History and Heritage of Coastal Engineering.* New York: American Society of Civil Engineers, 1996.

Lafferty, W.M. & Meadowcroft, J., *Democracy and the Environment: Problems and Prospects.* Cheltenham: Edward Elgar, 1996.

Lafferty, W.M., "The Politics of Sustainable Development: Global Norms for National Implementation", *Environmental Politics*, Vol. 5, No. 2., Summer 1996, pp. 185–208.

Langmore, J. & Quiggan, J., *Work for All: Full Employment in the Nineties.* Carlton, Victoria: Melbourne University Press, 1994.

Leiss, W. (ed.), *Ecology Versus Politics in Canada*. Toronto: University of Toronto Press, 1979.

Leitman, J., *Energy-Environment Linkages in the Urban Sector* (Urban Management Program Discussion Paper 2). Washington DC: The World Bank, 1996.

Leitmann, J., *Rapid Urban Environmental Assessment* (Urban Management Program Tool No. 15). Washington DC: The World Bank, 1994.

Lines, W.J., *Taming the Great South Land: a History of the Conquest of Nature in Australia*. North Sydney: Allen & Unwin, 1991.

Lloyd, C., *The National Estate: Australia's Heritage*. Adelaide: Savvas Publishing, 1983.

Local Government Management Board (LGMB), *Five Years On*. London: LGMB, 1997.

Low, N. (ed.), *Selected Electronic Proceedings presented to the Environmental Justice: Global Ethics for the 21 Century Conference*. University of Melbourne, 1–3 October 1997 (*http://www.arbld.unimelb.edu.au/envjust/papers/allpapers/crowley.home.htm*).

Lowe, I., "Towards a Green Tasmania: Developing the 'Greenprint'", *Habitat Australia*, August 1991, pp. 12–14.

Lowe, I. *Shaping a Sustainable Future: Science, Technology and Society*. Brisbane: School of Science, Griffith University, 1991.

Lowi, T., "American Business, Public Policy, Case-Studies, and Political Theory" (review article), *World Politics*, Vol. XVI, 1964, pp. 677–715.

M'Gonigle, R.M., "The 'Economising' of Ecology: Why Big, Rare Whales Still Die", *Ecology Law Quarterly*, Vol. 9, (1980) No. 1, pp. 120–237.

Maddison, D., Pearce, D., et al., *Blueprint 5: The True Costs of Road Transport*. London: CSERGE/Earthscan, 1996.

Maher & Associates, *An Approach to Environmental Management Systems for Local Government*. Brisbane: Maher & Associates, 1996.

Marsh, I. (ed.), *Governing in the 1990s: an Agenda for the Decade*. Melbourne: Longman Cheshire, 1993.

Marsh, I. (ed.), *The Environmental Challenge*. Sydney: Longman Cheshire, 1991.

Marsh, I. (ed.), *Australia's Emerging Industries: Achieving Our Potential*. Canberra: Growth 45 (Committee for the Economic Development of Australia [CEDA]), 1997.

Marshall, A.J. (ed.), *The Great Extermination*. London and Melbourne: Heinemann, 1966.

Martin, A., *The Last Generation*. Glasgow: Fontana/Collins, 1975.

Martin, P. & Woodhill, J., "Landcare in the balance: government rôles and policy issues in sustaining rural environments", *Australian Journal of Environmental Management*, Vol. 2, 1995, pp. 173–183.

May, P. "Policy learning and policy failure", *Journal of Public Policy*, Vol. 12, 1992, pp. 331–345.

Mazza, P., "Cooptation or Constructive Engagement?: Quincy Library Group's Efforts to Bring Together Loggers and Environmentalists Under fire", *Cascadia Planet*, http://www.cascadia@tnews.com, August 1997, p. 3.

McAllister, I., "Dimensions of Environmentalism: Public Opinion, Political Activism and Party Support in Australia", *Environmental Politics*, Vol. 3, No. 1, Spring 1994, pp. 22–42.

McEachern, D., "Environmental policy in Australia 1981–1991: a form of corporatism?", *Australian Journal of Public Administration*, Vol. 52, 1993, pp. 173–186.

McEachern, D., *Business Mates: The Power and Politics of the Hawke Era*. Sydney: Prentice-Hall, 1991.

McGregor, A., *Looking Forward — A guide to preparing a local conservation strategy*. Melbourne: Ministry for Planning and Environment, 1989.

McIntyre, G., "Freeholding, Resorts and Barrier Reef Islands", *Legal Service Bulletin*, Vol. 13, 1988, pp. 6–9.

McMaster, J.C. & Webb, G.R. (eds), *Australian Project Evaluation*. Sydney: ANZ Book Co., 1978.

McMichael, A.J., *Planetary Overload*. Cambridge: Cambridge University Press, 1993.

McQueen, H., *A New Britannia: an argument concerning the social origins of Australian radicalism and nationalism* (revised edn). Ringwood, Victoria: Penguin Books, 1975.

Meadows, D.H., et al., *The Limits to Growth*. New York: New American Library, 1972.

Mercer, D., "Beach Usage in the Melbourne Region", *Australian Geographer*, Vol. 12, 1972, pp. 123–139.

Milbrath, L. & Inscho, F.R., *The Politics of Environmental Policy*. Contemporary Social Science Issues, No. 18. California: Sage, 1975.

Milbrath, L., *Learning to Think Environmentally While There is Still Time*. Albany: State University of New York Press, 1996.

Mintzer, I.M. (ed.), *Confronting Climate Change: Risks, Implications and Responses*. Cambridge: Cambridge University Press.

Mobbs, M., "Fear and Loathing on the ESD Trail", *The Australian*, 18 September 1998.

Moore, P., "Consensus," *Greenspirit. http://www.pmoore@rogers.wave.ca*

Morrison, J. & West, R., "Chapter 8 — Estuaries and the Sea", *Australian Journal of Environmental Management*, Vol. 4, 1997, pp. 175–177.

Mosley, G., "Thirty Years of ACF Achievements", in "ACF: Protecting the Environment for 30 Years", supplement in *Habitat Australia*, Vol. 24, No. 6, 1996.

Mosley, G., "The Triumph of the Woodchip Mentality", *Age* (Melbourne), 10 February 1997.

Mount Isa Mines (MIM) Holdings Web Site: *http://www.mimholdings.com.au/3McArinfo.html*.

Murphy, D.J., Joyce, R.B. & Hughes, C.A., *Labor in Power: The Labor Party and Governments in Queensland 1915–1957*. St. Lucia, Queensland: University of Queensland Press, 1980.

Naisbitt, J., *Megatrends 2000*. New York: Warner Books, 1982.

National Local Government Environmental Resource Network (NLGERN), *Constructing Bridges out of Barriers — Strategic Alliances for Regional Integrated Environmental Management*, National Workshop. Canberra: NLGERN, 1994.

National Population Council, "Population Issues and Australia's Future: Environment, Economy and Society", *Proceedings*. Canberra: AGPS, 1991.

Nelkin, D. (ed.), *Controversy*. Beverly Hills, CA: Sage, 1979.

Newton, P.W. (ed.), *Re-Shaping Cities for a More Sustainable Future: Exploring the Link Between Urban Form, Air Quality, Energy and Greenhouse Gas Emissions* (Research Monograph No. 6). Melbourne: Australian Housing and Urban Research Institute, 1997.

Nijkamp, P. & Perrels, A., *Sustainable Cities in Europe*. London: Earthscan, 1994.

Noonan, D., "SA Government Excludes the Australian Public From a rôle in the Future of Coongie Lakes", ACF Media Release, Adelaide, 16 January 1997.

NSW. Government. "'Reform' of Commonwealth Environmental Law", NSW Environment Defender's Office, *http://www.edo.org.au/cthlrev.htm*.

NSW. Government. Environmental Defender's Office, *Brief commentary on the Commonwealth Environment Protection and Biodiversity Conservation Bill*. Mimeo. Sydney: EDO, 1998.

OECD, *OECD Environmental Performance Reviews. Australia: Conclusions and Recommendations.* OECD Group on Environmental Performance, November 1997, *http://www.erin.gov.au/portfolio/esd/intergovtunit/OECD/oecd.pdf.*

Oliphant, J. & Morley, P., "Goss backs zinc giant", *Courier-Mail* (Brisbane), 7 March 1991, p. 1.

Olson, M., *The Logic of Collective Action.* Cambridge, Mass.: Harvard University Press, 1965.

Olson, M., *The Rise and Decline of Nations.* New Haven and London: Yale University Press, 1982.

Olympic Dam Community Consultative Forum, "Terms of Reference and Membership for the Olympic Dam Community Consultative Forum", 1998.

Olympic Dam Environment Consultative Committee (ODECC), "Summary Record", *PIRSA*, 24 March 1998.

Orbach, M., "Social Scientific Contributions to Coastal Policy Making", *Improving Interactions between Coastal Science and Policy: Proceedings of the California Symposium.* Washington DC: 1995.

Orchard, L., "Managerialism, economic rationalism and public sector reform in Australia: connections, divergences, alternatives", *Australian Journal of Public Administration*, Vol. 57, 1998, pp. 19–32.

Organisation for Economic Cooperation and Development (OECD), *Environmental Performance Review of Australia*, Paris: OECD, 1998.

Osborne, F., *Our Plundered Planet.* Boston: Little, Brown, 1948.

Osborne, F., *The Limits of the Earth.* Boston: Little, Brown, 1953

Ostrom, E., *Governing the Commons*, Cambridge: Cambridge University Press, 1990.

Papadakis, E., *Politics and the Environment: the Australian Experience.* Sydney: Allen and Unwin, 1993.

Parenti, M., *Democracy for the Few* (3rd edn). New York: St. Martin's Press, 1980.

Park, C.C. (ed.), *Environmental Policies, an International Review.* London: Croom Helm, 1986.

Parkin, A., Summers, J. & Woodward, D., *Government, Politics and Power in Australia* (5th edn). Melbourne: Longman Australia, 1996.

Parkin, A., Summers, J. & Woodward, D., *Government, Politics and Power in Australia.* Melbourne: Longman Cheshire, 1980.

Patience, A. (ed.), *The Bjelke-Petersen Premiership.* Melbourne: Longman Cheshire, 1985.

Patmore, G., *Australian Labour History.* Melbourne: Longman Cheshire, 1991.

Pattenden, M., "A Global Perspective on Local Agenda 21", *Environment South Australia*, Vol 6, No. 4., 1998, pp. 8–9.

Patterson, W.C., *Nuclear Power.* Harmondsworth: Penguin, 1976.

Pearce, D., "Cost-Benefit Analysis and Environmental Policy: A Reply to Elliott and Yarrow and to Smith", *KYKLOS*, Vol. 30, 1977, Fasc. 2, pp. 314–318.

Pearce, D., "The Limits of Cost-Benefit Analysis as a Guide to Environmental Policy", *KYKLOS*, Vol. 29, 1976, Fasc. 1, pp. 97–112.

Pearce, D.W., *Environmental Economics.* London: Longman, 1976.

Pearce, F., "Can't stand the heat", *New Scientist*, Vol. 180, Nos, 2165/6/7, 19/26 December 1998–2 January 1999, pp. 32–33.

Pearson, L., "Planning and Land Use Decision-Making at State and Local Level: The Look-At-Me-Now Headland Ocean Outfall", *Environmental and Planning Law Journal*, Vol. 12, pp. 221–230.

Pfeiff, M., "Sydney, You Really Surprised Me This Time", *Reader's Digest*, August 1998, pp. 38–45.

Pfeiff, M., "The Mayor Who Built Brazil's City of the Future", *Reader's Digest*, March 1998, pp. 26–31.

Pierce, C. & Van De Veer, D. (eds), *People, Penguins, and Plastic Trees* (2nd edn). Belmont, CA: Wadsworth Publishing, 1995.

Pope, D., "Australia's Development Strategy in the Early Twentieth Century: Semantics and Politics", *Australian Journal of Politics and History*, Vol. 31, No. 2, 1985, pp. 218–229.

Powell, J.M., *Environmental Management in Australia, 1788–1914. Guardians, Improvers and Profit: an Introductory Survey*. Melbourne: Oxford University Press, 1976.

Powell, J.M., *Watering the Garden State*. Sydney: Allen & Unwin, 1989.

Prasser, S. & Starr, G. (eds), *Policy and Change: the Howard Mandate*. Sydney: Hale & Iremonger, 1997.

Prately, J.E., *Principles of Field Crop Production*. Sydney: Sydney University Press, 1980.

Prest, J. & Downing, S., *Shades of Green? Proposals to Change Commonwealth Environmental Laws*, Laws and Bills Digest Group, Research Paper 16. Canberra: Parliamentary Library, Parliament of Australia, 1997–98.

Prideaux, M., Horstman, M. & Emmett, J., "Sustainable Use or Multiple Abuse", *Habitat*, Vol. 26, No. 2, April 1998, p. 15.

Productivity Commission, *Implementation of Ecologically Sustainable Development by Commonwealth Departments and Agencies — Issues paper*. Melbourne: AGPS, 1998.

Pugh, C. (ed.), *Sustainability, the Environment and Urbanization*. London: Earthscan, 1996.

Puplick, C. & Southey, R., *Liberal Thinking*. Melbourne: Macmillan, 1980.

Purdue, D., "Hegemonic Trips: World Trade, Intellectual Property and Biodiversity", *Environmental Politics*. Vol. 4, No. 1., Spring 1995, pp. 88–107.

Pusey, M., *Economic Rationalism in Canberra*. Cambridge: CUP, 1991.

Pybus, C. & Flanagan, R., *The Rest of the World Is Watching*. Sydney: Pan Macmillan, 1990.

Pyne, S.J., *Burning Bush: A Fire History of Australia*. North Sydney: Allen & Unwin, 1992.

Queensland. Government. *The Queen State, A Handbook of Queensland Compiled under Authority of the Government of the State*. Brisbane: Queensland Government Printer, 1933.

Queensland. Parliament. Papers. *Annual Report* of the Bureau of Investigation for the year 1946, QPP, Vol. 2, 1947/48, pp. 654–662.

Queensland Cane Growers' Council, *Submission to the Sugar Industry Inquiry 1978*, Submission No. 1, 1978.

Rabinovitch, J., "Curitiba: Towards Sustainable Urban Development", *Environment and Urbanization*, Vol. 4, No. 2, 1992, pp. 62–73.

Rabinovitch, J. & Hoehn, J., *A Sustainable Urban Transportation System: the "Surface Metro" in Curitiba, Brazil*. EPAT/MUCIA Working Paper No. 19, Madison: University of Wisconsin, 1995.

Rabinovitch, J. & Leitman, J., "Urban Planning in Curitiba", *Scientific American*, March 1996, pp. 26–33.

Ratcliffe, F., *Flying Fox and Drifting Sand*. Sydney: Angus & Robertson, 1948.

Raymond, K., "The Long-term Future of the Great Barrier Reef", *Futures*, Vol. 28, 1996, pp. 947–970.

Redclift, M. & Benton, T., *Social Theory and the Global Environment*. New York: Routledge, 1995.

Reed, D.J., "Sea Level", *Progress in Physical Geography*, Vol. 20, 1996, pp. 482–486.

Rees, W.E., "Achieving Sustainability: Reform or Transformation?", *Journal of Planning Literature*, Vol. 9, No. 4, 1995, pp. 341–361.

Reeves, W. Pember, *State Experiments in Australia and New Zealand*. Melbourne: Macmillan, 1968; first published 1902.

Revelle, R., Khosla, A. & Vinovskis, M. (eds), *The Survival Equation*. Boston: Houghton Mifflin, 1971.

Richardson, G., *Whatever it Takes*. Sydney: Bantam Books, 1994.

Roberts, B.H., Stimson, R.J. & Taylor, S.P., *Monitoring a Sun-Belt Metropolis 1996: Evaluating the Performance of the Brisbane and South East Queensland Economy.* Bribane: Australian Housing and Urban Research Institute, Queensland University of Technology, 1997.

Roddewig, R.J., *Green Bans: The Birth of Australian Environmental Politics.* Sydney: Hale & Iremonger, 1978.

Rolls, E.C., *They All Ran Wild.* Sydney: Angus & Roberston, 1969.

Rosauer, D., *Conservation of Natural Forests: the Changing rôle of the Australian Heritage Commission.* Research Paper in the Department of the Senate, Canberra 1993.

Rose, R., "On the Priorities of Government: a Developmental Analysis of Public Policies", *European Journal of Political Research,* Vol. 4, 1976, pp. 247–89.

Roseland, M., *Toward Sustainable Communities — A Resource Book for Municipal and Local Governments.* Ontario: National Round Table on the Environment and the Economy (NRTEE), 1992.

Rothman, H., *Murderous Providence.* London: Rupert Hart-Davis, 1972.

Rowell, A., *Green Backlash: Global Subversion of the Environmental Movement.* London and New York: Routledge, 1996.

Russell, J.S. & Isbell, R.F. (eds), *Australian Soils: The Human Impact.* St. Lucia: University of Queensland Press, 1986.

Sabatier, P.A., "Toward Better Theories of the Policy Process", *PS: Political Science & Politics,* June 1991, pp. 147–156.

Sachs, W., *Global Ecology: a New Arena of Political Conflict.* London: Zed Books, 1993.

Sant, M. "Accomodating Recreational Demand: Boating in Sydney Harbour, Australia", *Geoforum,* Vol. 21, 1990, pp. 97–109.

Satterfield, D.R., "A Change in Academic Environmental Thought: From Paradigms to Ideology," *Sociological Inquiry,* Vol. 53, No. 2–3, Spring/Summer, 1983, pp. 136–149.

Scheberle, D., *Federalism and Environmental Policy: Trust and the Politics of Implementation.* Washington DC: Georgetown University Press, 1997.

Seigmann, H., *The Conflicts Between Labour and Environmentalism in the FDR and USA.* Berlin: Gower, 1985.

Select Panel of the Public Inquiry into Uranium, *The Report of the Public Enquiry into Uranium.* Adelaide: Conservation Council of South Australia, 1997.

Self, P., *Government by the Market? The Politics of Public Choice.* Basingstoke: Macmillan, 1993.

Serageldin, I., Barrett, R. & Martin-Brown, J. (eds), *The Business of Sustainable Cities.* Environmentally Sustainable Development Proceedings Series, No. 7. Washington DC: The World Bank, 1995.

Serageldin, I. & Cohen, M.A. (eds), *The Human Face of the Urban Environment.* Environmentally Sustainable Development Proceedings Series, No. 5. Washington DC: The World Bank, 1995.

Serventy, V., *Saving Australia: a Blueprint for Our Survival.* Frenchs Forest, NSW: Child & Associates, 1988.

Sierra Club, ""Local Control" a Smokescreen for Logging", *The Planet: The Sierra Club Activist Resource, http://www.sierraclub.org/planet/199711/delbert.html,* p. 1.

Silberman, J. & Klock, M., "The Recreation Benefits of Beach Renourishment", *Ocean & Shoreline Management,* Vol. 11, 1988, pp. 73–90.

Simeon, R., "Studying Public Policy", *Canadian Journal of Political Science,* Vol. 9, No. 4, 1976, pp. 548–580.

Skipper, H.D. (ed.), *International Risk and Insurance. An Environmental-Managerial Approach.* Boston, Mass: Irwin McGraw-Hill, 1998.

Smith, A.K. & Pollard, D.A., "The Best Available Information — Some Case Studies from NSW, Australia, of Conservation-related Management Responses which Impact on Recreational Fishers", *Marine Policy*, Vol. 20, 1996, pp. 261–267.

Smith, D. & Smith, R., *The Economics of Militarism*. London, Pluto Press, 1983.

Smith, D., *Continent in Crisis: a Natural History of Australia*. Ringwood, Victoria: Penguin, 1990.

Smith, D., *Saving a Continent: Towards a Sustainable Future*. Kensington, NSW: UNSW Press, 1994.

Smith, V.K., "Cost-Benefit Analysis and Environmental Policy: A Comment", *KYK-LOS*, Vol. 30, 1977, Fasc. 2, pp. 310–313.

South Australia. Parliament. House of Assembly. *Parliamentary Debates (Hansard)*, 5 November 1998, pp. 234–235.

Standards Australia/Standards New Zealand, ISO AS/NZS 14001, *Environmental management systems — Specification with guidance for use.* Homebush/Wellington: Standards Australia/Standards New Zealand, 1996.

Star, C. (ed.), *Proceedings* of the Ecopolitics XI Conference. Melbourne: Ecopolitics Society of Australia, 1998.

State of the Environment Advisory Council, *State of the Australian Environment*. Collingwood: CSIRO Publishing, 1996.

Steinmo, S., Thelen, K. & Longstreth, F., *Structuring politics*. Cambridge: Cambridge University Press, 1992.

Stewart, D. & McColl, G., "The Resource Assessment Commission: An Inside Assessment", *Australian Journal of Environmental Management*, Vol. 1, No. 1, June 1994, pp. 12–23.

Stewart, R. & Ward, I., *Politics One*, Melbourne: Macmillan, 1992.

Stone, D., *Policy Paradox: The Art of Political Decision Making*. New York and London: W.W. Norton, 1988. Second Edition; New York: W.W. Norton, 1997.

Stretton, H., *Capitalism, Socialism, and the Environment*, Cambridge: Cambridge University Press, 1976.

Strong, G., "The Green Game", *The Age* (Melbourne), 17 August 1998, (on line at *http://www.theage.com.au/daily/980717/news/news22.html*), p. 3.

The Sunday Age (Melbourne), "Australians Moving North", 19 July 1998.

The Sunday Herald-Sun (Melbourne), "Japan Firm Plans $2.5b Resort City", 10 May 1998.

Suzuki, D., "The Super Species", *Island Magazine*, No. 66, Autumn 1996, p. 104.

Taberner, J., "Management for the Protection of the Coastal Zone". Paper Prepared for the 13th. Annual National Conference of the National Environmental Law Association, Melbourne, 6–8 October 1994.

Tansey, G. & Worsley, T., *The Food System: A Guide*. London: Earthscan, 1995.

TASQUE, *The Rôle of Local Government in Environmental Management*. Hobart: University of Tasmania, 1992.

Taylor, M., *Anarchy and Cooperation*. London & New York: Wiley, 1976.

Taylor, M., *Community, Anarchy and Liberty*. Cambridge: Cambridge University Press, 1982.

The Ecologically Sustainable Development Process: Evaluating a Policy Process, Canberra: Academy of Social Sciences and Public Policy Program, Australian National University, 1998.

The Editors of Ramparts, *Eco-catastrophe!* New York: Harper and Row, 1970.

Timlin, J., "Megacorp and Westernport Bay", in Dempsey, R. (ed.), *The Politics of Finding Out: Environmental Problems in Australia*. Melbourne: Cheshire, 1974.

Toth, F.L. (ed.), *Cost-Benefit Analyses of Climate Change: The Broader Perspectives*. Basel: Birkhauser Verlag, 1998.

Toyne, P., *The Reluctant Nation: Environment, Law and Politics in Australia*. Sydney: ABC Books, 1994.

Travers, P., *Living Decently: Material Well-Being in Australia*. Melbourne: Oxford University Press, 1993.

Tsubaki, T. & Irukayami, K. (eds), *Minamata Disease: Methylmercury Poisoning in Minamata and Niigata, Japan*. Tokyo: Kodansha, 1977.

Union of Concerned Scientists, *The World Scientists' Warning to Humanity*. Cambridge, Mass.: Union of Concerned Scientists, 1992.

United Nations Conference on Environment and Development (UNCED), Rio de Janeiro, *The Earth Summit: Agenda 21: The United Nations Program of Action from Rio*, New York: United Nations Department of Public Information, 1992.

United Nations Development Programme (UNDP), *Monograph* on the Inter-Regional Exchange and Transfer of Effective Practices on Urban Management. New York: UNDP, 1995.

United Nations General Assembly Special Session (UNGASS), *Program for the Further Implementation of Local Agenda 21*. New York: United Nations Commission for Sustainable Development (UNCSD), 1997.

Victor, P.A., "Economics & the Challenge of Environmental Issues", in Leiss, W. (ed.), *Ecology Versus Politics in Canada*. Toronto: University of Toronto Press, 1979.

Victoria. Government. Department of Conservation and Natural Resources (DCNR), *"Localinks"*. Proceedings of National Conference on Local Environment Action. Melbourne: DCNR, 1995.

Vig, N.J., "Toward Common Learning? Trends in US and EU Environmental Policy", Lecture for Summer Symposium, "The Innovation of Environmental Policy", Bologna, Italy, 22 July 1997.

Viviani, N. & Selby, J., *The Iwasaki Tourist Development at Yeppoon*, Research Paper No. 5. Brisbane: Griffith University Centre for the Study of Australian-Asian Relations, 1989.

Voisey, H., Beuermann, C., Astrid, L. & O'Riordan, T., "The Political Significance of Agenda 21: the early stages of some European experiences", *Local Environment*, Vol. 1, 1997, pp. 33–50.

Wackernagel, M. & Rees, W., *Our Ecological Footprint*. Philadelphia: New Society Publishers, 1996.

Wakeford, T. & Walters, M., *Science for the Earth*. Chichester: John Wiley and Sons, 1995.

Walker, D., "State's Air Deal Under Attack," *The Age* (Melbourne), 23 March 1994, p. 1; and "Controversy over grant threatens airline plan", ibid., 25 March 1994, p. 3.

Walker, K.J., "Economic Growth & Environmental Management: The Dilemma of the State", paper presented at the 27th Conference of the Australasian Political Studies Association, Adelaide, 28–30 August 1985.

Walker, K.J., "Ecological Limits and Marxian Thought", *Politics*, Vol. XIV, No. 1, May 1979, pp. 29–46.

Walker, K.J., "Methodologies for Social Aspects of Environmental Research", *Social Science Information*, Vol. 26, No. 4, December 1987, pp. 759–782.

Walker, K.J., "The Environmental Crisis: A Critique of Neo-Hobbesian Responses", *Polity*, Vol. XXI, No. 1, Fall 1988, pp. 67–81.

Walker, K.J., "The State in Environmental Management: the Ecological Dimension", *Political Studies*, Vol. 37, March 1989, pp. 25–39.

Walker, K.J., *The Political Economy of Environmental Policy: An Australian Introduction*. Kensington, NSW: UNSW Press, 1994.

Walker, K.J. (ed.), *Australian Environmental Policy: Ten Case Studies*. Kensington, NSW: UNSW Press, 1992.

Walker, M.L., *Human Impact on Australian Beaches*. Sydney: Surfrider Foundation of Australia, 1998.

Warhurst, J., "Single Issue Politics: the Impact of Conservation and Anti Abortion Groups", *Current Affairs Bulletin*, Vol. 60, No. 2, 1983, pp. 19–31.

Warnken, J. & Buckley, R., "Coastal Tourism Development as a Testbed for EIA Triggers: Outcomes Under Mandatory and Discretionary EIA Frameworks", *Environmental & Planning Law Journal*, Vol. 13, 1996, pp. 239–245.

Warnken, J. & Buckley, R., "Major 1987–93 Tourism Proposals in Australia", *Annals of Tourism Research*, Vol. 24, 1997, pp. 974–1019.

Warnken, J. & Buckley, R., "Scientific Quality of Tourism Environmental Impact Assessment", *Journal of Applied Ecology*, Vol. 35, 1998, pp. 1–8.

Watson, I., *Fighting Over the Forests*. Sydney: Allen & Unwin, 1990.

Weale, A., *The New Politics of Pollution*. Manchester: Manchester University Press, 1992.

The Weekend Australian, 16–17 September 1995; 15–16 March 1997; 15–16 August 1998.

Wells, D., "Green Politics and Environmental Ethics: A Defence of Human Welfare Ecology", *Australian Journal of Political Science*, Vol. 28, No. 3, November 1993, pp. 515–527.

Wescott, G., "Reforming Coastal Management to Improve Community Participation and Integration in Victoria, Australia", *Coastal Management*, Vol. 26, 1998, pp. 3–15.

White, M.E., *Listen... Our Land is Crying. Australia's Environment: Problems and Solutions*. Kenthurst, NSW: Kangaroo Press, 1997.

Whittaker, S., "A Study of Local Government in Australia and Local Agenda 21", *Local Environment*, Vol. 1, No. 4, June 1997.

Whittaker, S., *Local Agenda 21 Survey 1996*. Compiled for Environs Australia. Liverpool: Edge Hill University College, 1996.

Whittingham, H.E., "The Bathurst Bay Hurricane and Associated Storm Surge", *Australian Meteorological Magazine*, Vol. 23, 1958, pp. 14–36.

Wildriver, S., "Mining Mt. Etna: A Case Study in Statist Developmentalism and Environmental Irresponsibility", paper delivered at the Ecopolitics VII Conference, Griffith University, 2–4 July 1993.

Wiltshire, K., *Planning and Federalism: Australian and Canadian Experience*. St. Lucia: University of Queensland Press, 1986.

Woodford, J., "MPs ignoring environment warning bells, say scientists", *Sydney Morning Herald*, 31 March 1997, p. 1.

Woodhill, J., "Natural resources decision making: beyond the landcare paradox", *Australasian Journal of Natural Resources Law and Policy*, Vol. 3, 1996, pp. 91–114.

World Commission for Environment and Development (WCED), *Our Common Future* (The Brundtland Report). Berlin: Gower Books, 1985; Oxford: Oxford University Press, 1987. Australian Edition; Melbourne: Oxford University Press, 1990.

World Resources Institute (WRI), *World Resources 1996–97: A Guide to the Global Environment — The Urban Environment*. Washington, DC: WRI, 1997 (*http:/www.wri.org/wri/wr-96–97/*).

Wotherspoon, G., "The Determinants of the Pattern and Pace of Railway Development in New South Wales, 1850–1914", *Australian Journal of Politics and History*, Vol. XXV, No. 1, April 1979, pp. 51–65.

Zajacek, R., "The Development of Measures to Protect the Marine Environment from Land-based Pollution: The Effectiveness of the Great Barrier Reef Marine Park Authority in Managing the Effects of Tourism on the Marine Environment", *James Cook University Law Review*, Vol. 3, 1996, pp. 64–92.

Zann, L.P., *Our Sea, Our Future. Major Findings of the State of the Marine Environment Report for Australia*. Canberra: Department of the Environment, Sport and Territories, 1995.

Zann, L.P. & Kailola, P. (eds), *The Marine Environment. Technical Annex 1. State of the Marine Environment Report for Australia*, Canberra: Department of the Environment, Sport and Territories, 1995.

INDEX

167, 174–75, 178, 180, 183, 185, 190, 193, 207, 213, 217–18, 250
society 170
tourism 146
yield 246
Sustainable Energy Development Authority (SEDA) (NSW) 176, 184
Sydney 7, 21, 88, 144, 152, 166, 174–75, 177, 183–84, 197, 243
Greater Sydney Metropolitan Region 179
Sydney Harbour 153
Sydney Harbour Bridge 95
symbolic policy 57
synergism 8, 50, 61
synoptic policy strategy 238

tailings 233
Tampere, Finland 173
tariffs 39, 68, 90–91, 232–33
Tasmania 4, 13, 31–32, 38, 43, 65–68, 72, 78, 80, 82–84, 105–107, 149, 151, 154, 200, 219, 234
Tasmanian Hydro Electric Commission 33
Tasmanian Labor Party 231, 234
Tasmanian Parliament 231
tax reimbursements 32–33, 42
taxation 32, 43, 86, 95, 195, 227, 236
taxpayers 32, 38
technocratic dreaming 31
technological change 227, 231
technological dependence 41, 234
technological fix 11
technology 9, 11, 18, 21, 24, 35, 88, 106–108, 152, 208, 215, 227–28, 244, 246
telecommuting 169
telegraph 27, 29, 227
Telstra 74, 76
terms of debate 235
terra nullius 16, 116
territorial sea 165
Territories, Australian 104, 109, 112, 115, 118
textile 91
Thatcher, M. 75, 236
The Injured Coastline 157
theorists, policy 48, 56, 58, 61
theory
ecopolitical 45, 50, 53–56, 58, 60, 63
public choice 75
scientific 9
"think globally, act locally" 188

Third Conference of the Parties to the UN Framework Convention on Climate Change (COP-3) 16, 168
threshold effects 8, 12
Tibet 5
tidal patterns 119
Tighe, P. 83
timber 18, 23, 38, 73, 78–79, 82, 234
Tombolo, Port Hacking, NSW 149
tool making 5
topography 84–85, 153
Toronto, Canada 173
totalistic state control 230
tourism 17, 21, 77, 100, 115, 142–45, 148, 151–52, 154, 159–60, 163–64, 234
Tourism Council of Australia (TCA) 143
Tourism Working Group 146
Townsville, Qld 87
toxic waste 4, 112, 160
toxins 8
Toyne, P. 48, 115, 118
trace elements 24
trade 18, 41, 145
trade unions *see* unions
Trades Hall machine politics 231
traffic 169, 181, 192
trams 173
Transcontinental Railway 29
transport 26–35, 86–87, 113, 153, 166, 169, 176, 181–85, 235
trolleybuses 173
Tropic of Capricorn 86
tropics 17, 21, 23, 81, 84–85, 89, 102, 161, 243
Tully River 95
tunnel vision 20, 229
turtles 112–13
Tweed River 160
Tweed Shire, Qld 145

Uluru National Park 150
uncertainty 9, 12, 13, 19, 162, 206, 217, 239
underwater "acid rain" 164
unemployment 68, 92–93, 97–98, 232–33
unions 7, 28, 66, 68, 70, 92, 126, 199, 209, 232
United Kingdom 15, 17, 27, 75, 151, 196, 213, 223–24, 236
United Nations Centre for Housing and Settlements (UNCHS) 167, 171
United Nations Commission on